Steam and Steel

The Eastern Shore of Virginia 1870-1884

Brooks Miles Barnes

Copyright © 2024 by Brooks Miles Barnes

All rights reserved.

ISBN 978-1-62806-451-3   (print | paperback)

Library of Congress Control Number 2025907741

Published by Salt Water Media
29 Broad Street, Suite 104
Berlin, MD 21804
www.saltwatermedia.com

Front cover map by Bill Nelson, design by Salt Water Media
Interior maps by Bill Nelson

In Memory of

William W. Abbot

Martin J. Havran

Thomas H. Fooks V

In Honor of

Edward L. Ayers

Contents

Acknowledgements i

Introduction v

Chapter I: The Eastern Shore in 1870 1
   Landscape 6
      Land, Water, Woods 6
      Climate 16
      Habitations 19
   Livelihoods 26
      On the Land 27
         Agriculture 27
         Lumbering 47
         Other Occupations 51
      On the Water 53
         Fisheries 53
         Tourism 80
         Mariners 82
   Society 85

Chapter II: Agents of Transformation 103
   Visions of Progress 104
   The Transportation Web 116

Chapter III: Economic Growth 135
    Agriculture 135
    Fisheries 146
        Oystering 146
            On the Bayside 146
            On the Seaside 166
        Finfishing 169
        Terrapin 172
        Clamming 173
        Crabbing 174
    Tourism 176
    Transformation 187

Chapter IV: Landscape Change 189

Chapter V: Social Change 219

Chapter VI: Bands of Steel 261

Index 293

Acknowledgements

I am indebted to the following individuals and institutions for help in the research and writing of *Steam and Steel*. Curtis Badger, David Bearinger, Kellee Blake, and Stacia Childers read and criticized the entire manuscript. The late Bernard Herman commented on the Introduction and Emily Grey on Chapter I. M. K. Miles drew on his knowledge of Eastern Shore of Virginia genealogy to answer questions pertaining to family relationships. Allen Hamilton shared his transcriptions from Northampton County land and personal property tax records. Edward Barnes reviewed passages on local architecture. Bill Nelson created the maps. Curtis and Lynn Badger advised on publishers and publishing.

The late James E. Mears's pioneering work on the history of the Eastern Shore in the late nineteenth century facilitated my research. I regret that I never met James Mears but am glad that I attended his funeral on a wet day in 1975. I am fortunate to have known the late Kirk C. Mariner, whose understanding of the Eastern Shore's past was unsurpassed. As friends and neighbors, we often exchanged ideas and source materials for local history. After his death, I continued to consult him through his files, articles, and books. The late Frances Latimer, another good friend, shared generously her knowledge of the black experience on the Eastern Shore.

Over the years, conversations with the late Furlong Baldwin, Grayson Chesser, Dennis Custis, Jerry Doughty, the late Edward Holland, the late Charles Landis, George McMath, Erin Putalik, Lou

Tanner, Barry Truitt, Jonna Yarrington, and, especially, Anne Barnes enriched my understanding of aspects of local history. *Steam and Steel* also benefited from weekly talks with Theodore Corbett about history and historians.

Among my duties as librarian at the Eastern Shore Public Library, I collected materials pertaining to local history and culture. I appreciate that the late W. Robert Keeney and Carol Vincent, the library directors under whom I served, supported my work. The collection, now housed in the library's Eastern Shore Heritage Center in Parksley, is the source of much of the information in *Steam and Steel*. The staff of the library cheerfully assisted me in building the collection and, after my retirement, in using it for research. *Steam and Steel* also benefited from the collections of the Cape Charles Historical Society, Duke University, the Hagley Museum, the Library of Virginia, the National Archives-College Park, the Parksley Railroad Museum, Salisbury University, Shore History, the University of North Carolina, the University of Virginia, and the Virginia Museum of History and Culture. Archivists at these institutions were most accommodating. I especially acknowledge the late E. Lee Shephard of the Virginia Museum of History and Culture.

Some years ago, I had the good fortune of assisting the staff of the University of Virginia's Virginia Center for Digital History in developing the website *The Countryside Transformed: The Railroad and the Eastern Shore of Virginia, 1870-1935* (eshore.iath.Virginia.edu). The knowledge that I gained while working on the project deeply informs *Steam and Steel*. I am grateful to Edward L. Ayers and William G. Thomas III for inviting me to work on the website and to the late Thomas H. Fooks V for helping to fund it. I am also grateful to Worthy Martin, formerly of the Institute for Advanced Studies in the Humanities at the University of Virginia, for ensuring that *The Countryside Transformed* remains available to the public.

I was fortunate in my mentors in history as an undergraduate and graduate student at the University of Virginia. The late William W. Abbot, the late Martin J. Havran, and Edward L. Ayers were model scholars – patient, generous, and encouraging. What I have achieved as an historian I owe to them.

The arguments advanced in *Steam and Steel* depend much on the iconoclastic writings of the Southern Agrarians and of historians Eugene Genovese, Raimondo Luraghi, William Marvel, and C. Vann Woodward. Their interpretations seem to me necessary to making sense of what happened on the Eastern Shore of Virginia during the post-Civil War years.

The cheerful professionalism of Stephanie Fowler, Andrew Heller, and Patty Gregorio at Salt Water Media made the publication of this book as painless as possible.

Edward Barnes and Elizabeth Krawczel indulged a father whose mind often was in another century. Anne Barnes's daily assumption of a myriad of domestic and social duties made possible my excursion into the past. Her willingness to listen to my account of what I found there made the journey worthwhile.

Brooks Miles Barnes
Onancock
Eastern Shore of Virginia
May 12, 2025

Introduction

The years following the Civil War were fraught with change for the people of the Virginia counties of Accomack and Northampton on the Eastern Shore of Chesapeake Bay. War had altered patterns of trade two hundred years old and had accelerated profound change in agriculture and the fisheries. Moreover, the end of slavery required new economic, social, and political arrangements. As Eastern Shoremen struggled with these challenges, Northern capitalists eyed investment opportunities on the conquered peninsula.

In 1867 the Eastern Shore Steamboat Company of Baltimore expanded steamboat service to the two counties. In 1884 entrepreneurs associated with the Pennsylvania Railroad built a nominally independent line, appropriately named the New York, Philadelphia and Norfolk, down the spine of the peninsula to a new man-made harbor capable of handling the world's largest railroad barges. In the ensuing decades the rate of change accelerated as improved transportation combined with innovative business practices, emerging technologies, and an influx of new people, capital, and ideas to stimulate the Eastern Shore's economy, transform its landscape, and subsume its traditional culture.

A booming economy made Accomack and Northampton among the most prosperous rural counties in the United States. Between 1870 and 1910, population nearly doubled. New towns appeared along the railroad while existing crossroad and waterfront communities thrived. An expanded network of roads linked the rail depots to the hinterland. Power and telephone lines paralleled the roads. The roar of the motor truck and boat broke the silence of field and wood, marsh and bay. Accumulating capital enabled the creation of banks, which in turn underwrote business expansion. Contractors erected new houses, stores, wharves, churches, and lodge halls in town and countryside.

Rapid transport and expanding markets engaged the people of the Eastern Shore more deeply with the outside world. Improved communications and increased personal income enhanced their access to household amenities and cultural diversions. They became more mobile, more aware of new ideas and fashions, and more dependent on products grown and manufactured elsewhere.

Change on the Eastern Shore owed much to the ambition, initiative, and capital of outsiders. The growth of Northern cities created demand for Eastern Shore foodstuffs, fuel, building materials, and recreational opportunities. Rail and steamboat companies out of Baltimore, Philadelphia and New York expanded service on the peninsula, bringing local produce hours, even days, closer to market. Outsiders developed new towns, involved themselves as investors and managers in the seafood industry, and facilitated the shipment of mine props to the anthracite fields of Pennsylvania. Hundreds of urbanites came annually to engage in field sports or to rusticate in the numerous resorts along the peninsula's waterfront. Some of the outsiders – railroad administrators and workers, farmers and farm laborers, watermen, lumbermen, merchants, retirees – settled on the Eastern Shore where they invested their lives and fortunes.

Customarily an enterprising people, Eastern Shore natives caught the tide of change. They cultivated new crops for new markets and applied new technologies to agriculture, the fisheries, lumbering, and market hunting. They established businesses and banks. They built an extensive tourism industry. They founded towns and developed new neighborhoods in existing communities. Most important, they created the Eastern Shore of Virginia Produce Exchange, a farmers' marketing organization so successful that it attracted the attention of agriculturalists from across the country and around the world.

Prosperity diffused throughout the community. With business booming in multiple sectors, labor enjoyed a seller's market. Some people benefited more than others but most substantially improved their standard of living. Black people lagged behind white but they too grew in population, accumulated real and personal property, and constructed homes and other buildings. The Eastern Shore was one of the few sections in the rural South where blacks were better off materially than they had been before the Civil War. In contrast to black economic advancement, however, black political power on the peninsula declined into impotence and aspirations to social equality remained unfulfilled.

Nonetheless, by the early twentieth century, the people of the Eastern Shore, white and black, enjoyed more comfortable lives, greater economic opportunities, and more mobility than most other people in the South and in much of the nation.

THIS STORY OF PROSPERITY, LOCAL INITIATIVE, AND material comfort across racial lines runs counter to the prevailing narrative of Southern history. The post-Civil War South functioned as an economic colony of the North, selling cheap and buying dear in an exchange of raw materials, usually cotton, for manufactured goods. As cotton prices fell on the international market, farmers became indebted for seed and supplies to local merchants who in turn were indebted to Northern wholesalers. Desperate to pay off their notes and often too far removed from urban markets to plant truck crops, farmers found themselves shackled to cotton. Falling ever deeper in debt, they frequently lost their land, and the land, relentlessly single-cropped, lost its fertility. With profits flowing Northward, scarcity of capital stifled local investment. Most Southerners lived poor, some beyond the threshold of debt peonage, and Southern blacks, at the bottom of the economic ladder, lived poorest of all.

The Eastern Shore, for a time, experienced an alternative history. Although also an economic colony of the North, the Eastern Shore was not of the staple-producing areas that so dominate Southern historiography. Accomack and Northampton enjoyed thriving seafood, lumber, and tourism industries. More important, the Eastern Shore counties lay at the heart of a coastal truck-farming region scarcely noticed by historians. Emerging in the 1870s, the region extended from north Florida to Long Island. It provided immense quantities of Irish potatoes, sweet potatoes, strawberries, and other fruits and vegetables to markets along the East Coast and in the Middle West. Eastern Shore truck farmers enjoyed the advantage of the Eastern Shore of Virginia Produce Exchange whose aggressive marketing and insistence on quality made its Red Star brand a preference of consumers across much of the nation. Directed by Eastern Shoremen, the Produce Exchange also served as a bulwark against the abuses of outside brokers and speculators. The peninsula's mixed and prospering economy shaped a society that in important ways differed from that of the staple South.

WORLD WAR I WAS A WATERSHED EVENT in Eastern Shore history. United States government officials, anxious to supply the Allied war effort, encouraged American farmers to expand the production of truck crops. As a result, in the post-war years Eastern Shore farmers encountered competition in hitherto secure markets. Meanwhile, hundreds of young people, white and black, left the peninsula to work in the war industries. Many of them, having earned city wages and experienced city life, never returned to their country homes. The wartime migration, coupled with the devastating influenza epidemic of 1918-1919, robbed the Eastern Shore of many of its more intelligent and ambitious youth.

In the 1920s, Eastern Shoremen learned that there was no enduring rural sweet spot within the colonial economy. Technological innovation, which for decades had favored the peninsula, now began to work against it. Overproduction, resource depletion, and competition from other regions undermined its position in the national markets. All sectors of its economy declined. Debt and foreclosure became commonplace and poverty endemic. The Great Depression deepened the misery and despair. Years passed and hard times continued. Population declined along with opportunity. Derelict homes appeared in the countryside and shuttered stores in the towns as generation after generation of young people fled to the cities.

THE EASTERN SHORE'S BRIEF PERIOD OF PROSPERITY came at a cost higher than bust following boom. Most of its people willingly embraced the modernist idea of economic and social progress through scientific knowledge, technological application, and business innovation. A long history of involvement in the market economy, the evangelical insistence on hard work and frugality, and the shock of Confederate defeat predisposed them toward modernism. So, too, did their sharing the eternal human longing for a better life. By putting their faith in progress, they welcomed a force that was inherently transformative and thus fundamentally anti-traditional. They exchanged the local for the national, independence for dependence, and God for Science. They exchanged gradual change for rapid transformation, leisure for busyness, and the burden of patience for the tyranny of the clock. They put aside the knowledge, hard earned by Southerners, of the cost of defeat. On occasion some of them resisted one or another aspect of the new regime, or they detected signs of cultural declension, or worried that something of ineffable value had been lost, but few regretted the passing of the old order. For good or for ill, labor-saving devices, domestic amenities, personal mobility, public amusements, and cash in the pocket had made stale the world of the fathers.

The experience of the Eastern Shore is not merely a regional phenomenon. Its history of boom and bust amidst economic colonization and cultural homogenization is the story of the descent of rural America into what the poet and essayist Donald Davidson called an "Americanized nowhere."

Onancock, June 15 – "Here everything is different, the face of the country, the water, the air, the people, the names, the crops, the stock, the vehicles, the houses, the housekeeping, the feeding, everything, and were it not for politics . . . you would not realize that you were a Virginian in Virginia." (T. C. Morton, "Life in a Level Land," *Staunton Vindicator*, June 23, 1882).

Chapter I

The Eastern Shore in 1870

In 1870, the people of Accomack and Northampton counties on Virginia's Eastern Shore were in the midst of profound economic, social, and political change. Throughout the antebellum period, nearby cities grew and the regional transportation system expanded. Increased urban demand for local produce encouraged rapid growth in the seafood industry and a shift in agriculture from grain to truck farming. Civil War brought federal invasion and a decade of military occupation. Emancipation of the peninsula's slaves required a readjustment in race relations. Blacks endeavored to find a way to solidify the benefits of their new status as citizens while whites, their self-confidence diminished by Confederate defeat, struggled against a world turned upside down.

Reconstruction, from which the Eastern Shore emerged in 1870, had unfolded in an atmosphere of distrust, bitterness, and uncertainty. It was, in Richard Weaver's apt description, a "sectional feud in which one side was trying to impose its will on the other, and the other was resisting that imposition with every device of policy, stratagem and chicanery that could be found." In the absence of settled authority, criminality flourished and interracial violence erupted with demoralizing frequency. Throughout the war years, the local economy had held its own thanks largely to trade enabled by profiteering federal military and customs officers. During Reconstruction, political strife and an unsettled labor situation begat what a citizen of Accomack described as "A want of confidence, a perfect stupor, and an indisposition to attempt anything, or to form any plans for the future." Federal census figures for 1870 reflected the malaise. Cash values declined from those of 1860 in every category. Particularly striking was the drop in the value of Eastern Shore farms from $6,163,870 to $3,876,458, a loss of 37.1 percent. "To hope longer appears like hoping against hope." lamented the Accomack man. "God only knows what is to become of us." Writing in 1901, "Waldo" described the area around the village of Atlantic in upper Accomack County immediately after the war as "backward in every essential almost that goes to make a modern up-to-date community. Then, farms, dwellings, churches and schools were much neglected. Education and culture, as a rule, was at a 'low ebb' indeed, and what then existed were confined to a few favored individuals only. The blighting effects of slavery still rested over the land; the energies of the older men paralyzed for the time by its abolition, and the young men, cradled amidst its surroundings and enervated by its influence, had not yet arisen to that degree of independence and self-reliance that now characterizes them."[1]

The Eastern Shore of Virginia is bordered on the north by Maryland, on the east by the Atlantic Ocean, on the west by Chesapeake Bay, and on the south by the confluence of bay and ocean. In 1870 the peninsula was a land of fields, woods, marshes, and tidal creeks where the great majority of its 28,455 people made their livings as farmers, woodsmen, and watermen. The population of Accomack, the northernmost county, was 20,409, and that of Northampton 8,046. More whites – 15,765 – than blacks – 12,690 – lived on the Virginia peninsula. Thirty-eight percent of the people residing in Accomack were black compared to sixty percent in Northampton. The population was widely and evenly

---

1 Richard M. Weaver, "The Southern Tradition" in *The Southern Essays of Richard M. Weaver*, eds. George M. Curtis III and James J. Thompson Jr. (Indianapolis: Liberty Fund, 1987), pp. 216-217; James Egbert Mears, "The Virginia Eastern Shore in the War of Secession and in the Reconstruction Period," typescript, 1957, in Eastern Shore Heritage Center, Eastern Shore Public Library, Parksley, Va., pp. 368-370; Ludwell H. Johnson III, "Blockade or Trade Monopoly?: John A. Dix and the Union Occupation of Norfolk," *Virginia Magazine of History and Biography* 93 (January, 1985), pp. 54-78; Stephen B. Sledge, "The Bitter Fruits of Secession: The Union Army's Wartime Occupation of Southeastern Virginia," Ph.D. dissertation, George Mason University, 2012, pp. 153-173; *Richmond Dispatch*, March 21, 1867 (quotation); Mears, Statistics from Federal Censuses in "Shoreline Column," Onancock *Eastern Shore News* (hereafter cited as *ESN*), November 8, 1940; Accomac C. H. *Peninsula Enterprise* (hereafter cited as *PE*), April 27, 1901 (quotes "Waldo").

distributed, the only thickly settled areas were those adjacent the oyster grounds on both shores of upper Accomack County.[2]

The Eastern Shore was as thoroughly Virginian as any region of the commonwealth. Its land had been taken up by early English colonists and jealously held by their descendants. Geographically isolated, it had experienced little in-migration since well before the American Revolution. In 1870, only 2.6 percent of the total population of its two counties had been born outside of Virginia. If those born in the adjacent state of Maryland are subtracted, the portion shrinks to 1.2 percent. Most of the newcomers had recently settled in upper Accomack County near the boundary with Maryland to work in the rapidly expanding oyster industry.[3]

Native Eastern Shoremen, both white and black, could follow their roots on the peninsula back as many as 250 years. A traveler noted of the white watermen of the bay islands that "If their 'caste' may not be so high, and their social condition certainly is not, they can trace a long and direct line of ancestry as any of the proudest of the 'First Families.'" Through generations of intermarriage, white Eastern Shoremen had created, in the words of novelist Mary E. Bradley, "an almost universal 'cousinship' throughout the community." Some families had multiplied prodigiously. "The Nottingham family is so numerous that there are not enough Christian names to go around," a Norfolk journalist observed. "They have to import Christian names, and after they are all exhausted they resort to descriptive prefixtions to the same names. ... 'Chatter Bill,' 'Long John,' 'Johnny Short,' 'Red-faced Bob,' 'Lean David,' 'Pussy Joe,' Cross-eyed Jimmy.'"[4]

---

2 Joseph Patrick Harahan. "Politics, Political Parties, and Voter Participation in Tidewater Virginia During Reconstruction, 1865-1890," Ph.D. dissertation, Michigan State University, 1973, pp. 14-15, 19, 111-112; E. H. Stevens, *Soil Survey of Accomac and Northampton Counties, Virginia*, United States, Department of Agriculture, Bureau of Soils (Washington: Government Priinting Office, 1920), pp. 10-11.

3 Avery Odelle Craven, *Soil Exhaustion as a Factor in the Agricultural History of Virginia and Maryland, 1606-1860* (Goucester, Mass.: Peter Smith, 1965 [reprint of 1926 ed.], p. 122, n. 1; Francis Bibbins Latimer, comp., *1870 Census for Northampton County, Virginia* (Eastville, Va.: Hickory House, 1996); Gail Walczyk, comp., *The Accomack County 1870 Census* (Coram, N.Y.: Peter's Row, 1999).

4 George Fitzhugh, "Eastern Shore of Virginia," *DeBow's Review* XXXIV (July and August,

The Norfolk man spoke for numerous other visitors when he described the peninsula's white people as "more English in speech, manners, habits and customs than any other part of our population." George Fitzhugh discovered that "Many old English words, out of use in other sections are still in common use here. Ox-carts are always called 'wains,' and farm-yards and stables called 'pounds.' The double negative is often heard from the lips of educated and refined men." English mores, albeit leavened by New World realities and weakened by the passage of time, still shaped the attitudes and practices of Eastern Shoremen in agriculture, architecture, government, and other aspects of daily life.[5]

At the outbreak of the Civil War, more than a third of the Eastern Shore's black population already was free. A handful of black families traced their freedom back into the seventeenth century but most to the years beginning in 1782 when the Virginia legislature legalized the manumission of slaves. Black people also had been on the peninsula long enough to develop a 'cousinship.' Indeed, Eastern Shore 'cousinship' was not segregated by race. Seldom acknowledged kinship ties found mute expression in the frequency with which the term mulatto appeared in the federal censuses. Nor were whites and blacks culturally discrete. African influences worked subtly almost everywhere but were most apparent in cookery, religion, and speech. The Wilmington journalist

---

1864), p. 84; "A Peninsular Tour: Tangier Sound and the Chesapeake Oyster Beds," *Wilmington News Journal*, June 19, 1878 (quotes "H. H. C."); Mary E. Bradley, "On the Eastern Shore," *The Aldine* 5 (April, 1872), p. 79; *Norfolk Landmark*, November 20, 1877. See also *Middletown (Del.) Transcript* July 23, 1870; and Howard Pyle, "A Peninsular Canaan," *Harper's New Monthly Magazine* 58 (May, 1879), p. 812.

5 *Norfolk Landmark*, July 26, 1876; Fitzhugh, "Eastern Shore of Virginia," p. 84; *Middletown (Del.) Transcript*, July 2, 1870. See also "The Eastern Shore of Virginia," *Forest and Stream* VII (November 16, 1876), p. 232; Pyle, "Peninsular Canaan," p. 805; and Orris A. Browne, "The Eastern Shore," *American Agriculturist* in *PE* April 11, 1885. For the persistence of English customs in the New World see David Hackett Fischer, *Albion's Seed: Four British Folkways in America* (New York and Oxford: Oxford University Press, 1989). For the effect of the New World on English customs see Willie Graham, Carter L. Hudgins, Carl R. Lounsbury, Fraser Nieman, and James P. Whittenburg, "Adaptation and Innovation: Archaeological and Architectural Perspectives on the Seventeenth-Century Chesapeake," *William and Mary Quarterly*, 3rd ser., LXIV (July, 2007), pp. 451-522; and Cary Carson, Joanne Bowen, Willie Graham, Martha McCartney, and Lorena Walsh, "New World, Real World: Improvising English Culture in Seventeenth-Century Virginia," *Journal of Southern History* LXXIV (February, 2008), pp. 31-88.

Howard Pyle recognized in the dialect of local whites "something of the negro twang."⁶

The end of slavery set the peninsula's black people in motion. Some left permanently to join escaped or emancipated kinsmen who before the war had sought new lives in Baltimore, Philadelphia, or New York. The majority, however, soon settled on or near the farms on which they had been brought up. Census figures for 1860 and 1870 reveal that the black exodus was real but limited. The Eastern Shore's black population registered a miniscule loss during the decade while the white increased by 8.7 percent. Indeed, Accomack and Northampton were the only counties in the Tidewater region not to lose population during the 1860s. The freedmen were hemmed in by poverty to the South and antipathy to the North. An influx of black laborers competing for jobs had not been a Northern war aim. Northerners remained sympathetic toward black folks as long as they remained politically useful and in the South. The Eastern Shore had its own type of racial antagonism but the peninsula offered a living from land, wood, and water, and more important, it was home. Here, for black as well as white, were family and friends, elders and ancestors, homeplace and graveyard, the familiar and the beloved.⁷

---

6 Kirk Mariner, *Slave and Free on Virginia's Eastern Shore from the Revolution to the Civil War* (Onancock, Va.: Miona Publications, 2014), p. 39; Pyle, "Peninsular Canaan," p. 805. According to Eva Sheppard Wolf, "there existed in Accomack, as nowhere else in Virginia, a true culture of manumission" (*Race and Liberty in the New Nation: Emancipation in Virginia from the Revolution to Nat Turner's Rebellion* [Baton Rouge: Louisiana State University Press, 2006], pp. 60-62).

7 Harahan, "Politics, Political Parties, and Voter Participation," pp. 16, 19, 2; C. Vann Woodward, "Seeds of Failure in Radical Race Policy" in *American Counterpoint: Slavery and Racism in the North-South Dialogue* (Boston and Toronto: Little, Brown and Company, 1976). p. 169. Israel Townsend of Delaware, who settled near Capeville shortly after the war and became active in politics as a Republican, believed that the reunion of blacks with relatives sold South during slavery was *not* a factor in the small decline in the peninsula's black population (*Wilmington Delaware Tribune*, February 24, 1870.).

Landscape

Land, Water, Woods

Virginia's Eastern Shore is a tapering peninsula seventy-five miles in length and only eight miles in mean width. "A neck of land so narrow," remarked Jesse J. Simpkins of Northampton County in 1865, "that one can almost seem to feel the undulation of ocean and bay." Accomack is much the larger of the counties, of 470 square miles of land mass compared to Northampton's 212.[8]

The Eastern Shore rises barely above sea level. The highest elevation is around fifty feet, and most of the land lies between the high water mark and thirty-five feet. The peninsula's topography from sea to bay is, in the words of another Northampton man writing in 1875, "as level as a Western prairie." Only where the watercourses make their way through relatively high ground does anything resembling a hill appear. Generally, the land is well drained by numerous tidal estuaries, known locally as creeks, which penetrate both sides of the peninsula. The principal exceptions are on the Accomack bayside – the swamps between Pungoteague and Onancock creeks and, farther north, the semi-swampy lands that characterize much of the countryside between Hunting Creek and the Maryland boundary.[9]

The land is the farmer's delight. The terrain is devoid of hills and rocks. The soil tills easily, drains well while retaining moisture, and responds gratefully to fertilizer. "It appears to be the most easily cultivated and the most readily improved soil in the world," exclaimed a Delaware

---

[8] Stevens, *Soil Survey*, p. 5; Jesse J. Simpkins, "Invalid Inklings by the Seashore, and on Sand-Shoal Island," *Norfolk Post*, October 23, 1865.

[9] W. O. Strong, "Agricultural Conditions on the Eastern Shore of Virginia," *ESN*, May 17, 1935; Stevens, *Soil Survey*, pp. 6, 9, 58; *Richmond Dispatch*, August 13, 1875 (quotes "H. T. J."); J. A. Bonsteel, "Soils of Eastern Virginia and Their Uses for Truck Crop Production," United States, Department of Agriculture, *Bulletin* 1005 (April 24, 1922), p. 47; Edmund Ruffin, "Sketch of a Hasty View of the Soil and Agriculture of Part of the County of Northampton," *Farmers' Register* III (August, 1835), p. 233.

visitor in 1884. The Eastern Shore farmer, in the same amount of time as his hill-country brethren, cultivated more acreage with less wear on man, beast, and implement. As a result, the fields of Accomack and Northampton impressed visitors as remarkably large. In 1920, E. H. Stevens of the United States Bureau of Soils found the sandy loams of the Eastern Shore particularly well suited to the culture of fruits and vegetables. They "are among the most productive soils of the Atlantic Coastal Plain," he reported. "The better drained, retentive types are the equal of any trucking soils in the country."[10]

Stevens declared the water supply for farm use "everywhere adequate." Springs were not abundant on the peninsula but well-diggers usually struck water at ten to twenty feet. Eastern Shoremen encased their wells with wood. Some drew water by bucket and rope or by a chain attached to pulley or windlass while others used the old-fashioned sweep and bucket. "Water may be found almost anywhere for the digging," the Delaware man remarked, "but the water usually tastes of the ground."[11]

Abundant agricultural advantages combined with associations and memories accumulated across the generations to make Eastern Shore landowners reluctant to part with their real property. Following a visit to the peninsula in 1835, Edmund Ruffin wrote that "the people are too many for the land," that the average price of real estate was three times that of other Tidewater counties, and that "the renting of land is extensively practiced." In 1870, 54.9 percent of Accomack County heads of household owned their own land while in black-majority Northampton only 32.6 percent were landowners. Moreover, two and a half centuries of partition among a sedentary people had made landholdings relatively

---

[10] T. C. Johnson, "Potato Growing in Eastern Virginia," *Potato Magazine* 2 (August, 1919), p. 8; Stevens, *Soil Survey*, pp. 9, 24, 33, 37, 60; Browne, "The Eastern Shore"; "Accomac and Northampton," *Richmond Enquirer*, August 27, 1858; *Middletown (Del.) Transcript*, July 23, 1870; "On the Peninsula," Wilmington *Morning News*, November 15, 1884; Frank P. Brent, *The Eastern Shore of Virginia: A Description of Its Soil, Climate, Industries Development, and Future Prospects* (Baltimore: Harlem Paper Company, 1891), p. 4; September 25, 1779, Robert Honyman Diary, September 9 – December 18, 1779, Virginia Historical Society, Richmond.

[11] Stevens, *Soil Survey*, p.10; Samuel Sanford. "The Underground Water Resources of Coastal Plain Province of Virginia," Virginia Geological Survey, *Bulletin* V (1913), pp. 118, 244; "On the Peninsula."

small. In Accomack, 81.1 percent of the 1,905 landowners held 199 or fewer acres; in Northampton 69.7 percent of 528. Of the 2,433 landowners in the two counties, only 127 (.05 percent) met the 500-acre minimum set by the United States Census in 1860 for plantation ownership and only 6 of those owned more than 2,000 acres.[12]

Of his native Accomack, John W. Gillet noted that "few persons in this County have accumulated much estate ... whilst at the same time very few are extremely poor. In other words, property is very equally distributed." Gillet believed that the small size of the landholdings in Accomack increased both upward mobility and land values: "the smallness of the tracts bringing them within the reach of many persons and thereby producing competition amongst the purchasers." The relatively larger holdings in Northampton often were the remnant of extensive land patents granted the gentry by the English crown in the mid-seventeenth century. The same gentry secured even larger patents in Accomack after its creation from Northampton in 1663 but many of these they obtained with sale rather than estate building in mind. As commodity rather than patrimony, the Accomack patents more often were subject to division into smaller tracts than the home plantations to the south. A Philadelphian passing through the two counties in 1865 found Accomack much the less attractive: "The growing crops do not look as well as in the lower county, nor has the county the same sylvan beauty. The plantations are generally smaller; the houses smaller and less pretentious, the roads in worse condition."[13]

The sandy soil gave the peninsula's roads a Jekyll and Hyde character.

---

12 Ruffin, "Sketch of a Hasty View," pp. 236, 239; "Quantity and Value of the Exports of the County of Accomac." *Farmers' Register* VIII (1840), p. 255. Percentages for landholding were computed from Accomack County Land Tax, 1869; Allen B. Hamilton, comp., *Northampton County, Virginia, Land Tax Records, 1851-1870* (Berwyn Heights, Md.: Heritage Books, 2021), pp. 397-423; Walczyk, comp., *The Accomack County 1870 Census*; and Latimer, comp, *The 1870 Census for Northampton County*. For the minimum acreage for a plantation see Clement Eaton, *The Growth of Southern Civilizaton, 1790-1860* (New York: Harper & Row, 1961), pp. 98-99, 154.

13 John W. Gillet, Accomac C. H., to John B. LaForge, February, 1869, Gillet-Wise Family Papers, 1834-1872, Library of Virginia, Richmond; Susie M. Ames, "Beginnings and Progress," in *The Eastern Shore of Maryland and Virginia*, ed. Charles B. Clark (New York: Lewis Historical Publishing Company, 1950), I, 81; *Philadelphia Inquirer*, August 19, 1865.

Outsiders, who usually visited in the summer months, marveled how horses (shoeless in the absence of stones) sped over the smooth, firm roads. Behind a good team and driver, a carriage might attain eight to ten miles per hour and travel the seventy-five miles from Cape Charles to the Maryland line in a single day. Eastern Shoremen preferred driving carriages to riding on horseback. "The roads are so good one horse can pull as much as you can put on an ordinary vehicle, and you may travel for days without seeing a two-horse conveyance. They call their buggies, carriages, if they have tops, and a whole family, I have seen seven, often go in a one-horse cart," observed a visitor from the Shenandoah Valley. "As a result of this one-horse mode of travel, the middle of the road wherever you go, presents the singular appearance of having been shoveled out, leaving a narrow, deepish track, and the horse always sticks to it, needing but little guidance." A Baltimore man declared that "The horses ... are all small and more or less fast. Every one drives rapidly, and even the darkeys drive good trotters at a slashing speed." A Richmond visitor warned that "The western shoreman who is accustomed to trying the speed of his horse whenever he finds a stretch of smooth, level road, would drive his horse to death over here, for every mile of road is smooth enough for a race track." Another Richmonder perceived the economic advantage that firm roads and level terrain conferred to the Eastern Shore farmer and teamster: "No breecher and breaks wanted. ... Imagine what big loads they haul, o' ye hill-country farmer."[14]

With cold, wet weather, Jekyll departed and Hyde arrived. Freezing and thawing played hob with the sandy roadbeds, and heavy-laden timber wagons making their way to the creekside wharves churned them into a quagmire. In early March, 1882, John W. Edmonds, editor of the Accomac C. H. *Peninsula Enterprise*, offered "a wager and a reward. We wager cakes and ale that no county in the State, soil considered, has such

---

14 T. [Israel Townsend], Capeville, to editor, April 23, Wilmington *Delaware State Journal*, April 23, 1867; *Philadelphia Inquirer*, August 8, 1865; *Richmond Dispatch*, April 13, 1874, April 10 (fourth quotation), August 18, 1875; Fitzhugh "Eastern Shore of Virginia," p. 80; T. C. Morton, "Life in a Level Land," *Staunton Vindicator*, June 23, 1882 (first quotation); *Baltimore Sun*, September 10, 1881 (second quotation); "The Eastern Shore," Richmond *State*, July 24, 1883 (third quotaton).

excreable roads. Offer open 20 years. We offer a reward for a road three miles long which is decently good. Offer open 30 days." Residents of some of the waterfront communities improved the roads by spreading oyster shells, which, in the summer sun, glistened blindingly white.[15]

The principal roads running north and south bore the obvious names of Seaside, Middle, and Bayside. The Seaside and Bayside roads extended the length of the two counties. The Middle Road passed southward through Accomack until it terminated before the swampy headwaters of Pungoteague Creek. Across these thoroughfares ran numerous east and west roads connecting the necks (small peninsulas) between the creeks on the bayside with those on the seaside. From the neck roads spread a web of shorter roads down to the wharves and landings on the creeks. Where the often narrow roads ran though long stretches of woods, cutouts facilitated the meeting and passing of vehicles. Everywhere travelers needed to be aware of free-ranging livestock lounging in the roadbed and to remember to close gates behind them.[16]

Forests covered forty percent of the Eastern Shore's farmland. Oak, hickory, sycamore, walnut, and cedar, among others, grew abundantly but pine – loblolly, and short-leaf – thrived best in the sandy soil. Travelers often remarked on their resinous odor. James H. A. Johnson, a black minister who visited the peninsula in 1865, recalled the "towering pines, beautiful beyond description, lifting their bushy heads far above the bases of their majestic trunks and humming out anthems of praise in every passing breeze. Their trunks were so gigantic, so straight and clear that they stood like temple columns in the magnificent and extensive groves. Their native soil was level and cleanly covered with a red carpet

---

15 Stevens, *Soil Survey*, p. 11; *PE*, March 2, 1882; "A Virginian Atlantis," *American Traveller and Tourist* in *PE*, October 8, 1887.

16 "The Eastern Shore," Richmond *State*, July 24, 1883; "On the Peninsula"; "A Virginian Atlantis"; H. Chandlee Forman, The *Virginia Eastern Shore and its British Origins: History, Gardens and Antiquities* (Easton, Md.: Eastern Shore Publishers' Association, 1975), p. 206. Noting the pattern of narrow roads with sharp turns and frequent intersections, Forman concluded that the Eastern Shore had a "medieval English road pattern still extant" (p. 5). Forman was partially correct. He took into account the peninsula's settlement by the English shortly after 1607 but ignored, or perhaps was unaware of, the extensive road building that occurred after the coming of the railroad in 1884.

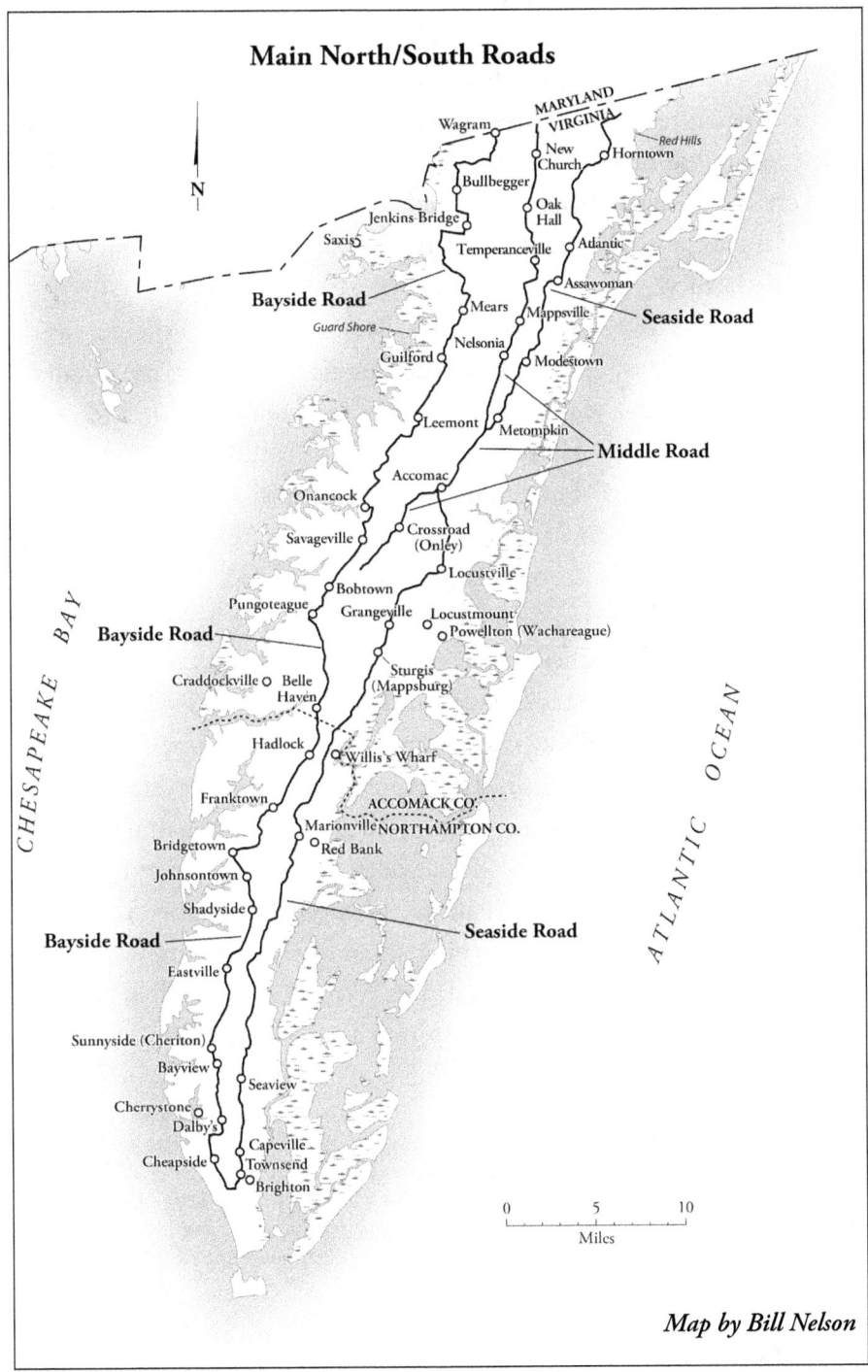

made by the abundance of their falling shatters [needles]." Travelers also noticed the open, park-like aspect of the forest understory. Farmers kept the floor clear of undergrowth by sweeping and gathering the shatters to use as manure for their sweet potato fields and by allowing their livestock to browse in the thickets. The blending of open wood and level field created an aesthetically and psychologically appealing landscape. In their daily doings the farmers and their families passed through scenes of serene beauty.[17]

The sea was as much a part of the lives of Eastern Shoremen as the land and the woods. "Down here," declared a visitor, "are most happily blended those great elements ... of man's existence, earth and water, tortuously entwined." He found the necks of land between the creeks "strangely disturbing" but granted that they formed "separate principalities, with the kindest and well-drained soils for cultivation and vast varieties of fish and also oysters and crabs for food." On the bayside southward from Hunting Creek the creek banks rise from five to thirty feet above high water. These bluffs provide home sites secure from storm surges and charming vistas of creek and bay.[18]

The creeks are shallow, with narrow, twisting channels, and often barred by sand at their mouths. In the post-bellum years even those with the deepest channels required a high tide to float vessels drawing more than ten feet. The creeks were not as deep as they once had been. Two centuries of hoe and plow agriculture had leached silt into the creeks, lowering the water level and turning some of their tributaries into dry gullies, known locally as "starved guts." In 1883 a small boat could hardly reach the site of a former shipyard on Assawoman Creek from

---

17 *The Statistics of the Wealth and Industry of the United States ... Compiled, From the Original Returns of the Ninth Census (June 1, 1870)* (Washington: Government Printing Office, 1872), pp. 266, 270; Browne, "The Eastern Shore"; Stevens, *Soil Survey*, p. 23; James H. A. Johnson, *The Pine Tree Mission* (Memphis, Tenn.: General Books, 2012 [reprint of 1893 ed.]), p. 1; *Philadelphia Inquirer*, August 8, 1865; "A Trip for Quail in Maryland," *Forest and Stream* 7 (February 1, 1877), p. 402. For the psychological appeal of the park-like landscape see Tom Horton, *Bay Country* (Baltimore: Johns Hopkins University Press, 1987), p. 179.

18 "The Old Man Takes a Cruise," *Richmond Dispatch*, December 13, 1883 (quotation); Stevens, *Soil Survey*, p. 42; Brent, *The Eastern Shore of Virginia*, p. 8. See also Curtis J. Badger, *Peninsulas in Repose: The Necks of Virginia's Eastern Shore* (Berlin, Md.: Salt Water Media, 2023).

which in antebellum years schooners and sloops had been launched. Fortunately, the shallow-draft steamboats of the bay and coastal trades could navigate most of the bayside creeks and some of those on the seaside.[19]

Tidal marsh accounts for around 30 percent of the total acreage of the two counties. On the bayside, marsh stretches the length of Accomack County, consuming to the northward more and more low-lying acreage until it culminates in the great Free School Marsh between Saxis Island and the mainland. On the seaside, the marsh extends the length of the peninsula between the mainland and the string of barrier islands confronting the Atlantic Ocean. In its lower reaches, the marsh and adjacent flats and water are known as the Broadwater. "The Broadwater," wrote the sportsman Alexander Hunter,

> consists of shoals and banks and sea-meadows, through which the sea forces its way in creeks and channels, with a width of an ordinary canal to that of a lesser river. At low tide these streams dwindle away to small rivulets, but when the ocean sends its vast volume of water surging inland, it soon fills them, and bursting its bounds, the sea-green fluid flushes over the meadows and sandbars. ... The surroundings change as if by magic. In minacious billows the incoming tide spreads itself over the level surface as fast as one can walk, and soon the eye rests upon a vast sheet of water that seems a part of the ocean itself.[20]

The Virginia barrier islands are some of the most dynamic landforms on earth. The sea is their master, and it is restless and resistless. Its

---

19 Petition of Citizens, December 13, 1859, Accomack County Legislative Petitions, 1776-1862, Library of Virginia, Richmond; A Hughlett Mason, *History of Steam Navigation to the Eastern Shore of Virginia* (Richmond: The Dietz Press, Inc., 1973), pp. 31, 35, 41, 42, 60, 65, 66; *Forest and Stream* 1 (October 23, 1873), p. 173; Jack Temple Kirby. *Mockingbird Song: Ecological Landscapes of the South* (Chapel Hill: University of North Carolina Press, 2006), p. 192; Forman, *The Virginia Eastern Shore and its British Origins*, p. 241; "The Eastern Shore," Richmond *State*, July 24, 1883.

20 Stevens *Soil Survey*, pp. 6, 36; Alexander Hunter, "Shore Birds off Cape Charles: I. Summer Shooting," *Forest and Stream* XXI (August 23, 1883), pp. 64-65.

gradual rise since the end of the last ice age has driven the islands slowly westward. Its shifting currents daily build each of the barriers up on one end and tear it down on the other. Its fierce storms wash away dunes, fill marshes, and cut new inlets. Under the suzerainty of the sea, individual

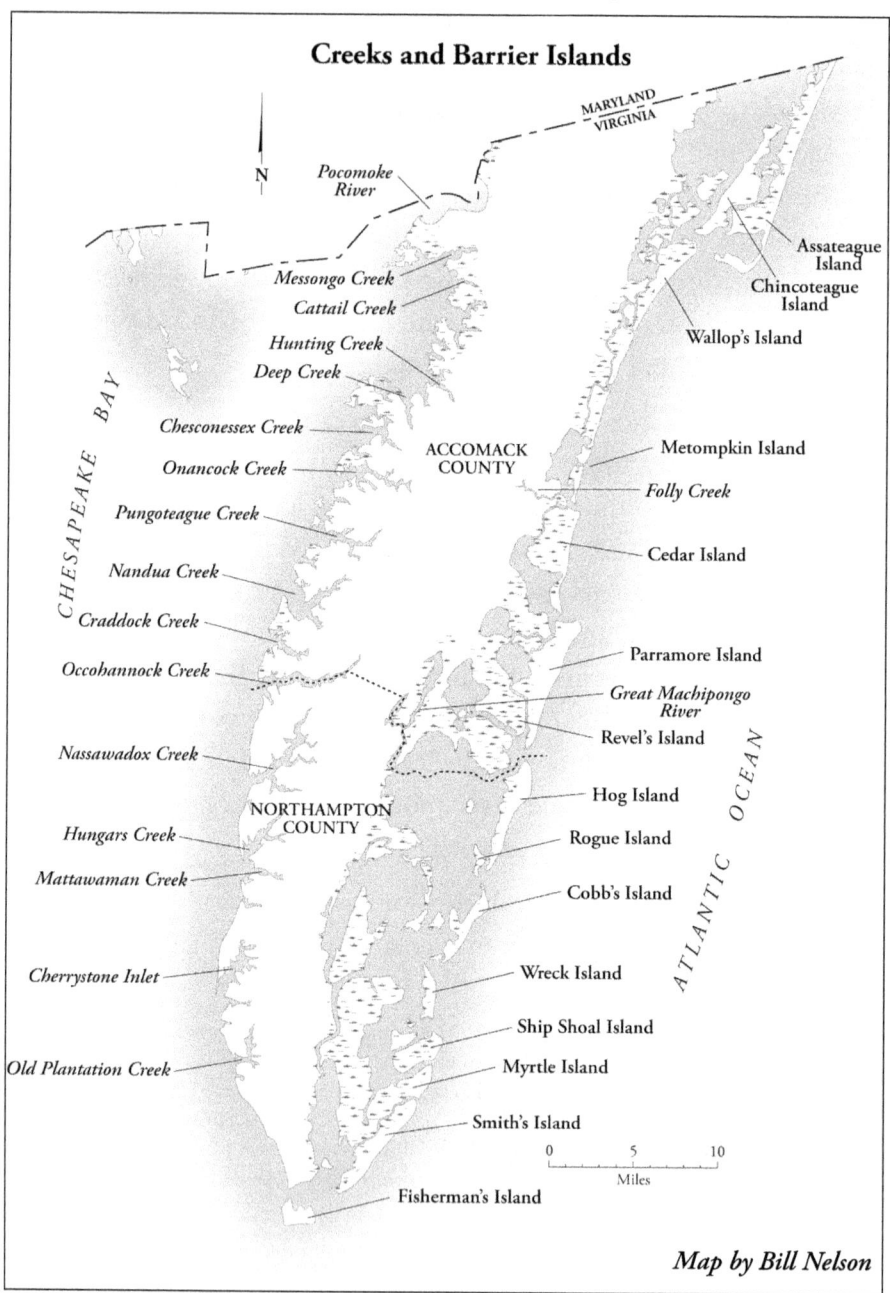

Map by Bill Nelson

islands flourish, whither, and flourish again. The experience of Cobb's Island in the late nineteenth century is typical. In a span of less than forty years storms divided and reunited the island while currents dramatically reshaped its shoreline.

The occasional barrier island is large enough to sustain stands of cedar, pine, and myrtle but most are mere strips of beach and dune. Thousands upon thousands of birds and waterfowl rest on or near the islands during their annual migrations. Nearby marshes are spawning ground for a multitude of marine organisms, and the islands themselves are rookeries for numerous species of shore and sea birds.[21]

On the Chesapeake Bay side of the peninsula, dozens of small islands known as hammocks are scattered in the marsh. Larger islands, such as Saxis, Job's, Tobacco, Tangier, Watts, and Fox are found near the mouths of the creeks and in Pocomoke and Tangier sounds. While the bay islands are more geologically stable than the barriers, they too have experienced the effect of sea level rise. In 1872, Isaac Sterling, aged eighty-one, testified that pine stumps littered the bottom of Pocomoke Sound, and Captain William Sterling, aged sixty-one, stated that Fox and Watts islands had "washed away some good deal in my remembrance." William Nelson, aged sixty-four, recalled family lore that at the time of the Revolution a man with a twelve-foot fence rail could have walked the five miles across what was now open water between Fox and Watts. In 1879, Charles W. B. Marshall, editor of the Onancock *Eastern Virginian*, observed that on Tangier Island the camp meeting ground of twenty-five years before was now submerged 250 yards from shore.[22]

---

21 Brooks Miles Barnes and Barry R. Truitt, "A Short History of the Virginia Barrier Islands," in *Seashore Chronicles: Three Centuries of the Virginia Barrier Islands*, ed. Barnes and Truitt (Charlottesville: University Press of Virginia, 1997), p. 6; "Brant Shooting on the Virginia Broad Waters," Wilmington *Daily Gazette*, November 12, 1881. See also Curtis J. Badger, *Wilderness Regained: The Story of the Virginia Barrier Islands* (Berlin, Md.: Salt Water Media, 2021).

22 Michael S. Kearney and J. Court Stevenson, "Island Land Loss and Marsh Vertical Accretion Rate Evidence for Historical Sea-Level Changes in Chesapeake Bay," *Journal of Coastal Research* 7 (Spring, 1991), pp. 413-414; *Final Report of the Virginia Commissioners on the Maryland and Virginia Boundary to the Governor of Virginia* (Richmond: R. F. Walker, Superintendent of Public Printing, 1874), pp. 159, 182 (quotes William Sterling), 188-190; Onancock *Eastern Virginian* (hereafter cited as EV) in *Richmond Dispatch*, July 8, 1879.

Climate

The Eastern Shore's weather in the post-bellum years was cooler and wetter than today. Tempered by the close proximity of salt water, the winters were mild but with periods of intense cold much in excess of early twenty-first-century experience. In 1881, for example, ice blockaded Cobb's Island from the mainland for the first time since 1857 and the bayside creeks froze so solid that people drove their carriages from shore to shore. The peninsula's surrounding waters ensured a frost-free period from early April to late October. The long growing season allowed Eastern Shore farmers frequently to grow two crops on the same land in the same year. Rainfall was ample and evenly distributed, usually falling most abundantly during the growing season. The bay country's high humidity refreshed the vegetation with heavy nocturnal dews.[23]

The Eastern Shore's growing season lasted about a month longer in lower Northampton than in upper Accomack. E. H. Stevens of the Bureau of Soils noted that "the moderating effect of the Gulf Stream is more marked near the lower extremity of the peninsula. ... Further, the narrowing of the peninsula in Northampton County intensifies the tempering influence of surrounding bodies of water, and also give more 'sweep' to the winds, resulting in freer air circulation. ... The peninsula is so narrow near its lower extremity that the modifying influence of the waters extends to all parts of the interior." As a result, Northampton farmers enjoyed the economic advantage of shipping their truck crops

---

[23] John E. Kutzbach and Thompson Webb III, "Climate and Climate History in the Chesapeake Bay Region," in *Discovering the Chesapeake: The History of an Ecosystem*, eds. Philip D. Curtin, Grace S. Brush, and George W. Fisher (Baltimore and London: The Johns Hopkins University Press, 2001), p. 23; *Richmond Dispatch*, January 2, February 2, 1881; *Forest and Stream* XV (January 27, 1881), p. 511; C. C. Taylor, "Agriculture," in *Virginia Economic and Civic*, eds. R. Lee Humbert, Willard H. Humbert, Melville L. Jeffries, and Clarence W. Newman (Richmond: Whittet & Shepperson for the Virginia Polytechnic Institute in collaboration with the Virginia State Chamber of Commerce, 1933), p. 171; Strong, "Agricultural Conditions"; Brent, "The Eastern Shore of Virginia," p. 5; Stevens *Soil Survey*, p. 12; *Baltimore Sun*, September 10, 1881; Wilmington *Morning News*, February 11, 1881.

earlier in the season than their Accomack neighbors. Both counties shipped sooner than Western Shore counties along the same latitude.[24]

The long, warm summers, although relieved along the waterfront by sea breezes, were a trial to the human spirit. Like a boiling pot, the shallow water of Chesapeake Bay suffused the peninsula in humidity. Eastern Shoremen endured heat and sweat, damp bedding and malodorous bodies. Flying through the moist air were mosquitoes and horseflies. Lurking in the summer woods were ticks and chiggers. "Mosquitoes!" complained Alexander Hunter. "Well, send your enemy to Cape Charles for summer shooting, and then remember him in your prayers." On seaside farms horseflies tormented horses and mules, and on bayside marshes swarms of mosquitoes harried the pastured cattle. Herdsmen protected the cattle during the night by burning piles, or "smothers," of marsh grass. To humans mosquitoes were more than an annoyance. "We have bilious and intermittent fever [of] a mild type," admitted Accomack attorney John W. Gillett in 1869. "For the 12 years, preceding the last two, no section of the Country was healthier, or freer of diseases usually proceeding from malaria. But the loss of labor, occasioned by the emancipation of the slaves, has prevented proper drainage of the lands and as good cultivation as was usual previous to the War and by these causes no doubt are to be attributed the unusual sickness of the two last years." Eastern Shore natives acquired a limited immunity to malaria, but summer visitors to the barrier islands occasionally went home with the 'shakes.'[25]

Extended drought was uncommon but not unheard of. In 1884, drought gripped the land from early August to late October. In mid-September, the Onancock *Eastern Virginian* reported that "The leaves on the trees are turning yellow and falling off; the grass looks brown like

---

24 Stevens, *Soil Survey*, p. 13; Wilmington *Morning News*, April 26, 1882.

25 Stevens, *Soil Survey*, p. 12; *Forest and Stream* XIX (August 17, 1882), p. 47; Edmund Ruffin, "A Trip to Some of the Sea Islands of Virginia," *Farmers' Register* III (1836), p. 531; *Baltimore Sun*, July 4, 1873, September 8, 1876; John W. Gillet, Accomac C. H., to John B. LaForge, February, 1869, Gillet-Wise Family Papers; "Chincoteague Island, Va.," *Baltimore Sun*, August 28, 1876. For the boiling pot analogy see climate expert Mike Allen quoted in Joanne Kimberlin, "We're Just Hot ... and Humid," Norfolk *Virginian-Pilot*, August 18, 2016. For acquired immunity to malaria see Peter H. Wood, *Black Majority: Negroes in Colonial South Carolina From 1670 through the Stono Rebellion* (New York: Alfred A. Knopf, 1974), p. 90.

winter, many streams have ceased to run, and some have dried up; the water in the wells is low, and there is imminent danger of a water famine. There will hardly be more than half a crop of corn, and sweet potatoes leaves wilt in the sun." Woods fires, some accidentally set by coon hunters, raged in both counties, consuming timber, fence rails, and pine shatters. A fire in Hack's Neck burned for more than a month, and the woods on Fox and Watts islands were completely destroyed. Overnight passengers on the bay steamers viewed the spectacle of a series of woods fires reflected on the water.[26]

An ordeal more often endured than drought was the northeast storm. Severe storms swept the Eastern Shore in 1867, 1868, 1876, 1878, and 1879. The storm of October 1878 brought the highest tides in memory, exceeding by three feet those of the Great September Gust of 1822. The worst damage occurred on the seaside. A tidal surge inundated the barrier islands and the new village of Powellton. On the islands, it flooded the recently constructed Life-Saving Service stations, lifting the Cobb's Island station off its foundation. Livestock died by the hundreds in the high water. The Chincoteague correspondent of the *Baltimore Sun* reported that he had "traveled by the little steamer *Widgeon* for over forty miles among the estuaries &c., of the Eastern Shore of Virginia, and the shores of the rivers, &c., were strewn with the carcasses of horses, cattle and sheep." A steamboat captain returned from the Eastern Shore told the *Sun* that "the coast for twenty miles north of Cape Charles has been swept almost entirely of stock, houses and grain." Shipwrecks littered the shore of Cobb's Island and in Chesapeake Bay and its Eastern Shore tributaries sunken, capsized, and beached vessels appeared seemingly everywhere. For days afterward, drowned sailors washed up on bayside and seaside beaches.[27]

---

26 *Norfolk Virginian*, October 11, 1884; *EV* in *Norfolk Weekly Landmark*, September 18, 1884; *Baltimore Sun* in *Norfolk Virginian*, September 12, 1884; *Baltimore Sun* in *Norfolk Landmark*, October 17, 1884; *Baltimore Sun*, October 17, 24, 1884; *PE*, October 18, 1884; Frederick (Md.) *News*, October 27, 1884.

27 *Richmond Dispatch*, April 30, 1867; William H. Fisher, "Cobb's Island, Virginia," *The Osprey* 1 (1897), p. 108; *Alexandria Gazette*, September 25, 1876; *EV*, October 26, November 2, 9, 1878; *Baltimore Sun*, October 26 (second quotation), 28 (first quotation), 29, 1878; August 22, 23, 1879.

Habitations

Human activity on the Eastern Shore of Virginia focused on the waterfront. From creek side wharves and landings people shipped their goods to market, and from creek, marsh, bay, and ocean they obtained seafood, shorebirds, and waterfowl for their tables. They most valued lands a short haul from the water and chose, if possible, to live in the necks between the creeks rather than in the "mid-woods," those often equally fertile lands lying along the spine of the peninsula.[28]

The homes of the large landowners often stood on or near the water. A few were of brick construction but most were of frame. The great majority consisted of sections of unequal size connected by curtains, known locally as colonnades. The stereotypical design consisted of a large, two-storey section attached to a smaller one-storey section, often the oldest part of the house, connected in turn by a curtain to a kitchen. Usually they had been in built in stages as the family prospered. However, Eastern Shoremen were enamored of the style and occasionally built new homes on the multi-sectional plan. Lacking the grandeur of the stereotypical Southern mansion, these houses nonetheless enchanted visitors. "Among the many creeks that deeply indent the shores of the Chesapeake stand numerous old mansions, outlooking over the beautiful waters of the bay, with lawns in front smooth as green velvet, dipping down to the placid water's edge," gushed the writer and illustrator Howard Pyle. "Roomy old-fashioned buildings are these mansions, an air of easy, careless gentility, somewhat decayed, hanging about them." The houses often were as redolent of "careless gentility" inside as out. Another traveler described the sitting room at The Folly near Accomac C. H.: "a heavy mahogany table, mahogany and plate glass side-board, luxuriant chairs, heavy framed pictures of ancestors, and a massive fireplace." Beyond the main houses stood tenant dwellings, smokehouses and granaries, sheds

---

28 Ruffin, "Sketch of a Hasty View," p. 233; Washington *National Republican*, November 1, 1879; "On the Peninsula"; "The Eastern Shore," New York *Evening Post*, April 25, 1885. For the frequent use of the term "mid-woods" see Hamilton, comp., *Northampton County, Virginia, Land Tax Records, 1851-1870*, pp. 397-426.

and stables thatched with straw or pine shatters, and dove-cotes and ice houses. A visitor from Delaware declared that "there are no barns in the sense of that word as it is understood in New Castle county."[29]

The homes and outbuildings of the small landowners and more prosperous tenants were lesser replications of gentry establishments. Most of their houses were of frame construction, but brick structures of two or three rooms occasionally served as the dwellings of small farmers. Much favored was the Siamese-twin house —sections of equal size connected by a curtain. John W. Gillet warned a wealthy client interested in settling on the Eastern Shore of the deficiencies of these houses: "The buildings and improvements are generally of an inferior character, and such as you would not consider as coming with your definition of 'comfortable.'"[30]

At the bottom of the housing scale were the habitations of the poorer families – tenants, laborers, and watermen – black and white. These structures, which comprised at least half of the peninsula's housing, were of one or two rooms with a loft and, sometimes, an attached shed. They included frame structures and log cabins and were characterized by wooden shutters rather than glass windows, fireplaces rather than stoves, and unplastered walls. Some featured brick chimneys; others a frame of logs parged with mud. The houses often were seated on cedar piers and, when painted, whitewashed. A visitor to Tangier Island noticed that its dwellings were "freshly painted white, with fancy colors to set off the contrast." Found within the main room of the homes were a bedstead, a chair or two, and some cooking utensils. Outside stood the ubiquitous

---

[29] Forman, *The Virginia Eastern Shore and its British Origins*, pp. 63, 209, 374-375; Pyle, "Peninsular Canaan," pp. 804-805 (first quotation), 816-817; "Virginian Atlantis" (second quotation); "On the Peninsula" (third quotation). The thatching of stables and sheds with pine shatters continued well into the twentieth century ("Presbyterianism Born at Accomac," *Baltimore American*, April 17, 1927). Discussions with Edward Miles Barnes greatly expanded my knowledge of Eastern Shore architecture.

[30] Forman, *The Virginia Eastern Shore and its British Origins*, pp. 275, 280, 329, 374-375; Ralph T. Whitelaw, *Virginia's Eastern Shore: A History of Northampton and Accomack Counties* (Richmond: Virginia Historical Society, 1951), I, 712; *Norfolk Landmark*, July 16, 1876; "The Eastern Shore," New York *Evening Post*, April 25, 1885; John W. Gillet, Accomac C. H., to John B. LaForge, February, 1869, Gillet-Wise Papers. Gillet also told his client that "The best class residences, - say houses of two stories containing three and sometimes four rooms on a floor, are rarely found on any tract containing less than from three to 500 acres."

smokehouse. As late as 1890, journalist John R. Spears reported that on Chincoteague Island "Dozens and scores of the kind of little shanties in which colored people live in the rural districts of Long Island and New Jersey are to be seen, and it is not without a mental shock that the New Yorker notices that the occupants are almost invariably white."[31]

Architectural historian H. Chandlee Forman identified the English origins of Eastern Shore housing. Subsequent historians and archeologists have shown how from the beginning of colonization the New World environment continually transformed the English prototypes. The homes in which Eastern Shoremen lived in 1870 were current iterations of an old idea. Mary E. Bradley, visiting the peninsula in 1872, approved of how the inhabitants drew on a combination of Old World and New when naming their homes – Chatham and Runnymeade, Wynona and Mattassippi. Nonetheless, she disapproved of the houses themselves:

> It is in architecture that the two counties bear off the palm for utter absurdity and inadequacy. One may ride for miles and miles, and see many wayside dwellings, but not one that answers, even in a remote degree, to Northern ideas of grace, neatness, or comfort. There are a number of fine old mansions, with lofty rooms and wide halls, and a general air of ancient grandeur; but apart from these, the ordinary Accomac or Northampton homestead is a forlorn-looking affair. There is a prevailing indifference to the beautifying

---

31 "Chincoteague Island, Va."; John R. Spears, "Life on Chincoteague," New York *Sun*, May 11, 1890; Nicholas M. Luccketti, Perry McSherry, Martha McCartney, Charles Hodges, and Carl R. Lounsbury, *Phase I Archaeological Survey, Accawmacke Plantation, South Tract at Old Plantation Creek, North Tract at King's Creek, Cape Charles, Virginia* (Williamsburg: James River Institute for Archaeology, Inc, 1993), p. 37; Alexander Hunter, *The Huntsman in the South, Volume I: Virginia and North Carolina* (New York: Neale Publishing Company, 1908), pp. 303-304; Maude Radford Warren, "The Island of Chincoteague," *Harper's Monthly Magazine* 127 (October, 1913), p. 782; *Richmond Dispatch*, August 13, 1875; Adam Wallace, *The Parson of the Islands: A Biography of the Rev. Joshua Thomas* (Cambridge, Md.: Tidewater Publishers, 1961 [reprint of 1861 ed.]), p. 44; "Peninsular Tour: Tangier Sound"; Howard Pyle, "Chincoteague: The Island of Ponies," *Scribner's Monthly* XIII (April, 1877), p. 739. A Northerner who settled near Capeville declared that "you can see plenty of houses twenty-five or thirty years old, that never was white-washed since built" (T. [Israel Townsend] to editor, October 27, Wilmington *Delaware State Journal*, November 8, 1867; A traveler noticed thatched roofs on some cabins and outbuildings ("Virginian Atlantis").

effects of paint and white-wash; barns, fences, dwellings have all the same dingy, weather-stained exterior; doors and windows seem to have been dropped accidently in their places, rather than arranged with definite purpose; rooms are thrown together in the oddest juxtaposition; staircases run down into principal apartments with no intermediate hall-ways or entries; pantries, closets, and other domestic conveniences, indispensable in the simplest Northern cottage, are comparatively unknown; and there is a general architectural stultification, incomprehensible to the stranger, but accepted with satisfied serenity by the native inhabitant.

Where the visitor saw disorder and unconcern, the Eastern Shoreman gazed with "satisfied serenity" on the beloved familiar. These were the homes of a people in touch with their past and comfortable with themselves and the world as it was. Writing a century after Bradley, Forman grasped the mystique of these rambling edifices: "How these Eastern Shore designs build up in simplified and harmonious masses. They do not show the restlessness of much of modern architecture."[32]

These houses, from the big house to the cabin, were filled with people – parents and children, grandparents and other relations, servants and hands. These folks passed their lives within the home circle. Most of their conversation concerned their small, immediate, and constant world. Meanwhile, domestic activities consumed the limited household space, and the bustle of the numerous children enlivened room and yard. Communal life was the only life that most Eastern Shoremen knew. They had acquired no need of privacy, and only an isolated few endured the private ordeal of loneliness.[33]

---

32 Fischer, *Albion's Seed*, pp. 264, 271; Graham *et al.*, "Adaptation and Innovation," pp. 466, 496, 502; Bradley, "On the Eastern Shore," p. 79; Forman, *The Virginia Eastern Shore and its British Origins*, p. 275.

33 Peter Laslet, *The World We Have Lost further explored* (New York: Charles Scribner's Sons, 1983), pp. 21, 119; Andrew Nelson Lytle, *A Wake for the Living: A Family Chronicle* (Nashville: J. S. Sanders & Company, 1992 [reprint of 1975 ed.]), p. 11-12; Rhys Isaac, *The Transformation of Virginia, 1740-1790* (New York and London: W. W. Norton & Company, 1988 [reprint of 1982 ed.], pp. 70-71, 72.

Even after death people remained close to the home. The living interred their dead in family graveyards or nearby churchyards or communal cemeteries. The burial grounds often were marked by a wooden railing or a grove of trees with the graves sometimes decorated with seashells. A Baltimore newspaperman disclosed his cultural blindness by declaring the graveyard on Chincoteague Island's Rattlesnake Ridge "a most extraordinary cemetery, for the reason that it has no memorial stones." A more careful observer might have noticed the absence of native stone on the peninsula and that most of its inhabitants had not the means to bring in tombstones from elsewhere. Perhaps, too, the bereft felt little need for permanent memorials. They preserved the memory of their ancestors in the stories told by the fireside or on the porch.[34]

Most Eastern Shoremen lived within a short distance of a village, most of which stood adjacent to a landing or where roads met at the head of a neck. A Northampton man observed that a village appeared about every six miles along the Bayside Road. These places were small, a handful of dwellings clustered around a store or two (one of which might house a post office), and, perhaps, a church. In upper Accomack County watermen made their homes along the shores of Pocomoke Sound and Chincoteague Bay. With a relatively dense population living on holdings of five acres or less, the countryside there assumed the aspect of a dispersed village. The only places on the peninsula resembling towns were Onancock, a collecting point for grain shipments, and the county seats of Accomac C. H. (also known as Drummondtown) and Eastville.[35]

The people of the Eastern Shore lived in a world of natural sound. They heard the wind through the pines, the song of birds and insects, and the lowing of cattle and bleating of sheep. They heard the muffled clop of horses passing on sandy roads and their neighbor calling her children. When wind and atmosphere were right, they heard the ocean breaking upon the beach and the boom of the sunset gun at Fort

---

34 "The Eastern Shore," New York *Evening Post*, April 25, 1885; Pyle "Peninsular Canaan," pp. 807-808; *EV*, July 27, 1878; J. P. Matthews, "Chincoteague Island," Baltimore *American* in Westminster (Md.) *Democratic-Advocate*, August 23, 1873.

35 *Alexandria Gazette*, September 25, 1876; Sue Brittingham, "New Church History is Given," *PE*, April 5, 1956; Wallace, *The Parson of the Islands*, p. 44; Accomack County Land Tax, 1869.

Monroe. The only alien sounds they suffered were the chug and whistle of the steamboats coming up the creek or the shriek of the steam sawmill in the thicket. Of a fall evening, standing in their doorways, they heard the music of the hounds and, through an otherwise inviolate darkness, saw the brilliance of the night sky and, perhaps, a light burning in a distant window.[36]

They also lived in a world of immense natural bounty. The soil was productive and the climate mild. The surrounding waters yielded seemingly inexhaustible harvests of seafood and of shorebirds and waterfowl. An observer noted that Eastern Shoremen "have a continuous crop in the fish, oysters, clams, crabs, &c. To an 'uplander' it is really curious to see a member of the family here go to the bay or sea-side to gather fish, oysters, &c., for each and almost every meal, just as they go their gardens for vegetables, or their poultry-yards for eggs and poultry." John S. Wise, an Accomack native, deemed the peninsula farm owner "the most contented and independent being in the world." Poorer people also fared well, seafood and wildfowl supplementing their high-protein, vitamin-rich diet of lean range pork and unrefined corn bread. Having considered the generosity of the peninsula's landscape, a Wilmingtonian declared that "The poor man who knows how to cultivate a garden can always make a living there, and if he knows how to use a gun, a trap, and a fishing net he need never suffer for want of meat."[37]

Most visitors believed the natives of the Eastern Shore lacked initiative. They echoed each other in labeling the peninsula a "Lazy Man's Paradise." A Richmonder acknowledged that Eastern Shore farmers

---

[36] Camp Wilkes (Accomac C. H.) *Regimental Flag*, January 16, 1862, in Darrell N. Middleton, comp., *The Second Regiment Delaware Volunteers* (Georgetown, Del.: By the Author, 2005); *Alexandria Gazette*, September 25, 1876; "Parksley's a Paradise," *New York Times*, September 15, 1895.

[37] Robert Wilson, "On the Chesapeake," *Appleton's Journal* X (October 11, 1873), p. 466; Fannie B. Ward, "Red Letter Days, No. III: Summering at Old Point Comfort," New Orleans *Daily Picayune*, July 21, 1878; *Richmond Dispatch*, August 13, 1875 (quotation); Brent, *The Eastern Shore of Virginia*, p. 5 (quotes John S. Wise); *Middletown (Del.) Transcript*, July 23, 1870; Pyle, "Chincoteague," p. 738; Pyle, "Peninsular Canaan," p. 811; Spears, "Life on Chincoteague"; Wilmington *Morning News*, November 15, 1884. For the high-protein, vitamin-rich diet of tenant farmers in the antebellum South see Grady McWhiney, "The Revolution in Nineteenth-Century Alabama Agriculture," *Alabama Review* 31 (January, 1978), pp. 27-28.

failed to exploit fully their advantages, but he discounted laziness as the cause. "Their lands have been so good they have not felt the necessity of improving them," he wrote. "Perhaps another cause of neglect of the land is the world of wealth of the seas that wash the shores." Nathaniel H. Bishop, who touched on the Eastern Shore during a canoe expedition along the Atlantic Coast in 1874-1875, maintained that "In no portion of America do the people seem to feel the burden of earning a livelihood more lightly. They get a great deal of social enjoyment out of life at very little cost, and place much less value on the 'mighty dollar' than do their brother farmers of the northern section of the states." John R. Spears took the analysis a bit further. "They do not hurry. ... They do not have to," he maintained. "They have everything they want. ... [L]acking hurry they lack also worry and anxiety – the Northern man wonders whether after all the peninsula farmer does not come as near solving the problem of life as any one."[38]

It is easy to romanticize this lost world, to overlook the inequalities of race and class, to ignore the ravages of disease and age, to forget that work was continuous, domestic conveniences few and for most people unobtainable, and rural life for some, even in the midst of family and friends, intellectually stultifying. And yet so pleasant seemed the life lived there that a newspaper editor, writing in 1858, might be excused the encomium:

> The best roads in the world; the gamest little horses to trot over them; taverns by the roadside where the best fare tempts the epicure at every stopping place; a sky and an atmosphere outrivaling those of Italy in all that tempts to indulgences in a *dolce far niente* [pleasant idleness], yet braced by breezes alternately laden with the murmurs of the Chesapeake and

---

38 "Chincoteague Island, Va."; Pyle, "Peninsular Canaan," p. 805; "My Own Trip: Cape Charles – The Eastern Shore," *Richmond Dispatch*, August 19, 1874 (first quotation); Nathaniel H. Bishop, *Voyage of the Paper Canoe: A Geographical Journey of 2500 Miles, From Quebec to the Gulf of Mexico, During the Years 1874-5* (Edinburgh: David Douglas, 1878), pp. 124-125; John R. Spears, "The Virginia Peninsula: It Is New York's Great Sweet Potato Patch," *New York Sun*, May 11, 1890. For "lazy man's paradise" see Wilmington *Morning News*, September 22, 1884; "On the Peninsula"; Spears, "Life on Chincoteague."

the roar of the Atlantic; bright sunshine scarcely dimmed by refreshing showers; moonlights cool and balmy - . ... the forests of gigantic pines, skirted with the brighter foliage of oak and maple, gum and beech, hawthorn, crab-apple, dogwood and laurel; and then the wide views of beach and marsh, sea and sky, which seem to melt into each other in one unbroken prospect.[39]

Livelihoods

The overwhelming majority of the people, black and white, made their livings from land, water, or woods. The comment of a journalist about the lands along the Rappahannock River applied equally to the Eastern Shore: "The prevalence of bold water throughout this region, in the shape of numerous and navigable bays, creeks and estuaries which indent the coast, has given a semi-amphibious character to the population." Thus, occupations given in the federal census – farmer, farm laborer, oysterman, fisherman, sailor, sawyer – did not necessarily indicate specialization. Someone working in the maritime trades might also pick strawberries, tend cattle grazing on the marsh, or raise a patch of potatoes for the market. A farmer or farm laborer might also rake clams or tong oysters for the local storekeeper. "Nearly everybody's house has a water-way to it," remarked a Baltimore man, "sailboats lie moored at the shore, fishing nets are hung on trees, and the oyster-tongs and field rake repose side by side in the tool-house when not employed." A working life begun on the water might move to the land and vice versa. In 1870, Oscar Coles Miles, a sailor, aged twenty-four, lived near Johnsontown in Northampton County on the farm of his father Richard Miles, himself a retired sailboat captain. Ten years later, Coles, as he was known, was the head of his own household and a farmer. At the time of his death in 1913, he was still listed in the census as a farmer but also was leasing

---

39 "Accomac and Northampton."

oyster planting ground. Meanwhile, in 1906, a son of Coles had married a near neighbor whose father's occupation was oyster planter.[40]

On the Land

Agriculture

For more than 150 years, grain had been the Eastern Shore's predominant crop. "Like Boniface," Abel Parker Upshur of Northampton County told a friend in 1824, "we eat our own grain, and drink our grain, and sleep upon our grain." In the late antebellum period, Accomack ranked among the commonwealth's leading counties in the production of oats and corn. Samuel T. Ross recalled of Onancock in the 1850s that grain houses and accompanying wharves stood as far up the creek as vessels could load. Beginning about 1820, first sweet potatoes and then Irish potatoes emerged as competitors to grain. Stimulated by urban demand, potatoes by 1870 rivaled grain for primacy among Eastern Shore farmers.[41]

---

40 "The Oyster at Home," *Southern Review* XXIV (October, 1878), pp. 391-392 (first quotation); "The Maryland Seaside," *Baltimore Sun*, August 16, 1876 (quotes "N. E. F."). For Oscar Coles Miles see Latimer, comp., *1870 Census for Northampton County*, p. 81; Allen B. Hamilton, comp., *The Northampton County, Virginia, 1880 Census* (Millsboro, Del., Colonial Roots, 2016), p. 111; Hamilton, comp., *Northampton County, Virginia, 1900 Census* (Berwyn Heights, Md.: Heritage Books, 2018), p. 98A; Northampton County, Virginia, Census of Population, 1910, district 94, p. 6A; Jean Merritt Mihalyka, comp., *Gravestone Inscriptions in Northampton County, Virginia* (Richmond: Virginia State Library, 1980), p. 56; *Annual Report of the Commission of Fisheries of Virginia, October 1, 1914 to September 30, 1915* (Richmond: Davis Bottom, Superintendent of Public Printing, 1916), p. 159; Phyllis Elmore, comp., *Northampton County Marriages, 1854-1922* (Coram, N. Y.: Peter's Row, 2007), p. 141.

41 Claude H. Hall, *Abel Parker Upshur: Conservative Virginian* (Madison: The State Historical Society of Wisconsin, 1964), p. 28 (quotes Upshur to William Kennon, September 29, 1824); "Virginia Agricultural Statistics," *The Virginia Historical Register and Literary Companion* V (July, 1852), p. 173; "Onancock and Accomack County," Richmond *Times-Dispatch* in Onancock *Accomack News*, October 30, 1909; Samuel T. Ross, "Recollections of Onancock," *PE*, February 13, March 20, 1942. Commercial sweet potato shipments from the Eastern Shore date from at least the 1760s (Purdie and Dixon Williamsburg *Virginia Gazette* December 3, 1767). John W. A. Elliott, writing as "Septuagenarian," mistakenly claimed that the first sweet potato shipment from the Eastern Shore occurred in 1827 (*PE*. March 7, 1891). Eugene Barnes claimed that the first Irish potatoes were shipped from the peninsula in the early 1840s (*ESN*,

In 1870 there were 1,456 farms in Accomack and 640 in Northampton. Average farm size in Accomack was 112 acres and in Northampton 167. Both were below the Virginia average of 246 acres. The pattern of farm size in the two counties mirrored the pattern of landholding. In Accomack 88.5 percent of the farms were of 99 acres or less; in Northampton 65.3 percent. Only 12.5 percent of the farms in Accomack were of 100 acres or more; in Northampton 34.7 percent. Northampton actually surpassed the larger and more populous Accomack by 222 to 182 in the number of farms of 100 acres or more. The farm operators were predominately white. The federal census listed only 186 black farmers in Accomack and 126 in Northampton. Though small, these figures illustrate the impact of emancipation. In 1860 free black farmers numbered 77 in Accomack and only 10 in Northampton. In April 1870 black politician Peter J. Carter of Northampton told the Washington *New Era* that "At the close of the late war the whites said they would neither 'sell nor rent their land to colored people.' But they soon found out that large plantations would not pay so well as they did when they had the negroes to cultivate them." The black-operated farms generally were of less acreage than the white.[42]

The agricultural census of 1870 neglected to note farm tenure – whether the farm operator owned the land he worked or whether he rented it for money or a share of the crop. The limited distribution of Eastern Shore land ownership and data from the 1880 census indicates that around 60 percent of the farmers in the two counties were tenants

---

March 18, 1921, June 22, 1928).

42 *The Statistics of the Wealth and Industry of the United States ... Compiled, From the Original Returns of the Ninth Census (June 1, 1870)*, pp. 266, 270, 364; Harahan, "Politics, Political Parties, and Voter Participation," p. 43; Frances Bibbins Latimer, comp., *1860 Census for Northampton County* (Eastville, Va.: Hickory House, 1994); Latimer, comp., *1870 Census for Northampton County*; E. Thomas Crowson and Susan Crowson Hite, comps., *Accomack County, Virginia, 1860 Census* (Bowie, Md.: Heritage Books, 1987 from copy corrected by Barry W. Miles, M. K. Miles III, and Phyllis Elmore, in Eastern Shore Heritage Center); Walczyk, comp., *The Accomack County 1870 Census*; Lt. Eld. Murphy, Drummondtown, to Brig. Gen. Orlando Brown, January 31, 1867, Records of the Bureau of Refugees, Freedmen, and Abandoned Lands, Drummondtown and Eastville, Virginia, United States, National Archives, Record Group 105, vol. 151, pp. 38-39 (microfilm copy in Eastern Shore Heritage Center); Peter J. Carter, Northampton County, to editor, Washington *New Era*, May 5, 1870; *Baltimore Sun*, September 10, 1881.

and that a substantial majority of them rented for money. Ownership among black farmers was rare, and they were more likely to rent on shares than their white counterparts. The agricultural census also failed to differentiate between the share tenant who himself disposed of his portion of the crop and the sharecropper who surrendered the disposition of the crop to the landowner. Tenants might rent for the year or lease for a number of years. They negotiated terms with the landowner about rent, improvements on the premises, and the supply of seed, fertilizer, and work stock. At Christmas tenants renewed their contracts or removed to a new situation. They were constantly on the lookout for better terms, better buildings, more woodland resources, and more fertile land. For their part, the landowners sought tenants who would treat the property responsibly and, especially if renting on shares, who would work the land diligently.[43]

Between 1850 and 1870 the number of farms on the Eastern Shore expanded while average farm acreage contracted. The most dramatic change occurred during the decade of Civil War and Reconstruction, 1860 to 1870, when the number of farms increased from 1,533 to 2,096 while the average farm acreage declined from 172 to 128.5. The changes in farm number and average farm acreage reflected not only the demise of the slave regime but also the shift from grain to potatoes. Truck farming generated significantly higher gross sales per acre than grain farming. Two acres of potatoes earned the same average return as fifteen acres of corn. While the shift to truck farming led to a decline in average farm acreage, it also contributed, along with the concurrent expansion of the seafood industry, to the growth in population. Eastern Shore population, which had grown by 9.5 percent in the four decades between 1800 and 1840, grew by 12.8 percent as the shift gained momentum in the three decades from 1840 to 1870. Requiring fewer acres to make a living under the new agricultural arrangement, farmers felt less need to

---

43 Barbara Jeanne Fields, *Slavery and Freedom on the Middle Ground: Maryland During the Nineteenth Century* (New Haven: Yale University Press, 1985), p. 177; Emmett B. Fields, "The Agricultural Population of Virginia, 1850-1860," Ph.D dissertation, Vanderbilt University, 1953, p. 182; E. R. Tatem to Philip A. Fitzhugh, August 5, 1872, Philip A. and William Bullitt Fitzhugh Papers, 1821-1939, Duke University, Durham, North Carolina.

keep their holdings intact. They sold or rented surplus land or subdivided their estates among their children by deed or testament. People, including freedmen, who might have emigrated chose to stay put.[44]

The change in number of farms and *average* farm acreage did not necessarily correlate with changes in *total* farm acreage. In the twenty years between 1850 and 1870, the number of farms in Accomack increased from 1,007 to 1,456 and average farm acreage decreased from 222 to 112. Total farm acreage in the county also decreased from 223,733 to 162,626, an astonishing loss of 27 percent. Meanwhile, Northampton also experienced an increase in the number of farms from 376 to 640 and a decrease in average farm acreage from 249 to 167. Although as involved in the transition from grain to truck farming as Accomack, Northampton's total farm acreage increased from 93,549 to 106,713, a gain of 14 percent. The decline in total farm acreage in Accomack occurred because rising sea level encroached on formerly arable land on the margins of Pocomoke Sound and because many of the county's farmers curtailed or abandoned farming in order to find employment in the burgeoning seafood industries.[45]

Ideally, Eastern Shore farmers desired a homeplace with good soil, a nearby wharf for shipping produce, and easy access to hunting, fishing, and the gathering of oysters. Perhaps most important, the farm must have a good stand of wood. Farmers valued woodland as hunting grounds and as windbreaks for their crops and houses, and they required lumber for building and repairs, stove wood, hot-bed frames, packaging, and fencing. As truck farming gained importance, they increasingly needed pine shatters to spread as manure on their potato fields. They calculated that they required about an acre of pine woods to supply every acre of plowed ground. They kept the understory free of briars and saplings and they guarded the boundary line running through their

---

44 Mears, Statistics from Federal Censuses; G. Terry Sharrer, "Farming, Disease, and Change in the Chesapeake Ecosystem" in *Discovering the Chesapeake*, p. 312; John Fraser Hart, *The Rural Landscape* (Baltimore: The Johns Hopkins University Press, 1998), p. 280.

45 Mears, Statistics from Federal Censuses; Erin Putalik and Brian Davis, "Bay Migrations," *Places Journal* (October, 2022) https://placesjournal.org/article/climate-and-migration-in-the-chesapeake-marsh. Accessed 21 October 2022.

woods as jealously as that crossing their most fertile field. They found a ready market in shatters to neighbors who lacked an adequate pine thicket. Eastern Shoremen deemed any farm deficient in shatters or, in local parlance, "resources," as undesirable. Accomack abounded in "resources." In 1870, the ratio of improved acreage to woodland in Northampton County was two to one while that in Accomack was nearly even. The difference between the two counties resulted from the presence in Accomack of large marshes and of tracts of poorly drained but heavily timbered land.[46]

Although in 1870 truck crops increasingly absorbed the attention of farmers, grain production remained significant. Corn led the way at 797,154 bushels, followed by oats at 476,528. Wheat, at 3,457, had become inconsequential. The corn harvest had declined by 20 percent since 1860, but Eastern Shore farmers continued to consider it of crucial importance. Nearly every farmer in Accomack and nine out of ten in Northampton planted corn. Eastern Shoremen sold some of the crop but used most of it to feed their livestock and themselves. "Corn is the staple grain," declared a visitor, "and pone is more frequently met with than white bread." The locals liked their cornbread coarse. John J. Townsend, a Delawarean who settled in Capeville just after the Civil War, told his hometown newspaper that "when we first run our steam grist mill, we had a sifter attached, like other mills, but the 'natives' quit coming to the mill, so we had to disconnect it and grind the meal a little finer than horse feed to please them. The negroes eat the meal without sifting at all."[47]

In tending their corn crop, Eastern Shore farmers generally followed

---

46 Wilbur O'Byrne, "More and Better Pines on the Eastern Shore,"; *ESN*, October 23, 1936; *Richmond Dispatch*, April 16, 1874; Will Payne, "Cooperation – Colorado Apples; Virginia Potatoes; Retail Stores," *Saturday Evening Post*, July 16, 1910, p. 41; *EV*, July 7, 1876; *Norfolk Landmark*, July 16, 1876; *Baltimore Sun*, September 10, 1881; Stevens, *Soil Survey*, p. 23; "Presbyterianism Born at Accomac"; *The Statistics of the Wealth and Industry of the United States ... Compiled, From the Original Returns of the Ninth Census (June 1, 1870)*, pp. 266, 270.

47 *The Statistics of the Wealth and Industry of the United States ... Compiled, From the Original Returns of the Ninth Census (June 1, 1870)*, pp. 267, 268, 271, 272; Mears, Statistics from Federal Censuses; Accomack County, Virginia, Census of Agriculture, 1870; Northampton County, Virginia, Census of Agriculture, 1870; "On the Peninsula"; *Middletown (Del.) Gazette*, July 9, 1870 (quotes John J. Townsend).

the ways of the fathers. Only a few employed modern machinery such as corn planters or cultivators. The farmers prepared the earth for the crop in February and planted in March. A New York reporter watched a farmer near Accomac C. H. "turning up the sandy loam with one mule power. He threw up a furrow, a colored woman followed dropping a kernel every two feet, and a negro came behind with a harrow to cover it – this was his method of planting corn." After the corn came up in April, they usually tilled the soil with a plow rather than a cultivator. In late autumn they harvested the ears. A Wilmingtonian viewing the fields before the fodder was gathered noted that "the old-fashioned method of topping the plant just above the ear is still in vogue, and hundreds of acres of dry sticks, standing about three feet apart, may be seen."[48]

Oat production had declined at nearly the same rate as that of corn. Nonetheless, oats remained valuable to Eastern Shore farmers as animal feed and cash crop. In 1870, 85.8 percent of the farmers in Accomack and 53.4 percent of those in Northampton grew oats. Townsend criticized local oat culture as caustically as he had that of corn. "Spring opens here about the last of February, when they commence plowing in the oats." he told his friends back in Delaware. "The oats are sown broadcast, and plowed in with one horse and a small plow, about 3 inches deep, the rougher they can get the land plowed the better. A harrow or roller is something they consider useless." At the harvest in July, "Oats are cradled altogether, as there is not a reaper in the county. I have seen 20 cradlers in one field at a time. The grain is not bound into sheaves but lie in the field until properly cured, then hauled in and stacked." A thrifty Philadelphian strongly disagreed with the insistence of most local farmers that the peninsula's mild climate made the erection of barns an unnecessary expense. "The grain is threshed in the open field, on the bare earth," he sniffed, "and I am assured, by competent authority, that one-tenth of the crop is wasted, while on a barn floor not a peck would be lost." Some farmers employed threshing machines but most used horses to tramp out the grain. They then stored the oats in granaries.[49]

---

48 *Middletown (Del.) Gazette*, July 2, 1870; "The Eastern Shore," New York *Evening Post*, April 25, 1885 (first quotation); Pyle, "Peninsular Canaan," p. 817; "On the Peninsula" (second quotation).

49 Mears, Statistics from Federal Censuses; Accomack County, Virginia, Census of Agricul-

In their dependence on manual labor, Eastern Shore farmers certainly seemed bound by tradition. Their critics, however, failed to take into consideration that under the antebellum regime farmers had little incentive to purchase expensive machinery that recalcitrant slaves might willfully sabotage and that, in the immediate postbellum years, even if farmers had discarded ingrained assumptions about black labor, they were too impoverished to purchase reapers, corn planters, and the like. Moreover, to farmers whose landholdings were small and whose labor was supplied by family members and a few hired hands, the acquisition of costly machinery seemed unnecessary.[50]

In the use of fertilizer, Eastern Shore farmers combined the old ways with the new. They drew on a tradition reaching back to England in improvising from local matter – excess or unpalatable fish, lime from burned or fragmented clam or oyster shells, and pine shatters, woods mould, creek mud, and seaweed composted with animal manure. They knew that woods and creek muck served as an effective plant food and that a ton of horse droppings when mixed with pine shatters could supply three or four tons of compost annually. Eastern Shore farmers had been among the first to use Peruvian guano following its importation into the United States in 1843. Israel Townsend of Capeville (John J. Townsend's father) complained in 1867 that Peruvian guano could not be had at "a reasonable price … as to phosphates of the different makes, the people have been so swindled that I doubt if there was a any real honest phosphate manipulator to make a present of a cargo of his best that any one would take it as a gift."[51]

---

ture, 1870; Northampton County, Virginia, Census of Agriculture, 1870; *Middletown (Del.) Transcript*, July 2 (quotes John J. Townsend), 23, 1870; *Philadelphia Inquirer*, August 8, 19 (quotation), 1865; Gabrielle M. Lanier and Bernard L. Herman, *Everyday Architecture of the Mid-Atlantic: Looking at Buildings and Landscapes* (Baltimore and London: The Johns Hopkins University Press, 1997), p. 193.

50 Eugene D. Genovese, *The Political Economy of Slavery: Studies in the Economy and Society of the Slave South* (New York: Vintage Books, 1965), pp. 54-55; Harold D. Woodman, comment on Jonathan M. Wiener, "Class Structure and Economic Development in the American South, 1865-1955," *American Historical Review* 84 (October, 1979), p. 1000.

51 Mildred Campbell, *The English Yeoman in the Tudor and Early Stuart Age* (London: Merlin Press, 1983 [reprint of 1942 ed.), p. 175; W. S. Eyre, "Farming and Manures of the Eastern

Outsiders also expressed surprise at the failure of the locals to plant clover. A newspaper correspondent who styled himself "Rambler" believed that "the greatest display of short-sightedness among the farmers, is the almost universal absence of the cheapest, fastest and best land improver that was ever put on the land, which is red clover." Earlier commentators had noted that peninsula farmers used the indigenous partridge pea, known locally as the Magothy Bay bean, as a cover crop. Like clover, the Magothy Bay bean provides browse for livestock and is rich in nitrogen upon which corn feeds heavily. Edmund Ruffin acknowledged the bean as "peculiarly adapted to sandy soil" and as "an improver of fertility" but lamented that it was "a scattered and thin cover compared to what is found under more favorable circumstances." When grain was the predominant crop, the typical crop rotation was corn, oats, and Magothy Bay beans. Available sources do not reveal the prevailing rotation used by farmers under the mixed grain and truck regime of 1870.[52]

By 1870 the production of sweet potatoes had reached 292,196 bushels and that of Irish potatoes 159,346 bushels. Eastern Shore growers preferred the sweet potato. It stored better than the Irish and its longer shipping period – four months to the Irish potato's two – inhibited price fluctuations. Most important, the flavor of the variety produced on the Eastern Shore made it a favorite in Northern markets. In 1870 97.8 percent of Accomack's farmers and 85.9 percent of Northampton's

---

Shore of Virginia," *Farmers' Register* I (March, 1834), p. 731; Ruffin, "Sketch of a Hasty View," 233; John H. Snead, "Remarks," appended to St. George's Parish, Accomack County, Virginia, Census of Persons Who Died During the Year Ending June 1, 1850; A. Oemler, "Truck Farming," in *Report of the Commissioner of Agriculture, 1885* (Washington: Government Printing Office, 1885), p. 593; F. M. L. Thompson, "Nineteenth-Century Horse Sense," *Economic History Review* 29 (February, 1976), p. 77; Rosser H. Taylor, "The Sale and Application of Commercial Fertilizers in the South Atlantic States to 1900," *Agricultural History* 21 (January, 1947), pp. 46, 50; Weymouth T. Jordan, "The Peruvian Guano Gospel in the Old South," *ibid.* 24 (October, 1950), pp. 217-218; T. [Israel Townsend] to editor, April 16, Wilmington *Delaware State Journal*, April 23, 1867.

52 "On the Peninsula"; "Through Accomac," Wilmington *Daily Republican*, June 2, 1885 (quotes "Rambler"); Ruffin, "Sketch of a Hasty View," p. 234; Joseph Martin, *A New Comprehensive Gazetteer of Virginia, and the District of Columbia* (Charlottesville: J. Martin, Mosley & Tompkins, 1835), pp. 249-250; Fitzhugh, "Eastern Shore of Virginia," p. 90. Stacia Childers drew my attention to the resemblance of the Magothy Bay bean to the partridge pea.

grew sweet potatoes. John J. Townsend discovered that raw sweet potatoes were served in the place of fruit: "In the fall, if you go to call on your neighbors, instead of apples being handed around, you will see a plate of pared sweet potatoes offered to you, a very good substitute."[53]

Sweet potato culture always was at hand. Even before the harvest was over, preparation of the soil for the next year's crop had commenced. In the fall and winter, farmers gathered immense quantities of pine shatters from the woods. Having brought in their livestock for the winter, they spread the shatters in the cattle pounds, hog pens, and stable yards. All through the winter, they added fresh shatters, woods mould, creek mud, and seaweed while removing the ripe compost to piles scattered about the farm yard. James H. A. Johnson watched Peter Savage, a prosperous black farmer living near Belle Haven, put into his hog pen "load after load of shatters, and keep on at it until he would have to take a little ladder to get up to his hogs." In March, Savage and his fellow farmers planted seed potatoes in hot-beds – narrow strips of pine board supporting a covering of shatters or sheets of oil cloth or, increasingly, panes of glass. Meanwhile, the farmers had hauled the piles of compost to the fields (500 to 2,000 cartloads per farm), spread it as thick as practicable, and plowed it under. In late April, they removed the potato slips from the hot-beds, planted them in the rich, friable soil, and continuously cultivated them until the harvest began in August. Thence, they began the cycle anew.[54]

Irish potatoes required less time and effort. Hot-beds were unnecessary. In late February and early March, farmers plowed their fields and dug trenches, which they filled with commercial fertilizer and ridged

---

53 *The Statistics of the Wealth and Industry of the United States ... Compiled, From the Original Returns of the Ninth Census (June 1, 1870)*, pp. 268, 272; "A Land of Promise," *Baltimore Rambler* in *Southern Planter* 44 (March, 1883), p. 151; James Egbert Mears, *Hacks Neck and Its People Past and Present* (Chicago: Author, 1937), p. 46; *Richmond Dispatch*, April 10, 1875; *Philadelphia Inquirer*, March 20, 1878; Accomack County, Virginia, Census of Agriculture, 1870; Northampton County, Virginia, Census of Agriculture, 1870; *Middletown (Del.) Transcript*, July 9, 1870 (quotes John J. Townsend).

54 *Baltimore Sun*, September 10, 1881, February 27, 1927; Richmond Dispatch, April 10, 1875, January 22, 1879; Johnson, *The Pine Tree Mission*, p. 16; *Middletown (Del.) Transcript*, July 2, 1870; Payne "Cooperation," p. 41.

over before planting seed potatoes. Irish potato farmers used fertilizer liberally – from 500 pounds to a ton per acre. Desiring to produce "new" potatoes for the Northern markets, they "forced" an early harvest by applying as much fertilizer as they could afford. The growers knew that potatoes sent North in May brought a better price than those sold in the glutted market of June. Immediately following the harvest, they planted a second crop that would be ready for shipment in the fall. In 1870, 83.6 percent of the farmers in Accomack and 63.9 percent of those in Northampton grew Irish potatoes. Enjoying the advantage of a climate favorable to early harvests, Northampton farmers who had the means to purchase sufficient quantities of the preferred fertilizers – Peruvian guano and ground fish meal – made new potato production a specialty.[55]

Eastern Shore farmers also marketed small quantities of other crops. Peach orchards were found on nearly every farm. Some of the peaches were picked by women and children, black and white, packed in ventilated wooden containers, and shipped North. Others the women pared and dried for barter with local storekeepers for household necessities. The men distilled the rest of the crop into a liquor famous along the eastern seaboard as Accomack Peach Brandy. A few farmers grew strawberries, which were sent to market in wooden pint or quart containers packed into crates of sixty- to seventy-quarts capacity. Some growers marketed plums, apples, quinces, and watermelons that sold readily in urban markets but generally brought low prices. Writing from Onancock in 1874, the correspondent "Viator" lamented that "Melons grow in such quantities that the people find it profitable to feed them to their hogs." A few farmers planted cotton but low yields, high fertilizer costs, and onerous federal taxes severely limited the acreage devoted to the crop.[56]

---

55 G. Terry Sharrer, *A Kind of Fate: Agricultural Change in Virginia, 1861-1920* (Ames: Iowa State University Press, 2000), p. 56; Charles P. Finney Day Book, 1871-1888, Eastern Shore Heritage Center; *Richmond Dispatch*, April 30, 1867, April 14, 1868, January 5, 1869; T. [Israel Townsend], Capeville, to editor, March 16, Wilmington *Delaware State Journal*, March 22, 1867; Accomack County, Virginia, Census of Agriculture, 1870; Northampton County, Virginia, Census of Agriculture, 1870.

56 *Philadelphia Inquirer*, August 19, 1865; "Onancock and Accomack County"; Ross, "Recollections of Onancock"; Robert Wilson, "On the Eastern Shore," *Lippincott's Magazine* XVIII

Before the Civil War, Eastern Shoremen marketed their produce from the Canadian Maritimes to the West Indies. "Every Atlantic market is open to their choice," Ruffin declared in 1835. The Union blockade cut off commerce with Southern ports, and, after the war, the South's impoverishment precluded the trade's immediate resumption. The Eastern Shore found itself firmly under the sway of markets to the North, principally Baltimore, Philadelphia, New York, and Boston.[57]

The farmers possessing schooners or sloops marketed their own crops. Some sold or consigned produce to mariners who resold in the urban markets. Others sold their crops to local merchants who supplied on credit their agricultural and domestic needs. The larger of the mercantile firms operated small fleets of sailboats and maintained large warehouses. The granaries of Hopkins & Bro. in Onancock had a capacity of 75,000 bushels. During the harvest months of 1871, Charles P. Finney operated three schooners from his wharf on Onancock Creek. Merchants, sailboat skippers, and those farmers who bypassed the local middleman sold direct to city retailers or consigned their produce to a handful of urban commission merchants who disposed of the goods and, after deducting their fees and expenses, remitted the balance to the client.[58]

Livestock were a critical source of food, fertilizer, and motive power. Cattle, sheep, and hogs supplied farmers with meat, dairy products, wool, hides, and manure. On an ascending scale, Eastern Shore farmers in 1870 kept sheep (21.5 percent), beef cattle (68.5 percent), milch cows (81 percent), and hogs (98.7 percent). They favored hogs over sheep and cattle because of their higher rate of reproduction and because the lower

---

(1876), pp. 364-365; Charles P. Finney Day Book; Washington *Evening Star*, September 27, 1866; *Richmond Dispatch*, April 14, 1868, April 13, 1874 (quotes "Viator"); T. [Israel Townsend], Capeville, March 16, May 27, to editor, Wilmington *Delaware State Journal*, March 22, May 31, 1867; Wilmington *Delaware Tribune*, February 24, 1870. For the federal taxation of cotton, see E. Merton Coulter, *The South During Reconstruction*, 1865-1877 (Baton Rouge: Louisiana State University Press, 1947), pp. 10-12.

57 Ruffin, "Sketch of a Hasty View," p. 233; Elizabeth H. Smith, "Century-Old Firm Retains Charm of Yester-Years," *Southern States Cooperative* in ESN, January 23, 1942.

58 Smith, "Century-Old Firm"; Benjamin T. Gunter, "Produce Exchange Keystone of Prosperity," *PE*, August 8, 1936; Charles P. Finney Day Book; Littleton T. LeCato to editor, October 19, *PE*, October 24, 1891.

water content of pork made it easier to preserve. These animals were not blooded stock. Antebellum farmers had little incentive to buy improved animals that might be abused by subversive slaves, and their postbellum successors lacked the financial resources to purchase the better breeds. Critics variously described Eastern Shore hogs as "long-nosed," "large-boned," razor-backs," which were "hard to fatten." "Nevertheless," maintained an Onancock man, "the cured meat of swine is good, and some of the hams have a reputation."[59]

Between 1850 and 1870, cattle, sheep, and swine enumerated in the federal censuses dropped by nearly one-half. The number of cattle fell from 10,124 to 6,696, sheep from 12,210 to 4,708, and swine from 37,506 to 20,183. Several factors contributed to the decline. The shift from general to truck farming meant that farmers had less grain and fodder for winter feed. During the Civil War, the occupying Union forces diverted local livestock into the federal commissary. At the end of the war, emancipation relieved slave owners of the obligation to stock their smokehouses every December with pork to feed their chattels throughout the ensuing year. With the effects of emancipation in mind, it should be noted that every federal agricultural census until the ending of the open range on the Eastern Shore at the turn of the twentieth century significantly undercounted livestock, particularly hogs and cattle. The official numbers did not include the livestock owned by non-farmers – laborers and watermen – whose animals ranged free in the woods and on the marshes and islands. Emancipated slaves – overwhelmingly laborers – now had to look to their own provision of pork and beef. The freedmen and other non-farmers might individually own only a hog or two but taken together the uncounted livestock added up.[60]

---

59 P. K. O'Brien, "Agriculture and the Industrial Revolution," *Economic History Review*, new ser., 30 (February, 1977); p. 169; Accomack County, Virginia, Census of Agriculture, 1870; Northampton County, Virginia, Census of Agriculture, 1870; Graham *et al.*, "Adaptation and Innovation," pp. 471, 510; Merrill K. Bennett, "Aspects of the Pig," *Agricultural History* 44 (April, 1970), p. 227; Genovese, *The Political Economy of Slavery*, pp. 112, 245; *Baltimore Sun*, September 5, 1881 (quotation); Wilmington *Morning News*, September 22, 1884; "Parksley's a Paradise."

60 Mears, Statistics from Federal Censuses. For the importance of hog killing to the slaveholder see the Plantation Books in the Tazewell Family Papers, 1623-1930, Library of Virginia, Rich-

The effect of the decades 1850 to 1870 on work stock was mixed. The number of mules increased marginally from 363 in 1850 to 370 in 1870 while that of horses declined somewhat from 3,868 to 3,537. As truck farming grew in importance, the attraction of the slow, clumsy ox diminished along with the amount of acres in need of cultivation. The number of working oxen, described by a Union invader as "miserably small and mean looking," plummeted from 2,846 to 1,327. Horses were now kept by 91.6 percent of the farmers and oxen by 41.8 percent. Mules appeared on only 12 percent of the farms. The horse, fast and nimble, had won the day with Eastern Shore farmers.[61]

Through the spring, summer, and fall, Eastern Shoremen allowed their animals to range free in woods, swamp, and marsh. Any unfenced mainland was legally considered commons. It was the responsibility of the farmer to fence in his crops, not his livestock. The open range originated in the early colonial period when the colonists found it efficient to use the surrounding forests as a boundless source of shelter and forage for animals. The practice allowed the landless and poor to own cattle and hogs. The owner need only mark his animals by branding their hides or slitting their ears. Cattle and hogs thrived on the Eastern Shore's marshes and in its woods. The animals facilitated the raking of shatters by grazing on briers, vines, pine seedlings, and hardwood shoots. Hogs were particularly voracious, consuming nearly anything. Near Woodberry in Accomack County in 1882, two young men used an ax to free a rooting hog that had become trapped in the carcass of a horse. The remains of animals littered the forest floor. Agricultural reformer Orris A. Browne believed that the old bones scattered across the two counties, if ground into fertilizer, would "make thousands of acres of land rich."[62]

---

mond.

61 Mears, Statistics from Federal Censuses; George C. Harding, *The Miscellaneous Writings of George C. Harding* (Indianapolis: Carlon & Hollenbeck, 1882), p. 236; Genovese, *The Political Economy of Slavery*, pp. 112-113; Accomack County, Virginia, Census of Agriculture, 1870; Northampton County, Virginia, Census of Agriculture, 1870.

62 Kirby, *Mockingbird Song*, pp. 120, 121; Douglas Helms, "Soil and Southern History," *Agricultural History* 74 (Autumn, 2000), p. 733; Steven Hahn, "Hunting, Fishing, and Forag-

When food was ample, livestock stayed close to home. During the warm months, their owners often took advantage of the animals' herding instinct to confine them at night on the farm where their manure might be gathered for compost. In the late fall, many owners impounded their animals for the winter, not only for the production of manure but also to fatten them for slaughter. The owners turned out their cattle into their fields to graze on Magothy Bay beans and corn stubble and their hogs to browse fallen orchard fruit and the remains of the sweet potato harvest. They also fed their livestock oats and corn, fodder and other offal. On a cold December day, the owners slaughtered enough animals to fill the smokehouse. With the coming of spring, they released their brood stock back onto the commons.[63]

The omnipresence of livestock necessitated miles of fence along roads and around fields, gardens, and house-yards. Eastern Shore landowners constructed their fences of pine rails and erected them in a worm pattern. They used pine because it was abundant and preferred the worm because it was easily assembled and disassembled. One observer considered their enclosures "excellent." The fences of Robert S. Costin of Northampton County stood ten rails high (about six feet) and ran in a worm of four or five feet. Costin estimated that a field of one hundred acres required two miles of fence (approximately 13,000 rails). Fence was as characteristic of the Eastern Shore landscape as open woods and large fields; its procurement, construction, and maintenance a constant burden on the landowner and tenant.[64]

---

ing: Common Rights and Class Relations in the Postbellum South," *Radical History Review* 26 (1982), p. 42; Ruffin, "Sketch of a Hasty View," p. 238; Washington *National Republican*, November 1, 1879; PE, February 16, 1882, March 8, 1883, September 6, 1890 (quotes Orris A. Browne); Carson *et al.*, "New World, Real World," pp. 45, 48-49.

63 Carson *et al.*, "New World, Real World," pp. 43, 44; Helms, "Soil and Southern History," p. 733; Ruffin, "Sketch of a Hasty View," pp. 234, 238; Mears, *Hacks Neck and Its People*, p. 48.

64 Drew Addison Swanson, "Fighting over Fencing: Agricultural Reform and Antebellum Efforts to Close the Virginia Open Range," *Virginia Magazine of History and Biography* 117 (2009), pp. 113, 114; Stephen H. Bogardus Jr., *Dear Eagle: The Civil War Correspondence of Stephen H. Bogardus, Jr., to the Poughkeepsie Daily Eagle*, ed. Joel Craig (Wake Forest, N.C.: The Scuppernong Press, 2004), p. 16; *Philadelphia Inquirer*, August 8, 1865; "Cobb's Island," Washington *Evening Star*, August 15, 1871; *Richmond Dispatch*, August 13, 1875; Frances Bibbins Latimer, comp., *Robert S. Costin of Northampton County, Virginia: Claims of a Loyal Citizen for*

Eastern Shore farmers were at once prudent and opportunistic, as interested in profit as in subsistence. They looked to smokehouse and corn crib first, but eyes open to the main chance, they planted a diversity of cash crops. Self-sufficiency filled their bellies and, by so doing, limited their debts to the storekeeper. Market produce enabled them to pay off their obligations for domestic and agricultural supplies while allowing them to set something aside for the future. The diversity of farm produce protected them from crop failure and market collapse and helped them keep their farm hands at work. In 1870, 98.7 percent of Eastern Shore farmers raised hogs and 97 percent grew corn. The very definition of a basic commodity, corn resisted pests and drought, required relatively little labor, and fed man and beast. Along with corn, potatoes and oats were sold or stored for family use. Sweet potatoes were grown by 94.2 percent of the farmers, Irish potatoes by 77.5 percent, and oats by 75.9 percent. No wonder that a journalist described the peninsula's landscape as "corn and potatoes, potatoes and corn, with tracts of woodland intervening." Dairy needs were met by the milch cows kept by 81 percent of the farmers. A perhaps typical holding was that of George T. Annis, a black farmer living in the mid-woods of upper Accomack County. Annis rented fifty acres – twenty-five arable and the remainder in resources – on which he grew corn for bread and sweet potatoes as a cash crop. He kept a mule, a horse, and two cows.[65]

When the two counties are compared, percentages in Accomack

Supplies Furnished During the Rebellion, Claim N. 55231 (Eastville, Va.: Hickory House, 1998), pp. 7, 35-36; John Wennersten, "Soil Miners Redux: The Chesapeake Environment, 1680-1810," *Maryland Historical Magazine* 91 (Summer, 1996), p. 168.

65 James Henretta, "Families and Farms: *Mentalite* in Pre-Indusrrial America," *William and Mary Quarterly*, 3rd ser., XXXV (January, 1978), p. 19; Barbara Jeanne Fields, "The Nineteenth-Century American South: History and Theory," *Plantation Society* II (April, 1983), pp. 14-15; Fields, "The Agricultural Population of Virginia," pp. 85-86; Helms, "Soil and Southern History," p. 731; John T. Schlotterbeck, "The 'Social Economy' of an Upper South Community: Orange and Greene Counties, Virginia, 1815-1860" in *Class, Conflict, and Consensus: Antebellum Southern Community Studies*, eds. Orville Vernon Burton and Robert C. McMath Jr. (Westport, Conn., and London: Greenwood Press, 1982), p. 6; Accomack County, Virginia, Census of Agriculture, 1870; Northampton County, Virginia, Census of Agriculture, 1870; David Maldwyn Ellis, *Landlords and Farmers in the Hudson-Mohawk Region, 1790-1850* (Ithaca and London: Cornell University Press, 1946), p. 106; *Philadelphia Inquirer*, August 19, 1865 (quotation); Wilmington *Morning News*, November 19, 1884.

are higher in every category except hogs than those in Northampton. Especially striking is the divergence in sweet potatoes – 97.8 percent of the farmers in Accomack to 85.9 percent in Northampton – and Irish potatoes – 83.6 percent in Accomack to 63.9 percent in Northampton. Freedmen made up a larger proportion of the farmers of Northampton than did those of Accomack. Their impoverishment, limited acreage, and immediate need for pork and cornbread discouraged their movement into truck farming.[66]

"THE WAY OF THE FARMER, LIKE THAT of the transgressor, is hard," wrote historian Avery Craven, himself the son of an Iowa farmer. "He must ever plant and await his harvest amid the uncertainties of weather, pests, and markets. Hope must ever be tempered with fear. The brightest prospects may at any moment turn to utter ruin. Heat and cold, rain and sun are both his fickle friends and his brutal enemies." The farmer's responsibilities seemingly were limitless. He tended livestock and managed the labor of his children and hired help. He repaired tools, carts, harness, and outbuildings. He built, replaced, and moved miles of fence. He cut firewood and split fence rails. He raked and hauled shatters and set out hotbeds. He spread manure, plowed, harrowed, planted, and harvested. He toiled in heat and cold, in rain and snow. His wife worked as hard as he. She bore and nurtured their children. She cooked, washed, cleaned, and sewed. She cared for the sick and those injured in the frequent farm mishaps. When necessary, she worked in pound and field.[67]

Debt, weather, and the supply of labor were forever on the farmer's mind. Even the most successful among them carried debt. He owed the storekeeper for seed, fertilizer, implements, and general supplies, and he might be obligated to neighbors for land or livestock bought on credit. A cold spring, a late frost, a surfeit of rain, or a long dry spell might make the payment of his debt a daunting prospect. Bad weather was of particular concern to the many Eastern Shore farmers who grew

---

[66] Accomack County, Virginia, Census of Agriculture, 1870; Northampton County, Virginia, Census of Agriculture, 1870.

[67] Avery Craven, "John Taylor and Southern Agriculture," in Craven, *An Historian and the Civil War* (Chicago and London: University of Chicago Press, 1964), p. 18; Sharrer, *A Kind of Fate*, pp. 84-87.

perishable crops for distant markets. "Unfavorable weather may not only very materially diminish the total yield," warned an agricultural expert, "but, more disastrous still to the prospects of the truck farmer, it may endow his produce with a nature so unstable as entirely to destroy its carrying capacity."[68]

Unlike in the cotton South where a majority of the freedmen farmed as sharecroppers, in Accomack and Northampton and the other counties of the Virginia Tidewater, most worked as laborers. Eastern Shore laborers were not dependent on agriculture alone. They could find work throughout the year on the farm or in the seafood and lumbering industries. At peak seasons, the industries vied with each other for help, creating a seller's market for labor. White farmers preferred to employ white hands, but beggars could not be choosers. The racial proportion of Eastern Shore farm labor varied with terms of employment and seasons of the year – for example, during their offseason white watermen and their families participated heavily as day laborers in the strawberry and Irish potato harvests – but blacks usually comprised the majority of agricultural laborers. Blacks who chose to work principally on the farm did so because they had driven a good bargain with the farmer, because they wanted to learn how to farm while putting aside some money toward the purchase of their own place, or because they felt an attachment to the farmer or his land. "I am about 66 years old, and work & live on Mr. [Robert S.] Costin's farm, & want to die on here," testified Peter Cox of Kendall Grove near Eastville in 1879. "I was here all during the war & belonged to Mr. Costin before freedom came & was a farm hand & worked in the fields. Since the war I have worked for him by the day." Most laborers, aware that the demand for labor often exceeded the supply, chose to work by the day, week, or month rather than by the year. A Freedmen's Bureau official explained to his superior officer that black laborers preferred to hire by the month "as the extended bay and seaside coasts of this peninsula afford them an opportunity to earn during the fall and spring months at oystering, a much larger sum per month than they could procure at any other labor."[69]

---

68 Oemler, "Truck Farming," p. 608.

69 Harahan, "Politics, Political Parties, and Voter Participation," p. 60; James R. Irwin, "Farmers

For the farmer, the supply of labor was a fraught variable. Even those with a small holding or children old enough to work were likely to need help at some time or other. Crops and weather waited for no one. The crucial demands for labor in the agricultural cycle occurred with the planting and, especially, the harvest. When not gathered promptly, oats would shatter and shed in the field in a dry year or become too damp to salvage in a wet. Perishable crops would rot in the field or in shipment if left too long in the heat or wet. At the harvest and all the year the farmer desired punctual, careful, and diligent hands. Those he usually employed seldom shared his sense of responsibility and thus were in need of his constant attention. The Alabama novelist and agrarian Andrew Lytle perhaps best articulated the farmer's anxiety: "The long slow dealing with the seasons, the care for and need to manage those who do the physical work often makes the head light as a gourd from strain and dwindling hope."[70]

White Eastern Shore farmers were used to managing autonomous black labor. For much of the antebellum period, they had drawn on the peninsula's large free black population for hired hands. From the farmer's perspective the results were unsatisfactory. In the early 1850s, white citizens of Accomack unsuccessfully petitioned the Virginia legislature to enable the mandatory hiring out of free blacks "in order to prevent them from idleing, and continuing bad habits" such as fencing produce stolen by slaves and selling liquor to slaves. At the war's end

---

and Laborers: A Note on Black Occupations in the Postbellum South," *Agricultural History* 64 (Winter, 1990), p. 59; Pyle, "Peninsular Canaan," p. 817; Washington *New Era*, May 5, 1870; Deposition of Peter Cox, September 23, 1879, Latimer, comp., *Robert S. Costin of Northampton County*, p. 8; Lt. Eld. Murphy to Brig. Gen. Orlando Brown, January 31, 1867, Montgomery S. Reed to Brown, June 29, 1868, Records of the Bureau of Refugees, Freedmen, and Abandoned Lands, vol. 151, pp. 38-39 (quotation), vol. 156, pp. 48-49; *Richmond Dispatch*, January 23, 1868.. For the attraction of freedmen to the oyster grounds adjacent Gloucester County on the Western Shore of Chesapeake Bay see George W. Munford to Thomas T. Munford, December 4, 1870, in James L. Roark, *Masters Without Slaves: Southern Planters in the Civil War and Reconstruction* (New York and London: W. W. Norton & Company, 1977), p. 164. In 1870 farm laborers in lower Northampton County received a monthly ration of a bushel of corn meal and twelve pounds of bacon (*Middletown (Del.) Transcript*, July 9, 1870).

70 E. J. T. Collins, "Harvest Technology and Labour Supply in Britain, 1790-1870," *Economic History Review* 22 (December, 1969), p. 465; Lytle, *A Wake for the Living*, p. 135.

Henry A. Wise told the *New York World* that "We knew just the size of the elephant you were getting by the freeing of the slave. Take Accomac County, for instance; we had, for thirty [eighty] years before the war, been engaged in the emancipation of the blacks, and had about thirty-four hundred of them on our hands who could, by the use of the oyster tongs for two days obtain sufficient to last them the rest of the week, which they spent in frolic." Throughout the 1860s, federal military and Freedmen's Bureau officers expressed similar opinions. In 1867 Lieutenant Eld. Murphy reported that the freedmen's "past education [in slavery] having taught them to have no care for the future, they only ask from the present a few of the necessaries of life that can be obtained by irregular labor, and time to indulge their strong social propensities." Murphy added, however, that "this class I am glad to say consists only of a very small minority." Delaware emigrant John J. Townsend complained at the end of the decade that "It generally takes five amendments to do three men's work. They will not go to work until the sun is about an hour high and quit a little while before sundown."[71]

As Lieutenant Murphy indicated, free black behavior was conditioned by the past. He might have added that it also was conditioned by the present. Landless and possessing little personal property, they had no estate or station in society to maintain. All classes of whites disdained them for their race, their poverty, and their status as former slaves. Some black laborers sought security by attaching themselves to a farmer or group of farmers. Others maintained their independence by moving from job to job. The living the casual laborer made was occasionally uncertain but usually adequate to immediate needs for food, clothing, and shelter and for providing more opportunities for leisure

---

71 February 18, May 17 (quotation), 1852, February 10, 1853, Accomack County Legislative Petitions; *Alexandria Gazette*, April 26, 1866 (quotes Henry A. Wise); Lt. Col. Frank J. White to Lt. Col. Horace Porter, February 28, 1865 in *Freedom: A Documentary History of Emancipation, 1861-1867, Selected from the Holdings of the National Archives of the United States; Series I, Volume II, The Wartime Genesis of Free Labor:: The Upper South*, eds. Ira Berlin, Steven F. Miller, Joseph Reidy, and Leslie S. Rowland (Cambridge: Cambridge University Press, 1993), pp. 223-231; Lt. Eld. Murphy to Brig. Gen. Orlando Brown, January 31, 1867, Lt. George P. Sherwood to Brown, January 25, 1868, Records of the Bureau of Refugees, Freedmen, and Abandoned Lands, vol. 151, pp. 38-39 (quotation), vol. 156, p. 8; *Middletown (Del.) Transcript*, July 23, 1870 (quotes John J. Townsend).

and conviviality than was granted them as slaves. The Eastern Shore was an ideal place for the laborer, black or white, to enjoy the good life. Its kindly soil made gardening easy; its woods, marshes, and waters supported an abundance of game and fish free for the taking; and its mix of natural resources created a competitive market for labor. Sadly, the mobile labor force encouraged a rootlessness that sometimes manifested itself in neglected or abandoned wives and children.[72]

White farmers felt deep frustration at their inability to procure an adequate supply of reliable labor. They too had to provide for families. The landowners among them strived to secure their livings, and all desired to maintain their social status. The great majority were yeomen who worked the land alongside their children and hired hands. For generations, the Eastern Shore had been the land of the small holder. Field work entailed no social stigma. "I have seen white men and their sons, worth thousands of dollars, working in the same field with their slaves," Representative Thomas H. Bayly of Accomack told Congress in 1848. "I have seen many as respectable men as are in my district or anywhere else, working side by side in their fields with slaves they hired. But they did not feel themselves degraded, nor does anybody consider them so." These were easy-going and hospitable people who valued friends and leisure, but they also tended to business and laid aside for the future. They were baffled and disgusted by those who were not as provident as themselves. For those who had owned slaves (over 50 percent of the householders in the two counties in 1850), the necessity of bargaining with their former chattels was an additional source of anxiety and annoyance. Tragically, both white farmers and black laborers were prisoners of the past. That blacks had been conditioned by the injustices of slavery to be evasive and dilatory only confirmed the whites in their opinion of black inferiority.[73]

---

[72] Donald Davidson believed that "Rather than being a sign of shiftlessness, this sense of life's priorities is one of the supreme virtues of African American culture in the South." (Mark Royden Winchell, *Where No Flag Flies: Donald Davidson and the Southern Resistance* [Columbia and London: University of Missouri Press, 2000], p. 305).

[73] Fields, "The Nineteenth-Century American South," pp18-19; Harold D. Woodman, "Sequel to Slavery: the New History Views the Postbellum South," *Journal of Southern History* 43 (November, 1977), pp. 541, 551-552; Thomas H. Bayly, *Slavery in the Territories: Speech of Hon. T. H. Bayly, of Virginia, in the House of Representatives, May 16, 1848* (Washington: Congressio-

Catastrophe in any number of forms – bad weather, labor scarcity, insect infestation, livestock disease, market collapse, creditor demand – singly or in combination might befall the farmer at any time. His reckoning came annually at the harvest. Attention to work alone was not enough to ensure success. He needed a measure of good fortune and, more important, he must learn from experience. Farming, according to Andrew Lytle, was as much mystery as skill:

> By turning the dirt, each moment surrounded by the concrete substance of the land, farmers learn the thing nature is, that no rule may measure it entirely nor foresight always anticipate its multitudinous aspects. Nevertheless, the master farmer must try to foresee. This burden cannot be transferred to another. It was his sense of this which gave strength and resilience to his rule and, in times of sorrow, fortitude to meet reverses. That is, if he was a good master.[74]

Lumbering

Wood was essential to the lives of Eastern Shoremen. They used it for buildings, boats, and bridges, for mile on mile of fence, for hot-bed frames and the handles of oyster tongs. They used it to fuel stoves, sawmills, steamboats, and brick-kilns. Annually, a family consumed fifty to one hundred cords for household purposes. A well-managed acre of woodland yielded a cord of firewood. In the region's mild climate, the average Eastern Shore farm's 51.6 acre woodlot probably provided an adequate supply. Chopping, splitting, and transporting deadfall was laborious and time-consuming. Farmers usually undertook the work themselves but might also hire it out. Additional demands, such as the construction and maintenance of buildings, fences, and hot-bed frames,

---

nal Globe, 1848), p. 15; Mariner, *Slave and Free*, p. 85.

74 Fields, "The Agricultural Population of Virginia," p. 158; Lytle, *A Wake for the Living*, p. 135. See also Mark Malvasi, "The Georgic Vision of Andrew Lytle." *Modern Age* 55 (Winter/Spring, 2013), p. 65.

taxed the resources of farmers possessing average or smaller woodlots. These met their needs by purchasing from wood dealers operating steam or water-powered sawmills in their neighborhoods.[75]

From the colonial period Eastern Shoremen had sold lumber along the Atlantic Coast. The trade had gradually declined as the peninsula's expanding grain production devoured its woodland. The trend toward deforestation reversed in the late antebellum period as vegetables replaced grains and as farmers curtailed or abandoned farming to work on the water. Loblolly and short-leafed pine colonized recently abandoned fields. Both species grew rapidly, but the peninsula's light soil especially suited the loblolly. The straight, cylindrical bole of the mature loblolly stood around 100 feet high. Each tree supplied at least three logs of sixteen feet with a diameter of two-and-a-half feet. Loblolly was used for construction and fencing and made superior kindling for stove and fireplace. Before harvesting, it bestowed upon the farmers an abundance of shatters for the making of compost.[76]

Meanwhile, the growing population of the urban North stimulated demand for firewood, which by the late 1840s the Eastern Shore supplied from its maturing woodlots. Cordwood production centered in the lowlands of upper Accomack County where abandoned fields and moist soil created an ideal environment for the loblolly. In the late 1840s and in the 1850s, six partnerships, with one exception composed of local men, contracted for timber rights on the 1,000-acre Sanford Charity tract between Pocomoke River and Messongo Creek. The contracts allowed the lessees to build roads and wharves to facilitate the shipping of lumber In 1857, Daniel D. Nash, the head of a New York

---

[75] Sharrer, *A Kind of Fate*, p. 84; *The Statistics of the Wealth and Industry of the United States ... Compiled, From the Original Returns of the Ninth Census (June 1, 1870)*, p. 270; *Baltimore Sun*, October 6, 1871.

[76] Peter V. Bergstrom, *Merchants and Markets: Economic Diversification in Colonial Virginia* (New York: Garland Publishing, 1985), pp. 143-145; Ruffin, "Sketch of a Hasty View," p. 235; O'Byrne, "More and Better Pines on the Eastern Shore," ESN, October 30, 1936; Mart A. Stewart, *"What Nature Suffers to Groe": Life, Labor, and Landscape on the Georgia Coast, 1680-1920* (Athens and London: University of Georgia Press, 1996), p. 213; W. D. Sterrett, "Forest Management of Loblolly Pine in Delaware, Maryland, and Virginia," U. S. Department of Agriculture *Bulletin* 11 (January 23, 1914), pp. 2, 3, 4, 6; Washington *National Republican*, November 1, 1879; Swanson, "Fighting over Fencing," p. 116.

syndicate backed by nearly $100,000 in capital, purchased 10,000 acres of timber land in Winder's Neck to the south of Swan's Gut Creek and to the west of Chincoteague Bay. Nash's Accomac Wood and Kindling Company employed in Winder's Neck more than a dozen people (none of whom was a Virginian), including woodcutters, sawmill workers, and boatmen. Nash's employees sent "fat" pine to the company's plant, which occupied an entire New York City block. There a circular saw and a mechanized axe cut and split the cordwood into kindling. The light wood sold in the city by the bundle or by the barrel.[77]

The Union occupation of the Eastern Shore created opportunity for Northern lumbermen. They might obtain fine stands of timber on estates confiscated from Confederate sympathizers. They might persuade a conquered and cash-strapped people to relinquish their timber rights. They might induce on-the-take federal military and customs officers to disregard inconvenient regulations. From August, 1864, to March, 1865, twenty-five Northern lumbermen registered at Drummondtown with the Union provost marshal. Fifteen of the men were residents of Maine. The Eastern Shore at that time was in the military district commanded by Major General Benjamin F. Butler, a Massachusetts politician whose talent for administration combined unwholesomely with a penchant for graft.[78]

The men from Maine were known as "timber birds," buyers and speculators circling over and flying through. A third wave of lumbermen – steam-sawmill operators and their assistants – arrived in the aftermath of the war. Every sawmill engineer in the two counties listed in the 1870 federal census was native to a state north of Virginia. Most were Marylanders. Some of the operators brought their families and settled

---

77 Moody K. Miles III and Mark S. Fisher, comps., *Sandford's Charity Ledger Book (1773-1874)* (Woodbridge, Va.: Authors, 2005), pp. 101, 114, 115, 117, 119, 130, 133; Mariner, *Slave and Free*, p. 141; Crowson and Hite, comps., *Accomack County, Virginia, 1860 Census*, p. 118; *New York Commercial Advertiser* in *New England Farmer* XIII (March, 1861), p. 107; *Brooklyn Times Union*, May 6, 1858.

78 Lists of Prisoners and Stragglers (1863-1865), Post at Drummondtown, Office of the Provost Marshal, Entry 1589, RG393, Records of U. S. Army Continental Commands, 1817-1947, National Archives-College Park, Md.; Mary Bandy Daughtry, *Gray Cavalier: The Life and Wars of General W. H. F. "Rooney" Lee* (Cambridge, Ma.: Da Capo Press, 2002), p. 288.

permanently on the peninsula. In lower Northampton, the village of Townsend grew around the saw and grist mill of Israel Townsend of Middletown, Delaware. In upper Accomack, James Witham of Maine established a sawmill at the Hammocks on Messongo Creek. A nearby community bears his name. Witham likely came to the Hammocks to saw timber harvested by E. Flye and Company of Maine from the Sanford Charity tract in 1866-1867. The interrelated families of Miles, Taylor, and Lankford of Somerset County, Maryland, also made homes on the Eastern Shore. They ran sawmills at Onancock and at Miles Wharf on Occohannock Creek.[79]

Around a half dozen steam sawmills operated in the two counties in 1870. The federal census listed 47 persons (of whom 21 were black) whose principal source of income was the lumber industry. Whites directed the enterprise, but sawyers and woodcutters included men of both races. Work in the woods was not for the weak, the careless, or the fastidious. One woodsman complained of ticks "that seem to be organized for the extermination of man. You may see them from the size of a bumble bee to that of a channel crab, and woe be to the man who comes within their reach." Woodcutters wore themselves out chopping, lifting, and hauling. They were injured by falling trees, misdirected axe strokes, and the inattention of the drivers of timber-laden ox-carts. Sawmill work was even more dangerous. Circular saws took off fingers and legs, ripped open arms and thighs, and sent handspikes flying with deadly effect. The explosion of an overheated boiler created horrific scenes of men and animals scalded, mutilated, and blown to bits, entrails and body parts festooning the branches of trees.[80]

---

79 Lists of Prisoners and Stragglers (1863-1865) ("timber birds"); Walczyk, *The Accomack County 1870 Census*, I, 82, 128, II, 6, 24, 25, 27, 30; Latimer, *1870 Census for Northampton County, Virginia*, pp. 1, 55, 99; Wilmington *Delaware Tribune*, February 24, 1870; Mariner, *Almost an Island*, p. 38; Miles and Fisher, comps., *Sandford's Charity Ledger Book (1773-1874)*, p. 157; *Baltimore Daily Commercial*, November 25, 1865; *Baltimore Sun*, October 7, 1918; "Aged Shore Colored Civil War Vet Says First to Open 'Old Dutch Gap,'" *ESN*, September 5, 1930. Moody K. Miles III has traced the genealogies of the Miles, Taylor, and Lankford families in the Miles Files (espl-genealogy/org/MilesFiles/site/index.htm).

80 Walczyk, *The Accomack County 1870 Census*; Latimer, *1870 Census for Northampton County, Virginia*; *PE*, June 22, 1882 (quotation); April 26, June 14, July 26, 1883, April 5, May 3, 24, July 5, 1884; Philadelphia *Times* July 10, 1878.

— Steam and Steel —

Other Occupations

Almost every Eastern Shoreman lived within a short distance of a country store. They had only to walk to the closest wharf or to the crossroads at the head of the neck. Although a few of the stores were large establishments such as Hopkins & Bro. in Onancock with its row of granaries, fleet of schooners, and varied stock of merchandise, most were smaller, less well capitalized, and more vulnerable to failure. The small operators supplied their customers with the basic household commodities, nautical supplies, and farm necessities such as seed and fertilizer. Merchants, great and small, served as the peninsula's bankers. They bought on credit from wholesalers in Baltimore, Philadelphia, and New York merchandise, which they sold on credit to their customers. On the one hand the cost of interest and bookkeeping raised consumer prices while on the other competition among merchants limited the increase. In 1870 at least eighty mercantile houses served Accomack and twenty Northampton (two of which were operated by blacks).[81]

The Eastern Shore's economy was based on barter. Very little money was in circulation. Customers retired their debts on payment of goods and services or through the proffering of "due bills" that merchants were willing to accept. "A person had to know the market to keep from losing money in the barter business," recalled Onancock storekeeper Thomas S. Hopkins. Merchants usually extended credit without demanding collateral to those customers they considered trustworthy. When supplying fertilizer, a particularly costly commodity, they sometimes required that the farmers give them a mortgage on their crop. The merchants themselves were a link in a chain of debt. Their survival depended not only on their knowledge of markets but also on their knowledge of their neighbors.[82]

---

81 William Cronon, *Nature's Metropolis: Chicago and the Great West* (New York and London: W. W. Norton & Company, 1991), p. 294; Ellis, *Landlords and Farmers*, pp. 89, 90; Walczyk, *The Accomack County 1870 Census*; Latimer, *1870 Census for Northampton County, Virginia*.

82 Sharrer, *A Kind of Fate*, p. 92; Mears, *Hacks Neck and Its People*, p. 70; Smith, "Century-Old Firm" (quotes Hopkins). See also Aubrey C. Land, "Economic Behavior in a Planting Society:

Also working on the Eastern Shore were small contingents of craftsmen – shoemakers, blacksmiths, wheelwrights, carpenters, brick masons – and professionals – doctors, lawyers, teachers, ministers of the gospel. Whites dominated all of these callings. No black person was listed as doctor, lawyer, or wheelwright, and only a few as brick mason (1 of a total of 17), shoemaker (2 of 43), blacksmith (6 of 23), or carpenter (11 of 137). On first appearance either the peninsula's slave regime failed to produce many black craftsmen or some were discouraged from using their skills in the post-war years. More likely, they practiced their craft in freedom much as they had practiced it on the small farms on which they had been enslaved – not exclusively, but occasionally amidst other labor. Blacks monopolized a few occupations. They toiled as stevedores at the steamboat wharves and as drivers of passenger carriages and delivery carts. James H. A. Johnson considered the passenger trade "a profitable business ... followed by a number of the colored men on 'The Shore.'"[83]

Black women worked as domestic servants and as washers and ironers of clothes. A few earned a living as bakers and purveyors of cakes. White women seldom served as domestics or baked commercially (at least not for sale beyond their immediate neighborhood), but some worked from home as seamstresses. Women, white and black, who kept house labored in the home and in the farmyard or garden. Their work, while not as physically demanding or dangerous as that of the men, was unceasing. Doubtless, some took satisfaction in making a home while others felt condemned to a sentence of sustained tedium.[84]

The Eighteenth-Century Chesapeake," *Journal of Southern History* XXXIII (1967), pp. 479-480, and Susie M. Ames, "A Typical Business Man of the Revolutionary Era: Nathaniel Littleton Savage and His Account Book," *Journal of Economic and Business History* 3 (May, 1931), p. 421.

83 Walczyk, *The Accomack County 1870 Census*; Latimer, *1870 Census for Northampton County, Virginia*; Johnson, The Pine Tree Mission, p. 12. "Rare indeed was the skilled slave who had not performed some sort of farm labor" (Orville Vernon Burton, *In My Father's House Are Many Mansions: Family and Community in Edgefield, South Carolina* (Chapel Hill and London: University of North Carolina Press, 1985), p. 36.

84 Walczyk, *The Accomack County 1870 Census*; Latimer, *1870 Census for Northampton County, Virginia*.

— Steam and Steel —

On the Water

Fisheries

Although waterman was not used as an occupational term by those taking the federal censuses of population of Accomack and Northampton counties in 1870, it best describes the economic opportunists who made their livings by taking from the sea and wetlands whatever was available at the moment. Watermen, wrote a journalist, were "in turn fishermen, crabbers, terrapin-catchers, and oyster-tongers, according to the season and the exigencies of the weather; and they literally scoop, tong, seine, dredge, and drag their living from the waters of the great bay." Watermen also salvaged wrecks, tended cattle on the islands and hammocks, and hunted shorebirds and waterfowl for the restaurant and feather trades. They occasionally worked as woodsmen or farm laborers, and they kept hogs and patches of corn and vegetables. Robert Wilson knew "one who manages ... three distinct callings, discretely varied according to days and seasons. While the fish are running, he occupies a shanty on the shore – except when he is up to the waist in water, which is four hours out of every five. Through the rest of the year he 'follows' carpentering, while his Sundays are faithfully given to the loudest kind of preaching."[85]

About one-fifth of the Eastern Shore's people derived most of their income from the fisheries. The 1870 census for the two counties listed 938 persons working as fishermen or oystermen – 794 in Accomack and 144 in Northampton. Oystermen outnumbered fishermen by 862 to 76 – in Accomack 777 to 17 and in Northampton 85 to 59. Unlike in many Western Shore counties, whites dominated the seafood industry

---

85 David Bruce Fitzgerald, "With the Oyster Police," *Lippincott's Monthly Magazine* LVI (1895), p. 699 (quotation); "Chincoteague Island, Va.," *Baltimore Sun*, August 28, 1876; Matthews, "Chincoteague Island"; Marshall McDonald, "The Oyster Industry" in *Second Annual Report of the Bureau of Industrial Statistics of Maryland* (Annapolis: King Bros., State Printers, 1894), p. 270; Wilson, "On the Chesapeake," p. 466.

803 to 135. In Accomack white watermen outnumbered black by 722 to 72 and in black-majority Northampton by 81 to 63.[86]

Finfishing – The waters of the Eastern Shore abounded with fish – shad, herring, trout, mackerel, hogfish, roach (spot), weakfish (sea trout), sheepshead (drum), and numerous others. Thomas T. Upshur of Brownsville in Northampton County recalled that during the summer of 1873 the owner of a farm at Battle Point in Occohannock Neck and his friends "made an average catch of from ten to twenty sheepshead per day at the end of his wharf ... and that they did not have to enter a boat, but simply sat on the wharf and hauled them up." Hogfish, according to Upshur "were frequently on the tables of our citizens, and for a bushel to be caught in a day by one fisherman with his hand line was no uncommon occurrence. Roaches (or spots) too, were plentiful, anyone could get as many as they needed, and to go fishing on a Saturday, as relaxation for mind and body after a week's work in the fields, was beneficial and enjoyable." Northern newcomer Israel Townsend primly disapproved of the natives' zest for fishing. He believed that "our September and October chills and fever ... are brought on by laziness and exposure, for almost every one is out night and day fishing."[87]

Eastern Shoremen fished from beach or wharf or from a canoe hewn from one or more pine logs and powered by sail or oars. Most caught their fish with hook and handline but some, especially during the spring and fall runs, used seines, gill nets, and, on the lower Northampton bayside, pound-nets. In the spring they harpooned sheepsheads and in the winter speared eels hibernating in the mud at the heads of the creeks. The excess catch they gave or sold fresh to their neighbors, stored salted in crocks for the own use or in barrels for urban sale, and spread on their fields for fertilizer. Black farmer Peter Savage used the oil he took from sharks caught in a nearby creek to grease the axles of his carts. Federal

---

86 Browne, "The Eastern Shore"; Walczyk, comp., *The Accomack County 1870 Census*; Latimer, comp, *The 1870 Census for Northampton County*.

87 *Philadelphia Inquirer*, August 8, 1865; Spears, "Life on Chincoteague"; Thomas T. Upshur, "Waste of Fishes, Etc.," *ESH*, June 23, 1905; T. [Israel Townsend], Capeville, to editor, Wilmington *Delaware State Journal*, November 8, 1867.

census takers listed only 76 professional fishermen on the peninsula – 59 in Northampton and 17 in more populous Accomack. Whites dominated the occupation in both counties – 51 to 8 in Northampton and 14 to 3 in Accomack. The great majority of Northampton fishermen lived on the barrier islands of Hog and Smith's and on the bayside near Cherrystone Creek.[88]

Terrapin Gathering, Clamming, Crabbing – The surrounding waters also supplied a profusion of terrapin, clams, crabs, and oysters, all of which were popular local fare. In 1870 some terrapin and clams were sold in the cities, but limited supply of the former and demand for the latter retarded the development of substantial markets. Crabs, although relished by Eastern Shoremen, found little favor with diners in the urban North. On the other hand, the demand for oysters was robust and transportation readily available.

Oystering – Oystering was by far the largest and most lucrative of the Eastern Shore's fisheries. It was also the most complex and contentious. Conflict raged (not too strong a word) between tongers, dredgers, and planters over the management of the public oyster grounds, between Maryland and Virginia over control of the boundary waters, between legislators from the Tidewater and from the rest of Virginia over taxation and expenditure, and between state officials and the oystermen and their political allies over the enforcement of regulations and the collection of revenues. To add further complication, the oystering industry developed differently in Accomack than in Northampton and differently on the bayside than on the seaside.

---

[88] Frank B. Jess, "Fishing on Cherrystone Creek," *Outing* XX (April, 1892), pp. 52-54; Wallace *The Parson of the Islands*, p. 43; *Richmond Dispatch*, April 13, 1874; Wilson, "On the Eastern Shore," pp. 236-237; Leonard Treherne, A *Sketch of the Life and Work of Rev. L. Treherne* (undated pamphlet in Eastern Shore Heritage Center) pp. 6-7; L. Eugene Cronin, "Chesapeake Fisheries and Resource Stress in the 19th Century," *Journal of the Washington Academy of Sciences* 76 (September, 1986), p. 190; Pyle, "A Peninsular Canaan," pp. 810-811; George Shiras 3rd, *Hunting Wild Life with Camera and Flashlight: A Record of Sixty-Five Years' Visits to the Woods and Waters of North America* (Washington: National Geographic Society, 1935), II, 81; Johnson, *The Pine Tree Mission*, p. 16; Walczyk, comp., *The Accomack County 1870 Census*; Latimer, comp., *The 1870 Census for Northampton County*.

The local waters were an ideal environment for the growth of oysters. Water temperatures fell within the appropriate range, an abundance of sea grass concealed spawn, known locally as "spat," from predators, and salt tide and fresh water influx provided a continuous supply of nutrients. In the shallow, brackish waters of Chesapeake Bay and its tributaries and in the seaside bays and Broadwater, oysters grew on "rocks" composed of shells and live oysters. The oyster's spawning season occurred during the summer months, the spat "striking" to cultch – the rock or any other clean, hard, and rough surface – and becoming mature oysters in around three years. Well-situated rocks were prolific. In 1858 an Accomack oysterman testified that he knew of a single rock of three acres yielding a harvest of from 70,000 to 105,000 bushels of oysters. The largest rocks were given names such as Bird, Brig, and California.[89]

A succession of oyster rocks was known as grounds. The most extensive grounds worked by Eastern Shore oystermen were adjacent the upper Accomack bayside in Pocomoke and Tangier sounds. Tangier Sound extended north for thirty-six miles from Watts Island. Most of the sound's 69.12 square nautical miles were in Maryland waters, leaving only about a quarter of its 28 named rocks legally available to Virginians. Pocomoke Sound, running north-northeasterly for over twelve miles from Watts, was only half the size of Tangier Sound but its seventeen named rocks lay on Virginia bottom. Observing that Pocomoke Sound was shielded from the wind by Tangier, Fox, and other islands to its west and possessed of a "uniform and favorable depth," a Maryland oyster policeman declared that "certainly not in the Chesapeake, perhaps not in the United States, would it be possible to find a bit of ground so well adapted to the laying down of oysters."[90]

---

89 "Oysters of the Chesapeake – Their Propagation and Culture" in *Report of the Commissioner of Agriculture for the Year 1868* (Washington: Government Printing Office, 1869), p. 341; "The Oyster Trade," *New-York Tribune*, August 3, 1871; Francis Winslow, "Deterioration of American Oyster-Beds," *Popular Science Monthly* XX (November, December, 1881), pp. 145, 146, 148; *Richmond Enquirer*, March 5, 1858.

90 Francis Winslow, "Report on the Oyster Beds of the James River, Va., and of Tangier and Pocomoke Sounds, Maryland and Virginia" In *United States Coast and Geodetic Survey Report for 1881*, Appendix No. 11 (Washington: Government Printing Office, 1882), pp. 15, 28, 33; "Oysters of the Chesapeake," p. 343; Fitzgerald, "With the Oyster Police," p. 701 (quotation).

While the Pocomoke and Tangier grounds were the dynamo of the Eastern Shore's bayside oyster industry, oysters might be taken almost anywhere along the peninsula. "The saltier the water the better the flavor" was the guiding axiom when consumers rated the provenance of local oysters. A *New-York Tribune* reporter asserted in 1871 that the "Cherry-stone Inlet oyster must be ranked first among all the oysters of the world. It is a large, fat white oyster of exquisite salty, oyster flavor. It is thick, and of firm, solid substance, so that it may be sliced, when steamed, like a veal cutlet or breast of turkey." Unfortunately, he continued, "the genuine Cherry-stone oyster is almost extinct as the Dodo. Less than a hundred bushels were 'caught' and sent to the market last year." Demand for Cherrystones was so high and supply so limited that oystermen sold most of the harvest at exorbitant prices to hotels, restaurants, and private clubs. Oysters taken from the sounds and creeks of the Accomack bayside, though enjoying a reputation as "something beyond the common run of bivalves," rated below the Cherrystone and other oysters gathered in the more saline waters of the Northampton bayside. Nonetheless, according to the *Tribune* reporter, the oysters of Pocomoke and Tangier sounds accounted for "the larger proportion of the oysters used in all except the extreme Eastern cities of the United States." Seaside oysters received a mixed reception in the urban markets. Some diners considered them delicious while others dismissed them as too small and, surely to the amazement of Eastern Shoremen, too salty.[91]

Eastern Shore watermen gathered oysters from shallow water with rakes and from deep water with tongs or dredges. Tongers or tongmen, as they were known, traveled in log canoes to the oyster grounds. "The canoes of these [Saxis] islanders are the fastest, most seaworthy, and most beautiful boats I have ever seen," exclaimed a Marylander. "They

---

91 Winslow, "Report on the Oyster Beds," p. 40 (first quotation); *Baltimore Sun*, October 10, 1857; "Oysters of the Chesapeake," pp. 341, 343-344; George Alfred Townsend, "The Chesapeake Peninsula," *Scribner's Monthly* III (March, 1872), pp. 519-520; "The Oyster Trade" (second and fourth quotations); Alexander Hunter, "Duck Shooting off the Virginia Capes," *Forest and Stream* XVI (March 10, 1881), p. 106; Elkton (Md.) *Cecil Whig*, October 25, 1884 (third quotation); *Alexandria Gazette*, September 25, 1876; "Washington's Oyster Trade," Washington *Evening Star*, January 26, 1889.

are built from the largest heart pine trees from the beautifully streamlined model of a forgotten genius." The boats averaged around twenty feet in length, four feet across the gunwales, and eighteen inches deep. A preacher visiting Tangier Island noted that the canoes "are rigged with two masts, with sails attached, which can be easily taken down or put up, and can out sail every vessel on the water that is not propelled by steam. When there is not sufficient wind for them to sail, the islanders are very dexterous in managing them with paddles." A man or two and a boy served as the canoe's crew.[92]

Robert Wilson described the tonger at work: "Arrived on the ground, the oysterman furls up his sail, unships his mast. ... A stout board provided with side-guards is fixed across the boat to hold the oysters; the tongman stands and plunges his long rakes to the bottom, opening and closing them with a peculiar motion of the arms until a sufficient number of oysters has been brought together, and then raises them 'hand over hand,' and deposits the load upon his cross-board." The wooden shafts of the tongs were from twelve to twenty-eight feet in length. Attached to the ends were metal rakes with from ten to eighteen teeth. Much of what the tongers brought to the surface was trash, which the "cull-boy" (most oystermen began their work on the water as cull-boys) removed from the culling board and dumped over the side. A tonger's daily catch usually amounted to ten or twelve bushels of marketable oysters, which the tongers might sell to the skippers of 'buy boats," larger vessels anchored in the grounds with empty baskets fixed to their masts signaling that they were ready to receive oysters. The buy boat captains in turn sold the oysters to dealers in urban markets or waterfront railheads. Wilson noticed buy boats anchored in Pocomoke Sound near the railroad town of Crisfield, Maryland, "and long canoes, loaded to the gunwales ... approaching them from every quarter." The tongers might also barter their catch to neighborhood merchants who

---

92 John Value Dennis, *The Dennises of Beverly and Their Kin* (Delmar, Del.: Evans-Coates Printing, 1992), p. 88 (first quotation); McDonald, "The Oyster Industry," pp. 268, 269; Wallace, *The Parson of the Islands*, p. 41 (second quotation); Ernest Ingersoll, "The Oyster Industry" in *The History and Present Condition of the Fishery Industry*, by G. Brown Goode (Washington: Government Printing Office, 1881), p. 181.

disposed of the oysters on contract with city dealers. The oyster season lasted from September through April, but during the summer months some tongers moved oysters from the public grounds such as those in the sounds and spread them on the private rocks of oyster planters.[93]

Dredgermen worked the oyster grounds in large sailboats such as conventional schooners and sloops. They also used pungies and bugeyes, double-masted vessels indigenous to the bay country. Both pungies and bugeyes were decked-over from stem to stern with capacious holds below. A Baltimore reporter described them as an epitome of elegance and speed:

> The pungy ... is little different in appearance from the schooner, except that there is no waist. There is an absence of the graceful, sweeping curve from stem to stern, but when the pungy is under sail and heeling over with the lee rail awash and sails drawing well there is a gracefulness and beauty in plenty. But the bugeye is the one type that is expressive of the Chesapeake. Built of logs and sharp at the bow and stern, there is a buoyancy to the hull that makes her an exceptionally fine sailer. Few bugeyes carry topmasts, but the fore and mainmasts are inclined at an angle that is almost violent. Leg-o'-mutton sails are used and before a wind of any volume the average buyeye can show a clean pair of heels to many steamers plying on the bay.

Dredger crews consisted of captain, mate, cook, and from two to nine hands depending on the size of the vessel. Often the mate aspired to one day command a vessel himself. Crewmen hired out by the trip, which might extend from ten to forty days.[94]

Once the boat was under sail on the oyster ground, dredges were

---

93 Wilson "On the Eastern Shore," 240, 242; McDonald, "The Oyster Industry," pp. 268, 319; "The Oyster at Home," p. 399; Winslow, "Report on the Oyster Beds," p. 42; *Journal of the Senate of the Commonwealth of Virginia, 1859-1860* (Richmond: James E. Goode, Senate Printer, 1859), Doc. No. 35, p. 3; Ingersoll, "The Oyster Industry," p. 164; "The Oyster Trade."

94 McDonald, "The Oyster Industry," pp. 279, 280, 284, 285; "Sailing Trade is Active," Baltimore Sun, July 27, 1906; Ingersoll, "The Oyster Industry," p. 160.

thrown overboard from both sides and dragged across the rock until the crew recognized that their trailing bags of linked iron rings were full. Deck hands then manned winches to haul aboard the dredges, now heavy laden with live oysters, shell, mud, sea grass, and other debris. Small oysters and trash were culled and thrown overboard, and the dredges were lowered for another pass across the rock. Dredger captains considered sixty bushels a good day's haul. They expected to load their vessels within one to four weeks. The captains sold the catch to dealers in markets such as Crisfield, Baltimore, Philadelphia, and New York or to the skippers of the buy boats. They tended to limit their trade to cities where they were sure of obtaining a return cargo. Most of the Eastern Shore captains owned a part or full interest in their boats. Some farmed during the closed season but others remained on the water freighting wood, fertilizer, farm produce, and other commodities.[95]

Dredging was at once beneficial and detrimental to the oyster rocks. By breaking up solidified virgin rock, it allowed the growth of larger, more marketable oysters. Its scraping action expanded the area of the rock. Conversely, scraping also broke off and otherwise damaged healthy oysters. Perhaps more pernicious, the culling of dredged oysters lacked the precision of that of tonged oysters. Often, oysters too small for market were wasted when, rather than thrown immediately back onto the rock, they were cast onto barren ground at the completion of the dredger's run or stowed in the vessel's hold to be discarded at the packing house. Tongers believed that the dredgermen robbed them of employment by looting the oyster grounds. They also resented the dredgermen's access to technology denied themselves for want of means. Tongers were not incipient conservationists. Nor were they cultural traditionalists wedded to a subsistence lifestyle. Had they the wherewithal they too would have been dredgermen.[96]

---

95 Ingersoll, "The Oyster Industry," 158; Winslow, "Deterioration of American Oyster-Beds," pp. 34-35, 42; McDonald, "The Oyster Industry," pp. 279, 280, 283-85; Washington *National Republican*, November 20, 1866; "The Oyster Trade."

96 Victor S. Kennedy and Linda L. Breisch. "Sixteen Decades of Political Management of the Oyster Fishery in Maryland's Chesapeake Bay," Center for Environmental Science, University of Maryland, Contribution No. 1332, p. 6; Ingersoll, "The Oyster Industry, pp. 158,

Riparian rights of landowners living on Virginia's Atlantic coast and on Chesapeake Bay and its tributaries extended to the ordinary low water mark, excepting waters considered commons. On bayside and seaside, on private and public domains, landowners, lessees, and squatters staked out bottom barren of oysters on which they spread shells and other clean refuse. The "planters" then took from the common grounds such as Pocomoke and Tangier sounds young oysters known as "seed" and spread them along the newly created rock. A tourist found Cherrystone Creek "a great place for oysters. The wide, shallow harbor quite bristles with poles, showing the locality of the numerous oyster beds." The planters sowed the seed at different times on different sections of their rock to ensure a supply of oysters in various stages of development. They encouraged maximum growth by annually scattering the oysters by "combing" them with mesh dredges. They also thinned the rock by removing and breaking up large clusters of oysters and moving them to less crowded bottom. By the time that they matured, transplanted oysters had assumed the salinity of the host waters. Thus, whether native or transplanted, oysters taken from Cherrystone Creek were sold as Cherrystones.[97]

Oyster planting was not for the feckless. In 1868 a newcomer to the peninsula, the son of a Union general, dumped but neglected to spread a large quantity of seed oysters in the shallow waters of his father's property on Occohannock Creek. Huge, stinking piles of decaying oysters memorialized his folly. Planters included tongers who supplemented

---

168; Winslow, "Deterioration of American Oyster-Beds," pp. 35, 37; George D. Santopietro and Leonard A. Shabman, "Common Property Rights in Fish and Water Quality: The Oyster Fishery of the Chesapeake Bay," paper presented at the International Association for the Study of Common Property, Duke University, Durham, North Carolina, September 1990, p. 8. For a view of tongers as cultural traditionalists, see Bradford Botwick and Debra A. McClane, "Landscapes of Resistance: A View of the Nineteenth-Century Chesapeake Bay Oyster Fishery," *Historical Archaeology* 39 (2005), p. 109.

97 *Acts Passed at a General Assembly of the Commonwealth of Virginia, 1818-1819* (Richmond: Thomas Ritchie, 1819), pp. 40-41; Wallace *The Parson of the Islands*, pp. 42-43; "A Trip to Cobb's Island – There or Thereabout," Washington *Evening Star*, September 7, 1870; James Richardson, "American Oyster Culture," *Scribner's Monthly* XV (December, 1877), pp. 230-231, 232; *Baltimore Sun* in Philadelphia *Times*, May 6, 1882; "Oysters of the Chesapeake," pp. 343-344.

their incomes by planting on an acre or two of bottom and entrepreneurs who counted their acreage in the hundreds. Throughout the year, the latter employed tongers and dredgermen to replenish, maintain, and harvest their rocks.[98]

Oystering on the Bayside – In the seventeenth and eighteenth centuries the Eastern Shore's oyster trade was almost exclusively local. Nearby coastal cities were small and well supplied with oysters from adjacent waters. Potential inland markets were too distant for fresh delivery. Development of a Chesapeake Bay oyster industry began at the turn of the nineteenth century. By that time the growth of Northern cities had created a demand that increasingly depleted local rocks could not supply. About 1808 Yankee oystermen from Fair Haven, Connecticut, the center of the national oyster trade, turned their attention to the bay country. Initially working in the lower Chesapeake, they obtained cargoes of mature oysters by purchase from natives or by dredging. The dredge was the first of a series of scientific, technological, and business innovations introduced by Northerners that enabled a more thorough exploitation of the Eastern Shore's natural resources.[99]

The commerce in bay oysters grew steadily. By 1830 the trade also included seed oysters to replenish the ravaged rocks of Fair Haven and other Northern grounds. The commencement of operations of the Baltimore and Ohio Railroad in 1828 and the construction of national turnpikes opened interior markets. To meet growing demand, dealers from Fair Haven and other New England ports in the mid-1830s established shucking houses in Baltimore. In the 1840s the discovery of the fecund grounds in Pocomoke and Tangier sounds provided new sources of supply while the commencement of oyster canning in Baltimore extended market range. Surging urban growth and rail construction in the following decade further stimulated production. A committee of

---

98 James A. Ward, *That Man Haupt: A Biography of Herman Haupt* (Baton Rouge: Louisiana State University Press, 1973), p. 190.

99 Cronin "Chesapeake Fisheries," p. 193; McDonald, "The Oyster Industry," p. 223; Kennedy and Breisch, "Sixteen Decades of Political Management of the Oyster Fishery," pp. 3-4.

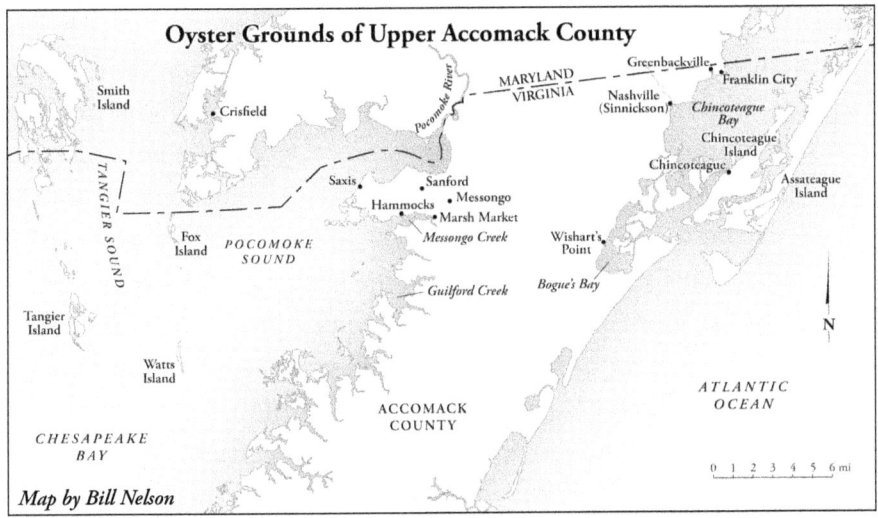

Map by Bill Nelson

the Virginia House of Delegates estimated that during the season of 1857-1858 a minimum of 6,000,000 bushels of oysters valued at $1 per bushel were taken from the commonwealth's waters. A year later, a Richmond reporter reckoned that Tangier and Pocomoke sounds accounted for half of Virginia's total harvest.[100]

The opening of the sounds dramatically stimulated the oyster industry in Accomack County. From 1850 to 1860, the population of the mid-bay island of Tangier leaped from 178 to 411. Including seaside as well as bayside, the number of oystermen in the Accomack grew during the decade from 35 (5 of whom were free blacks) to 341 (18 free blacks). The latter figure included 51 men whom the oyster boom had lured to Accomack. Most were natives of coastal states extending northward from Maryland to New York. There is a grain of truth in the barb aimed at Henry A. Wise during his 1855 gubernatorial campaign that he lived "among the fishmongers and free negroes of Accomac." The participation of Northampton County in the boom of the 1850s is difficult to gauge. A petition of its citizens in 1831 informed the General Assembly

---

[100] David M. Schulte, "History of the Virginia Oyster Industry, Chesapeake Bay, USA," *Frontiers in Marine Science* (www.frontiersin.org) 4 (May, 2017), article 127, pp. 2-3; Cronin "Chesapeake Fisheries," pp. 193-194; Kennedy and Breisch, "Sixteen Decades of Political Management of the Oyster Fishery," pp. 4, 5; McDonald, "The Oyster Industry," pp. 226, 327, 329; Winslow, "Report on the Oyster Beds," p. 40; *Richmond Enquirer*, March 5, 1858; *Richmond Dispatch*, April 22, 1859.

that "very few" of the county's whites engaged in supplying oysters to Northern vessels "so that they are chiefly dependent on our slaves & free negroes." The 1860 census listed only 7 oystermen (3 of whom were free blacks), up from 5 (no free blacks) in 1850. The censuses were silent on whether the number of slaves gathering oysters commercially for their masters or moonlighting for themselves (quite literally moonlighting according to the petition) increased in the late antebellum period.[101]

From the moment a Fair Haven skipper first lowered a dredge, Chesapeake oystering became a free-for-all. Ensuing acts of the Virginia legislature prohibited dredging and reserved to Virginians the export of oysters out of the commonwealth. Unfortunately, frugal legislators neglected to allocate funds for effective enforcement and pirate-hearted Yankees, Marylanders, and Virginians violated the laws with impunity. In the late 1840s and early 1850s, as the wealth, actual and potential, generated by the oyster industry became evermore apparent, a movement arose to discourage the flaunting of the law, prevent the destruction of the rocks, and protect Virginia's vested interest against interlopers.[102]

The boundary between Virginia and Maryland across Chesapeake Bay became a point of contention. Ominously, a joint commission of the two states reported in 1858 that it could not agree on where the line came ashore in Pocomoke Sound. More pressing at the moment were the depredations of Northern oystermen. A petition of Northampton citizens in 1842 informed the General Assembly that the oysters in most of its creeks already had been "greatly diminished." John W. Winder of Accomack County told a House committee in 1858 that in a single day

---

[101] Kirk Mariner, *God's Island: The History of Tangier* (New Church, Va.: Miona Publications, 1999), pp. 53, 78; Patricia Scherzinger, comp., *Accomack County, Virginia, 1850 Census* (Bowie, Md.: Heritage Books, 1988, from copy corrected by Barry W. Miles and M. K. Miles III in Eastern Shore Heritage Center); Crowson and Hite, comps., *Accomack County, Virginia, 1860 Census*; Frances Bibbins Latimer, comp., *The 1850 Population Census & 1850-1880 Mortality Schedules, Northampton County, Virginia*, ed. Doris Adler (Eastville, Va.: Hickory House, 1999); Latimer, *1860 Census for Northampton County, Virginia* (Eastville, Va.: Hickory House, 1994); Lynchburg *Virginian* in *Richmond Enquirer*, March 23, 1855 (quotation); Petition of Citizens, December 6, 1831, Northampton County Legislative Petitions, 1776-1862, Library of Virginia, Richmond. Slaves labored for Northerners "only in the night."

[102] Petition of Citizens, March 11 and April 23, 1852, Accomack County Legislative Petitions; *Richmond Enquirer*, March 5, 1858.

he had seen 150 vessels, many of them out of Philadelphia, dredging in Pocomoke and Tangier sounds. He declared that the rocks there had been "very much broken up" and lamented the passing of the day "when there was more money realized from the oysters of the Chesapeake than from all the farms bordering on the Chesapeake." Further testimony before the committee revealed that Yankee buy boat captains paid less than twenty cents for a bushel of Chesapeake oysters which when resold in Northern markets brought a dollar. To add insult to injury, some Yankee skippers were bringing along their own labor to work the rocks, thus cutting out Virginia tongers altogether. "While few Virginians have made more than a bare subsistence from the oyster beds of their State, Northern men have amassed princely fortunes," asserted the *Norfolk Argus*. "Northern communites ... have been built up by the oyster trade. Fair Haven owes its existence and prosperity to it; its street are paved with Virginia oyster shells, and its people's pockets are filled with the profits of their contents."[103]

Where Virginian resentment confronted Yankee rapacity violence might ensue. In February, 1849, the sheriff of Accomack County raised a posse, mounted cannon on sailboats, and intercepted a fleet of Philadelphia dredgers at work in Pocomoke Sound. When the dredgermen resisted arrest, the Accomack artillerymen commenced fire. The Philadelphians replied with small arms but the cannon, loaded with nails and slugs and directed by a veteran of the war with Mexico, tore to shreds the riggings of their vessels. An oyster pirate was killed and seventy or more captured and jailed in Drummondtown. A Virginian suffered a buckshot wound to the cheek. In the aftermath of the battle an Accomack man pointed out that had the legislature funded an oyster police force it might have prevented the illegal dredging and resultant combat.[104]

---

103 Louis N. Whealton, "The Maryland and Virginia Boundary Controversy (1668-1894)," Ph.D dissertation, Johns Hopkins University, 1897, p. 37; Petition of Citizens, March 17, 1842, Northampton County Legislative Petitions (quotation); *Richmond Enquirer*, March 5, 1858 (quotes Winder); *New York Times*, June 18, 1858; *Norfolk Argus* in "Oyster Trade of Virginia," p. 260.

104 *Richmond Enquirer*, February 27, March 6, 1849.

In 1855, Henry A. Wise of Accomack County won election as governor of Virginia. Brilliant, ambitious, and audacious, Wise proposed that the legislature provide for the policing and taxation of the oyster industry. He recommended that the taking of oysters be restricted to Virginians, that the time and method of their taking be regulated, that their taking and transport require an annual license and fee, that barren ground in the public domain be leased to planters, and that a police force of four steamers patrol the grounds and enforce the statute. Wise predicted that the revenue from fees and rentals would pay for the oyster navy and leave a handsome surplus that might help fund Virginia's program of building railroads and other internal improvements. His proposal was stillborn. Tidewater legislators almost unanimously rejected it. Eastern Shoremen abhorred the idea of being taxed for an activity that they considered a right and believed that their geographically remote peninsula would see not a cent in internal improvements money. The poorer among them suspected that most of the public bottom leased for planting would fall into the hands of the wealthy. They found the pill more bitter coming from a native son whose apostasy they never forgave.[105]

Federal army and naval forces occupied the Eastern Shore of Virginia in November, 1861. The *New York Herald* joyfully anticipated plunder: "Now, with old Accomac and Northampton in our possession, the entire eastern side of the bay is ours. ... [W]e have the lion's share of the good things of the Chesapeake, including ... an abundance of oysters, to the end of the war." Under Federal rule the free-for-all continued. The occupiers ignored Virginia laws restricting the dredging and transport of oysters by non-citizens, and military and customs officers seized the opportunity for some plundering of their own. From oystermen and

---

[105] Craig M. Simpson, *A Good Southerner: The Life of Henry A. Wise of Virginia* (Chapel Hill: University of North Carolina Press, 1985), p. 146; Henry A. Wise, "Message on Miscellaneous Subjects to the General Assembly of Virginia, December 7, 1857" in *Journal of the House of Delegates of the State of Virginia for the Session of 1857-58* (Richmond: William F. Ritchie, Public Printer, 1857), pp. cxxxvii-cxxxviii; *Richmond Enquirer*, March 5, 1858; *Journal of the Senate of Virginia for the Session of 1859-60* (Richmond: William F. Ritchie, Public Printer, 1859), Doc. No. 35, p. 3; William Mayo, The Hague, to William Mahone, September 8, 1882, William Mahone Papers, William R. Perkins Library, Duke University, Durham, N.C.

mariners they collected fees and extorted bribes and kickbacks. "I sure hated that Commodore [John] McGowan," recalled Tangier waterman John W. Dize. "He was very fond of the choicest oysters, and every day I had to cull over the whole day's tonging to pick him out the best specimens." During the five years of war, Washington, D.C. alone received annually an estimated 500,000 bushels of oysters. In 1871, Eastern Shoreman Orris A. Browne of the Virginia Oyster Police deplored the consequence of Yankee peculation in the area under their control: "[T]he oyster beds were scraped bare, and it was two years before they could recuperate."[106]

The Civil War left the South impoverished. It left the North and West flush with money and with a transportation system capable of delivering oysters most anywhere people were willing to pay for them. The price of Chesapeake oysters jumped from 15 to 20 cents per bushel at the beginning of the 1860s to 25 to 30 cents at the end of the decade. In 1867 a railhead soon known as Crisfield touched the bay on the lower Eastern Shore of Maryland. Sited on a high place in the Annemessex marshes, the town literally was built on oyster shells. Oystermen from both Maryland and Virginia sold their catch to Crisfield dealers who in turn shipped boxcar after boxcar northward. By 1870 the town's oyster trade was well on its way to surpassing that of Baltimore. "The huge oyster-packing houses line the shore for half a mile, all built upon shells; canoes, under sail or oar, are moving in every direction, all intent upon one idea – oysters," Wilson reported. "Sloops, schooners, pungies, steamers, barges, cat-boats, craft of every kind, are moving or at anchor, loading oysters or discharging shells."[107]

---

106 *New York Herald*, November 23, 1861; Wilton P. Moore, "Union Army Provost Marshals in the Eastern Theater," *Military Affairs* 26 (Autumn, 1962), p. 124, 125; ESN, June 21, 1935; Thomas Crockett, *Facts and Fun: The Historical Outlines of Tangier Island* (Berkley, Va.: Berkley Daily News, 1890), p. 34; Bayly Ellen Marks, "Rakes, Nippers, and Tongs: Oystermen in Antebellum St. Mary's County," *Maryland Historical Magazine* 90 (Fall, 1995), p. 319; "The Oyster Trade"; Orris A. Browne, *A Report to the Auditor of Public Accounts on the Oyster Beds of Virginia* (Richmond: Shepperson and Graves, 1872), p. 6.

107 John R. Wennersten, "The Almighty Oyster: A Saga of Old Somerset and the Eastern Shore, 1850-1920," *Maryland Historical Magazine* 74 (March, 1978), pp. 81-82; Francis Winslow, "Present Condition and Future Prospects of the Oyster Industry," *Forest and Stream* XXIII (September 18, 1884), p. 148; Wilson, "On the Eastern Shore," p. 240.

In late 1865 Governor Francis H. Pierpont resuscitated Governor Wise's plan to tax the oyster industry. Ironically, Pierpont desired revenue not to fund a program of internal improvements but to provide Virginia with means to retire the debt incurred by the antebellum program. "The recommendation of Governor Pierpoint [sic] that the shell fish shall bear a fair share of the onerous burthen of taxation is just and proper, and we hope will be acted on with promptness by the Legislature," the *Richmond Dispatch* declared. "The wealth and ability of the State to pay its debts have been fearfully diminished by the war and its assets have nearly all been swept away and in this emergency we must avail of every resource which has been spared the ravages of war." The legislature acted promptly and thoroughly. In its two sessions before Congressional imposition of military reconstruction on the commonwealth in 1867, it adopted almost every part of Wise's plan. It declared the summer months a closed season, prohibited non-citizens from taking oysters, required licenses and fees for taking and for transporting, restricted dredging to Tangier and Pocomoke sounds, and created an oyster police force. It also confirmed to landowners and lessees their exclusive right to their planted oysters. Irony upon irony, the legislation soon lost much of its effectiveness as a revenue measure. Irate oystermen successfully lobbied delegates to the constitutional convention of 1867-1868 to insert an article stating that "No tax shall be imposed on any of the citizens of this State for the privilege of taking or catching oysters from their natural beds with tongs, in the waters thereof."[108]

The Virginia oyster police force organized during the summer of 1867. The force consisted of three small, armed steamers captained by inspectors and under the overall command of Chief Inspector William H. C. Lovett of Norfolk. As the price of oysters climbed and as more and more men took to the waters of the bay, depredations increased in

---

[108] *Journal of the Senate of the Commonwealth of Virginia, 1865-1866* (Richmond: James E. Goode, Senate Printer, 1865), pp. 15-17; *Richmond Daily Dispatch*, December 29, 1865 (quotation), January 23, 1868; *Acts of the General Assembly of the State of Virginia, 1865-1866* (Richmond: Allegre & Goode, 1866), pp. 74-77, 155-157; *Norfolk Virginian*, August 28, 1867; *The Constitution of Virginia: Framed by the Convention which met in Richmond, Virginia, on Tuesday, December 3, 1867, Passed April 17, 1868* (Richmond: Printed at the Office of the *New Nation*, 1868), Article X, Sec. 2, p. 32.

Tangier and Pocomoke sounds along the Maryland-Virginia boundary. The oyster navy seems quickly to have driven out Northern pirates but interloping tongers and dredgermen from Maryland, enjoying sanctuary a short sail away, continued to rob Virginia rocks (just as Virginians robbed Maryland rocks). In early November, 1868, twenty or more Smith Islanders fired from the shore at Virginia police steamers crossing into Maryland in pursuit of fleeing pirates. The steamers' crewmen returned fire but no one on either side was injured. A Maryland-Virginia legislative commission having recently failed in another attempt to establish an official boundary, Chief Inspector Lovett and Commander Hunter Davidson of the Maryland oyster police on December 11 jointly designated an unofficial line demarcating their respective areas of jurisdiction. The Lovett-Davidson line aided the oyster police in defining limits of operation but oystermen bent on plunder considered it nothing more than a mark on a sheet of paper.[109]

The expansion of the Eastern Shore oyster industry gained momentum in the 1860s. Including both bayside and seaside, the number of Northampton oystermen listed in the federal census grew from 7 in 1860 to 85 (of whom 55 were black) in 1870 while that in Accomack jumped from 341 to 777 (69 black). Those born outside of Virginia increased in Accomack from 51 to 114. Emancipation partially accounts for the dramatic increase in the number of oystermen in Northampton while the early decimation of the county's bayside rocks helps explain the lagging performance of the county's oyster industry in comparison to that of Accomack. Around half of the oystermen in Accomack and two-thirds of those in Northampton worked the bayside grounds. Along the upper Accomack bayside, farmers abandoned the land for the water. In 1850 Saxis Island on Pocomoke Sound was a farming community. Only one Saxis oysterman appeared in the federal census. That number grew to 23 in 1860 and 48 in 1870. In the latter year only three farmers, average age 69, lived on the island. Near the end of the 1860s

---

109 R. W. M., "The Oyster Trade," *New-York Daily Tribune*, March 27, 1869; *Baltimore American* in *Richmond Dispatch*, November 9, 17, 1868; Whealton, *The Maryland and Virginia Boundary Controversy*, pp. 34-41; *Baltimore Sun* November 9, 1868; *Norfolk Virginian*, January 1, 1869.

Accomack with 350 licensed oystermen ranked fourth among the nineteen Tidewater counties behind Norfolk (486), Gloucester (404), and York (352). Northampton ranked twelfth with 85.[110]

Oystering on the Seaside – Oysters on the Eastern Shore seaside grew in immense quantities – "enough to feed the world," exclaimed a visitor to Cobb's Island. Tightly clustered on their native rocks, the oysters were too small to find much of an urban market but when separated and transplanted they attained a marketable size. Up to 1870 Chincoteague Bay was the focus of the seaside oyster trade. To its south navigation of the shallow inlets separating the barrier islands was continuously at the whim of current and storm. With oysters readily available in Chincoteague and Chesapeake bays, Northern mariners usually avoided their inhospitable waters. Trade to the south of Chincoteague was mostly in seed oysters. Mature oysters put on the market had themselves been transferred from natural rocks to planting grounds at the heads of seaside creeks.[111]

The Chincoteague oyster industry began about the same time as that of the Chesapeake. Most of Chincoteague Bay's early oyster trade probably was in seed to replenish depleted Northern rocks. Around 1840 people living along the bay began to plant oysters for themselves. Planting seems an inevitable development in the shallow waters of the Eastern Shore seaside. Acres of mudflats extending from shore lay exposed at low water, placing a premium value on riparian rights (and thus provoking decades of litigation). Chincoteague oystermen refused to sell to outsiders mature oysters from their planting grounds. Instead, they carried their harvest in schooners and large bateau (sloop-rigged vessels indigenous to the seaside) to New York and Philadelphia. Prices

---

110 Crowson and Hite, *Accomack County, Virginia, 1860 Census*; Latimer, *1860 Census for Northampton County, Virginia*; Walczyk, comp., *The Accomack County 1870 Census*; and Latimer, comp., *The 1870 Census for Northampton County*; Kirk Mariner, *Almost an Island: The History of Saxis, Virginia* (Onancock, Va.: Miona Publications, 2011), pp. 22, 23, 24; "The Oyster Trade."

111 *Richmond Enquirer*, March 5, 1858; Fitzhugh, "Eastern Shore of Virginia," p. 81; McDonald, "The Oyster Industry," 379; T. [Israel Townsend, Capeville, to editor, March 16, Wilmington *Delaware State Journal*, March 22, 1867; "Cobb's Island," Washington *Evening Star*, August 15, 1871; Petition of Citizens, January 25, 1834, Accomack County Legislative Petitions.

rose with demand. Chincoteague oysters sold from 12 cents per bushel in 1844 to 50 cents in 1850 to $1 in 1861. By the late 1850s, thirteen vessels carried northward an estimated 40,000 bushels per annum. The population of Chincoteague Island grew from around 150 in 1800 to around 350 in 1830 to more than 700 in 1860.[112]

Voters on Chincoteague almost unanimously opposed the Virginia ordinance of secession and when war came affirmed their devotion to the Union. "All our interests were in the north," island patriarch John A. M. Whealton later admitted. "We sold nearly all the oysters we raised in Philadelphia. It would have meant starvation to us to have seceded and cut us off from that market." The islanders flattered themselves that their patriotism induced the federals to reopen quickly the Chincoteague Bay oyster trade. More likely, Northern consumers and businessmen had the greater influence. Also, federal military and customs officers desired to exploit the opportunities for graft presented them by the war to preserve the Union. Chincoteague oyster dealer John W. Bunting boasted that during the war he "would enter and go out of New York harbor without any trouble, when the other fellows could not do it; that he took along with him some $10.00 bills."[113]

Just as opportunists followed the Union military into occupied areas of the cotton South, so too they came to Chincoteague Bay. The number of island residents born in the North leaped from 40 in 1860 to 184 in 1870. The Yankee "spirit of industry and enterprise" stimulated newcomer and native alike to seed the mudflats in mid-bay from which they harvested a more desirable grade of oyster that those grown along the shore. Signs of prosperity abounded. On the island the population

---

112 *PE*, April 26, 1940; McDonald, "The Oyster Industry," p. 306; Bishop, *Voyage of the Paper Canoe*, p. 139; Spears, "Life on Chincoteague"; Kirk Mariner, *Once Upon an Island: The History of Chincoteague* (New Church, Va.: Miona Publications, 1996), p. 41; *New-York Daily Tribune*, December 20, 1861; James G. Paxton, "Oyster Fundum of Virginia," *Richmond Enquirer*, June 4, 1858; Matthews, "Chincoteague Island"; *Richmond Dispatch*, April 22, 1859; Crowson and Hite, *Accomack County, Virginia, 1860 Census*, pp. 129-141, 153-157.

113 Pyle, "Chincoteague," pp. 744-745; Susie M. Ames, "Chincoteague Island During the Civil War," *PE*, June 15, 1961 (quotes Whealton); Martin Parks Burks, *Reports of Cases in the Supreme Court of Appeals of Virginia, Vol. CVII, from June 1, 1907, to March 1, 1908* (Richmond: Davis Bottom, Superintendent of Public Printing, 1908), p. 181 (quotes Bunting).

grew from 704 in 1860 to 1,122 in 1870. On the western side of the bay a new town, appropriately named Greenbackville, emerged just below the boundary with Maryland. By 1870, 224 persons, of whom 113 were born in Union states, lived in and around Greenbackville. On mainland and island, waterfront property increased in value. A Baltimore journalist visiting Chincoteague in 1873 exclaimed that "Every house now on the island, except two or three, has been built since 1859."[114]

And yet there was a worm in the bud. By the late 1860s, Chincoteague islanders began to worry about the depletion of the public oyster rocks. Planters fretted about the expense of having to bring in seed from elsewhere, but the chief concern was that of the tongers who understood that the destruction of the bay's natural rocks meant for them a greater dependence on work provided by the planters.[115]

Livestock Herding, Market Hunting, Wrecking – Eastern Shore watermen worked also as herdsmen, wreckers, and market hunters. The peninsula's wetlands served as pasture for hogs, goats, sheep, cattle, and horses. Marsh grass provided livestock with browse, and on the adjacent islands natural pools and shallow wells supplied them with water. Herds of livestock sheltered on nearly all the islands and at the appropriate time according to species were penned, marked or branded, gelded, sheared, slaughtered, and the surplus sold. Most of these events passed without more than local notice, but the separate pennings of sheep on Assateague and Chincoteague and the combined penning on Chincoteague of ponies from both islands attracted buyers and spectators from as far away as New York. The most famous of the pennings was that of the ponies. Around thirty persons owned herds on the two islands. The only investment necessary was in a few brood-mares; the

---

114 Crowson and Hite, *Accomack County, Virginia, 1860 Census*, pp. 129-141, 153-157; Walczyk, *The Accomack County 1870 Census*, I, pp. 28-29, 31-34, 97-123; Matthews, "Chincoteague Island" (quotations); T. W. Taylor Jr., "An Oyster Gold Mine: How Planting Prospered in Accomac County, Virginia," *Baltimore Sun*, January 23, 1906; *The Statistics of the Population of the United States ... Compiled From the Original Returns of the Ninth Census (June 1, 1870)* (Washington: Government Printing Office, 1872), p. 278; *Baltimore Sun*, December 12, 1865.

115 *Richmond Dispatch*, February 12, 1867.

only regular labor required was at the penning. The owners turned their stock onto the commons and let nature do the rest. The combined Assateague and Chincoteague herds numbered from four to five hundred animals. Inbred and from birth exposed to the elements and coarse fare, the ponies were small, strong, and tough. An observer described them as "mongrels, if such a term may be employed in respect to horses." The larger ponies were used on the mainland for the saddle and for light farming. All were well suited to the use of children for riding and for pulling light buggies. Wealthy folks attending the penning often purchased the prettier ponies as family pets.[116]

Eastern Shoremen also hunted wildfowl and shorebirds for the Northern restaurant and millinery markets. The birds stood not a chance. The market hunters used traps and nets, blinds and sinkboxes, breech-loading shotguns, battery guns, and mammoth puntguns. They spread bait and shot birds on the water and by torchlight. The slaughter was immense. In 1860, citizens of Accomack County warned the General Assembly that the use of traps augured the "total destruction of wild fowl." Legislation in the *Code of Virginia* of that year prohibited night shooting, hunting from skiff or sinkbox, and hunting of wildfowl in the Tidewater by non-residents. Lacking provisions for effective enforcement, the acts no more deterred depradators than antebellum statutes regulating the oyster industry.[117]

The Eastern Shore's treacherous Atlantic coast inspired fear and respect. Ocean currents and rough weather continually reconfigured shoals and inlets. Navigational ignorance or error might be severely punished. Northeast storms pushed ships shoreward. Waves beat to pieces wooden vessels stranded on shoals or beaches. Their cargo cast

---

116 *Richmond Dispatch*, April 16, 1874, August 18, 1875; *Alexandria Gazette* in New York *Evening Post*, February 27, 1844; PE, May 24, 1884; Pyle, "A Peninsular Canaan," pp. 813, 814; Pyle, "Chincoteague," p. 741; "Chincoteague Island, Va," *Baltimore Sun*, August 28, 1876 (quotes N. E. F.) "Chincoteague Island," Elkton (Md.) *Cecil Whig*, September 9, 1876; Matthews, "Chincoteague Island";

117 Barnes and Truitt, "A Short History of the Virginia Barrier Islands," p. 12; Petition of Citizens, January 11, 1860, Accomack County Legislative Petitions; *The Code of Virginia, Second Edition, Including Legislation to the Year 1860* (Richmond: Ritchie, Dunnavant & Co., 1860), pp. 505-506.

ashore; their sailors and passengers drowned. Mariners had little more than experience on which to rely. Lighthouses on Assateague, Hog, and Smith's islands provided some security, but navigational charts became quickly out of date and other aids were rudimentary. Not until 1876 would United States Life-Saving Service stations offer succor to the shipwrecked. The most dangerous shoals were Winter Quarters off Chincoteague Island, Dawson's (Dorson's) off Cedar and Parramore, and those off Cobb's, deplored by Alexander Hunter as "the scene of scores of shipwrecks, and many sailors are buried here [on Cobb's], the victims of some terrible disaster."[118]

The practice of wrecking, the salvage and plunder of stranded vessels, epitomized the opportunism of those who worked on the water. If the sea gave it up, watermen considered it theirs for the taking. Most wreckers were islanders who rushed to the booty-strewn beach to collect and conceal the ship's cargo and appurtenances before owners, government agents, or professional wreckers arrived on the scene. In 1836, men sent to Hog Island to secure the cargo of the shipwrecked sloop *Capital* "found several persons on the Island who had already committed great depredations." Casual wreckers might loot the bodies of the drowned and rob defenseless survivors. Conversely, they might rescue the endangered at the risk of their lives and take care to bury the dead safely beyond the breakers. Edmund Ruffin discovered that the inhabitants of Hog Island "have never accounted smuggling and wrecking (in a decent way) among the things prohibited by the Decalogue – but rather consider the opportunities for both as among the bounties of Providence, which are to be enjoyed temperately and thankfully."[119]

Professional wrecking companies from as far away as New York also hastened to Eastern Shore shipwrecks. The professionals salvaged ship and cargo or, if the vessel was beyond saving, as much of the cargo as possible. Under contract or through negotiation, they obtained from ship

---

118 *Baltimore Sun*, January 28, 1875; Hunter, T*he Huntsman in the South*, p. 301; Hunter to editor, August 2, *Alexandria Gazette*, August 7, 1875 (quotation).

119 Alexander Hunter to editor, July 23, *Alexandria Gazette*, July 30, 1879; *Charleston Southern Patriot*, February 10, 1836 (quotation); *New York Herald*, April 19, 1870; Ruffin, "A Trip to Some of the Sea Islands of Virginia," pp. 533-534.

owners or insurance underwriters a percentage of the value of the salvage. The most successful of the local professionals was the Cobb family of Cobb's Island. The Cobbs, who came to Northampton County from Cape Cod in the early 1830s, engaged in a number of seaside businesses including hunting wildfowl and shorebirds for the market and keeping a resort hotel, but they made their fortune as wreckers. From the time of their arrival, they undertook the salvage of at least thirty-seven wrecks. In 1870, the Cobbs earned $10,000 or more when they salvaged from a sand bar opposite Cobb's Island the stranded bark *Crickett* and its cargo of Brazilian coffee. The hurricane of 1876 brought the Cobbs "a rich haul," which they estimated by the thousands of dollars.[120]

WATERMEN, WROTE NEW YORK REPORTER JOHN R. Spears, "dress in long-legged rubber boots, twilled cotton overalls, and jackets, and sou'westers which they wear on their heads at this [summer] season with the flannel lining out. ... They wear their beards full, their faces are red, their hands hard, and their manners bluff." Alexander Hunter considered watermen "a class of humanity different from what we see in our every day world, rough, uncouth, and uneducated, but honest and hospitable." Spears discerned that their honesty had a limit: "They never lock their doors at night, because there is not a man [in their communities] who would steal money, though they do say that unaccountable mistakes are made when gathering the oyster harvest, by which under-water farm lines are crossed and the reaper gathers where he did not sow." Most watermen were illiterate but they were not ignorant. They knew the ways of the water – "all expert boatmen, boatbuilders, and sailmakers," observed Spears; they knew the fluctuations of the fisheries markets; and they knew to enlist the aid of the better educated among them when transacting business with outsiders. Class divisions existed among them but, as a visitor to Chincoteague noted, "there being fewer artificial conditions, the dividing lines are less arbitrary and more consistent with

---

120 Hunter, *The Huntsman in the South*, p. 141; Alexander Hunter to editor, August 2, *Alexandria Gazette*, August 7, 1875; Amine Kellam, "The Cobb's Island Story," *Virginia Cavalcade* XXIII (Spring, 1975), p. 22; *ESH*, January 30, 1932; A. S. M., Hungars Parish, to editor, October 21, *Alexandria Gazette*, October 23, 1876 (quotation).

reason than in more populous and polished communities." They did not possess equal abilities, but their individualistic calling encouraged a tacit equality.[121]

Watermen worked in small boats on open water in heat and cold. They suffered the effects of exposure and of hard physical labor. If they avoided drowning, they usually had to quit the water by middle age. "It is a man's work in every sense of the word," a retired watermen declared. "There is money to be made in the water, but it's worth every dollar a man gets out of it." John B. Baylor, who surveyed the Virginia oyster grounds in the 1890s, came to admire the bay oystermen: "[They] are inured to hardship and exposure from boyhood. The force of circumstance has taught them to be cool and collected in the hour of danger, for their own safety often demands that they should be so. Strong in their friendships, bitter and relentless in their hatred, they are a body of men from which heroes have sprung. No one could live long amongst them without feeling for them and with them."[122]

Most watermen owned an acre or so close to the shore, a small house and garden, and a canoe or an interest in one. Their expenses – equipment, labor, taxes – were light, and their work usually close at hand. Offsetting these advantages were hiatuses imposed by rough weather and closed seasons. During the eight-month oyster season, oystermen expected 120 to 140 working days. A week of below-freezing temperature, not uncommon in the late nineteenth century, might force the families of oystermen to economize for the rest of the year. Watermen generally earned adequate livings. Some accumulated more property than most, but only the few who ventured successfully into seafood dealing or oyster planting became wealthy.[123]

---

[121] John R. Spears, "A Curious Virginia City," New York *Sun*, May 7, 1890; Alexander Hunter, "Cobb's Island in Summer," *Forest and Stream* VII (August 31, 1876), p. 49; Washington *National Republican*, November 20, 1866; Matthews, "Chincoteague Island" (quotation).

[122] Ingersoll, "The Oyster Industry," p. 181; "The Oyster at Home," p. 397; "While Farmers Plan for Spring, Water Industry is Benefactor," ESN, January 19, 1923 (quotation); J. B. Baylor, *The Oyster Industry: A Series of Letters Written for the Richmond "Dispatch" and "Times" During the Winter of 1892-'93* (Richmond: Whittet & Shepperson, 1893), p. 7.

[123] Ingersoll, "The Oyster Industry," p. 162; McDonald, "The Oyster Industry," p. 270; "The

Steam and Steel

Richard H. Edmonds, a Baltimore journalist who preached a Northern-style "gospel of work" to the recovering South, believed that watermen lacked ambition. With some overstatement, Edmonds described what he considered the problem:

> A tongman can, at any time, take his canoe or skiff and catch from the natural rocks a few bushels of oysters, for which there is always a market. Having made a dollar or two, he stops work until that is used up, often a large part of it being spent for strong drink. When his money is all gone he can repeat the same course. Unless spent in the indulgence of intemperate habits, a small amount of money will enable an oysterman to live in comparative comfort. He can readily, and at almost no expense, supply his table in winter with an abundance of oysters and ducks, geese and other game, while in summer, fish and crabs may be had simply for the catching. So long as they are able to live in this manner, it is almost impossible to get them to do any steady farm-work.

Edmonds provided a generally accurate description of the watermen's work habits, but their meaning escaped him. They were not ruled by clock or farmyard rhythm. Their days were determined by the cycle of the tides and by the caprice of the wind. The daily impress of chance – the varying weather, the size of the catch, the daily fluctuations of the market – shaped their attitude toward work. Fisheries expert Ernest Ingersoll believed that "The influence of these uncertainties upon the habits and thrift of the men is plainly marked, particularly in dislike of steady industry." The prospect of a poor catch as the price of grueling labor might make the idea of tomorrow's work unpalatable. Their families need not starve or want for shelter. For sustenance, they could fall back on the immense natural bounty around them. If times were hard on the water, temporary work was available in the fields or in the woods. Instead of criticizing them for their laziness, Edmonds might

---

Teagues of Accomack," Wilmington *Delaware State Journal*, April 7, 1881; "Wickedness of the Frozen Up Oystermen," New York *Sun*, February 19, 1905; Wallace, *The Parson of the Islands*, p. 44; "A Peninsular Tour: Tangier Sound and the Chesapeake Oyster Beds," Wilmington *News Journal*, June 19, 1878.

have praised them for their diligence. Marshall McDonald, a fisheries administrator who studied the Chesapeake watermen closely, insisted that they "compare favorably in industry and morals with any body of men *similarly situated* [emphasis added]." The economist and agrarian George Fitzhugh understood the logic and the temptation of the waterman's hand-to-mouth strategy: "It is somewhat remarkable, and much to the credit of the people of this section, that they are not generally tempted to quit farming and betake themselves to the more fascinating and less laborious pursuits of fishing, oystering, and ducking."[124]

Eastern Shore watermen usually passed their lives in or near shorefront communities. As their children came of age, they divided and sub-divided their already small holdings. Their villages became more crowded, interrelated, and insular. The newcomers who continued to come from Maryland and other states shared the native waterman's mentality. Psychologically and sometimes physically separated from the mainland, they prided themselves on their independence while holding in contempt those who were tied to the soil. White watermen also exhibited what a politician called "an intense feeling of hostility to the negro." A bred-in-the-bone attitude of racial superiority was affronted by post-Civil War competition with large numbers of freedmen aggressively defending what they regarded as their territory in Western Shore rivers. Thomas "Sugar Tom" Crockett of Tangier Island related that immediately after the war several of the islanders "went to the Rappahannock river oystering, and there were 5 to 10 niggers for one white man, and that made those niggers very saucy and mean." The record reveals little overt racial conflict in the Eastern Shore fisheries. The commons offered space enough for all. Blacks and whites avoided those grounds considered reserved for the other race. Tar Bay on the seaside of black-majority Northampton County had its name for a reason.[125]

---

124 Ingersoll, "The Oyster Industry, pp. 157 (quotes Edmonds), 181; McDonald, "The Oyster Industry," p. 270; Fitzhugh, "Eastern Shore of Virginia," p. 81; T. H. Bayly Browne, Drummondtown, to William Mahone, November 30, 1884, Mahone Papers, Duke. For Edmonds and the "gospel of work," see Paul M. Gaston, *The New South Creed: A Study in Southern Mythmaking* (New York: Alfred A. Knopf, 1870), pp. 50-51, 108. Historian Barbara Jeanne Fields noted that newsmen such as Edmonds criticized oystermen in the same terms in which they criticized blacks (*Slavery and Freedom on the Middle Ground*, p. 164).

125 Wallace, *The Parson of the Islands*, p. 44; Botwick and McClane, "Landscapes of Resis-

Watermen regarded the bounty of the aquatic commons as a gift of God for which He required only gratitude. Human abstractions such as game laws, catch limitations, state boundaries, and private planting grounds were problematic, their legitimacy contingent on the individual waterman's need, opportunity, and fear of punishment. Tangier Islanders told officers of the Reconstruction government that "oysters, being the handiwork of the Creator should be exempt from taxation." Having acknowledged the dominion of God, they added that "as citizens of a Democratic country they ought not to pay taxes for the use of their own property." On the other hand, Tangier and other watermen howled when Marylanders descended into Virginia waters or when miscreants stole oysters from their private beds. A journalist acidly remarked that the watermen's "abhorrence of restriction here resembles closely that of the 'Pilgrim Fathers' in the matter of [freedom of] religion – being directed against the practice rather than the principle." The commons encouraged individualism and opportunism while it discouraged stewardship. Historian Harry Walsh sadly recalled a conversation with a veteran market hunter: "In his mind, the proudest moment of a duck's life was when he shot it. The thing he knew and did best was hunting wildfowl. Conservation and survival of a species were foreign thoughts to him – the Lord had placed the fowl here for the benefit of man and the Lord helped those who helped themselves." Unlike the land, the commons belonged to everyone and to no one. Constantly replenishing their soil and preserving their woodland, the farmers whom the watermen held in such contempt were the better stewards of their God-given patrimony.[126]

---

tance," p. 102; Dennis, *The Dennises of Beverly*, p. 88; William Mayo, The Hague, to William Mahone, September 8, 1882, Mahone Papers, Duke; Crockett, *Facts and Fun*, p. 38

[126] John R. Wennersten, *The Chesapeake: An Environmental Biography* (Baltimore: Maryland Historical Society, 2001), p. 134; R. W. M., "The Oyster Trade" (second and third quotations); "The Oyster at Home" (fourth quotation); Harry M. Walsh, *The Outlaw Gunner* (Centreville, Md.: Tidewater Publishers, 1971), p. 67.

Tourism

Beginning in the 1840s, Eastern Shoremen and other Virginians began to dream of seashore resorts catering to the growing number of vacationers and sportsmen, North and South. Proposed resorts on the barrier islands of Bone, Mockhorn, and Smith's and on the mainland near Cape Charles proved, in the words of a promoter, nothing more than "a very large Air Castle." Dream became reality only on Prout's and Cobb's islands on the lower Northampton seaside and on Tangier Island in mid-Chesapeake Bay. The hotels on Prout's and Tangier, the latter "well conducted on temperance principles," failed to survive the Civil War but that on Cobb's endured.[127]

Besides wrecking, market hunting, and other maritime enterprises, the Cobbs of Cobb's Island also housed and guided sportsmen who came to their island to hunt shorebirds and wildfowl. In the 1850s, the Cobbs used their savings to expand their hunting lodge into an all-seasons resort. The island enjoyed the advantages of a smooth beach, abundant vegetation, and freedom from mosquitoes. By the end of the decade, the Cobbs entertained a hundred or more vacationers daily during the summer. Despite its growth, the resort retained the rusticity of the sportsman's retreat. Travel from Norfolk to the island required an exhausting day's journey beginning with a steamer across Chesapeake Bay to Cherrystone, followed by a carriage ride of six miles across the peninsula, and culminating with a sailboat trip, tide and weather permitting, another eight miles over the Broadwater to the island. The resort's

---

[127] Petition of Citizens, January 6, 1858, Northampton County Legislative Petitions; "Letter from Mockhorn Island," *Forest and Stream* I (September 4, 1873), p. 52; George Washington Parke Custis, Arlington House, to Henry A. Wise, October 15, 1850, PE, May 9, 1947; William H. Parker, Capeville, to Ellis, January 21, 1853, Garrett Family Papers, 1811-1943, Albert and Shirley Small Special Collections Library, University of Virginia, Charlottesville (first quotation); *Acts of the General Assembly of Virginia, Passed in 1852* (Richmond: William F. Ritchie, 1852), pp. 207-208; Latimer, *1860 Census for Northampton County*, p. 26; Wallace, *The Parson of the Islands*, pp. 40-41 (second quotation); *Baltimore Sun*, May 29, 1860, July 8, 1862, August 2, 1866; Norfolk *Day Book*, September 20, 1866; Mariner, *God's Island*, p. 63.

accommodations and atmosphere were primitive. A Richmonder advised that "The house is tolerable, but the fare is indifferent except the fish, crabs, and oysters, which are very fine. There are no baths for the ladies and the way the salt water is taken is by walking right down into the surf from a low sandy beach. This is very fine; but may not suit ladies not used to that kind of bathing. ... I am of opinion that it is a very fine place for young men ardent in the pursuit of amusement of a manly sort ... but I hardly suppose it would suit the ladies, unless the more romantic and energetic kind."[128]

During the Civil War, the federal military requisitioned the Cobb's Island resort for use as a concentration camp where it incarcerated without benefit of habeas corpus local men and women suspected of disloyalty to the Union and other crimes against the state. The military also quartered soldiers at the resort. In late 1865, Jesse J. Simpkins described the hotel in the aftermath of Yankee occupation:

> [N]orthern troops were often quartered there, in loafing idleness, and soon various apartments were gutted, and their naked wall begrimed with black paint and charcoal caricatures, which it required many appliances of the whitewash brush to efface. Most of the portable furniture was taken away under the orders from a post officer whose name will live in infamy here while the present generation lasts. ... [T]hese petty spoliations were never known at district headquarters, and the enriched beneficiary was permitted to depart 'unwhipt of justice.' No human foresight could have

---

128 Curtis J. Badger, "The Golden Age of Gunning Clubs," *Virginia Wildlife* 77 (January/February, 2018), pp. 6-7; Kellam, "The Cobb's Island Story," p. 23; "Cobb's Island," Washington *Evening Star*, August 15, 1871; Alexander Hunter, "Hog Island," *Alexandria Gazette*, July 30, 1879; Simpkins, "Invalid Inklings by the Seashore"; J. A. Cowardin, Richmond, to Robert Lewis Dabney, July 7, 1858, Charles W. Dabney Papers, Southern Historical Collection, University of North Carolina, Chapel Hill. Useful histories of Cobb's Island are Ron M. Kagawa and J. Richard Kellam, *Cobb's Island Virginia: The Last Sentinel* (Virginia Beach: The Donning Company, 2003) and S. Lloyd Newberry, *Wings of Wonder: The Remarkable Story of the Cobb Family and the Priceless Decoys They Created on Their Island Paradise* (Columbia, S. C.: Sporting Classics, 2020). An informative short study is Curtis J. Badger, "Nathan Cobb's Island," in *Wilderness Regained: The Story of the Virginia Barrier Islands* (Berlin, Md.: Salt Water Media, 2021), pp. 78-87.

guarded against the secret rascalities that were perpetrated by some of these subordinate officers when left alone.[129]

The Union military having left the island at the end of the war, the Cobbs drew on money earned from the fortuitous beaching of a whale to restore and improve their resort. They enlarged the hotel and expanded the dining room to a capacity of 250. They built a bakery, a bowling alley, a billiard room, and new bathing houses. They connected the complex with new plank walkways. They hired a string band to give nightly concerts in the ballroom. Perhaps more important, they relieved much of the traveler's tedium by replacing their sailboat with a small steamer, which three times weekly transported guests back and forth across the Broadwater. A Washingtonian applauded the Cobbs' efforts: "[F]rom being a resort of a few eager sportsmen seeking good fishing and shooting, it has now become the point of attraction for numbers of pleasure-seekers of both sexes, mainly Virginians and Marylanders, and including many family parties, who find healthful enjoyment here with very little fashionable display to vex the soul and bleed the pocket." By 1870 the Cobb's Island hotel required a summer staff of eleven – two white hotel keepers, a white clerk, and eight black waiters and chambermaids. The Cobbs were said to have turned down a recent offer of $100,000 for the island, which Nathan Cobb Sr. had purchased for $150 in 1839.[130]

Mariners

Virtually everything and everyone entered and departed the Eastern Shore by water. In 1870, officers of the Cherrystone federal customs district, which embraced both counties, enrolled and licensed 211 vessels. Among Virginia's seven districts, Cherrystone was second in

---

129 Simpkins, "Invalid Inklings by the Seashore."

130 Washington *National Republican*, August 10, 1875; *Baltimore Sun*, July 10, August 2, 1866, June 9, 1868, July 22, 1869; *Richmond Dispatch*, April 30, 1867; *Washington Critic-Record*, August 11, 1870; "Cobb's Island," Washington *Evening Star*, August 15, 1871 (quotation); Latimer, *1870 Census for Northampton County, Virginia*, p. 110; March 11, 1839, Northampton County Deed Book 31, Circuit Clerk's Office, Eastville, p. 66.

number of vessels only to Norfolk-Portsmouth. Sailboats – large canoes and bateau, pungies, bugeyes, sloops, and schooners – predominated. An average tonnage of 16.9 indicates that most of them were small. Mariners themselves usually built the smaller craft. Some of the large sailboats were constructed locally by a handful of resident boat builders and by anyone possessed of sufficient skill and confidence. Between 1865 and 1872, Captain John Kelso built in the yard of his home on Pungoteague Creek two large schooners for his own use. Urban boatyards supplied the remainder of the vessels.[131]

Most of the boats were owned by Eastern Shoremen individually or in partnership. The owners were usually mariners, farmers, or merchants. The boat captains owned their vessels or worked for hire. They shipped their own cargoes or handled those of others. The sailboats carried lumber, seafood, and agricultural produce to Norfolk, Baltimore, and Washington and to Philadelphia, New York, and other Northern ports. They brought homeward barrels, fertilizer, farm implements, and general merchandise. In the cool months, they dredged and transported oysters; in the warm they hauled fruits, grains, and vegetables. From July 24 through November 6, 1871, the three schooners of Charles P. Finney of Finney's Wharf made a total of twenty-nine runs to Baltimore. Through August 14, the schooners carried apples, peaches, peas, plums, quinces, watermelons, and sweet potatoes. For the rest of the period, they carried sweet potatoes exclusively. Finney purchased the bulk of the produce from local farmers, black and white. On a single trip one of his schooners transported sweet potatoes purchased from forty-nine farmers. He also shipped produce consigned to Baltimore merchants for which he charged freight. After expenses and upkeep, Finney cleared $2,318.92 (an average of $79.96 per voyage). His most lucrative month was September, the height of the sweet potato harvest.[132]

---

131 *Annual Report of the Chief of the Bureau of Statistics on the Commerce and Navigation of the United States for the Fiscal Year Ended June 30, 1870* (Washington: Government Printing Office, 1871), p. 750; Walczyk, *The Accomack County 1870 Census*, II, 105, 208; McDonald, "The Oyster Industry," p. 267; Hugh and Esther Kelso, *The Kelso Family of Virginia's Eastern Shore* (n.p.: Author, 1983), p. 30.

132 *Philadelphia Inquirer*, August 19, 1865; Wallace, *The Parson of the Islands*, p. 43; *Richmond*

Eastern Shore sailors were overwhelmingly white. The 1870 census listed in Accomack County 272 white sailors compared to 28 black and in Northampton 47 white to 5 black. Had the census been taken in the winter rather than in the summer, the number of sailors, especially black sailors, probably would have been higher. Sailboats required a larger crew for dredging oysters than for transporting cargo, and blacks frequently worked as dredger crewmen. The crew of the average Eastern Shore sailboat, dredgermen excepted, consisted of a captain, mate, cook, and deck hand. The cooks and deck hands moved frequently from vessel to vessel. During 1870-1871, Leonard S. Tawes, aged seventeen, of Accomack, sailed on two schooners and three pungies as cook or dredger hand. While serving as cook on the Crisfield schooner *Lizzie Bell*, Tawes made two trips to Baltimore carrying oysters and four to New York carrying watermelons, Irish potatoes, and sweet potatoes.[133]

Sailors endured the hard labor involved in handling ropes, sails, and cargo and the tedium of the constant maintenance that the boats required. They suffered exposure to drenchings in cold weather and long watches on rough seas that made sleep a matter of catch as catch can. Sailors faced the ever-present threat of death by drowning. They slipped on wet decks and plunged over the rails, were knocked overboard by wind-driven booms and bowsprits, or perished in shipwrecks (a fate not uncommon in the days of sail). A gale on the night of February 12, 1877, capsized two dredgeboats in Tangier Sound. The crew of the schooner *Delmay* of Messongo Creek escaped in a small boat, but the seven men of the Onancock schooner *J. T. H. Colburn* were lost. Some of the bodies of drowned sailors were recovered and returned to loved ones for burial. Other bodies fed the crabs and fishes or washed up on an alien shore to be interred by strangers. Although perilous, the sailing life had its compensations. Sailors enjoyed good pay relative to day laborers and the opportunity to witness in the cities a life far different than that

---

Dispatch, April 13, 1874; Charles P. Finney Day Book, Eastern Shore Heritage Center.

133 Walczyk, *The Accomack County 1870 Census*; Latimer, *1870 Census for Northampton County, Virginia*; John R. Waddy, Eastville, to William Mahone, December 1, 1881, Mahone Papers, Duke; "Sailing Trade is Active"; Leonard S. Tawes, *Coasting Captain: Journals of Captain Leonard S. Tawes*, ed. Robert H. Burgess (Newport News, Va.: The Mariners Museum, 1967), pp. 5-7.

lived on their rural peninsula. They also experienced the exhilaration of speeding before a trailing wind in a world of infinite sea and sky.[134]

Society

In 1870 society on the Eastern Shore of Virginia was remarkably homogenous. Its people, of British and African stock, had roots in the peninsula going back as much as two hundred and fifty years. Their progenitors had enmeshed them in a web of kinship that sometimes crossed the racial divide. No matter their race or economic status, the farmers and farm laborers who comprised the majority of the population shared perennial concerns over weather and markets. They were Protestants, the great majority Methodists and Baptists. Their white ancestors had come to the New World largely from the southwest of England, a region noted for its traditionalism, and they, too, kept many of the old ways. A visitor from New Orleans believed that "living remote from the cities, and comparatively isolated from their fellow men, [they] do not get their oddities so toned down and their idiosyncrasies polished off by the friction of society." George Fitzhugh described the manners of the local gentry as "somewhat provincial – direct, frank, open, manly, resembling those of the English country gentlemen of a century ago." Firmly imbedded in place, community, and tradition, Eastern Shoremen, in the words of a Wilmington Methodist minister, "think something of themselves, and, as a matter of course, are well thought of by others."[135]

"The population of the Eastern Shore is essentially a working element," declared a Baltimore man. Most heads of household were landowners, of whom 80 percent held fewer than 100 acres. Only 0.5

---

134 *PE*, September 8, 22, October 6, 1881, June 7, 1883, April 12, 1884; Norfolk *Weekly Virginian and Commercial*, April 14, 1884; *Baltimore Sun*, February 17, 1877.

135 Fitzhugh, "Eastern Shore of Virginia," pp. 84 (quotation), 86; Land, "Economic Behavior in a Planting Society," p. 482; Fischer, *Albion's Seed*, pp. 236, 253; E. P. Thompson, "The Moral Economy of the English Crowd in the Eighteenth Century" in *Customs in Common* (New York: New Press, 1991), p. 195; Ward, "Red Letter Days" (first quotation); "Seashore Gossip," *Richmond Dispatch*, August 16, 1872 (third quotation).

percent owned 500 acres or more. An Accomack County man claimed to perceive the subtle gradations of class among the white inhabitants of this republic of small farmers: "Should you meet a man walking along the road with bare feet, he is a poor white; if he has shoes, he possesses a potato patch, and perhaps a corn field; if you see one driving a cart with one ox harnessed to it, he is a middle-class farmer; if you see one driving an open wagon, he is a gentleman; but if you see one driving a gig, *he* is a prince." To which a Northampton County man retorted: "If every man here who possessed a gig was a prince, there would be enough princes in this small county ... to govern the world." Howard Pyle was struck by "the superficial conglomeration of all castes; all are hail-fellow-well-met with each other and with any visitor whom chance might fling among them; all have the same peculiarities of speech; all dress alike roughly. ... [A]t first it is difficult to distinguished between classes." The democratic nature of white society also found expression in the widespread custom of calling friends and acquaintances "captain" as an indication of familiarity and respect irrespective of social status. Fitzhugh believed that the ease of making a living on the peninsula promoted "the feeling of independence." A member of the Western Shore gentry, Fitzhugh paid Eastern Shoremen the backhanded compliment of deeming them "aristocrats, in the Yankee sense of the term." Dr. Edward W. Marshall of neighboring Worcester County, Maryland, used similar terminology but in a way that would have confounded Fitzhugh. "There is more aristocracy in the two counties of Northampton and Accomac than in all the rest of Virginia," Marshall asserted. The Wilmington minister discerned how ties of kinship weakened class distinctions: "One of the peculiarities of the Eastern Shore Virginians is that each one is almost every other one's cousin. Like a colony of rabbits inhabiting the same thicket for a succession of generations, they have got things so mixed up that they bid defiance to the genealogical tables of the oldest inhabitant. Perhaps this almost universal relationship may account for their social free-and-easiness, as also for the interest they manifest in strangers."[136]

---

136 *Baltimore Sun*, September 10, 1881 (first quotation); Pyle, "A Peninsular Canaan," (second and fourth quotations); *Richmond Dispatch*, May 8, 1879 (third quotation); Fitzhugh, "Eastern

The predominance of small farmers also shaped race relations. The typical antebellum slave holding was in single digits, and farmers lived and worked beside their slaves and their black hired hands. "On the Eastern Shore of Virginia few people either white or black were rich, farms were small, and in the day-to-day struggle to make a living people were rarely segregated from one another by race," wrote Kirk Mariner, the historian of slavery on the peninsula.

> Blacks and whites, slaves and free lived in close proximity, knew each other and dealt with each other, often on a daily basis. They regularly mingled together, worked together, farmed together, and sailed together. They went to church together, drank together, and celebrated together. They hatched crimes together, and stood together before the courts. Not infrequently they lived in the same houses, even slept in the same rooms. It was hardly a unified, classless society, but it was in practice very different from the ideal enshrined in the law and logic of slavery, for at ground level the laws and customs of a slave society often proved unworkable or impractical, and they could be and frequently were ignored.

Given the racial propinquity of the Eastern Shore's slave regime and the bounty supplied by land and sea, the typical patriarch of a small peninsula farm probably worked his family of bondsmen and servants no harder than he worked himself and his family of blood kin. In 1867, Northern settler Israel Townsend told the *Delaware State Journal* that "an old freedman now with me declares the times were not so bad under the old rule, if they did not sell them South once in a while; and that,

---

Shore of Virginia," p. 85; George Alfred Townsend, "Eastern Shore Men," Philadelphia *Times*, November 12, 1877 (quotes Marshall); "Seashore Gossip" (last quotation). My thanks to Curtis J. Badger for reminding me of the frequency with which the term captain was used on the Eastern Shore of Virginia in the 1950s and 1960s. The use of captain on the Eastern Shore was nautical in origin (*Middletown (Del.) Transcript*, July 23, 1870; "The Teagues of Accomack"). Its use on the peninsula apparently had little, if anything, to do with the rank of members of slave patrols (Joel Williamson, *The Crucible of Race: Black-White Relations in the American South Since Emancipation* (New York and Oxford: Oxford University Press, 1984), p. 20).

and that alone, appears to have been the great evil of negro servitude here." Townsend added that "Northern men who came here have proven harder task-masters than the original owners, and now the negroes look on them with suspicion." He complained that he had to recruit black labor for his saw and grist mill from Hampton on the Western Shore. Townsend's son John J. echoed his father. Eastern Shore blacks, he told the *Middletown Transcript* "won't work for northern people, if they can help themselves, they think themselves above them."[137]

Eastern Shore slavery was paternalistic. It required the fulfillment between master and slave of reciprocal responsibilities. When at the end of the Civil War the emancipated slaves exercised their freedom by leaving the farms and refusing to work, the peninsula's whites, displaying what historian Peter Laslett called "social opacity, the blank inability to realize the situation of the other individual," felt betrayed as if by disobedient children. By 1870, the freedmen had returned to the farms, but a change had begun. Social equality denied them, freedmen wished to escape white oversight. They desired to self-segregate, to live, worship, and fraternize in separate homes and institutions. For the former masters, the demise of slavery meant a loss of investment capital and of bound labor, but it also meant a diminishing sense of responsibility for feeding, housing, and providing medical care to their former chattels. Northern notions of labor relations gained a foothold. Paternalism began gradually to give way to the cold logic of the wage nexus. In 1867, Israel Townsend attended the annual holiday that was August court in Eastville. There he found

> not less than fifteen hundred negroes ... all well dressed and happy as dogs. The District Attorney [Northampton Commonwealth's Attorney William G. Riley], a reconstructed Rebel, now a very fair Union man, remarked to

---

[137] Mariner, *Slave and Free*, pp. 15-16 (quotation), 87, 228; T. [Israel Townsend], Capeville, to editor, March 16, Wilmington *Delaware State Journal*, March 22, 1867; John J. Townsend, Capeville, to editor, June 21, *Middletown (Del.) Transcript*, July 9, 1870. For the comparatively benign treatment of slaves on small farms and for the small farmer's greater susceptibility to economic crisis that might necessitate the sale of his slaves, see Burton, *In My Father's House Are Many Mansions*, pp. 183, 184.

me that when they were slaves and come into town on such days, (for they always come) he always noticed they brought fiddles and banjos, and engaged in dancing; now he always sees the men in small groups talking apparently like so many white men – he supposes discussing politics. He says this great change in the negro behavior has been remarked to him by several Rebels as a sign that they are plotting devilment. ... [H]e always laughs at them and tells them it is a sign the negro is emerging from barbarism, and that it is a credit to them."[138]

Eastern Shoremen cherished a strong sense of place. Those living on the peninsula in 1870 were descended from generations on the soil. They primarily regarded land not as an end but as a means, not as a commodity to be bought and sold but as a foundation for home, family, and way of life. It was where ancestors lay at rest, where the living worked, played, loved, and grieved, and where their progeny, God willing, would feel the presence of those who had come before. Their neighbors were of the "cousinship," kinsmen whom they had known from childhood and with whom they socialized, worshiped, and married. Conflict, always present in human society, was restrained by ties of blood and memory. They lived in a contained, comfortable, and traditional world.[139]

---

138 Keith Thomas, "Work and Leisure in Pre-Industrial Society," *Past & Present* 29 (December, 1964), p. 52; Elizabeth Fox-Genovese, "The Anxiety of History: The Southern Confrontation with Modernity," *Southern Cultures* Inaugural Issue (1993), p. 67; Roark, *Masters Without Slaves*, pp. 84, 89, 198, 199; Laslet, *The World We Have Lost further explored*, p. 214; C. Vann Woodward, "The Strange Career of a Historical Controversy" in *American Counterpoint*, pp. 251-252; Coulter, *The South During Reconstruction*, p. 92; T. [Israel Townsend], Capeville, to editor, September 23, Wilmington *Delaware State Journal*, October 1, 1867; Bayard Taylor, "Down the Eastern Shore," *Harper's New Monthly Magazine* XLIII (October, 1871), pp. 704-705.

139 John W. Gillet, Accomac C. H., to Jno. B. LaForge, February, 1869, Gillett-Wise Family Papers, September 23, 1879; Deposition of Peter Cox, *Robert S. Costin of Northampton County*, p. 8; *Baltimore Sun*, August 31, 1882; Fischer, *Albion's Seed*, p. 393; Hall, *Abel Parker Upshur*, p. 4; Peter Laslett, "The Gentry of Kent in 1640," *Cambridge Historical Journal* 9 (1948), p. 148; Avery Craven, *The Coming of the Civil War*, 2nd ed. (Chicago: University of Chicago Press, 1942, 1957), pp. 34-35, 37-38; Robert Finch, *Outlands: Journeys to the Outer Edges of Cape Cod* (Boston: David R. Godine, 1986), pp. 18-19, 20. In the case of the Eastern Shore of Virginia, historian Jack Temple Kirby is mistaken when he bemoans "sentimental myths of home-sweet-home, stability, continuity, 'old families,' and obsessive land-loving in the South, and perhaps

Eastern Shoremen possessed a surfeit of riches – a pleasing landscape, an extensive "cousinship," a plentitude of food and drink. They were at ease with themselves and others and, although their estates were not large, they famously offered hospitality to neighbors and strangers alike. Their geographic isolation both attracted travelers and made travelers attractive to them. "Are you fortunate enough to be intimately acquainted with a family on the Shore? That is enough. Go there immediately," advised a Richmonder. "You will be feasted on something better than a fatted calf. You will be visited by everybody. You will have pressing invitations to stay everywhere, and everywhere you will find a hearty welcome and all the delights which the receipt of country hospitality implies." Orris A. Browne greeted a group of strangers at his home on Folly Creek with the salutation: "Get down gentlemen, very glad to see you; make yourselves at home." Browne entertained his guests with conversation and cigars, a sail on Metompkin Bay, and supper of fish, oysters, and terrapin. Mary E. Bradley warned that dining at an Eastern Shore table might test the capacity of the guest: "I remember various visits at certain delightful houses, where I grew to dread the dinner-hour, knowing that I should be compelled to eat fish, oysters, game, poultry, pastry with all manner of sauces, dainty sweets, and 'lucent-syrups,' not at my own option, but that of a hostess who had no remorse for my limitations." Geniality was not restricted to the upper reaches of society. Passing among the oystermen of the upper Accomack seaside, Bayard Taylor discovered that "The poorer classes of all this region are rough and ignorant, but very good-natured and hospitable."[140]

These relaxed and generous people, not surprisingly, were "greatly

---

over the continent" (*Mockingbird Song*, p. 93).

140 "Accomac and Northampton"; "The Future State," Wilmington *News Journal*, February 28, 1878 (quotes Browne); Bradley, "On the Eastern Shore," p. 79; Taylor, "Down the Eastern Shore," *Harper's New Monthly Magazine* XLIII (October, 1871), p. 708. See also Simpkins, "Invalid Inklings"; T. [Israel Townsend], Capeville, to editor, March 16, Wilmington *Delaware State Journal*, March 22, 1867; *Baltimore Sun*, January 1, 1869; *Norfolk Virginian*, August 22, 1871; *Wilmington Daily Commercial*, September 26, 1872; *Richmond Dispatch*, April 13, 1874; "My Own Trip"; Pyle, "Chincoteague," p. 738; Washington *National Republican*, November 1, 1879; J. T. B. Middleton to editor, May 9, Wilmington *Every Evening* in *PE*, May 17, 1884; "A Virginian Atlantis."

given over to festivity and frolic." They traditionally had reserved Easter, Whitsuntide, and the week spanning Christmas and New Year's as days of rest and merriment. After their emancipation blacks continued to claim as a right the enjoyment of a long Christmas break. "Christmas is all most gone," grumbled the manager of a large Northampton farm on December 30, 1869, "and I am glad for you can't get anny thing dun as long as it last." On Hog Island the white watermen and their families gathered annually for a Christmas Eve dance that "rocked and trembled" the host's cabin from foundation to roof. As anticipated as the Christian holidays was the first day of the August meetings of the county court in Drummondtown and Eastville. Their crops having been laid by, the farm families felt the urge to escape their routine for a day. "Our August court is looked upon as the great day of the year for the gathering of our Farmers," observed Accomac C. H. lawyer T. H. Bayly Browne. "The custom has been kept up so long that it has almost grown to be a law." In 1868, an officer of the Freedmen's Bureau told a superior that on court day the main street of Drummondtown "was crowded with wagons of different descriptions, tables with provisions for sale, and people, principally colored." Eastern Shoremen also relished Saturday night dances to the tune of fiddle or banjo and summertime beach parties featuring surf bathing, oyster roasts, and moonlight sails.[141]

The peninsula's geographic isolation, dispersed population, and low literacy rate (probably less than half of its people could read) threw its inhabitants upon themselves for news and other mental stimulation. Bradley discovered an intellectually circumscribed community : "There are no printing presses, no newspapers, no lectures or public entertainments. ... The average male mind finds food sufficient in the affairs of

---

141 *Norfolk Virginian*, April 20, 1868; *Alexandria Gazette*, September 25, 1879 (quotes A. S. M.); Henry Howe, *Historical Collections of Virginia* (Baltimore: Regional Publishing Company, 1969 [reprint of 1845 ed.], pp. 158-159; Edward P. Wescoat, Old Plantation, to Sally Tazewell, December 30, 1869 (second quotation), Tazewell Family Papers, LVA; Alexander Hunter, "A Summer Idyl in Virginia," *Forest and Stream* XI (October 31, 1878), p. 257 (third quotation); Johnson, *The Pine Tree Mission*, p. 4; *Middletown (Del.) Transcript*, July 9, 1870; T. H. Bayly Browne to William C. Elam, August 17, 1880, Mahone Papers, Duke; D. B. White, Eastville, to Gen. S. C. Armstrong, August 27, 1868, Records of the Bureau of Refugees, Freedmen, and Abandoned Lands, vol. 156, pp. 55-57; "When Armed Riders Patrolled 'Singing Wires,'" *PE*, August 8, 1936; *Richmond Dispatch*, February 2, 1867; "Parksley's a Paradise."

the farms, and the county politics; the average female intellect occupies itself with poultry, servants, and gossip." News passed mostly by word of mouth. People talked with kinsmen and neighbors in parlors and kitchens, in stores and on wharves, and in churchyards and on courthouse greens. An impatient Cobb's Island-bound vacationer traveling between Cherrystone Wharf and Cobb's Landing (now Oyster) in a convoy of hacks observed the local grapevine in operation:

> Then there came along the road towards us a colored boy seated in a wagon drawn by a single steer, harnessed up horsewise in the shafts. He drew up in a corner of the worm fence to allow us to pass, and our driver also drew up – perhaps to rest his horses. "Hallo, Dave," said he, "whar ye goin' in such a hurry?" "Goin' for the doctor," responded Dave; "Missus took very bad." Whereupon our driver settled himself down for a good long talk with Dave about all the particulars of the case ending with an inquiry of what his boss was giving for sweet potatoes. Then we started again, and Dave, nothing loath, was intercepted at various fence corners by the other drivers, and the parties of each part settled comfortably to give and get all the particulars of the sudden illness of missus, and the way she was "tuck." It is to be hoped that the doctor reached the afflicted lady before all was over.

According to John J. Townsend, the locals punctuated their discourse with profanity: "Swearing seems a universal habit of the men and indulged in to a great extent by the women."[142]

Eastern Shore males were known for their robust living. The Richmond man who advised his readers to visit their friends on the peninsula insisted to those who had no acquaintances there that they "don't hold back. Go, stay at the taverns and mix with the bachelors. ... These same bachelors enjoy life, and know how to communicate enjoyments

---

142 Bradley, "On the Eastern Shore," p. 79; "Cobb's Island"; *Middleton (Del.) Transcript*, July 9, 1870 (quotes Townsend). "Within these neighborhoods whites knew each other and each other's business, whether first-hand or thorough gossip, to a greater extent than most of us today can imagine." (Burton, *In My Father's House Are Many Mansions*, p. 32).

to others, all in their own peculiar manner, about as well as any other set of mortals. They drive good horses, drink good beverages, talk politics amazingly, dance, laugh, love and hate with an uncommon fervor." A Norfolk businessman described Eastern Shoremen as "fishermen, truckers, fast horse & card-playing men, love whisky & jolly good fellows." They enjoyed drink and conversation at cards, over oyster and terrapin suppers, or on the porch or around the stove of neighborhood stores.[143]

Eastern Shoremen hunted as avidly as they fished (see above, pp. 52-53) and for the same reasons. Hunting provided respite from the monotony of the farm, meat for the tables of family and friends, and a commodity for sale or barter. The Eastern Shore's mild climate, its level terrain, large fields, and open woods, its creeks, marshes, and islands were a standing invitation to its sportsmen. The mainland provided an ideal locale for partridge (quail) hunting, the supreme test of the wing-shot's prowess. A hunter rejoiced in the countryside between Horntown and Franklin City on the upper seaside: "There were good thick stubbles and cornfields and brushy fence rows and much of the timber was the original growth, not matted with undergrowth, and practicable to shoot in." Another noted that the good roads enabled rapid transit from covert to covert and that vegetation along the creek banks protected the birds from predators. Robert Wilson remarked that "The stranger cannot fail to be struck with astonishment by the number of setter dogs which he sees in the streets of every town, leaving the impression – which is not far from the truth – that every other man at least indulges in the manly and healthful recreation of partridge-shooting."[144]

On bayside and seaside, hunters built along the water's edge blinds

---

143 "Accomac and Northampton" (first quotation); H. W. Burton, Norfolk, to William Mahone, July 25, 1877, Mahone Papers, Duke (second quotation); *Middletown (Del.) Transcript*, July 9, 1870; Snead, "Remarks"; *Alexandria Gazette*, September 25, 1876; *Forest and Stream* XV (August 5, 1880), p. 10.

144 Thomas, "Work and Leisure in Pre-Industrial Society," p. 53; Charles P. Roland, "The South of the Agrarians," in *A Band of Brothers: The Vanderbilt Agrarians after Fifty Years*, eds. William C. Havard and Walter Sullivan (Baton Rouge and London: Louisiana State University Press, 1982), p. 25; "A Trip for Quail in Maryland," p. 402 (quotation); "The Eastern Shore of Virginia," *Forest and Stream* VII (November 16, 1876), p. 232; Wilson, "On the Eastern Shore," p. 370.

of cedar brush or they improvised by nailing cedar boughs two or three feet high onto the sides of their boats. In the dim light of a winter's morning, they arranged in the water near the blinds hand-carved stools (decoys) or live stools tethered to a raft. They then loaded their shotguns – 8- or 10-guage, double-barreled, muzzle-loaders – and, dog at their side and warming dram at hand, awaited the heart-stopping moment when a flight of doomed ducks or geese settled gently around the stools. On the seaside when the early spring tides filled the marshes they polled their boats in pursuit of marsh hens (clapper rail), and later in the spring and into in the fall they hunted shorebirds on barrier island beaches.[145]

Other game also attracted the attention of local sportsmen. By daylight they hunted rabbits, delighting when a clean shot dispatched a rabbit before the nose of the coursing hound. In twilight they waited patiently for careless squirrels. On fall nights they sat by a camp fire, drank whisky, and enjoyed the music of the dogs on the trail of a raccoon or opossum. The 'possum, treed and captured, would next day be served for dinner "in a wide iron pan in which it was baked, and lying under and around it, where they could absorb the juices of the game, are such golden beauties from the sweet potato patch as make a man's mouth water to think of."[146]

Immediately after the Civil War, freedmen and free blacks seized on the opportunity to hunt, a privilege not widely permitted them under slavery. Many former black soldiers had retained their firearms when mustered out of the Union army. They saw their weapons as means to procure food and to engage in sport. They also regarded them as means to protect themselves and to intimidate others. In this time of social and political uncertainty that frequently dissolved into lawlessness, many whites feared the presence in their midst of numerous and armed former

---

145 "Brant Shooting on the Virginia Broad Waters,"; Wilson, "On the Chesapeake," p. 467; "Letter from Mockhorn Island," p. 52; "Honk! Honk! Honk!," *Forest and Stream* I (December 25, 1873), pp. 308-309; *Richmond Dispatch*, April 16, 1874; Alexander Hunter, "Birds at Cobb's Island," *Forest and Stream* XVIII (March 23, 1882), p. 146; "The Eastern Shore of Virginia," *Forest and Stream* VII (November 16, 1876), p. 232.

146 *PE*, November 15, 29, 1883, February 2, 1884; Marinus James, "The Raccoon Hunt," *PE*, February 20, 1926; Spears, "The Virginia Peninsula" (quotation).

slaves. White landowners were particularly disturbed by blacks hunting on their property without bothering to seek permission. In 1870, hunting was another area of Eastern Shore life where racial parameters were under negotiation.[147]

The peninsula's smooth, level roads invited fast driving and racing. Both whites and blacks prided themselves on their knowledge of horseflesh. Small farmers, they eschewed costly saddle horses in favor of those capable of pulling plow and carriage. Sportsmen, they valued in their animals speed as well as durability. "The horses," a Staunton visitor remarked, "are fine travelers, and some of the negroes with their carts, drive trotters that would astonish an Augusta [County] farmer." Israel Townsend considered "the native breed ... fast roadsters and hardy work horses." The swiftest trotters might be trained for match races at neighborhood tracks. The center of local horse racing in 1870 was the St. Charles Trotting Park at Pungoteague, owned by Thomas M. McConnell, a driver and promoter recently of Philadelphia. The Pungoteague oval, which dated from 1835, had for years attracted not only local enthusiasts but also excursionists who came by steamboat from Baltimore. The strength and beauty of the horses, the dramatic spectacle on the home stretch, and the enthusiastic crowds appealed to race goers, but its popularity owed much to the inevitable drinking and gambling. A Norfolk man related how he was cajoled into placing a bet on the opponent of the legendary Eastern Shore trotter Sadie Bell: "There were refreshments on the grounds, and the more refreshments people took the less refreshed they seemed to be. A gentleman from Accomack presented me with a whisky straight and half a pint of peanuts, for which I thanked him profusely. I took all the thanks back afterwards, because he persuaded me to bet on the losing horse, and won my money himself."[148]

147 Lt. Eld. Murphy, Drummondtown, to Brig. Gen. Orlando Brown, October 31, 1866, Records of the Bureau of Refugees, Freedmen, and Abandoned Lands, vol. 151, pp. 7-8.

148 "Future State"; *Baltimore Sun*, September 2, 1867, July 19, 1868, September 10, 1881; Morton, "Life in a Level Land" (first quotation); T. [Israel Townsend], Capeville, to editor, April 13, Wilmington *Delaware State Journal*, April 23, 1867; James Egbert Mears, "The Eastern Shore of Virginia in the Nineteenth and Twentieth Centuries" in *The Eastern Shore of Maryland and Virginia*, ed. Charles B. Clark (New York: Lewis Historical Publishing Co., 1950), II, 620; *Norfolk Landmark*, April 8, 1877 (quotation). For professional horse drivers and trainers, see

Refreshments were ever present. A Union soldier considered rum and tobacco "the necessaries of peninsular life." Liquor was a social lubricant and a medicinal balm. It was a solace against despair, an antidote to monotony, and a reward for labor. "If you don't drink, stranger, up your way, what on airth keeps your buddies and soulds together?" a Chincoteague oysterman asked the visiting canoeist Nathaniel Bishop. Although a teetotaler, Henry A. Wise seemed delighted to inform a Maine newspaperman that his district was "proverbial for 'honey drams,' 'mint juleps,' 'hail-stones,' 'slings,' 'dew-drops,' and every description of nectared drinks." Stores at every crossroad and wharf dispensed liquor by the drink or bottle. At the foot of Cherrystone wharf stood "a white building of multifarious uses – grocery and variety store, post office, county treasurer's office, &c., while a portion of the busy counter curtained off affords opportunity for customers to imbibe the semi-occasional cocktail or whisky straight."[149]

Liquor encouraged conviviality but, taken in excess, might turn a card game into a bacchanal or court day into a pandemonium of swearing and violence. Men, otherwise amicable, might under the influence of liquor wound each other with words or fists or other weapons. Liquor also exacerbated racial conflict. Many of the affrays of Reconstruction were fired by drink. A Freedmen's Bureau agent lamented that "the Freedmen often repair [to neighborhood stores] and sometimes indulges too freely in liquor when he becomes noisy and turbulent. Some of the whites often indulge in the same way and the condition of both parties, should they happen to meet, leads to difficulties."[150]

Latimer, comp., *1860 Census for Northampton County*, p. 24; Latimer, comp., *1870 Census for Northampton County*, p. 41; Walczyk, comp., *The Accomack County 1870 Census*, II, 214.

149 Harding, *The Miscellaneous Writings*, p. 237 (quotation); Maj. George H. French, Drummondtown, to Gen. S. C. Armstrong, August 20, 1866; Lt.. Eld. Murphy, Drummondtown, to Brig. Gen. Orlando Brown, October 31, 1866, Records of the Bureau of Refugees, Freedmen, and Abandoned Lands, vol. 149, pp. 108-109; vol., 151, pp. 7-8; Bishop, *The Voyage of the Paper Canoe*, p. 136; *Portland (Me.) Advertiser and Gazette*, July 18, 1837; "Trip to Cobb's Island"; "Cobb's Island" (quotation).

150 Snead, "Remarks"; "When Armed Riders Patrolled 'Singing Wires'"; George R. Mapp, Johnsontown, to Thomas M. Scott, March 11, 1861, Albert and Shirley Small Special Collections Library, University of Virginia; Lt. Eld. Murphy, Drummondtown, to Brig. Gen. Orlando

The people of the Eastern Shore were conventionally religious. Their basic convictions were those that historian Douglas Southall Freeman ascribed to Confederate soldiers: "Acceptance of traditional Christianity was almost universal. Mild and reverent deism was viewed with horror. Doubt was damnation. Agnosticism was service to Antichrist. What was believed was professed." Eastern Shoremen were almost exclusively Protestant. The majority of those who participated in religious services adhered to evangelical denominations. Of the fifty-seven churches on the peninsula in 1870, two were Presbyterian, five Episcopalian, twelve Baptist, and the remaining thirty-eight Methodist.[151]

A series of Methodist and Baptist revivals between 1772 and 1814 routed a moribund Anglican establishment, but most male Eastern Shoremen resisted revivalist doctrines. God having provided them with an abundance of sustenance and leisure, they recoiled from the abstemiousness and moral discipline demanded by the evangelicals. Daily watching Eden's light play on field, wood, marsh, and bay, they needed no direction from a Methodist exhorter on how or where to find Heaven. Their God being a demonstrably beneficent God, simple belief was enough for them. A retired minister described Holmes Presbyterian Church at Bay View in lower Northampton County before the Civil War as "unique in one respect – for many years it had only fifteen ladies and not one male member. The men had a perfect Elysium for unregenerate human nature. They had hunting, fishing, oystering, fast horses, public houses and days, and a plenty of that which is said to soothe, and certainly does inebriate. They went to church, talked politics, supported the Gospel by liberal contributions. But they sadly needed the sermon of old Dr. [Frederick Augustus] Ross, preached in his own church in Huntsville, Ala., to prove that men had souls."[152]

Brown, Records of the Bureau of Refugees, Freedmen, and Abandoned Lands, vol. 151, pp. 7-8.

151 Douglas Southall Freeman, *Lee's Lieutenants: A Study in Command, Volume One, Manassas to Malvern Hill* (New York: Charles Scribner's Sons, 1942), p. xxviii; *The Statistics of the Population of the United States ... Compiled From the Original Returns of the Ninth Census* (June 1, 1870), pp. 557, 558.

152 Kirk Mariner, *Revival's Children: A Religious History of Virginia's Eastern Shore* (Salisbury, Md.: Peninsula Press, 1979), pp. 18-52; "Old Time Politics," *Richmond Dispatch*, March 31,

The religious division between Eastern Shoremen was not between believers and non-believers, but between the churched and the unchurched. Or, more precisely, between the churched and those who attended services perfunctorily, occasionally, or not at all. Over the years, revival's fire cooled to embers. In 1841, a Northern schoolmaster living near Belle Haven entered in his diary a self-satisfied homily. Noting as typical a sparse attendance at public worship, the preaching of a single sermon, and an aftermath of drinking and visiting, he concluded that "the people in this part of the country are far behind those of N. England in respect [to] morality and religion. They probably never had such examples to imitate as we have had handed down to us by our puritan fathers. If they have, they have certainly degenerated from the wisdom of their ancestors." In 1858, devout Episcopalian Maria S. Joynes of Montpelier near Drummondtown lamented that "deadness to spiritual things is apparent in all different denominations." A few years later a Union soldier discovered in Drummondtown "three Churches, but judging from the attendance on Sabbath I am led to believe the good spirit does not burn any too strong in our friends' hearts." During Reconstruction, a correspondent of the *Richmond Dispatch* found Eastern Shore churches "desolated and worn out by the war and stagnations thereof."[153]

The evangelical minority considered nature's bounty less a gift of God than a devilish delusion and snare. Earthly enjoyments interposed between God and man and promoted licentious behaviors such as sloth, fornication, drinking, gambling, swearing, and fighting. Evangelicals believed that salvation required a renunciation of the ways of man and a personal engagement with God. The engagement was ratified by a conversion experience and maintained by a strict discipline that included church attendance, study of the scriptures, prayerful self-examination,

---

1895 (quotation).

153 William H. Williams, *The Garden of American Methodism: The Delmarva Peninsula, 1769-1820* (Dover, Del.: Scholarly Resources for the Peninsula Conference of the United Methodist Church, 1984), pp. 168, 170; September 19, 26 (quotation), 1841, J. Milton Emerson Journal, 1841-1842, Duke; Maria S. Joynes, Montpelier, to Susan S. Fackler, April 5, 1858, Satchell Family Papers, 1839-1894, Eastern Shore Heritage Center; Camp Wilkes *Regimental Flag*, January 23, 1862, in Middleton, comp., *The Second Regiment Delaware Volunteers; Richmond Dispatch*, July 18, 1867.

upright living, and the cultivation of one's God-given talents. It also required living in a spirit of charity and acting as thy brother's keeper. Frequent meetings, extempore prayers and preaching, and shared emotional enthusiasm knit the evangelicals together and gave them heart that they might redeem a world of lost souls.[154]

Despite empty pews on Sunday, the church represented an ideal. "[T]he church," intoned a Northampton man, "the fountain of doctrine and morals, of taste and sentiment, of social maxims and culture." Its maxims, however, were often honored in the breach; its influence largely latent. At their best the churched set an example of service to God, family, and community. A visiting minister met at Cokesbury Methodist Church "a polished graduate" of Wilmington's Wesleyan Female College, "a delicate, tender girl [who] has the supervision of her father's family, leads a class of youthful Christians, teaches in the Sabbath morning school in Onancock, attends service, gets through dinner and its bustle, [and] drives her pony several miles to a destitute neighborhood, where she has instituted and has charge of a school for the benefit of the neglected little ones." At their worst the churched demanded that others join them in lives of abnegation. They committed what Andrew Lytle considered "the great Puritan heresy." They "put evil in the object, in a deck of cards, in a woman's hair, in dancing, in that great invention whiskey." Lytle insisted that "Evil cannot be in the object. It must be in the mind and heart. That's the only place it can be." Evangelical hectoring guaranteed that Eastern Shoremen would never be fully at ease when enjoying their ease.[155]

In its mixture of faith and frolic, the Methodist camp meeting epitomized the division between the churched and the unchurched. The first camp meeting on the Eastern Shore occurred in August, 1805, near Pungoteague when, after pitching tents for shelter and erecting a frame

---

154 Williams, *The Garden of American Methodism*, pp. 97-98; Isaac, *The Transformation of Virginia*, pp. 260-261, 264.

155 *Alexandria Gazette*, January 22, 1878 (quotes A. S. M.); "Seashore Gossip" (second quotation); Andrew Nelson Lytle, "A Christian University and the Word," in *From Eden to Babylon: The Social and Political Essays of Andrew Nelson Lytle* (Washington: Regnery Gateway, 1990), p. 164.

tabernacle large enough to accommodate a half dozen preachers, the faithful commenced several days of almost around-the-clock religious services. In the ensuing years, camp meetings convened annually at numerous locations on the peninsula. Especially popular were waterfront sites such as Tangier Island and Cherrystone that could be reached by sailboats and by steamers carrying day-tripping excursionists from Norfolk, Baltimore, and Washington. The campers included black people as well as white. After emancipation some blacks established separate camp meetings while others continued to worship with the whites. In 1874, excursionists from Washington witnessed at Cherrystone "the white and black brethren ... alternately singing, dancing, and 'getting religious.'"[156]

A camp meeting in some respects resembled an August court. People gathering from a distance took the opportunity to socialize with friends and kinsmen. Entrepreneurs set up booths near the grounds from which they dispensed food and liquor. Courting couples promenaded around the grounds or slipped into the woods to pursue better their amours. Noisy and belligerent drunks sometimes disturbed the worshipers. A traveler on a Chesapeake Bay steamer noticed that "[S]ome gentlemen, going to the camp meeting at Cherrystone, sung 'You'll never miss the lager till the keg runs dry,' embellished with a tambourine solo." Most people, however, attended camp meetings not to court or gossip or drink but to merge themselves with something greater than themselves. The meeting provided them with the intense religious experience that they craved – a crowd yearning for divine sanction, a succession of ministers engaged in almost continuous preaching, interludes of hymn singing, the building of spiritual tension culminating in the mass ecstasy of the altar call. Howard Pyle described a scene that harked back across the millennia: "In among the great pines of Chincoteague is a noble place for such a gathering, when at night their huge trunks are illuminated by the light of the 'pine chuck' bonfires, in the gleam of which the distant

---

156 Mariner, *Revival's Children*, pp. 42-49; *Baltimore Sun*, August 2, 1867; "Seashore Gossip"; Matthews, "Chincoteague Island"; Washington *National Republican* in *Norfolk Landmark*, August 15, 1874.

trees flash forth for a moment and then vanish into obscurity again, and when the solemn measured chant of the Methodist hymns is heard and the congregation sways with the mighty religious passion that stirs them, while over all hang lurid wreathings of resinous smoke."[157]

---

[157] "Seashore Gossip"; *PE*, August 18, 1881; *Washington Chronicle*, August 11, 1872 (quotation); Pyle, "Chincoteague," pp. 742-743. An excursion party visited "the fair and camp-meeting at Cherrystone" (Washington *National Republican* in *Norfolk Landmark*, August 15, 1874). One evening a couple attending a camp meeting ventured into the dark woods where they accidentally sat upon a pitch pine, the pitch two inches thick and still warm from the summer sun. To extricate themselves, the woman had to remove her dress and the man his pants and drawers (*EV*, September 1, 1877). For a description similar to Pyle's of a Chincoteague camp meeting see Spears, "Life on Chincoteague."

Chapter II

Agents of Transformation

Civil War and Reconstruction, 1861-1870, altered the course of Eastern Shore of Virginia history. The events of the decade at once accelerated and impeded ongoing economic and social change while initiating new developments. The Union naval blockade cut off the peninsula from its Southern markets and diverted trade northward. War-driven railroad expansion enabled the rise of Western competition in coastal grain markets, thereby hastening the local shift to truck crops. Meanwhile, the growth of Northern cities created demand for Eastern Shore seafood, lumber, and agricultural produce. Emancipation brought an abrupt culmination to slavery's gradual demise on the peninsula while necessitating a renegotiation of race and labor relations. The granting to blacks by Congress of the rights of citizenship transformed the political landscape. Union victory encouraged Northern capitalists to envision the region as an imperial province. Confederate defeat called into question the suppositions of the white majority. Occurring with bewildering speed, these events compelled Eastern Shoremen to acquire new habits of thought and to adopt new systems of value. The next decade and a half, the period between 1870 and the coming of the railroad in 1884, saw the Eastern Shore's landscape – mental, economic, and physical – begin to take its modern shape.

Visions of Progress

The Northern vision of America's economic future was rooted in New England Puritanism. Puritans held that godliness, industriousness, sobriety, and the application of one's God-given talent would indicate personal salvation while bringing ever closer the millennial utopia. By the antebellum period, the Puritan fixation on election and damnation survived, if at all, in remote corners of rural New England. Pietism, undermined by Transcendentalism, Unitarianism, and Mammon, had been replaced by a supercilious moralism. What remained were belief in personal discipline, human perfectibility, and Northeastern cultural and moral superiority. Power resided with urban capitalists – bankers, merchants, and industrialists of the Eastern seaboard and their Western allies. In their minds, the millennium had become conflated with materialism and stockholder dividends. The capitalists would do good for mankind and for themselves by providing an ever-expanding supply of consumer products, the appetite for which would be satisfied by exploiting America's seemingly boundless natural resources. In 1840, Maine native Nathaniel Parker Willis captured the inherent restlessness of the cult of progress:

> He who journeys here [America] ... must feed his imagination on the future. The American does so. His mind, as he tracks the broad rivers of his own country, is perpetually reaching forward. Instead of looking through a valley, which has presented the same aspect for hundreds of years – in which live lords and tenants, whose hearths have been surrounded by the same names through ages of tranquil descent, and whose fields have never changed landmark or mode of culture since the memory of man, he sees a valley laden down like a harvest wagon with virgin vegetation, untrodden and luxuriant; and his first thought is of the villages that will soon sparkle on the hill-sides, the axes that will ring from the woodlands, and the mills, bridges, canals, and

railroads, that will span and border the stream that now runs through sedge and wild-flowers.¹

Willis typically expropriated for his own region the term "American." Antebellum Southerners were unlikely to devote their "first thought" to villages, mills, canals, and railroads. Their ancestors had come to America to claim a freehold, not build a utopia. A life close to the soil, having been good enough for their fathers, was good enough for them. They were a traditional people, content with the steady rhythms of farm and plantation and with the leisurely enjoyment of the world as is. Southerners saw money as a means to the end of living the good life on their own land. If that life seemed backward to progressives, so be it. "Southerners of all social classes," observed historians Forrest McDonald and Grady McWhiney, "would have rejected the naïve and culture-bound assumption that people naturally seek to better their condition." Southerners knew that Northern cultural imperatives threatened not only slavery but their agrarian way of life. As they rejected the demand of Northern abolitionists for the eradication of slavery, they also opposed the aspirations of Northern businessmen for protective tariffs, hard money, and federal support for internal improvements.²

The modernizing North emerged from the Civil War victorious over the traditionalist South. The power of the South to thwart Northern ambitions had been broken by military defeat and by wartime federal legislation advantageous to Northern commerce, banking, and

---

1 Van Wyck Brooks, *The Flowering of New England, 1815-1865*, rev. ed. (n.p. E. P. Dutton & Co., 1937), pp. 21-45; Lewis P. Simpson, *Mind and the American Civil War: A Meditation on Lost Causes* (Baton Rouge: Louisiana State University Press, 1989), pp. 47-48; Raimondo Luraghi, *Five Lectures on the American Civil War, 1861-1865* (Rome: John Cabot University Press, 2013), p. 6; David Herbert Donald, *Liberty and Union* (Boston and Toronto: Little, Brown and Company, 1978), p. 24; Jeremy Beer, "Limits, Risk Aversion, and the Technocracy," *Local Cultures* 2 (September, 2020); Judith Hansen O'Toole, *Different Views in Hudson River School Painting* (New York: Columbia University Press in association with Westmoreland Museum of American Art, 2005), p. 114 (quotes Willis).

2 Eugene D. Genovese, *The Southern Tradition: The Achievement and Limitations of an American Conservatism* (Cambridge and London: Harvard University Press, 1994), p. 4; Raimondo Luraghi, *The Rise and Fall of the Plantation South* (New York and London: New Viewpoints, 1978), p. 75; Avery Craven, *The Coming of the Civil War*, 2nd ed. (Chicago: University of Chicago Press, 1942, 1957), pp. 90-91; Forrest McDonald and Grady McWhiney, "The South for Self-Sufficiency to Peonage: An Interpretation," *American Historical Review* 85 (December, 1980), p. 1095.

transportation. The South was now a conquered province and the North treated it as such. In the succinct phrase of historian Pekka Hamalainen, the South was "demilitarized, transformed, and harnessed for profit." The region became an economic colony of the North. Its function was to supply to its conqueror foodstuffs and raw materials in return for processed and manufactured goods. The trade favored the North, which invested the surplus extracted from the South in further industrial expansion. The South's autonomy destroyed, its economic base co-opted, its independent and fractious spirit tamed, its people became dependent on the national market and many of them, white and black, descended into serfdom. While the story of the South was dramatic and tragic (so dramatic and tragic that it spawned a great literature), it was only another chapter in the world history of the subordination by capital of the countryside to the metropolis.[3]

The Northern colonization of the South occurred in an era described by Walt Whitman as one of "brazen effrontery." The Civil War occasioned previously unimaginable federal expenditures, which in turn encouraged fraud and peculation. "The demoralizing effect of this civil war is plainly visible in every department of life," wrote a former member of Lincoln's cabinet. "The abuse of official powers and the thirst for dishonest gain are now so common that they cease to shock." The war initiated a career of corporate freebooting, exacerbated by Darwinian competition, which continues to this day. "During the Civil War, business had its arm up to the elbow in the fleshpots, and when the War ended, was not willing to accept any readjustment," commented Robert Penn Warren. "[M]odern America, whether or not conceived in sin, was born in corruption."[4]

---

3 Donald Davidson, "Federation or Disunion: The Political Economy of Regionalism," in *Regionalism and Nationalism in the United States: The Attack on Leviathan* (New Brunswick and London: Transaction Publishers, 1991 [reprint of 1938 ed.], p. 112; Raimondo Luraghi, "The Civil War and the Modernization of American Society: Social Structure and Industrial Revolution in the Old South before and during the War," *Civil War History* 18 (September, 1972), p. 233; Pekka Hamalainen, *The Comanche Empire* (New Haven and London: Yale University Press, 2008), p. 313; P. K. O'Brien, "Agriculture and the Industrial Revolution," *Economic History Review*, new ser., 30 (February, 1977), p. 172; Joe Persky, "Regional Colonialism and the Southern Economy," *Review of Radical Political Economics* IV (Fall, 1972), p. 71; Beer, "Limits, Risk Aversion, and the Technocracy"; Luraghi, *The Rise and Fall of the Plantation South*, p. 87.

4 David Goldfield, *America Aflame: How the Civil War Created a Nation* (New York: Blooms-

The outcome of the Civil War seemed to confirm to Northerners and Southerners alike the superiority of the millennial vision. Had not God granted victory to the industrial North over the agrarian South? Had not the result of the war proved the Yankee capitalists worthy of emulation? Did not the future belong to the ambitious and wide awake? "The people of the South," predicted the editor of the *Richmond Whig* in 1869, "as the delusions of the past decade wears off, will perceive that their material interests will be best subserved by the re-establishment of business intercourse with the North, and by recognizing the reciprocal relations between the two sections. They will hereafter invite, rather than repel, 'Yankee' energy, industry, and capital; and when the 'era of good feelings' is restored, prosperity and contentment will everywhere prevail."[5]

The bloody demise of the Confederacy and the morally corrupting ordeal of Reconstruction had left white Southerners embittered against the North. The bitterness would remain for generations but its passion was soon spent. Hatred gave way before the necessity of making a living. "What most Southerners felt, or came to feel,' noted the agrarian essayist John Donald Wade, "was that they were desperately poor, while the North was becoming almost desperately rich. They wanted to be rich too." Historian Jack P. Maddex Jr. delineated the process of reconciliation: "Working to integrate their homeland into the structure of the contemporary United States, [Southerners] adopted 'Yankee' institutions and ideas: industrial capitalism, American nationalism, Gilded-Age political practices, and a system of race relations that made the

---

bury Press, 2011), p. 466 (quotes Whitman); Jeffrey Rogers Hummel, *Emancipating Slaves, Enslaving Free Men* (Chicago and La Salle, Ill.: Open Court, 1996), p. 314 (quotes Edward Bates); Vernon L. Parrington, *Main Currents in American Thought, Volume Three: The Beginnings of Critical Realism in America*, 1860-1920, p. xxv; Robert Penn Warren, "The Second American Revolution," *Virginia Quarterly Review* 7 (April, 1931), p. 286.

5 John Donald Wade, "Old Wine in a New Bottle," in *Selected Essays and Other Writings of John Donald Wade*, ed. Donald Davidson (Athens: University of Georgia Press, 1966), p. 156; Wade, "Profits and Losses in the Life of Joel Chandler Harris," in *ibid.*, p. 98; Richard M. Weaver, "Agrarianism in Exile," in *The Southern Essays of Richard M. Weaver*, eds. George M Curtis III and James J. Thompson Jr. (Indianapolis: Liberty Fund, 1987), pp. 41-42; Wilmington *Daily Republican*, December 3, 1866; George B. Vaughan, "Politics in Virginia During Redemption with Special Emphasis on the Tidewater Area," M.S. thesis, Radford College, 1965, p. 19 (quotes *Richmond Whig*, April 11, 1869).

Negro a freeman and officially a citizen but not an equal. They looked forward to a new South modeled in many respects on the pattern of the conquering North." In effect, they embraced the most pernicious aspects of Northern culture – nationalism, imperialism, political corruption, and industrial capitalism – while retaining the most pernicious of their own culture – racial inequality.[6]

A small minority of Southerners rejected the idea of reconciliation. In Union victory they saw only the triumph of materialism and of an atomized individualism at war with organic society. They found nothing to emulate in the conqueror. They rejected pragmatism, opportunism, and Darwinian competitiveness. They recoiled from the cult of progress, from constant dissatisfaction with life as is, and from the juvenile craving for the trappings of success. The dissenters cherished family, the continuities of memory and tradition, and the natural rhythms of an unhurried life lived close to the soil and under the cope of heaven. They believed in the subordination of individual appetites to the social responsibilities required by personal honor. They shared with Southerners who dreamed of a New South only a commitment to white supremacy. Few in number, lacking in influence, and dismissed by their peers as fossils, the dissidents were men without a country. They could not slow, much less stem, the tide of modernism. They could only preserve the idea that the end of man's living was something greater than perpetual motion and endless longing. Writing in 1903, Virginia dissident Berkeley Minor declared that the United States was ruled by a plutocracy for the benefit of the North. Minor pointed to the Civil War as a turning point in American history. He told the editor of the *Baltimore Sun*: "Lincoln conquered the South and built up a powerful nation, in which true lovers of liberty cannot rejoice, for it cost the lives of two noble republics, the old United States of America and the Confederate States of America."[7]

---

6 John Donald Wade, "What the South Figured: 1865-1914," in *Selected Essays and Other Writings of John Donald Wade*, pp. 82, 83 (quotation), 88; E. Merton Coulter, *The South During Reconstruction, 1865-1877* (Baton Rouge: Louisiana State University Press, 1947), pp. 188, 210; Jack P. Maddex Jr., *The Virginia Conservatives, 1867-1879: A Study in Reconstruction Politics* (Chapel Hill: University of North Carolina Press, 1970), pp. xii (quotation), 84, 276, 278.

7 Wade, "What the South Figured," pp. 84-85; C. Vann Woodward, "A Southern War Against

Northerners were cultural imperialists who knew little about the South and were not interested in learning more. They considered the region a backward and menacing nuisance in need of a transfusion of Yankee brains, money, and morals. At the beginning of the Union occupation of the Eastern Shore in November, 1861, a Philadelphia journalist lamented "the isolated, unvisited, unenterprising condition of the people." He anointed invading Union troops as "THE PIONEERS OF KNOWLEDGE. ... [W]e may call their march but the invasion of knowledge, and say that their bayonets are all tipped with light." After a decade under the rule of "bayonets all tipped with light," Eastern Shoremen, white and black, still seemed unenlightened to Northern settlers and visitors. Delawarean Israel Townsend complained that "they are really dozing away an easy, lazy life, not improving the time, but letting the time take care of itself waiting for something to turn up that will enable them to live without work of any kind." Despite acknowledging the locals' geniality, hospitality, and love of leisurely pastimes, Israel's son John J. Townsend declared that "the natives, do not know the real comforts of civilization. They do not *live*, but simply *stay* here."[8]

Northerners had an unquestioning faith in their own cultural superiority. While the Townsends and others closely observed and reported on local mores, they often failed to understand what they had seen. Eastern Shoremen were far from unenterprising. From the early colonial period, they had traded in the produce of farm and forest along the

---

Capitalism," in *American Counterpoint: Slavery and Racism in the North-South Dialogue* (Boston and Toronto: Little, Brown and Company, 1976), p. 107; Stark Young, *Stark Young: A Life in the Arts: Letters, 1900-1962*, ed. John Pilkington (Baton Rouge: Louisiana State University Press, 1975), I, 508 (note by Pilkington); Berkeley Minor to editor, January 19, *Baltimore Sun*, February 4, 1903. See also Simpson, *Mind and the American Civil War*, p. 93, and Mark Royden Winchell, *Where No Flag Flies: Donald Davidson and the Southern Resistance* (Columbia and London: University of Missouri Press, 2000), p. 180.

8 Howard R. Floan, *The South in Northern Eyes, 1831 to 1861* (New York, Toronto, and London: McGraw-Hill for the University of Texas, 1958), p. 89; *Philadelphia Inquirer*, November 30, 1861; T. [Israel Townsend], Capeville, to editor, October 27, Wilmington *Delaware State Journal*, November 8, 1867; John J. Townsend, Capeville, to editor, June 14, *Middletown (Del.) Transcript*, July 2, 9 (quotation), 1870; "A Trip to Cobb's Island – There or Thereabout," Washington *Evening Star*, September 7, 1870; *New York Herald*, November 23, 1861; Volunteer, Camp Wilkes, Drummondtown, to editor, December 9, Milford (Del.) *Peninsular News and Advertiser*, December 20, 1861.

Atlantic seaboard and among the islands of the Caribbean. In the late antebellum period, they supplied coastal ports with seafood, pine wood, and grain and truck crops. In 1843, John Beauchamp Jones, a Maryland native who married into a peninsula family, told a Washington newspaper that "Eastern Shoremen are called the *Yankees* of Virginia; that is, they are a people emphatically of enterprise and trade. They are the only people in lowland Virginia among whom there has been no dilapidation and decay. There is no moss on their roofs; there are *no nabobs and no paupers* among them. Hardy and independent, and improving daily in their condition, Accomac has nearly quadrupled her agricultural productions in the last ten years." In 1867, Israel Townsend admitted that his Northampton neighbors were shrewd men who could drive a hard bargain. The seeming lack of initiative that so irritated Townsend might partly have been due to the effects of Civil War and Reconstruction. The Union naval blockage had sealed off the peninsula's Southern trade, government red tape and graft had discouraged commerce with Northern ports, emancipation had deranged labor relations, and political uncertainties had diminished confidence in the future.[9]

The Townsends and other Northerners were so culturally progressive that they reflexively dismissed as evil the idea of "not improving the time." Eastern Shoremen might want more and entered the market to get more, but the bounty of the earth and its waters relieved the doing and getting of much of its necessity. "No people have lived more abundantly, and few have lived so much within themselves," remarked George Fitzhugh. Eastern Shoremen were agrarians to whom the land at once enabled their independence and bound them to their ancestors. They suspected that the Yankee cult of progress would lead inevitably to personal dependence and demoralization and to the destruction of traditional society. Their observation of Northern ethics during military

---

9 Kirk Mariner, *Slave and Free on Virginia's Eastern Shore from the Revolution to the Civil War* (Onancock, Va.: Miona Publications, 2014), pp. 4, 189-190; Craig Simpson, *A Good Southerner: The Life of Henry A. Wise of Virginia* (Chapel Hill: University of North Carolina Press, 1985), p. 20; Subscriber, Accomack, to editor, June 26, *Southern Planter* 15 (August, 1855), p. 232; John Beauchamp Jones, Wythe County, to editor, January 23, Washington *Daily Madisonian*, January 27, 1843; T. [Israel Townsend], Capeville, to editor, May 27, Wilmington *Delaware State Journal* May 31, 1867.

occupation and Reconstruction persuaded them that Yankee claims to a higher morality were spurious. George Alfred Townsend, the most perceptive of the Delaware Townsends, concluded that Eastern Shore history had "produced in the end a self-esteeming democratic philosophy to reflect upon the wealth of a more industrial society. The desert tribes never loved the tribes of Yemen."[10]

Yet, even as Eastern Shoremen adhered to old habits of mind and old ways of living, they adjusted to the reality of the current situation. They admitted to themselves that the Yankees had won the war and had seized control of the national economy. They acknowledged the competitive superiority of the industrial North and modified accordingly their traditional attitudes. They adapted labor organization and political practice to the realities of black emancipation and citizenship. They saw the refusal to change as a guarantee of economic isolation and poverty (with which few people can be satisfied). A Northampton man preached that his fellow Eastern Shoremen must endure, persevere, and look to the future: "Under our new *regime* determination to make the best of things as they come along, without dreaming and worrying over the past, will contribute much towards making bright and cheerful many a fireside, and in the end will make them proud to think that they are capable of stemming the tide against difficulties."[11]

The post-war popularity of the proposed construction of a railroad down the peninsula indicated a change in local opinion. Before the war, the railroad and other internal improvements had failed to win the support of a majority of the citizens of Accomack and Northampton counties. Dr. George Teackle Yerby, who represented Northampton in the Virginia House of Delegates from 1839 to 1861, led the opposition. Yerby and his allies argued that state financial support for internal improvements meant higher taxes, that the rails would bring abolitionist

---

10 George Fitzhugh, "Eastern Shore of Virginia," *DeBow's Review* XXXIV (July/August, 1864), p. 84; George Alfred Townsend, "Townsend's Letter," *Boston Globe*, August 16, 1903.

11 *Richmond Dispatch*, November 30, 1867, January 21, 1873 (quotes "Observer"). See Robert Tracy McKenzie, "From Old South to New South in the Volunteer State: The Economy and Society of Rural Tennessee, 1850-1880," Ph.D. dissertation, Vanderbilt University, 1988, pp. 268-269.

ideas southward, and that water transportation would remain sufficient to the needs of Eastern Shoremen. Yerby's antagonists exclaimed "that it is no wonder the Doctor opposed improvements since he wanted none; for he visited his patients in a canoe and brought back his fees in oysters!" Yerby died at the close of the Civil War. A few years later, a Northampton correspondent told the *Richmond Dispatch* that "These old anti-internal improvement people, headed in time back by the lamented Dr. G. T. Yerby, have turned a complete somerset on the subject of internal improvements. We hope to have the railroad down here."[12]

Younger leaders were also coming to the front. The post-war men were mostly professionals – lawyers, educators, newspaper editors. Some had learned the benefits of efficiency and regimentation in the Confederate and Union armies while others had been non-combatants introduced to the modern world by the practical, if sordid, example of the federal occupiers. The new leaders genuflected to the past by memorializing the valor of Confederate soldiers, but their only enduring continuity with antebellum experience was their commitment to white supremacy. They looked forward to a new and prosperous Eastern Shore created in the image of the modernized North. They convinced themselves that Northern investors were benefactors rather than exploiters.[13]

The demand for a railroad was an early stage in a gradual process of conversion to the cult of progress. Eastern Shoremen would continue to taste the bitterness of defeat. They would retain for years traditional ways of living and thinking. They would delude themselves that they resembled their forefathers – *in* the national market but not *of* it. They

---

12 *Richmond Enquirer* April 27, August 28, 1838; Arthur Watson, "Speech of Dr. A. Watson, of Accomac, Delivered in the House of Delegates, Wednesday, February 29th, 1860, on the Bill to amend the Charter of the North and South Railroad," *Richmond Enquirer*, March 13, 1860; Staunton *Valley Virginian*, August 21, 1890; "My Own Trip: Cape Charles – The Eastern Shore," *Richmond Dispatch*, August 19, 1874 (first quotation); *Richmond Dispatch*, April 14, 1868, January 21, 1873 (quotes "Observer"); *Newtown (Md.) Record* in *Baltimore Sun*, January 1, 1869; T., Accomac C. H., to editor, August 18, *Norfolk Virginian*, August 22, 1871.

13 Brooks Miles Barnes, "Triumph of the New South: Independent Movements in Post-Reconstruction Politics," Ph.D. dissertation, University of Virginia, 1991, pp. 248-254. See also Maddex, *The Virginia Conservatives*, p. 290, and Peter S. Carmichael, *The Last Generation: Young Virginians in Peace, War, and Reconstruction* (Chapel Hill: University of North Carolina Press, 2005), pp. 215-216.

would on occasion consciously resist the modern leviathan. They would discover, however, that the railroad and the culture that it represented increased their dependency on the outside world while robbing them of the ability to shape their own destiny. Eastern Shoremen had accepted the supremacy of the nation over the provinces. They had not reckoned on the reduction of local autonomy and their assimilation into the national culture.

IN THE IMMEDIATE AFTERMATH OF THE CIVIL War, the Eastern Shore's mild climate, kindly soil, abundant natural resources, and close proximity to fast growing urban markets attracted a small number of Northern settlers. The newcomers sought opportunity as farmers, watermen, lumbermen, and merchants. A few came to gain the prestige and emoluments of public office by organizing the freedmen as Republican voters. Some, such as former Union General Herman Haupt, whose ambitions as farmer and oyster planter were quickly blasted, left after a short time, but most made a life for themselves on the peninsula, intermarrying and assimilating with the natives.[14]

Paying only brief visits were speculators, their purses heavy with wartime profits, and railroad and steamboat magnates looking to expand their corporate empires. In 1865, William H. Kimberly of Old Point Comfort bought several hundred acres on Cherrystone Creek. Originally of Baltimore, Kimberly had come to Virginia during the war to oversee his company's provisioning of Union naval vessels. He opened a store at the steamboat wharf at Cherrystone where he dealt in general merchandise, farm produce, and seafood. He also sold real estate, leased oyster planting grounds, and operated a cannery. Joseph P. Power, also a Maryland native, resided at Cherrystone for a decade before departing for Baltimore. He ran the store for Kimberly and acted as agent at the wharf for the Adams Express Company, the Eastern Shore Steamboat Company of Baltimore, and the Old Dominion Steamship Company of New York. A Republican, Power served in the early 1870s

---

14 For example, see above, pp. 49-50. For Haupt see James A. Ward, *That Man Haupt: A Biography of Herman Haupt* (Baton Rouge: Louisiana State University Press, 1973), pp. 189-190.

as treasurer of Northampton County and from 1866 to 1875 as postmaster at Cherrystone.[15]

In July 1867, New York financier Nathaniel L'Hommedieu McCready visited the Eastern Shore along with "other metropolitan capitalists and businessmen" to investigate "commercial and agricultural resources." McCready had recently organized the Old Dominion Steamship Company whose ocean-going steamers connected New York with Norfolk, Portsmouth, City Point, and Richmond. McCready was interested not only in the James River trade but also in the goods supplied the river cities by railroads linking them to points south and west. He now was looking to expand his operations to the Delmarva Peninsula. In 1869, the Old Dominion Steamship Company took over steamboat service between Cherrystone and Norfolk. By 1876, it controlled rail traffic running from Lewes on Delaware Bay to Franklin City on Chincoteague Bay.[16]

A few weeks after the departure of McCready's party, "an excursion of railroad and steamboat men" traveled on the new steamer *Sue* from Norfolk to Cherrystone where they were greeted with a salute from an old brass field piece. After an inspection of Cherrystone harbor, the *Sue* steamed up the bay to the new railhead at Crisfield where the excursionists took the cars home to Wilmington and Philadelphia. One of the visitors remarked that he was "thoroughly convinced of the ultimate extension of the Delaware [Rail] Road to Cherrystone, there to connect with boats for Norfolk."[17]

Among the Wilmington transportation executives interested in the

---

15 *Richmond Dispatch*, April 8, 1868; Staunton *Valley Virginian*, August 21, 1890. For Kimberly see Ralph T. Whitelaw, *Virginia's Eastern Shore: A History of Northampton and Accomack Counties* (Richmond: Virginia Historical Society, 1951), I, 179; Fannie B. Ward, "Red Letter Days, No. III: Summering at Old Point Comfort," New Orleans *Daily Picayune*, July 21, 1878; Newport News *Daily Press*, August 16, 1898. For Power see *Baltimore Sun*, May 5, 1885.

16 *New York Times*, July 6, 1867. For the Old Dominion Steamship Company's activities in Virginia see *New York Daily Herald*, February 17, 1867; *Richmond Dispatch*, April 13, 1867; *New York Times*, June 28, 1867; *Norfolk Virginian*, August 26, 1867, May 11, 1870; Kirk Mariner, *Once Upon an Island: The History of Chincoteague* (New Church, Va.: Miona Publications, 1996), p. 70. For McCready see *Boston Globe*, October 10, 1887.

17 Wilmington *Delaware Tribune*, September 19, 1867.

Eastern Shore were Samuel Harlan Jr., and other officers of the Harlan and Hollingsworth Company, manufacturers of railroad cars and iron steamships. During the antebellum period, Harlan and Hollingsworth were, according to maritime historian Alexander Crosby Brown, "the one truly important shipbuilding establishment in America." In the post-war years, the company's executives served on the boards of corporations intent on developing the lower Delmarva Peninsula. From 1866, Harlan was a director of the recently constructed Eastern Shore Railroad of Maryland, a subsidiary of the Philadelphia, Wilmington and Baltimore Railroad on the board of which he served from 1869 to 1882. The Eastern Shore Railroad terminated at Crisfield on Somers's Cove on the Little Annemessic River. On the road's completion, Harlan, New York steamboat magnate Charles Morgan, and other investors put into operation the Great Southern Inland Navigation Company (better known as the Annemessic Line), which ran steamers connecting Crisfield with Norfolk and a few wharves on the Eastern Shore of Virginia bayside. In 1867, Harlan and Hollingsworth organized the Eastern Shore Steamboat Company of Baltimore, which eventually linked Baltimore and Crisfield with wharves on bayside tributaries from Pocomoke River on the Maryland boundary to Mattawaman Creek in Northampton County. All of the steamboats permanently in service on the Annemessic and Eastern Shore lines were built by Harlan and Hollingsworth. Between 1870 and 1884, no individual or corporation did as much as the Harlan and Hollingsworth Company to transform the economy, society, and landscape of the Eastern Shore of Virginia.[18]

The activities of Kimberly and Power and of the Old Dominion and Harlan and Hollingsworth companies represented not only the exploitation of a conquered province but also its incremental integration

---

18 Wilmington *Delaware State Journal*, March 19, 1867; Alexander Crosby Brown, "Notes on the Origins of Iron Shipbuilding in the United States, 1825-1861," M. A. thesis, College of William and Mary, 1951, p. 149; Princess Anne (Md.) *Somerset Herald* in *Baltimore Sun*, July 13, 1866; John C. Hayman, *Rails Along the Chesapeake: A History of Railroading on the Delmarva Peninsula, 1827-1978* (n.p.: Marvadel Publishers, 1979), p. 212; Wilmington *Delaware Tribune*, May 9, 1867, January 14, 1869; *Baltimore Sun*, January 10, 1882; Robert H. Burgess and H. Graham Wood, *Steamboats Out of Baltimore* (Cambridge, Md.: Tidewater Publishers, 1968), p. 48. For Harlan see Wilmington *Morning News*, February 7, 1883.

into the emerging nation. "The enduring bonds of union were not a common heritage nor even a common speech," wrote historian Charles M. Wiltse, "but the steamboat, the railroad, the telegraph, and all the scientific progeny that followed."[19]

The Transportation Web

The Civil War enriched and empowered Northern steamboat and railroad corporations. The defeated South became a cockpit of their rivalries. Transportation companies looked on the Eastern Shore of Virginia as virgin territory. No railroad hitherto had penetrated the peninsula and antebellum steamboats called regularly at only two of its landings. After the war, the Eastern Shore's numerous creeks and inlets lured steamboat men and its level terrain invited their railroading counterparts. Its harvests of seafood, lumber, and agricultural produce and its recreational potential whetted the appetites of both. Competition for control of the peninsula's commerce developed between corporations and between cities, principally Baltimore, Philadelphia, and New York. Although interested in tapping the local market, the railroad men saw the peninsula primarily as a thoroughfare over which the crops and natural resources of the Southeastern seaboard might quickly be transported via Norfolk to the burgeoning cities of the North. Believing that steamboats and railroads would bring them renewed prosperity, Eastern Shoremen encouraged and abetted the schemes of the corporations. They attempted and sometimes briefly succeeded in maintaining a degree of autonomy amidst the change transforming the peninsula, but the ultimate fate of their homeland had slipped beyond local control.[20]

Before the Civil War, Baltimore dominated the trade of the

---

[19] Charles M. Wiltse, *John C. Calhoun, Sectionalist, 1840-1850* (Indianapolis and New York: Bobbs-Merrill, 1951), p. 482.

[20] For examples of the Eastern Shore as a link between Northeast and Southeast see Wilmington *Delaware Tribune*, May 21, 1868, and William Mahone, President, Atlantic, Mississippi & Ohio Railroad, Lynchburg, to Dear Sir, April 19, *Wilmington Daily Commercial*, April 29, 1873.

Chesapeake Bay country, including the extensive Southern traffic through the port of Norfolk. From the Southern interior, cotton, tobacco, and lumber traveled by rail into Norfolk and thence by sail and steamboat up the bay to Baltimore where the Baltimore and Ohio Railroad transshipped the produce north and west. In return, Baltimore and its hinterland supplied the South with hardware, processed foods, and general merchandise. In the war's immediate aftermath, Baltimore's antebellum rivals expanded their footholds in the region. N. L. McCready's Old Dominion Steamship Company and other lines diverted some of Baltimore's Southern commerce to Philadelphia and New York while the new railhead at Crisfield siphoned off another portion of the trade for the benefit of Philadelphia.[21]

Baltimore's loss of Chesapeake Bay traffic to Philadelphia was the consequence of an "absurd blunder." In 1835, the Maryland legislature subscribed $1,000,000 to the capital stock of a proposed Eastern Shore Railroad to run the length of Maryland from Somers's Cove on the Little Annemessic River northward to Elkton where it would connect with the Philadelphia, Wilmington and Baltimore Railroad. Lieutenant Colonel James Kearney, the engineer who in 1836 surveyed the line, also made a preliminary study for a branch line running from near Princess Anne to the boundary with Virginia where it might link with another projected road extending down the peninsula to Cherrystone. Nearly fifty years would pass before the Cherrystone vision became reality. The legislators hoped that the Eastern Shore Railroad would bring the Eastern Shore of Maryland into closer communication with Baltimore. The Eastern Shoremen who served as the railroad's directors thought less in regional than in national terms. They saw the success of their road as dependent not on an around-the-head-of-the-bay connection with Baltimore but on the forging via steamboat of a direct link with Norfolk, a gateway to the South. Lieutenant Colonel Kearney explained to Congress in 1837 that the assurance of the railroad's viability was "based mainly upon the

---

21 Philadelphia *North American*, December 23, 1851; *Norfolk Post*, October 10, 1865; Wilmington *Daily Republican*, December 3, 1866; *New York Daily Herald*, February 17, 1867; *Richmond Dispatch*, April 13, 1867.

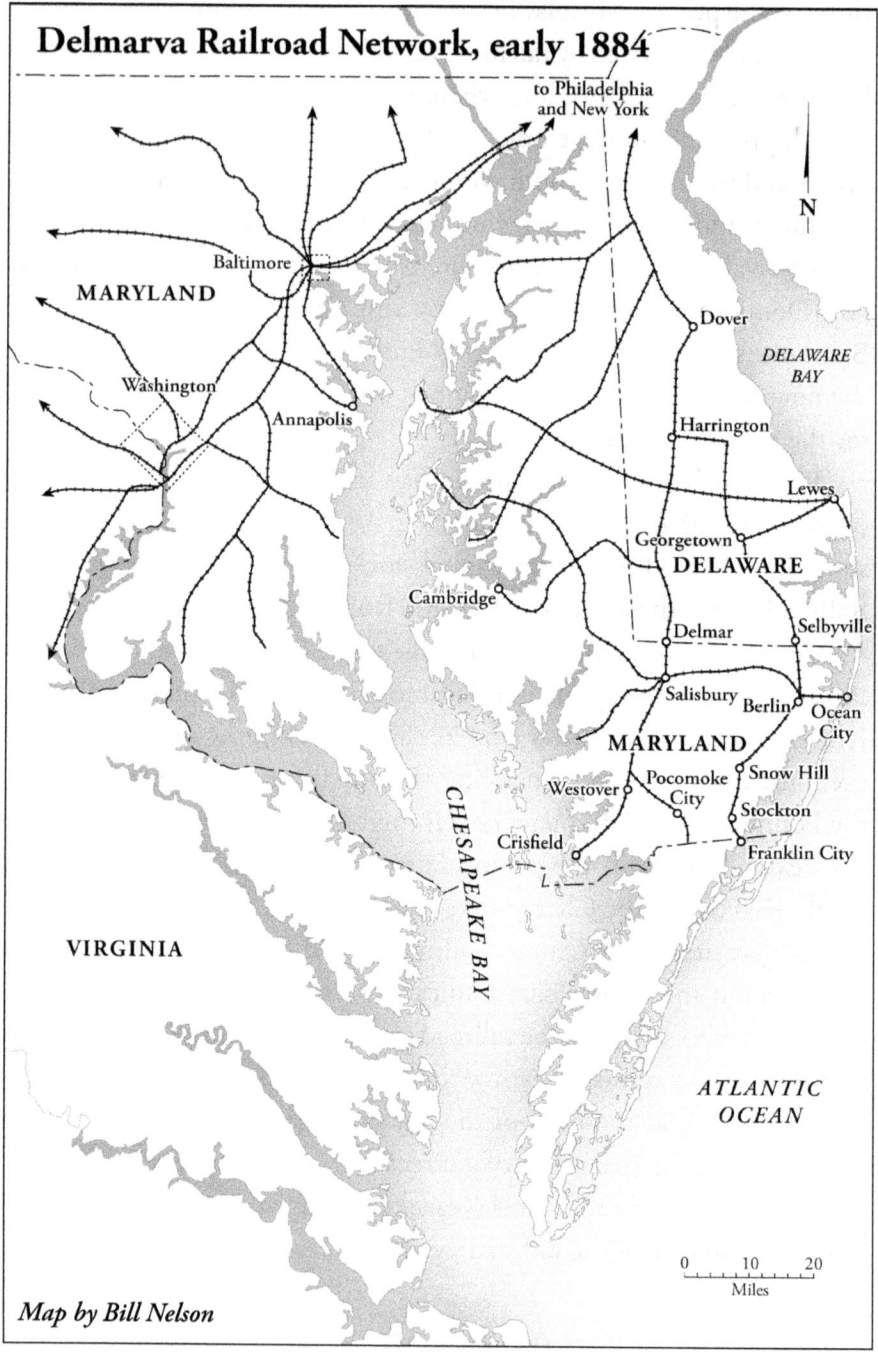

Map by Bill Nelson

expectation that it will very largely participate in the general travel of the Union, and in the business which the railroads of the South will bring towards the Eastern cities." Unfortunately, stockholder scandals and squabbles combined with the Panic of 1837 and a resulting state budget crisis to compel the legislature to suspend the project indefinitely.[22]

While Maryland hesitated, Delaware moved forward. Completed in 1859, the Delaware Railroad, a subsidiary of the Philadelphia, Wilmington and Baltimore, spanned the state from Wilmington to its terminus at Delmar on Delaware's southern boundary with Maryland. Ironically, during the 1850s and 1860s, Maryland legislative subscriptions helped finance the construction of several feeder lines connecting the Maryland Eastern Shore bayside with the Delaware Railroad. The re-chartered Eastern Shore Railroad running from Crisfield to its connection with the Delaware Railroad at Delmar enabled Philadelphia to grab a share of the Norfolk traffic. Perhaps more important, the Eastern Shore Railroad and the other feeders allowed Philadelphia entrée into the Maryland Eastern Shore bayside from the Chester River to the Little Annemessic. In 1866, the Smyrna (Del.) *Times* described the Delaware Railroad as "the grand trunk of all railroads on the Peninsula." A decade later, the *Times* attested to the Delaware Railroad's regional influence: "Baltimore, which used to have almost unlimited command of the Chesapeake side [of the Delmarva Peninsula], has had to surrender much of it to Philadelphia, by reason of the greater railroad enterprise of the latter. While water communication still gives Baltimore a large share, Philadelphia has all the rail communication, and has thus evenly divided with the Monumental City, a trade that used to go all one way."[23]

The impact on the Eastern Shore of Virginia of the feeder line to

---

22 Hayman, *Rails Along the Chesapeake*, pp. 15-18; Snow Hill (Md.) *Democratic Messenger*, June 10, 1882 (first quotation); James Kearney, "Report of the Engineer of the Eastern Shore Railroad," *Farmers' Register* 4 (1836-1837), p. 554; Report and Estimate in Reference to the Survey of the Eastern Shore Railroad, Senate, 24th Congress, 2d Session, Doc. 218 (1837), pp. 10-11 (quotes Kearney); *Baltimore Sun*, December 18, 1883.

23 Hayman, *Rails Along the Chesapeake*, pp. 19-32; "The Sussex Railroads," Wilmington *News Journal*, July 17, 1877; *Smyrna Times* in Wilmington *Daily Republican*, June 11, 1866; *Smyrna Times* in Wilmington *News Journal*, May 3, 1877; Snow Hill (Md.) *Democratic Messenger*, June 10, 1882; *Baltimore Sun*, December 18, 1883.

Crisfield was mostly confined to Pocomoke Sound. Watermen living on the sound found it convenient and profitable to sell their catch at Crisfield. Eastern Shoremen living at a distance discovered that shipping via the Delaware Railroad secured them no economic advantage. Down in lower Northampton County, Israel Townsend chaffed at the idea of Crisfield. He derided the place as "a miserable hole ... for a railroad terminus. ... the Heavenly abode of mosquitoes, bull-frogs and musk-rats." Townsend wondered "how an intelligent railroad engineer could recommend Crisfield as a terminus for the Delaware Railroad when he had such a country and such a terminus as Cherrystone or Cape Charles." He dismissed Crisfield as "only a temporary halting place; it will have to be given up ... and the road eventually run here; it is only a question of time." The editor of the Wilmington *Delaware Tribune* chided Townsend for his fit of pique, reminding him that Crisfield "was made the terminus not from choice, but because those interested had not sufficient funds to carry the road to Cherrystone. ... Everybody interested admits ... that the road *must* run to Cherrystone before it can ever realize the hopes of its projectors." The raising of money was essential to the extension of the railroad down the peninsula, but so too was the settlement of regional and corporate rivalries, the consolidation of railroad companies, the procurement of legislative approval, the resolution of engineering problems, and the securing of rights of way. It would take nearly two decades to answer Townsend's "question of time." By default, the interim between the coming of the railroad to Crisfield in 1866 and to Cape Charles City in 1884 was the heyday of the steamboat on the Eastern Shore of Virginia.[24]

WITH THE OPENING IN EARLY NOVEMBER 1866 of the Eastern Shore Railroad to through traffic, Crisfield became the transportation hub of the lower Eastern Shore of Chesapeake Bay. The Philadelphia, Wilmington and Baltimore Railroad, of which the Eastern Shore

---

24 Wilmington *Delaware Tribune*, May 9, 1867; T. [Israel Townsend], Capeville, to editor, June 24, Wilmington *Delaware State Journal*, June 28, 1867 (second quotation); T. [Israel Townsend], Capeville, to editor, June 20, Wilmington *Delaware Tribune*, June 23, 1870 (first and third quotations).

Railroad and Delaware Railroad were subsidiaries, connected Crisfield with Wilmington, Philadelphia, and New York. The waters of the Chesapeake linked Crisfield with the cities of Norfolk and Baltimore and with innumerable landings along the bay and its tributaries. No one was more aware of the business opportunities presented by the new railhead than the executives of the Harlan and Hollingsworth Company. For three decades, Harlan and Hollingsworth had supplied railroad cars to the Philadelphia, Wilmington and Baltimore. Pioneers in building iron-bottomed steamships, they knew the bay country and the type of boat best suited to its shallow waters. They had vision, experience, inside knowledge, and access to sources of capital.[25]

To every railroad speculator interested in the Delmarva Peninsula, Norfolk was the ultimate objective. From Norfolk branched the railroads that would bring northward the crops and natural resources of the Southern seaboard. Samuel Harlan Jr. and other executives at Harlan and Hollingsworth joined Charles Morgan and his associates in organizing the Annemessic Line of steamboats to run between Crisfield and Norfolk. Well before the last rail was laid, the Annemessic Line had erected a wharf and placed in readiness the steamboats *City of Norfolk* and *Lady of the Lake*. The steamboats "look like floating palaces," exclaimed a Wilmington newspaperman. "They are both built at the establishment of ... Harlan & Hollingsworth & Co., whose fame has become almost worldwide. The *City of Norfolk* is 230 feet long, thirty-two over her guards, and fourteen feet deep. Her cabins are handsomely furnished and her dining room is very inviting. She has forty-four state rooms, about forty berths, and is every way calculated to accommodate passengers. Some idea may be formed of her character from the fact that she cost as she now floats, about $200,000."[26]

Shortly after the Eastern Shore Railroad went into operation in late 1866, the Annemessic Line arranged an excursion to Norfolk for more

---

[25] *Baltimore Sun*, November 1, 1866; Wilmington *Morning News*, February 7, 1883; *Norfolk Virginian*, November 29, 1869.

[26] Wilmington *Delaware Tribune*, May 9, 1867; *Smyrna (Del.) Times* in Wilmington *Daily Republican*, June 11, 1866; Wilmington *Daily Republican*, December 3, 1866 (quotation); *Norfolk Virginian*, December 12, 1866.

than eighty prominent citizens of Wilmington, including the mayor, aldermen, and councilmen. The Norfolk City Council and Board of Trade warmly entertained the excursionists with speeches of welcome at the Opera House, tours of Fort Monroe and the Navy Yard, and a closing banquet. The purpose of the excursion was to promote as well as entertain. "Our business men can send [from Wilmington to Norfolk] over the new line, carriages, car wheels, castings, furniture, boots and shoes and various other articles," noted a reporter. "In return they may receive cotton, vegetables, and other products which the fertile soil of the sunny South is capable of producing, at an earlier period in the season than can be grown in more Northern situations."[27]

In 1867, the Harlan and Hollingsworth Company organized the Eastern Shore Steamboat Company of Baltimore. Samuel Harlan Jr. served as its president. Along with Harlan and Hollingsworth executives, the company's board included John W. Crisfield and Dr. George R. Dennis, prominent Maryland Eastern Shore politicians and leading stockholders in the Eastern Shore Railroad. The Eastern Shore Steamboat Company was initially capitalized at $160,000. Willard Thompson, who had married into the Harlan family, acted as its agent at Baltimore. Harlan and his associates intended to create a transportation web between Baltimore, Crisfield, Norfolk, and the towns and wharves along the Pocomoke River and the creeks of the Virginia Eastern Shore bayside. The company's steamers would carry Eastern Shore produce for distribution by rail westward via Baltimore and northward via Crisfield, Wilmington, and Philadelphia. Meanwhile, they would stimulate demand on the Eastern Shore for return cargoes of processed and manufactured goods.[28]

The Eastern Shore Steamboat Company absorbed the Annemessic Line in 1868 and operated it until its demise in 1873. A Wilmington newspaperman recalled that the line's steamers were "withdrawn because

---

27 Wilmington *Daily Republican*, November 29, December 3 (quotation), 1866.

28 Burgess and Wood, *Steamboats Out of Baltimore*, p. 48; "History of the Steamboat on the Chesapeake – XXIV: The Eastern Shore Company," *Baltimore Sun*, June 21, 1908; Hayman, *Rails Along the Chesapeake*, pp. 67-68; Wilmington *Morning News*, February 7, 1883; "Pungoteague" to editor, Accomac C. H. *Peninsula Enterprise* (hereafter cited as *PE*), September 21, 1882.

of some legerdemain of capitalists unknown to the writer. I was informed by a reliable party here [Crisfield], that a large quantity of cotton, rice and products of the Gulf States found their way to Philadelphia by this route, and I infer that the competition to the Old Bay Line was too great for that old monopoly to permit its continuance." The Old Bay Line, officially the Baltimore Steam Packet Company, dominated the steamboat trade between Norfolk and Baltimore. Between 1871 and 1874, the company purchased four steamers from the Harlan and Hollingsworth Company. Perhaps the Old Bay Line eliminated a rival for its Norfolk commerce by requiring Harlan and Hollingsworth to abandon the Annemessic route in exchange for securing contracts for the construction of the new vessels. Steamboat service continued between Crisfield and Norfolk after the demise of the Annemessic Line but not at the same level of organization.[29]

Harlan and Hollingsworth built the Eastern Shore Steamboat Company's steamers for the shallow waters of Chesapeake Bay. They were light-draft, three-deck side-wheelers, steel-hulled with a frame superstructure painted white. They carried cargo on the first deck. Passenger quarters – around thirty staterooms, saloon, and dining room – occupied the second deck and pilot house and life boats the hurricane deck. As territory expanded and commerce grew, the company added new boats – the *Sue* (1867), the *Maggie* (1869), the *Helen* (1871), the *Tangier* (1875), and the *Eastern Shore* (1883). With a single exception, each new boat was larger than its predecessors. Displacing 515 tons, the *Maggie* was the smallest of the steamers. She was 139 feet in length and was capable of carrying 1,200 barrels of potatoes. The *Eastern Shore*, built more than a decade later, displaced 792 tons. She was 176 feet in length and could carry 3,500 barrels of potatoes. The boats' crews numbered about thirty, including officers, stewards, deck hands, and engine room stokers. Their captains were of necessity experienced mariners, cool and resourceful in any situation. "The roughness of the weather in

---

29 Wilmington *Delaware State Journal*, August 9, 1867; *Norfolk Virginian*, July 22, 1872, September 4, October 3, 1874; "The Future State," Wilmington *News Journal*, February 28, 1878 (quotation); *Baltimore Sun*, April 22, 1882; Burgess and Wood, *Steamboats Out of Baltimore*, pp. 19, 50, 162-163; *Norfolk Landmark*, March 8, 1876; *Philadelphia Inquirer*, May 14, 1877.

this part of the bay, and the sandbars at the mouth of the different creeks being a terror to most all steamboat men," explained Tully A. T. Joynes of Accomack County, clerk of the *Maggie*.[30]

Before the Civil War, steamboat service from Baltimore to the Eastern Shore of Virginia was limited to a weekly stop at Dock Point on Pungoteague Creek near present-day Harborton. During the war, Union soldiers burned the wharf at Dock Point and otherwise interdicted steamboat commerce. The steamers returned to the peninsula shortly before the close of hostilities in the spring of 1865. The old, small, wooden-hulled *Massachusetts* of the Individual Enterprise Steamboat Company called twice weekly at Pungoteague Creek, at a rudely constructed former military wharf on Chesconnessex Creek, at Pitts's Wharf, and at several landings on the Maryland bank of Pocomoke River.[31]

The Eastern Shore Steamboat Company began operations by chartering the *Massachusetts* and taking over its route. The *Massachusetts* sufficed until Harlan and Hollingsworth launched the *Sue*, the first light-draft, iron-hulled side-wheeler on Chesapeake Bay. The company gradually expanded its territory southward along the Eastern Shore bayside while placing on its line steamers designed to carry ever larger cargoes on the shallow waters of the Eastern Shore creeks. When the *Maggie* came on line in 1869, the *Baltimore Sun* noted that "The increasing freight and travel on this route rendered the construction of a first-class steamer for it a necessity. The Baltimore market will receive by her, twice a week during the coming season, greater quantities of fruit and vegetables than have ever before reached it from that quarter, it is supposed." The addition of the *Helen* in 1871, the *Tangier* in 1875, and the *Eastern Shore* in 1883 enabled the company to serve more wharves on more creeks with greater frequency. By 1884, the *Helen*, the *Tangier*, and the *Eastern Shore* divided a territory extending from Snow

---

[30] Burgess and Wood, *Steamboats Out of Baltimore*, p. 48; James Egbert Mears, *Hacks Neck and Its People Past and Present* (Chicago: Author, 1937), pp. 37, 38; A. Hughlett Mason, *History of Steam Navigation to the Eastern Shore of Virginia* (Richmond: The Dietz Press, Inc., 1973), pp. 31, 35, 41, 65, 66; Joynes to editor, PE, April 6, 1882.

[31] Burgess and Wood, *Steamboats Out of Baltimore*, pp. 18-19; Whitelaw, *Virginia's Eastern Shore*, I, 697-698; *Philadelphia Inquirer*, August 19, 1865; Mason, *History of Steam Navigation*, p. 44; *Baltimore Daily Commercial*, March 26, 1866.

— Steam and Steel —

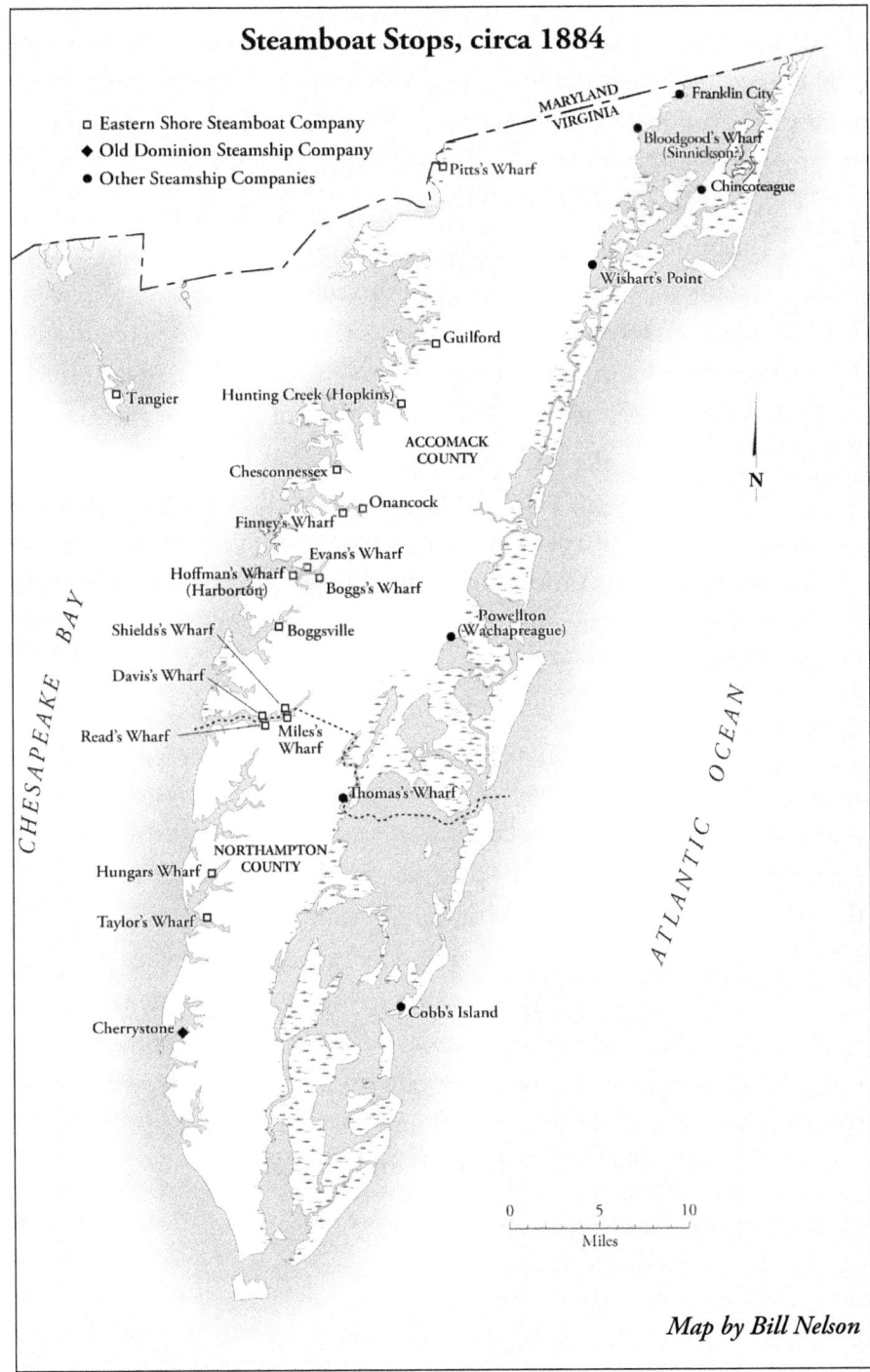

Hill, Maryland, on the upper Pocomoke River to Taylor's Wharf on the north bank of Mattawaman Creek in central Northampton County. The *Maggie* remained in service as a reserve boat. The vessels called at a total of twenty-five wharves on Pocomoke River and Eastern Shore of Virginia creeks. They made rail connections at Baltimore, at Crisfield for Wilmington and Philadelphia, and at Snow Hill for New York via Lewes, Delaware, and the Old Dominion Steamship Company. Harlan and Hollingsworth had spun its transportation web.[32]

Developing a territory underserved by steam navigation, the Eastern Shore Steamboat Company accepted initial loss in anticipation of future profit. It spent money to make money. In 1882, a Pungoteague man declared that the company had "Through a long succession of discouragements and difficulties ... persistently adhered to their original policy of confidence in the future of the Eastern Shore, and have spared no money or effort to develop the various industries as well as the wonderful natural resources of the peninsula, in the hope of building up a permanent and flourishing business between this section and the city of Baltimore." The company regularly overhauled existing vessels and added new. It built the *Helen* in the hope of expanding trade in upper Northampton. When Irish potato production increased dramatically on the *Helen*'s route it replaced her with the much larger *Eastern Shore*. It recognized the importance of keeping a regular schedule and of maintaining its wharf at the foot of South Street in Baltimore. "A steamer arriving every day, the buyers know where to go and what to depend on," boasted Tully Joynes. "It is convenient and roomy, and every effort has been made to make it the best dock in Baltimore for the sale of produce." The company also bought and leased, built and improved wharf facilities throughout the company's territory. Some Eastern Shore wharves failed to stimulate the anticipated trade, but most met company expectations.[33]

---

[32] Mason, *History of Steam Navigation*, p. 44; *Baltimore Sun*, May 9, 1867, March 27, 1869 (quotation), June 20, 1881; "History of the Steamboat"; *PE*, October 18, 1883, July 6, 1884; Snow Hill *Democratic Messenger*, July 8, 1882; Burgess and Wood, *Steamboats Out of Baltimore*, p. 49; "The Future State."

[33] Citizen to editor, *PE*, February 2, 1882; Pungoteague to editor, *PE*, September 21, 1882; Snow Hill *Democratic Messenger*, April 15, 1882; "History of the Steamboat"; Joynes to editor, *PE*, April 20, 1882; *Acts and Joint Resolutions Passed by the General Assembly of the State of Virgin-

In 1882, a group of Accomack County businessmen and attorneys organized the Accomac Steamboat Company. Promising low fares and shipping rates, the Accomack men, among whom were merchants engaged in the sailboat trade, at first set up as a rival to the Eastern Shore Steamboat Company. They assumed that the peninsula's growing economy would provide business sufficient for both steamboat lines. However, before beginning operations, they commenced negotiations with the Harlan and Hollingsworth Company for the purchase of the Eastern Shore Steamboat Company. The Accomack syndicate apparently believed that the threat of competition from themselves and from the increasingly imminent construction of a railroad down the peninsula might induce Harlan and Hollingsworth to sell their subsidiary. John Taylor Gause, the Harlan and Hollingsworth executive acting in the place of ailing company president Samuel Harlan Jr., coolly defined his company's position. After intimating that he "wished to narrow his business affairs to shipbuilding solely," he expressed the opinion that "the future of Accomac and Northampton counties is very promising." He said that "there will be a steady increase of population and business, and that the new railroad from Pocomoke City, Md., to Cherrystone ... will not damage the Eastern Shore Steamboat Company's business in the least, as there will be more than enough for both. If, however, the railroad should make war against the steamboat it would be worsted, as the history of such fights had demonstrated that water carriers can hold their own to advantage." Because Gause wished "to oblige" the people of the Eastern Shore "for whom the company had done a great deal, and from whom they had made money," he would sell the Eastern Shore Steamboat Company to them for "a reasonable price" of $221,500. The figure probably was more than double what the directors of the Accomac Steamboat Company were able to pay. Their dreams having encountered the reality of corporate finance, their company forthwith dissolved. Steamboat service to the Eastern Shore of Virginia would remain for its duration in the hands of outsiders.[34]

---

ia at its Session of 1876-77 (Richmond: R. F. Walker, Superintendent of Public Printing, 1877), p. 131; *PE*, July 12, 1883.

34 *PE*, February 23, March 9, April 13, 1882; Tully A. Joynes to editor, *PE*, April 6, 1882;

Rivaling the Harlan and Hollingsworth Company as principal agent for the initial expansion of steam transport on the Eastern Shore of Virginia was N. L. McCready's Old Dominion Steamship Company of New York. Before the Civil War, a steamer from Norfolk called every other day at Cherrystone. Immediately after the war, the Old Bay Line of Baltimore placed the old, wooden, side-wheeler *Eolus* on a thrice weekly circuit from Norfolk to Cherrystone to Old Point Comfort where she connected with the line's larger Baltimore steamers before returning to Norfolk. For a short time in the late 1860s, the Eastern Shore Steamboat Company's *Sue* ran to Cherrystone from Baltimore via Crisfield. Both Baltimore-based companies withdrew their boats from Cherrystone in 1869. They apparently discovered that they could not compete successfully with New York via Norfolk for the lower Northampton trade.[35]

The Old Dominion Steamship Company filled the breach. Its steamer *N. P. Banks* returned from Cherrystone directly to her wharf in Norfolk where freight and passengers might be transferred to company steamers bound for New York. The *N. P. Banks* continued on the Cherrystone route until replaced in 1880 by the new, wooden, side-wheeler *Northampton*. In the mid-1870s, Old Dominion also operated the Piankitank Line. Semi-weekly the company's screw-steamer *Olive* ran a route from Norfolk to five wharves in Gloucester, Middlesex, and Mathews counties on the Western Shore and to Hungars and Taylor's wharves in Northampton.[36]

Baltimore Sun, March 1, April 22, May 6, 9, 12 (quotes Gause), 30, 1882. For the high shipping rates charged by the Philadelphia, Wilmington and Baltimore Railroad see Wilmington *Delaware State Journal*, December 6, 1867, and Wilmington *Delaware Tribune*, April 14, 1870. For Gause see *Baltimore Sun*, December 2, 1898.

35 M., off Cobb's Island, to editor, July 26, *Staunton Spectator*, August 7, 1860; Mason, *History of Steam Navigation*, pp. 12, 33; *Baltimore Daily Commercial*, November 10, 1865; T. [Israel Townsend], Capeville, to editor, November 25, Wilmington *Delaware State Journal*, December 6, 1867; T. (Israel Townsend], Capeville, to editor, October 25, Wilmington *Delaware Tribune*, November 5, 1868. In late 1865, the steamer *Mattano* ran for a short time between Norfolk and Cherrystone (*Norfolk Post*, October 10, 1865).

36 *Norfolk Virginian*, May 11, 1870, July 12, 1874; Mears, *History of Steam Navigation*, p. 48; James E. Mears, "The Eastern Shore of Virginia Produce Exchange," Onancock *Eastern Shore News*, June 29, 1961; *Baltimore Sun* in Wilmington *Delaware Gazette and State Journal*,

As Harlan and Hollingsworth expanded its operations to include a steamboat company, Old Dominion expanded theirs to include railroad companies. By 1875, Old Dominion had assembled a rail network on the eastern side of the upper Delmarva Peninsula. The aptly named Junction and Breakwater Railroad connected Harrington on the Philadelphia, Wilmington and Baltimore Railroad via Georgetown with Lewes on Delaware Bay. From Georgetown, the Frankford and Breakwater extended southward to Berlin, Maryland, where the Worcester Railroad linked Berlin to Snow Hill on the Pocomoke River. Local produce went northward by rail through the junction at Harrington or by the company's ocean-going steamships from Lewes to New York. At Snow Hill the company transshipped Southern commodities from the port of Norfolk. In the long term, it planned to build a rail line from Snow Hill down through Accomack and Northampton to Cherrystone where boats would cross to Norfolk. For the time being, though, the company would extend the Worcester Railroad southeastward from Snow Hill to a terminus just over the Virginia line where at a new town called Franklin City it would tap the oyster grounds of Chincoteague Bay.[37]

Old Dominion had been involved in the Chincoteague Bay oyster trade since the fall of 1874 when it placed one of its steamers on a run between Chincoteague and New York. "These are considered the greatest oysters in the world, and Philadelphia has heretofore chiefly consumed them," observed a Wilmington reporter in October, 1875. "But now the New York epicures have had some of them put upon their plates by the Old Dominion Steamship Company, and they want them all." The Philadelphia, Wilmington and Baltimore Railroad proposed to safeguard the trade for Philadelphia by building a branch line from Newtown (now Pocomoke City), Maryland, to Bloodgood's Wharf on Chincoteague Bay below Nashville (now Sinnickson), but the project never developed beyond a preliminary survey. By November,

---

September 11, 1884.

37 *Norfolk Virginian*, July 28, 1874; *Baltimore Sun*, January 28, 1875; Wilmington *Delaware Tribune*, February 4, 1875; Wilmington *News Journal*, May 24, November 20, 1875; *Middletown (Del.) Transcript*, October 2, 1875; "The Sussex Railroads."

construction of the Worcester Railroad had advanced close enough to the bay that oysters might be carted to the waiting trains. On April 7, 1876, the depot at Franklin City opened for business.[38]

At Franklin City and on Chincoteague Island, the Old Dominion Steamship Company built piers to accommodate vessels transporting passengers and freight. The pier at Franklin City extended two hundred feet into Chincoteague Bay and was wide enough to admit the main track and a siding to facilitate the loading of oysters directly from the boats to the cars. In April 1882, railroad agent Harry McLeary installed a telephone line between his home and his office on the pier. McLeary thus became the first person on the Eastern Shore of Virginia to enslave himself to that infernal instrument. Old Dominion also improved the piers at Bloodgood's Wharf and at Wishart's Point near the village of Atlantic.[39]

The small side-wheeler *Alice* was the first steamboat to run between the Old Dominion piers. After the *Alice* burned at her dock in early 1877, Old Dominion replaced her with the larger *Accomack*, a new, iron-hulled side-wheeler. The company envisioned the *Accomack* as connecting the railhead at Franklin City with wharves at least as far south along the coast as the new town of Powellton (now Wachapreague). Unfortunately, the *Accomack* drew too much water for the shallow and shifting bottoms of the Eastern Shore seaside. In September, the company withdrew her from service. Her replacement, the much smaller *Widgeon*, called only at Chincoteague, Wishart's Point, and Bloodgood's Wharf before meeting the daily train at Franklin City.[40]

---

38 *Norfolk Landmark*, August 30, 1874; Wilmington *Daily Gazette*, October 23, 1875; Wilmington *News Journal*, November 12, 1875; *Wilmington Commercial* in *Baltimore Sun*, November 17, 1875; Hayman, *Rails Along the Chesapeake*, p. 34.

39 *Middletown (Del.) Transcript*, March 4, 1876; *Acts and Joint Resolutions Passed by the General Assembly of the State of Virginia during the Session of 1879-80* (Richmond: Superintendent of Public Printing, 1880), pp. 275-276; Wilmington *Daily Republican*, December 9, 1879; Snow Hill *Democratic Messenger*, November 26, 1881, April 15, 1882; Wilmington *Delaware State Journal*, July 22, 1880; *PE*, April 5, 1883.

40 *Baltimore Sun*, January 15, 22, April 25, 1877; Mason, *History of Steam Navigation*, pp. 18, 75; Wilmington *News Journal*, February 26, June 4, October 18, 1877; Onancock *Eastern Virginian* (hereafter cited as *EV*), September 22, 1877; *PE*, September 8, 1881, February 9, 1884.

As urban demand for Eastern Shore produce increased, so too did corporate interest in the seaside below Chincoteague Bay. In the summer of 1882, the Key Port Steamboat Company of New Jersey ran a screw steamer from Powellton and three wharves on the Machipongo River to New York. Key Port envisioned a fleet of steamers eventually serving the seaside from Custis's Neck near Drummondtown to Cape Charles. The plan failed to materialize perhaps because of fear of competition from the projected railroad down the peninsula or, more likely, because of the difficulties of navigating the treacherous seaside waters. In 1883, a steamer traveled regularly between New York and Thomas's Wharf in upper Northampton County. The following summer, the Old Dominion Steamship Company returned to the seaside. The ocean-going steamer *Newberne* plied between New York and wharves on the Machipongo while the small, wooden, screw-steamer *Tuckahoe* twice weekly carried potatoes from Powellton to Lewes where the cargo was transferred to larger Old Dominion boats for shipment to New York and Boston.[41]

THE STEAMBOAT WAS THE RIVAL RATHER THAN the nemesis of the sailboat. Expanding crop and seafood production on the Eastern Shore increased the demand for transportation. The number of sailing vessels enrolled in the Cherrystone (Eastern Shore) customs district grew from 211 in 1870 to 358 in 1880 (an increase of 69.7 percent). In the latter year, Cherrystone enrolled the most vessels among Virginia's six customs districts. Reflecting the importance of the oyster grounds of Pocomoke and Tangier sounds and of Chincoteague Bay, the great majority of the boats were based in Accomack County. New boats were built in the boatyards of Baltimore and at landings along the peninsula. Jenkins Bridge near Pocomoke Sound and Chincoteague and Greenbackville on Chincoteague Bay were boatbuilding centers. An active trade in used vessels involved the purchase of boats locally and from off the

---

41 *PE*, March 2, 16, April 27, May 11, 18, 1882, June 28, July 19, 1883, June 7, 21, August 9, 23, 30, September 13, 1884; Snow Hill *Democratic Messenger*, June 24, 1882; Wilmington *Gazette and State Journal*, August 21, 1884; Wilmington *Morning News*, August 26, 1884; Mason, *History of Steam Navigation*, p. 70.

peninsula. Despite the rapid expansion of steamboat service, sailboats carried to market at least half of the oyster harvest and a preponderance of that of agricultural produce. A statistical analysis of the commerce on Onancock Creek in 1882 revealed that sailboats handled more than 60 percent of the potatoes shipped from its wharves.[42]

WATER TRANSPORTATION BY SAIL AND STEAM WAS a dominant feature of Eastern Shore life in the post-Civil War years. The Virginia Commissioner of Fisheries grasped its scope, its glamour, and its meaning. "One has but to spend a week by the shores of the Chesapeake to realize that it is a great artery of the world's traffic," he wrote in 1882. "Day and night, in sunshine and storm, the stream of commerce flows steadily on. The smoke of the ocean and coasting steamers hangs a perpetual veil over the line between sky and water. By day ten thousand sails gleaming in the sunlight, by night ten thousand lights dancing on the waters, tell of the ceaseless flow of the interchange of human wants for *luxuries*."[43]

Steamboats and trains put urban America in touch with the Eastern Shore of Virginia. Sailboats put the Eastern Shore in touch with urban America. A crucial difference lay within the seemingly small distinction. Sail transportation on the peninsula went back to English settlement in the early seventeenth century. Sailboats were owned mostly by local people whose customers were their neighbors. The boats sailed to the great cities but also to smaller ports such as Alexandria and Williamsport. Dependant on the confluence of wind and tide, their comings and goings required a flexible schedule and a patient crew. Proceeding under

---

[42] *Annual Statements of the Chief of the Bureau of Statistics on the Commerce and Navigation of the United States, June 30, 1880* (Washington: Government Printing Office, 1880), p. 847; John W. H. Parker to William Mahone, May 19, 1883, William Mahone Papers, William R. Perkins Library, Duke University, Durham, N.C.; *Baltimore Sun*, September 12, 1870, December 22, 1881, November 6, 1882; Snow Hill *Democratic Messenger*, June 24, September 23, 1882; *PE*, June 15, 22, 1882, March 8, June 7, 14, 21, July 5, August 16, October 11, December 20, 1883, February 23, March 15, April 19, 26, May 24, June 21, July 5, August 30, October 4, November 15, 1884; Surveys of Certain Rivers in Virginia and North Carolina, United States, House of Representatives, 45th Congress, 3rd Session, Ex. Doc. 68 (1879), p. 12.

[43] *Annual Report of the Commissioner of Fisheries, 1882* (Richmond: R. F. Walker, Superintendent of Public Printing, 1882), p. 11 (italics in original). See also T. [Israel Townsend], Capeville, to editor, August 5, Wilmington *Delaware State Journal*, August 16, 1867.

sail, the vessels gave an impression of quiet and leisure. In no hurry to depart at a scheduled time, they were unloaded without bustle. The few passengers they carried to and fro were mostly locals.

Steam transportation was an entering wedge of economic and cultural transformation. Steamboats and trains were owned by corporations whose customers were strangers. The boats and trains directed local commerce to a handful of major markets – Baltimore, Norfolk, Boston, New York, Philadelphia, and Wilmington. They operated on industrial time, keeping a schedule dictated by the clock. They came to their docks and depots in cacophonous busyness and disgorged and loaded their cargoes in a rush. They carried Eastern Shoremen at cheap rates to the cities while bringing to the peninsula problematic outsiders – drummers, tourists, evangelists, lyceum orators, temperance advocates.

The railroad depots at Crisfield and Franklin City and the steamboat offices along both sides of the peninsula were agencies of empire. They linked the surrounding colonial landscape to the national market and attached its inhabitants to the metropolis. They were both conduits of trade and of cultural homogeneity. To the steamboat pier at the Hammocks near the mouth of Messongo Creek, sailboats brought seafood, lumber, and agricultural produce from nearby communities such as Saxis Island, Hall's Wharf, Marsh Market, and Skin Point. The sailboats returned to these communities with the stuff of the industrialized North – hardware and dry goods, newspapers and market intelligence, fashionable clothes and urban mores. The depots and offices also were a means through which the Yankee cult of material progress gained acceptance in the minds of Eastern Shoremen. The Eastern Shore Steamboat Company "*has provided for our wants even before our people have made any formal expression of them,*" marveled a Pungoteague man in 1882. "[T]heir keen foresight and liberal management have not failed to awaken a spirit of progress and thrift throughout the peninsula, which redound to the lasting benefit of the farmers and merchants of this locality."[44]

---

44 William Cronon, *Nature's Metropolis: Chicago and the Great West* (New York and London: W. W. Norton & Company, 1991), pp. 48, 54; Mary Frances Carey, *The Messongo Traders: A Family History* (Melbourne, Fl.: Edward L. Trader, 1980), p. 35; Tully A, Joynes to editor, PE, April 20, 1882; "Pungoteague" to editor, *PE*, September 21, 1882 (italics added).

Chapter III

Economic Growth

Between 1860 and 1890 the population of American cities grew from 6.2 million to 22.1 million. Population growth created demand for foodstuffs, fuel, building material, and recreational opportunity. Unlike much of the South, the Eastern Shore of Virginia was well positioned to meet demand. The peninsula benefited from close geographic proximity to major cities of the Eastern seaboard, from an expanding regional transportation network, and from the varied produce of its fields, waters, and woods. In addition, the readmission of Virginia to the Union in 1870 had reestablished the political stability necessary to a flourishing commerce. During the 1870s and early 1880s the Eastern Shore became increasingly an exception to the rule of Southern immiseration under the colonial economy. However, despite its prosperity relative to the rest of the South, the peninsula every day became more deeply involved in the Yankee empire.[1]

Agriculture

The expansion of steam transportation was a national phenomenon. Its effect on Eastern Shore of Virginia agriculture was

---

1 James L. McCorkle Jr., "Moving Perishables to Market: Southern Railroads and the Nineteenth-Century Origins of Southern Truck Farming," *Agricultural History* 66 (Winter, 1992), pp. 42-43; Howard N. Rabinowitz, *The First New South, 1865-1920* (Arlington Heights, Ill.: Harlan Davidson, Inc., 1992), p. 9; E. H. Stevens, *Soil Survey of Accomac and Northampton Counties, Virginia*, United States, Department of Agriculture, Bureau of Soils (Washington: Government Priinting Office, 1920), p. 17.

transformative, suddenly ending the nearly three centuries' importance of grain as a cash crop. New railroad lines, more powerful locomotives, and more capacious freight cars combined with shipping rates driven downward by competition between the great trunk lines to stimulate Middle Western grain production. As the 1870s advanced, crops grown on the immense bonanza farms of the prairies of Minnesota and the Dakotas came onto the market. To the consternation of East Coast farmers, ease of transport and economy of scale enabled cheap Western grain to flood their customary markets. In 1876 a *Baltimore Sun* correspondent complained that "Grain delivered in Baltimore at fifty cents a bushel from Chicago cuts the throat of Eastern Shore farmers." Eight years later, a Leemont man told the Accomac C. H. *Peninsula Enterprise* that "Very many in this community are having corn brought from Baltimore at 60 and 65 cents per bushel, instead of paying 80 cents per bushel for it, to those having it to sell at home." Commercial grain production on the peninsula collapsed. Between 1869 and 1879 oat production declined by 82 percent, from 476,528 bushels to 86,749. Corn production, however, declined only by 9 percent, from 797,154 bushels to 716,792. Corn had lost commercial value, but the farmer must still feed his family and livestock. The deflated grain market especially aggrieved Eastern Shore of Maryland farmers. Aid provided by the Maryland legislature had helped the Baltimore and Ohio compete with other major railroads for cheap Western grain. Peninsula farmers were reminded that legislatures do the bidding of corporations and that corporations know no regional loyalties.[2]

As railroad expansion pushed Eastern Shore grain out of the national market, changing dietary preferences of city dwellers pulled its truck

---

2 Barbara Jeanne Fields, *Slavery and Freedom on the Middle Ground: Maryland During the Nineteenth Century* (New Haven: Yale University Press, 1985), p. 170; David Goldfield, *America Aflame: How the Civil War Created a Nation* (New York: Bloomsbury Press, 2011), p. 390; "The Maryland Seaside," *Baltimore Sun*, August 16, 1876 (quotes N. E. F.); Accomac C. H. *Peninsula Enterprise* (hereafter cited as *PE*), July 5, 1884; T. C. Morton, "Life in a Level Land," *Staunton Vindicator*, June 23, 1882; *The Statistics of the Wealth and Industry of the United States ... Compiled, From the Original Returns of the Ninth Census (June 1, 1870)* (Washington: Government Printing Office, 1872), pp. 267, 268, 271, 272; *Report on the Productions of Agriculture as Returned at the Tenth Census (June 1, 1880)* (Washington: Government Printing Office, 1883), pp. 208-209; Wilmington *News Journal*, February 25, 1882.

crops more deeply into that market. The maturation of the peninsula's fruits and vegetables occurred at an opportune time to fulfill seasonal demand while a short haul brought the produce quickly to nearby cities. "The great idea now is trucking," wrote a correspondent of the *Richmond Dispatch* in 1875. Eastern Shore farmers, he continued, "are willing to take their place in the line of earliness. Charleston, S.C., leads off, Norfolk next, then the Eastern Shore, then Delaware, then Jersey." So rapidly did local growers come to adopt fruits and vegetables for cash purposes that in 1881 another *Dispatch* writer declared the peninsula "now dependent upon trucking for its money income."[3]

Potatoes became the Eastern Shore's primary cash crop. Both Irish and sweet potato production more than doubled between 1869 and 1879. The Irish potato harvest rose from 159,346 bushels to 344,897 and that of sweet potatoes from 292,196 bushels to 613,457. Accomack County trailed only Norfolk in Irish potato production in Virginia while Northampton placed fourth. Accomack led the commonwealth in sweet potato production with Northampton third. Peninsula farmers generally profited more from sweet potatoes than from Irish. They made money from sweet potatoes at $1.50 per barrel but usually received a higher price. "We raise yaller backs, nothing else," asserted a farmer living near Drummondtown, "plant 'em in March, set 'em out in May, dig 'em in August, cart 'em down to Nancock and send 'em all over the world. Net us $3 a barrel early, and $2 later. A right smart drap is fifty bushels to an acre; some farmers make a thousand barrels to a crop." By the early 1880s the estimated value of the crop in Accomack alone was $1,000,000.[4]

The cost of fertilizer discouraged Irish potato production. Sweet

---

3 McCorkle, "Moving Perishables to Market," p. 43; Fields, *Slavery and Freedom on the Middle Ground*, pp. 174-175; *Richmond Dispatch*, April 10, 1875, February 2, 1881; *Baltimore Sun*, July 13, 1875.

4 *The Statistics of the Wealth and Industry of the United States ... Compiled, From the Original Returns of the Ninth Census (June 1, 1870)*, pp. 268, 272; *Report on the Productions of Agriculture as Returned at the Tenth Census (June 1, 1880)*, pp. 319, 321; Morton, "Life in a Level Land"; Wilmington *Morning News*, September 21, 1881, November 19, 1884; "The Old Man Takes a Cruise," *Richmond Dispatch*, December 13, 1883; "The Eastern Shore," New York *Evening Post*, April 25, 1885 (quotation).

potatoes thrived on a limited admixture of commercial fertilizer to the customary compost of pine shatters, marsh mud, and barnyard muck. On the other hand, the preparation of Irish potatoes for an early market required copious applications of costly commercial fertilizer. To "force" the early harvest of Irish potatoes, Eastern Shore farmers continued to use Peruvian guano, sometimes in a mixture with fish scrap and ground bones. By the mid-1870s the diminishing supply of guano turned the farmers' attention to emerging superphosphate mixes derived from fish, bones, sulfuric acid, and phosphate rock. The growers purchased commercial fertilizer from manufacturers in Baltimore, Norfolk, and Pocomoke City and, increasingly, from home establishments.[5]

Eastern Shore manufacturers relied on menhaden, or alewives, a small fish useless for the table but when pressed or ground an excellent source of oil or fertilizer. The origin of the domestic fertilizer industry contained elements common to the Yankee penetration of the peninsula: depletion of natural resources in Northern waters and the exploitation of local resources with the willing aid of local people. In 1866 New England fishermen, having exhausted the supply of menhaden off their coast, established "fish factories" at Cape Charles. The New Englanders discovered the local supply of menhaden abundant and well suited for rendering into fertilizer. The Cape Charles factories operated only a short time but others soon appeared at numerous points in the Chesapeake Bay region.[6]

In 1873 a fish factory opened on Tangier Island. By 1884 thirteen factories operated in Eastern Shore localities – six on Tangier, three on Chincoteague Island, two on Cedar Island, and others on Assateague Island and at Hoffman's Wharf (now Harborton). The factories were small concerns owned by natives and newcomers, residents and outside

---

5 *PE*, August 31, 1882, February 9, July 6, 1884; Richard C. Sheridan, "Chemical Fertilizers in Southern Agriculture," *Agricultural History* 53 (January, 1979), pp. 308, 309, 313-314; Rosser H. Taylor, "The Sale and Application of Commercial Fertilizers in the South Atlantic States to 1900," *Ibid.* 21 (January, 1947, p. 48; Snow Hill (Md.) *Democratic Messenger*, May 7, 1881, August 26, 1882.

6 G. Brown Goode, "History of the Menhaden Industry" In *The History and Present Condition of the Fishery Industry* (Washington: Government Printing Office, 1881), p. 117; New Haven (Conn.) *Register* in *Washington Post*, August 2, 1882.

speculators. The resident owners often had their fingers in other pies. On Cedar Island, native agriculturalist and oyster planter Orris A. Browne partnered with Benjamin S. Rich, a pre-war emigrant from Massachusetts. From 1875 Rich served as the superintendent of the U. S. Life-Saving Service stations on the barrier islands. Also on Cedar Island, newcomer Edwin J. Foote of New York managed Fowler, Foote and Company for himself and his Connecticut investors. When Foote retired from the fertilizer business in 1894, he remained at his home in nearby Powellton where he planted oysters, kept store, and served as postmaster. At Hoffman's Wharf, Albro J. Morse of Connecticut enjoyed the financial backing of local merchant-shippers John T., George W., and Henry Powell and William and John P. L. Hopkins. On Chincoteague in 1884 Long Islander John A. Gum sold his Sea Fish and Oil Company to a consortium of natives and recent arrivals, among whom was Joseph T. Kenney, Union veteran, politician, merchant, and postmaster.[7]

A Chincoteague man considered the coming of the factories a boon to oystermen: "This is a new industry for Chincoteague, and will give employment to all of our surplus labor that has heretofore been idle during the summer months." The factories employed about a dozen men on site. The alewives were caught by Northerners operating steam trawlers and pound-nets and by local seine-hauling fishermen. The season extended from April to October and the catch varied from week to week and from year to year. In 1882 a Cedar Island factory processed 100,000 to 500,000 fish daily. The rendering of the fish into fertilizer exuded a pervasive stench that to factory owners and employees smelled like money. Boasting that "At no point on the Eastern Shore is fish manure manufactured more largely than with us," a Tangierman commented that its factories gave "employment to many persons at lucrative prices."[8]

---

7 Goode, "History of the Menhaden Industry," pp. ix, 169; Accomack County Court Order Book, 1881-1883, pp. 280-281; Kirk Mariner, *Once Upon an Island: The History of Chincoteague* (New Church, Va.: Miona Publications, 1996), pp. 76-77; Nannie W. Ames, "Harborton" in *An Economic and Social Survey of Accomac County*, eds. J. B. Carter, C. W. Hollarnd Jr., W. E. Johnson, and C. L. Miller. University of Virginia Record Extension Series XIII (March, 1929), p. 17; John Frye, *The Men All Singing: The Story of Menhaden Fishing* (Norfolk, Va.: Donning, 1978), p. 60; *PE*, July 14, 1881, February 16, March 1, 1884, June 29, 1901, May 7, 1921.

8 "The Teagues of Accomack," Wilmington *Delaware State Journal*, April 7, 1881; Wilmington

Local manufacturers offered their fertilizers in various grades to farmers on the Eastern Shore and in the Norfolk area. Fowler, Foote and Company marketed grades ranging in price from $15 to $24 to $30 per ton. The companies supplied the farmer direct or through merchants. Fowler, Foote sold from its factory on Cedar Island, from the wharf at Powellton, or by delivery to any landing on the seaside. Henry L. Crockett of Tangier sold from his schooner moored at wharves on Onancock and Pungoteague creeks. The larger the projected Irish potato crop, the greater the demand for fertilizer. In 1884 a Mappsville man predicted for upper Accomack County a planting "of round potatoes on a more gigantic scale than was ever known before. We hear of nothing now almost but fertilizers, and nearly every other man is an agent."[9]

The Colorado potato beetle, which arrived in the Chesapeake region in 1874, ignored the vines of sweet potatoes but ravaged those of Irish potatoes. Remarkably prolific, the bugs covered fields and floated on adjacent waters. In Northampton County in 1882 potato "fields were entirely ruined by them, plowed up and planted in corn." Farmers struggled to deal with the onslaught. They loosed guinea fowl on their fields and hired laborers to pick the bugs at six cents a quart. By 1877 some farmers sprayed their vines with a solution that included the compound Paris green. The pesticide proved effective, but the arsenic-based Paris green was dangerous to man, beast, and environment.[10]

Morning News, May 12, 1881 (first quotation); Snow Hill (Md.) *Democratic Messenger*, March 19, 1881, August 5, 1882; *PE*, July 14, 1881, July 13, 1882, May 17 (second quotation), June 14, 28, July 5, 1883; "The Chesapeake Shore" *Forest and Stream* XIX (August 17, 1882), p. 264; James Egbert Mears, *Hacks Neck and Its People Past and Present* (Chicago: Author, 1937), pp. 39, 43-44, 70. Historian Jack Temple Kirby recalled the paper mill in his boyhood home of West Point, Virginia: "Smoke and foul odor signified stability and prosperity – my father's Madeleine – and the mill was welcome" (*Mockingbird Song: Ecological Landscapes of the South* [Chapel Hill: University of North Carolina, 2006], p. 264.

9 *Norfolk Virginian*, February 2, 1884; Onancock *Eastern Virginian* (hereafter cited as EV), September 15, 1876, November 9, 1878; Snow Hill (Md.) *Democratic Messenger*, August 12, 1882; *PE*, February 22, September 13, 1883, February 16, March 1 (quotation), June 7, July 6, 1884.

10 James E. McWilliams, *American Pests: The Losing War on Insects from Colonial Times to DDT* (New York: Columbia University Press, 2008), pp. 65-66, 95-96, 150; Wilmington *Morning News* June 7, 1881, November 19, 1884; *Baltimore Sun*, February 17, 1877, May 3, June 10 (quotation), 1882; *PE*, May 11, June 1, 1882, May 31, 1884; Snow Hill (Md.) *Democratic*

Eastern Shore farmers marketed other truck crops including onions, peanuts, sugar beets, watermelons, peas, and black-eyed peas. They also sold blackberries, whortleberries, and strawberries. During the 1870s strawberries became a major crop. Growers annually shipped 50,000 quarts from the wharves of Onancock Creek alone. Valuing a prolific, firm berry that shipped well, they generally grew the "Wilson" and "Hoover" varieties. Local horticulturalists also developed the early ripening "Hyslop" and "Will's Extra Early." Meanwhile, a disease called the "yellows" destroyed the peach crop that had once made Accomack County nationally famous for its brandy. In 1879 a Delaware man on crossing the Maryland-Virginia boundary observed that "the orchards begin to thin out, and lose themselves altogether in the great potato fields of Accomac."[11]

MOST LOCAL AGRICULTURAL PRODUCE MOVED TO MARKET in discrete routes to a handful of urban hubs. The trade of the upper bayside from Mattawaman Creek northward generally went by sailboats and by the Eastern Shore Steamboat Company to Baltimore and, in smaller quantity, by railroad via Crisfield to Philadelphia and Wilmington. Sailboats and the Old Dominion Steamship Company carried the produce of lower Northampton County to Norfolk from whence it was transshipped by ocean-going steamboat to Philadelphia, New York, and Boston. The upper seaside also served the Northeastern cities by direct waterborne transport or from the railhead at Franklin City via Harrington junction or the Old Dominion Steamship Company at Lewes. Yet, it should be noted that the peninsula's narrow girth provided its farmers with

---

Messenger, May 7, 1881.

11 *Alexandria Gazette*, July 29, 1884; Wilmington *Delaware Tribune*, February 3, 1876; "Through Accomac," Wilmington *Daily Republican*, June 2, 1885; Washington *National Republican*, November 1, 1879; Westminster (Md.) *Democratic Advocate*, June 29, 1878; *Richmond Dispatch*, April 23, 1875, June 7, 1876; *Baltimore Sun* in *Salisbury (Md.) Advertiser*, June 2, 1877; *Baltimore Sun*, June 5, June 10, 1882; *PE*, May 4, 25, June 1, 15, August 10, 1882, March 15, 1884; Robert Wilson, "On the Eastern Shore," *Lippincott's Magazine* XVIII (1876), p. 364; G. Terry Sharrer, *A Kind of Fate: Agricultural Change in Virginia, 1861-1920* (Ames: Iowa State University Press, 2000), p. 52; Wilmington *News Journal*, May 6, 1879 (quotation), June 24, 1882; "On the Peninsula," Wilmington *Morning News*, November 15, 1884.

alternative points of shipment. "Few sections are more convenient to market," stated T. C. Morton of the *Staunton Vindicator*. "At Onancock and Pungoteague it is only about eight miles from the bay-side to the seaside landings, and at Belle Haven only two or three miles – the deep salt water creeks running up into the interior everywhere, so that the farmer has the choice on the one side of the Baltimore and Western markets and on the other of the New York and Northern."[12]

Baltimore, Norfolk, and New York were the principal destinations for national distribution. "Baltimore beyond question is one of the most solid and prosperous of American cities," a Richmonder conceded. "She pushes her hands out, perhaps, a little too violently, and with too little consideration for generosity at least, if not justice towards communities not so able to fend off as she is to invade. But there is no use abusing her. She is going ahead, no matter what is said." The tentacles of the Baltimore and Ohio Railroad and its tributaries grasped for Baltimore an extensive national trade. The Eastern Shore Steamboat Company linked the peninsula with the B&O and thus with Pittsburgh, Cincinnati, and points north and west. "Accomac sweet potatoes go West in vast quantities by way of Baltimore," a correspondent told the *Richmond Dispatch* in 1875. "The Chicago children cry for them." Baltimore merchants also benefited from a long history of trade and social relations with Eastern Shoremen. Surprised that "Four out of five drummers met with in the lower part of the Maryland and Virginia peninsula are sent out by Baltimore firms," a Philadelphian grumbled that "All of this trade belongs naturally to Philadelphia." In return for the lion's share of the peninsula's produce, the Baltimore merchants supplied groceries, dry goods, and footwear.[13]

---

12 Morton, "Life in a Level Land."

13 *Richmond Dispatch*, May 11, 1870 (first quotation), April 10, 1875 (second quotation), February 2, 1880; *Baltimore Sun*, June 21, 1876, October 9, 1883; J. H. Chataigne, ed., *Virginia Business Directory and Gazetteer, 1880-1881* (Richmond: Baughman & Bros., 1880), p. 399; "My Own Trip: Cape Charles – The Eastern Shore," *Richmond Dispatch*, August 19, 1874; *Philadelphia Inquirer*, October 2, 1884 (quotes R. B. Cooke). According to Orris A. Browne, around 1880 Eastern Shore Irish potatoes lost their Chicago market to those grown in Tennessee (*Report of the State Board of Agriculture of Virginia, 1890* [Richmond: J. H. O'Bannon, Superintendent of Public Printing, 1889), p. 131.

After the Civil War, Northern capitalists envisioned Norfolk as an outpost of empire. They looked with appreciation on the magnificent port and its railroad connections extending through the upper South and into Georgia and Alabama. They saw Norfolk as a conduit through which the agricultural produce, principally cotton, and natural resources of the South would flow to the Northeast and through which these goods, processed and value added, would return southward. The capitalists invested heavily in steamboats, among them first-class, iron, screw steamers built by the Harlan and Hollingsworth Company, which would travel regularly between Norfolk and the great Northern ports. By the mid-1870s steamboat companies connected Norfolk tri-weekly with Boston, Providence, Philadelphia, and Washington and daily with Baltimore via the Old Bay Line and New York via the Old Dominion Steamship Company. The cost of waterborne transport from Norfolk, exclaimed the Capeville correspondent of a Richmond newspaper, "either by sail or steamer, is almost nominal. Just think of it: the farmers here are sending their potatoes and other truck to New York and Boston at a cost of 30 cents per barrel. The same distance on any of the railroads leading to our city [Richmond] would cost at least $1.50 per barrel."[14]

Lower Northampton County maintained an economic and social relationship with Norfolk similar to that the upper bayside maintained with Baltimore. John R. Waddy of Eastville informed William Mahone that "we have a tri-weekly line of steamers to that city ... & nearly all of our sail vessels run there." Some lower Northampton produce was shipped from Norfolk up Chesapeake Bay to Baltimore and Washington but most went to Boston or New York. Israel Townsend told a Wilmington editor that "All our business is with Norfolk or with New York and Boston via Norfolk, where good steamship lines take all our produce to market." Never shrinking from engaging in hyperbole (or from delivering an insult), Townsend added that "We have no more

---

14 Washington *National Republican*, October 11, 1875; A. Oemler, "Truck Farming," in *Report of the Commissioner of Agriculture, 1885* (Washington: Government Printing Office, 1885), p. 604; *Richmond Dispatch*, August 13, 1875.

to do with Philadelphia or Wilmington markets than we have with Port Penn or Mount Pleasant."[15]

With its large population New York was a major market for Eastern Shore produce. Its wealthy epicures were famous for their willingness to pay "fancy prices" for delicacies such as oysters, terrapin, and strawberries. More important, the great rail and steamboat networks emanating from the city made it the premier transportation hub of the East Coast. In the early post-Civil War years, the upper seaside sent its crops to New York and Philadelphia and to Baltimore through Snow Hill on the Pocomoke River. The extension of the Old Dominion Steamship Company's railroad to Franklin City in 1876 enabled the company to capture a larger portion of the seaside trade for New York via Lewes. Baltimore was the big loser. "New York has opened a line ... through the Old Dominion Steamship Company, and offers more than Baltimore can afford to pay. ... [T]his route makes freights from New York lower than from Baltimore. Flour is 30 cents from New York and 65 cents from Baltimore via Snow Hill to Chincoteague," a writer for the *Smyrna (Del.) Times* observed. In the early 1880s the Old Dominion and other New York steamboat companies further cut into the commerce of Baltimore and Philadelphia by inaugurating service from wharves at Powellton and other points on the seaside.[16]

Until 1873 Eastern Shore farmers sold their sweet potatoes in bulk to buyers at the wharves. In that year, farmers at Powellton began to ship potatoes in barrels, which, in hope of obtaining high prices, they consigned to urban commission merchants. Consignment became commonplace, and every spring swarms of commission merchants with their cards and stencils descended on Accomack and Northampton counties. "Luckily for Pharaoh, commission agents were unknown in his day, or else he would

---

15 Waddy to Mahone, January 23, 1882, Mahone Papers, Manuscript Department, William L. Perkins Library, Duke University, Durham, N.C.; June 28, July 17, 1877, Charles Albert Van Ness Journals, 1874-1885, transcription in Eastern Shore of Virginia Heritage Center, Eastern Shore Public Library, Parksley, Va.; Washington *Critic*, June 28, 1883; Wilmington *News Journal*, August 10, 1877 (quotes Townsend).

16 Oemler, "Truck Farming," p. 626 ("fancy prices"); *Baltimore Sun*, April 25, 1877; *Smyrna (Del.) Times* in Wilmington *News Journal*, May 3, 1877; Morton "Life in a Level Land"; Wilmington *Morning News*, August 26, 1884; *PE*, July 6, 1884.

no doubt have enjoyed the pleasure of their acquaintance, when all other plagues had failed to soften his heart," groaned a Mappsville man. "They have appeared this year far in advance of the potato bugs, and are as pertinacious in their attacks as mad bees. The relief for a poor farmer is to promise unreservedly, a consignment." Some of the agents were Eastern Shore natives representing urban firms. Nathaniel J. W. LeCato, originally of Accomack, represented the New York house of J. L. Chadwick. The principals of Waddy & Saunders were both Northampton natives. Saunders solicited consignments from his home at Cherrystone while Waddy tended the office in New York. Most of the concerns, however, were owned and represented by persons from off the peninsula.[17]

The performance of the commission merchants varied. Some spoke frankly, pursued the market price, and promptly returned payment less commission. Others made inflated promises, sold short, and tendered late remittances. Many worked both sides of the street by representing not only the sellers of produce but the buyers as well, a conflict of interest that usually favored the large accounts (the buyers) over the small (the sellers). Some farmers sought to protect themselves by apportioning consignments among several commission merchants. In 1878 George B. Mapp, a farmer living on the lower Accomack seaside, employed the services of three New York firms. Other growers gambled that they could catch the market at its height by resisting consignment until their produce was at the wharf and ready to ship. In a good year the commission merchants might even buy their produce outright. The commission houses customarily remitted payments via check. In the absence of banks on the Eastern Shore, farmers used the checks as bills of exchange, turning them over to local storekeepers to settle debts or to purchase credit. As farmers and shippers were drawn ever deeper into the national market, they increasingly depended on the competence and honesty of middlemen, the majority of whom were outsiders.[18]

---

17 Littleton T. LeCato, Concord, to editor, October 19, *PE*, October 24, 1891; *Philadelphia Inquirer*, October 2, 1884; *PE*, July 20, 1882; March 1, 1883; April 19 (quotation), July 6, 1884; Norfolk *Weekly Virginian and Carolinian*, July 5, 1877.

18 *EV*, July 7, 1876; *PE*, August 25, 1881; *Baltimore Sun*, May 12, 1882; George B. Mapp memorandum, 1878, Mapp Papers and Artifacts, 1782-1896, Eastern Shore of Virginia Her-

Fisheries

Oystering

On the Bayside – The Chesapeake Bay oyster industry continued to boom in the years after 1870. Contemporaries estimated that in the early 1880s oystermen took from the bay fifteen to twenty million bushels annually. Oysters for the table went to the burgeoning Northern cities where they were consumed in homes or in restaurants or were shipped onward to every point in the country accessible by the trunk line railroads. Meanwhile, seed oysters were sent northward to replenish the ravished grounds of the Yankee coast. Under the pressure of growing Northern population and wealth, the price of oysters advanced from around 30 cents per bushel in the late 1860s to over 40 cents in 1879 to nearly 50 cents in 1884. The Chesapeake Bay was at the heart of American oystering. The bay accounted for 77 percent of the industry's national production, 75 percent of its work force, and 66 percent of its capital. The Eastern Shore played a leading role in Virginia's portion of the industry, providing 21 percent of both men and vessels involved in the trade. Bay oysters were harvested along the length of the peninsula but most were taken in Pocomoke and Tangier sounds astride the boundary with Maryland.[19]

---

itage Center; Snow Hill (Md.) *Democratic Messenger*, June 24, July 22, 1882; July 25, 1877, Charles Albert Van Ness Journals.

[19] John R. Wennersten, "The Almighty Oyster: A Saga of Old Somerset and the Eastern Shore," *Maryland Historical Magazine* 74 (March, 1978), p. 86; Francis Winslow, "Present Condition and Future Prospects of the Oyster Industry," *Forest and Stream* XXIII (September 18, 1884), p. 148; Donald W. Pritchard and Jeffrey R. Schubel, "Human Influences on the Physical Characteristics of the Chesapeake Bay" in *Discovering the Chesapeake: The History of an Ecosystem*, eds. Philip D. Curtin, Grace S. Brush, and George W. Fisher (Baltimore and London: The Johns Hopkins University Press, 2001), p. 75; Ernest Ingersoll, "The Oyster Industry" in *The History and Present Condition of the Fishery Industry*, by G. Brown Goode (Washington: Government Printing Office, 1881), p. 182. Recently, marine scientist David M. Schulte estimated the 1880 oyster harvest at slightly over eight million bushels ("History of the Virginia Oyster Industry, Chesapeake Bay, USA," *Frontiers in Marine Science* (www.frontiersin.org) 4 [May, 2017], article 127, p. 4).

Oystermen on the Eastern Shore bayside sold their catch to buy boats and to local dealers who in turn re-sold or consigned to restaurants and commission merchants in urban markets. Most of the oysters harvested on the lower bayside went to Philadelphia and New York either directly or via Norfolk. The upper bayside trade went to Baltimore and Crisfield or to Philadelphia and New York directly or via Crisfield. Baltimore was "the great oyster-market of the United States." Its dealers sold raw oysters packed in barrels, shucked oysters packed in jars, and steamed oysters packed in hermetically-sealed cans. Daily during the season, they sent the containers on trains of forty or fifty cars as far west as Detroit. The dealers usually used large oysters gathered by tongers for raw stock and small oysters indiscriminately harvested by dredgers for steamed. In words fraught with implications for the sustainability of the industry, an expert on Chesapeake Bay oystering noted in 1881 that "nothing in the shape of an oyster is too small to be available for the 'steamed' trade."[20]

Northern dealers quickly recognized Crisfield as the gateway to the great oyster grounds of Pocomoke and Tangier sounds. They established packing houses along the waterfronts of Crisfield and nearby communities within easy haul of the railroad. By the late 1870s twenty-six packing houses operated in Crisfield and vicinity from which annually around 650,000 bushels of shucked oysters and 62,500 bushels (25,000 barrels) of raw oysters were shipped by fast train to Philadelphia, New York, and cities as far north as Canada. The best of the oysters were reserved for barrel stock. The less desirable shucked oysters were shipped in tubs and buckets which were not hermetically sealed. Upper bayside oystermen preferred Crisfield to Baltimore because heavy demand in Philadelphia and New York generally warranted higher prices. A Wilmington journalist described Crisfield as "the Eldorado of the oysterman. Here we find a city a half-mile from the main, or fast land, with a population

---

20 *PE*, March 30, 1882, October 11, 1883, July 6, 1884; *Baltimore Sun*, February 2, 1882; *EV* in Philadelphia *Times*, December 24, 1884; Ingersoll, "The Oyster Industry," p. 168 (quotes Richard H. Edmonds); Francis Winslow, "Report on the Oyster Beds of the James River, Va., and of Tangier and Pocomoke Sounds, Maryland and Virginia," *United States Coast and Geodetic Survey Report for 1881*, Appendix No. 11 (Washington: Government Printing Office, 1882), p. 42.

of 2,500, a custom house registering over 700 vessels, ranging from 10 tons upwards, all engaged in the oyster trade. The streets are oyster shells. The dwellings, stores, shucking houses, railroad depot and warehouse, hotels, barber shops, are all built upon pilings and filled in with oyster shells, and two shipyards are built upon the same foundation. Not a tree is found in all the place."[21]

During the oyster season, sloops and schooners from up and down the East Coast crowded the wharves at the end of Spruce Street in Philadelphia. In 1878 the Philadelphia *Times* observed that on "a busy day, from two to three million oysters are sold at these wharves and the daily average is more than one million." Hucksters who peddled fruit, vegetables, and seafood from carts preferred small, cheap Chesapeake oysters as did the kettle men and women who sold them door-to-door. The big dealers who supplied the Western states, the Pennsylvania interior, and the Philadelphia eating establishments demanded premium oysters taken from Pocomoke Sound and Chincoteague Bay. The *Times* estimated that seasonal sales in Philadelphia restaurants, saloons, and cellars amounted to $30,000,000 per annum.[22]

New York dealers had less regard for Chesapeake oysters than their counterparts in Philadelphia. Alexander Frazer, a dealer in the market at the foot of Broome Street on East River, declared that "The Virginia oysters are inferior to those raised in this vicinity. ... There is as much difference between Blue Points and Virginias, as between a domestic and a Havana cigar." (Frazer spoke hastily and without a sense of irony. The revered Chincoteagues and Cherrystones were Virginia oysters, and the Blue Points likely grew from Virginia seed.) New York nonetheless used Virginia oysters along with those from Long Island Sound to build a growing trade with the West in cheap, shucked oysters shipped in non-hermetically-sealed containers. Mr. Porter, another Broome Street

---

21 Ingersoll, "The Oyster Industry," pp. 168-169, 186; "Peninsular Tour: Tangier Sound and the Chesapeake Oyster Beds," Wilmington *News Journal*, June 19, 1878; "The Lenten Oyster," Philadelphia *Times*, March 9, 1878; "The Future State," Wilmington *News Journal*, February 28, 1878 (quotation); *Baltimore Sun*, September 10, 1881.

22 "The Lenten Oyster"; Philadelphia *Times* in *Forest and Stream* XIII (October 30, 1879), p. 765.

dealer, believed that New York supplied better stock to the Western trade than Baltimore and that as a result was challenging Baltimore's national supremacy. "New-York is gaining on the trade of Baltimore right along," Porter averred. "Western people are getting educated to eat better oysters than Baltimore sends them." He conceded that Baltimore still led in national sales but boasted that the demands of hucksters, kettle men, hotels, oyster bars, and the Fulton Fish Market made populous New York the leading urban market in the country.[23]

THE SOARING DEMAND FOR OYSTERS AND THE concomitant investment of Yankee capital in transportation and packing facilities meant increased trade, employment, and income for the Chesapeake Bay region. Because good money could be made from common ground belonging to everyone and thus to no one, the Chesapeake, especially the boundary waters of Pocomoke and Tangier sounds, became a kind of aquatic Kentucky, a "dark and bloody ground." Oystering on the bay and in its tributaries in the post-Civil War years was an often violent free-for-all pitting Marylanders against Virginians and tongmen against dredgermen. It involved the ruthless exploitation of the resources of the oyster grounds by everyone. It provoked contention not only between states but in the Virginia legislature between representatives from the Tidewater and those from the upland counties of the commonwealth. "I commenced to learn that the oyster was a politician as well as an edible fish, and was opposed to any innovations," recalled Orris A. Browne, superintendent of the Virginia oyster police in the early 1870s. "[T]he time of those who made the laws was occupied in settling the contentions among those who were anxious to get all they could day by day, regardless of the future."[24]

---

23 "Oysters in Abundance," *New-York Tribune*, August 30, 1881. "The Fair Haven, the Blue Point, the Shrewsbury, and Saddle Rock oysters, all so popular in our markets, are, in most cases, natives of the Virginia waters transported from the natural beds in the rough and planted at the points enumerated above ("Oysters of the James: Chincoteague Bay's Great Industry," *New York Times*, May 16, 1880).

24 *Proceedings of the Convention Called to Consider and Discuss the Oyster Question, Held at the Richmond Chamber of Commerce, Richmond, Va., Jan. 12, 1894 with Papers Issued in Calling the Convention* (Richmond: J. W. Ferguson & Son, 1894), p. 39.

The unremitting contention and sporadic violence that characterized the oyster grounds cannot be ascribed solely to greed. Oystermen battled with each other because of the need to make a living for their families, because of pride in their states, because of occupational solidarity, and because of the conviction of independent men that they should not be bullied or defrauded. As important was the custom of the aquatic commons. Unlike an agrarian freehold, the commons was not private property the fertility of which must be maintained for future generations. Nor was it enclosed by discernible metes and bounds. On the vast expanse of the bay, laws and boundaries seemed trivialities easily ignored and the usages of time immemorial the only license necessary. The oyster grounds were seemingly inexhaustible. What was not taken by one oysterman today would be taken by another tomorrow. And had not God created an abundance of oysters for the use of man?

The dispute between Maryland and Virginia involved the location of the boundary between the states in Chesapeake Bay and the alleged right of Marylanders to take oysters from the waters of Pocomoke Sound. Much of the strife on the oyster grounds of the upper bay resulted from the inability of the states to resolve the issues. The conflict has its origin in the Compact of 1785 which established a boundary and granted joint rights to both states in the fisheries of the Pocomoke River. Over time shoreline migration had altered landmarks and thus rendered imprecise the 1785 boundary. Until the oyster industry began its rapid expansion in the 1830s, the existence of a boundary line meant little, if anything, to watermen. In 1872 Severn Bradshaw of Smith Island, Maryland, testified that "thirty or forty years ago, there was scarcely any talk about the line of the two states on this island; the taxes were small, and the oysters in the bay were not counted of great value, and we oystered in the creeks [rather than in the sounds], but since dredging commenced ... oysters have become valuable, and people began to look more closely after the line of the two states." Also in 1872 former Virginia Governor Henry A. Wise described for present Governor Gilbert C. Walker the valuable commerce in oysters at Crisfield and warned that "The stakes in this boundary question ... are worth, on the whole line in dispute, too many millions of dollars to be lightly relinquished or to be neglected."[25]

Oyster production having become a lucrative industry and a source of revenue to the states, the exact location of the boundary became of increasing importance to oystermen and government officials. So, too, the issue of equal rights in the Pocomoke River. Marylanders argued that the historic line lay farther southward than Virginia claimed, and Marylanders also asserted that Pocomoke Sound and its immense oyster grounds were part of the Pocomoke River. Virginians responded that the true line lay north of Crisfield and that Pocomoke Sound was a part of Chesapeake Bay, not of Pocomoke River. Failing to reach a mutually acceptable agreement, Maryland and Virginia in 1874 submitted the controversy to a board of arbitration consisting of members from Pennsylvania, Georgia, and Kentucky. In regard to the location of the Chesapeake boundary, the board's ruling in 1877 largely favored Virginia. Although denied sovereignty over Crisfield, Virginia received the larger share of the oyster grounds in Tangier and Pocomoke sounds. The arbitrators, however, did not find it in their purview to rule on the geographic limits of Pocomoke River. Other than embittering Marylanders, the board's ruling had little practical effect. Oystermen had scant respect for imaginary boundaries, and Marylanders still considered the grounds of Pocomoke Sound as much theirs as they were the Virginians'. To men on both sides of the line, taking oysters from Pocomoke Sound was a right worth fighting for.[26]

---

25 Wennersten, "The Almighty Oyster," p. 89; Wennersten, *The Chesapeake: An Environmental Biography* (Baltimore: Maryland Historical Society, 2001), pp. 126-127; Deposition of Severn Bradshaw, May 31, Deposition of Edward Tawes, June 4, 1872, *Final Report of the Virginia Commissioners on the Maryland and Virginia Boundary to the Governor of Virginia* (Richmond: R. F. Walker, Superintendent of Public Printing, 1874), pp. 194, 202-203; Wise to Walker, December 18, 1872, *Report and Accompanying Documents of the Virginia Commissioners Appointed to Ascertain the Boundary Line between Maryland Virginia* (Richmond: R. F. Walker, Superintendent of Public Printing, 1873), pp. 5-6; *Baltimore Sun*, December 31, 1873; Louis N. Whealton, "The Maryland and Virginia Boundary Controversy (1668-1894)," Ph.D dissertation, Johns Hopkins University, 1897, p. 41.

26 Wennersten, "The Almighty Oyster," p. 89; Wennersten, *The Chesapeake*, pp. 126-127; Marshall McDonald, "The Oyster Industry" in *Second Annual Report of the Bureau of Industrial Statistics of Maryland* (Annapolis: King Bros., State Printers, 1894), p. 245; Whealton, "The

The depredations of Maryland oystermen in Tangier and Pocomoke sounds were continual but usually clandestine. In the vast reaches of the sounds a discreet interloper in canoe or dredge boat might take oysters without attracting attention. Conflict erupted when fleets of vessels descended and lingered on the grounds for days. The intruders often came armed with rifles. So too the locals. In human interaction firearms are used more often to intimidate or dissuade than to injure. Most shots fired on the oyster grounds were meant as a warning. Wounds and fatalities occurred occasionally, but one side's superiority over the other usually was determined by relative volume of firepower. Under sail on open water, a dredge boat armed with half a dozen rifles or a small cannon had the advantage of any number of tongmen's canoes. Richard H. Edmonds described how in the winter of 1879-1880 about forty dredge boats descended on public rock reserved for tongers in the Rappahannock River: "The native tongmen, incensed at this depredation upon their beds, undertook to drive the dredgers away. In this, however, they signally failed. The dredgers, being well supplied with rifles, opened fire upon the tongmen. For several weeks the appearance of a tongman at any time, was certain to draw forth a volley from the dredgers." The fast, heavily armed steamers of the Virginia oyster navy were an adequate defense against invaders but they sometimes were absent in distant corners of the Chesapeake. Lack of policing led to vigilantism. Aggrieved tongmen commandeered schooners and, armed with rifles, defended their territory.[27]

For the Virginia General Assembly the oyster industry promised golden opportunities for taxation and job creation. Insuring these benefits, however, required that the legislature provide protection from over-harvesting and security from marauders. Sectional divisions and the pressure of rival constituencies hindered the legislature's ability to develop a coherent policy. Representatives from the upland portion of the state prioritized revenue gathering and were reluctant to expend funds on an oyster police force. They resented the article in the state

---

Maryland and Virginia Boundary Controversy," pp. 41-44.

27 Ingersoll, "The Oyster Industry," p. 158.

constitution prohibiting a license tax on tongmen. "The Oyster rocks are a *jus publicum*," Henry Wise told gubernatorial candidate James Lawson Kemper in 1873. "If in addition to their advantages of being near to them & having the monopoly of their use, the tide water people desire to have it free from an fiar [*sic*] and just tax, then they desire to have the public property without paying anything for its use & profits which are very large, and thereby to increase the taxes by so much on the people at large."[28]

Although exempt from a license tax, tidewater oystermen nonetheless paid what they regarded as an onerous levy on oysters harvested. They resented the tax (and Wise's perceived betrayal of their interests). Tidewater members of the General Assembly wanted to provide security for the oystermen who made up a large proportion of their electorate. They listened attentively to demands for police protection but struggled to balance the conflicting demands of their oystermen constituents. Tongmen would deny dredgermen access to the oyster rocks while both believed that planters, often wealthy and influential men, plotted to privatize the public grounds.

The legislature was further constrained by Virginia's large public debt. In the antebellum period Virginia had borrowed heavily to finance the construction of railroads and other internal improvements. The ruin inflicted upon the state during the Civil War destroyed her capacity to repay easily the debt, and in the unsettled post-war years unpaid interest accumulated until by 1870 the debt had reached $45,000,000. In 1871 lobbyists for the Northern and European financiers holding the bonds suborned the legislature into refunding the principal plus accrued interest. Some of the legislators who voted for the funding bill had been bribed while others believed the appeasement of outside capital necessary to Virginia's economic recovery. Harrison H. Riddleberger, editor of the Woodstock *Shenandoah Democrat*, grasped the inherent irony and pathos:

These bonds are held with very few exceptions, by the very

---

28 Wise to Kemper, August 18, 1873, in James A. Bear Jr., ed., "Henry A. Wise and the Campaign of 1873: Some Letters from the Papers of James Lawson Kemper," *Virginia Magazine of History and Biography* 62 (July, 1954), p. 337.

people who robbed us of one-third of our territory [West Virginia], robbed us of our property, burned our homes, devastated our lands, killed our fathers, sons and brothers, and by foreign capitalists, who aided and abetted this crusade upon all that was holy and sacred in the South – Wall Street brokers and stock gamblers who acquired them by payment of a few cents on the dollar. Still there are Virginians who would take the last pound of flesh from the carcass of their poor old mothers to give to these cormorants – strange indeed!

The refunded debt continued to grow despite the severe curtailment of government spending and the imposition of high taxes on real and personal property (but not on the property of large corporations).[29]

Penury, debt, and sectional and occupational rivalries resulted in constant legislative revision of the oyster laws. Political expediency rather than considered policy drove the legislation. By the early 1880s the oyster laws had become what Orris A. Browne condemned as "batches of red tape and nonsense." A Chincoteague man identified the chief beneficiaries of the legislation: "The oyster laws so twisted up and dovetailed are a conundrum to the attorneys of the Accomac bar, and no two lawyers can agree as to their interpretation except in the channel which leads to their own individual pocketbooks."[30]

By the fall of 1870 the *ad hoc* agreement creating the Lovett-Davidson boundary between Maryland and Virginia had effectively dissolved. Oystermen from Somerset County, Maryland, having laid waste to the oyster rock in the waters of their county began to drop down regularly into what Virginia claimed as its territory in Pocomoke and Tangier sounds. On September 27, Orris A. Browne, commanding the

---

29 Brooks Miles Barnes, "Triumph of the New South: Independent Movements in Post-Reconstruction Politics," Ph.D. dissertation, University of Virginia, 1991, pp. 42-48 (Riddleberger quoted on pp. 44-45).

30 *Norfolk Landmark*, January 23, 1874; Ingersoll, "The Oyster Industry," pp. 156-157; George Alfred Townsend, "The Chesapeake Peninsula," *Scribner's Monthly* 3 (March, 1872), p. 520; *Richmond Dispatch*, January 4, 1884 (quotes Browne); "Independent Candidate for the House of Delegates, Col. Frank Hollis" in Hollis to James D. Brady, September 27, 1883, Mahone Papers, Duke (quotation).

Virginia police steamer *Tredegar*, captured ten Maryland vessels, which he escorted to Onancock. Browne impounded the boats and turned their captains and crews over to Accomack County authorities for trial. After an exchange of correspondence between the governors of the two states, the Virginia legislature authorized Governor Walker to release the imprisoned oystermen and their vessels. "This act," Browne noted, "was prompted by the friendly relations that have always existed between the people of the two States, and a desire to maintain the good, neighborly feeling between them." "Friendly relations" and "neighborly feeling" abided in the sounds for six months. In March, 1871, Maryland encroachments began anew.[31]

In 1873 the General Assembly considered a general revision of the oyster laws with an eye toward increasing revenue. The oystermen smelled an upland rat. Peter J. Carter, black delegate from Northampton County who claimed practical experience as an oysterman, condemned the proceedings:

> We have petitioned, we have implored, we have begged our rights from this House; but our pleadings have been disregarded, and we have been overridden by force in whatever amendments have been proposed by those who understood the oyster question. Our rights have been trampled on, our very bread is taken from us by this onerous taxation. ... You have as much right to tax the birds in Shenandoah and Fauquier counties as you have to tax the oysters. ... This bill calls for the last pound of flesh, and the last drop of blood, and I tell you, sir, we won't stand it.

Carter's warning was disregarded. The bill became a law honored principally in its breach.[32]

---

31 Hunter Davidson, "The Maryland Oyster Trade," *Baltimore Sun*, January 8, 1870; John R. Wennersten, *The Oyster Wars of Chesapeake Bay* (Centreville, Md.: Tidewater Publishers, 1981), p. 49; *Richmond Dispatch*, January 8, 1870; *Baltimore Sun*, October 13, 1870; *Acts of the General Assembly of the State of Virginia, 1869-1870* (Richmond: James E. Goode, 1870), p. 518; Orris A. Browne, *Report to the Auditor of Public Accounts on the Oyster Beds of Virginia* (Richmond: Shepperson and Graves, 1872), pp. 1-2; Whealton, "The Maryland and Virginia Boundary Controversy," pp. 45-46.

32 *Acts and Joint Resolutions Passed by the General Assembly of the State of Virginia at its Session of*

In the spring of 1874 uplanders in the legislature, disappointed with the amount of revenue generated by the oyster tax and under pressure to pay the state debt, resolved to reduce expenditures. They passed acts eliminating state inspectorships and ordering the state auditor to sell the steamers of the oyster police force. They shifted the entire burden of collecting the tax and protecting the oyster grounds to part-time inspectors appointed by the county courts. The inspectors derived their income from a commission for taxes collected and a fee for every miscreant arrested. They had the authority to issue warrants and raise posses. In effect the oyster grounds were now protected not by a heavily-armed, professional police force in fast steamers but by lightly-armed amateurs in sailboats crewed by posses of either reluctant conscripts or potentially overzealous vigilantes.[33]

Cardinal Richelieu observed that "To make a law and not to see it in execution is to authorize what you have yourself forbidden." The Virginia oyster police having been defunded, Maryland pirates ran wild in Pocomoke Sound. On September 11 Accomack Oyster Inspector William P. Custis formed a posse and set out in two or more boats to apprehend encroaching Marylanders. In the ensuing melee, one of the posse discharged a shotgun at the boat of Marylander Thomas Riggin. Struck in the breast, neck, and face, Riggin collapsed against the washboard, his unattended boat drifting onto the Maryland shore where compatriots came to his aid. (Nearly two months later, Riggin died of his wounds.) Meanwhile, Custis and his party escorted four captured vessels into Onancock where they were impounded and their crews sent to jail at Drummondtown to await trial.[34]

1871-'72 (Richmond: R. F. Walker, Superintendent of Public Printing, 1872), p. 449; *Acts and Joint Resolutions Passed by the General Assembly of the State of Virginia at its Session of 1872-'73* (Richmond: R. F. Walker, Superintendent of Public Printing, 1872), pp. 310-327; *Richmond Dispatch*, January 23, 1873 (quotes Carter); *Proceedings of the Convention Called to Consider and Discuss the Oyster Question ... 1894*, p. 39.

33 Wilmington *News Journal*, February 25, 1882; *Acts and Joint Resolutions Passed by the General Assembly of the State of Virginia at its Session of 1874* (Richmond: R. F. Walker, Superintendent of Public Printing, 1874), pp. 238-249, 447.

34 C. V. Wedgwood, *Richelieu and the French Monarchy*, rev. ed. (New York: Collier Books, 1962), p. 142; *Correspondence of the Governor of Virginia with the Governor of Maryland and the*

Maryland Governor James Black Groome complained lustily to his Virginia counterpart James Lawson Kemper. Groome's complaints fell on receptive ears. Kemper, from Albemarle County in the Piedmont, apparently little understood the history of the boundary controversy or the value of the Pocomoke Sound oyster grounds to the Eastern Shore's economy. In light of the Riggin shooting, he might have dismissed the interests of Eastern Shore oystermen as those of homicidal thugs from an obscure corner of the commonwealth. Unlike governors Wise and Walker, Kemper accepted Maryland's argument that Pocomoke Sound was an extension of Pocomoke River. An incredulous Onancock editor believed that Kemper had put the cart before the horse: "Pocomoke river is no more Pocomoke sound than Delaware river Delaware bay; the river is simply tributary to the sound, which is really a part of the waters of the Chesapeake bay."[35]

Kemper and other administration officials pressured Accomack County authorities to free the prisoners and prosecute Riggin's assailants. Accomack Commonwealth's Attorney T. H. Bayly Browne (brother of Orris) refused to accept the contention that Pocomoke river and sound were one and the same: "You will find that there is a marked difference between Pocomoke *sound* and river. The sound has always been held exclusively Virginia water, while the river, under the old compact, between the two states has been held in common for the purposes 'of *fishing*.'" As for the shooting of Riggin, Browne declared that "Our next grand jury will thoroughly investigate the matter." The Accomack County Court tried and convicted three Maryland oystermen (two whites and one black), fined them $500, and confiscated their vessels. Having upheld the jurisdiction of the local court, Accomack authorities released the prisoners and remitted their fines because of inability to

---

Authorities of Accomac County, Va.; also, the Opinion of the Attorney-General of Virginia in Relation to Recent Difficulties in the Waters of the Pocomoke (Richmond: R. F. Walker, Superintendent of Public Printing, 1874), pp. 4-11, 24.

35 *Correspondence of the Governor of Virginia with the Governor of Maryland and the Authorities of Accomac County, Va.*, pp. 3-6, 14, 18; *EV* in *Baltimore Sun*, October 28, 1874 (quotation). For Kemper's tortured reasoning see *Journal of the House of Delegates of the State of Virginia, For the Session of 1875-5* (Richmond: R. F. Walker, Superintendent of Public Printing, 1875), pp. 10-12.

pay and allowed the owners to redeem their boats at public auction at an undervalued price. The grand jury took no action in regard to the shooting of Thomas Riggin.[36]

In the face of peninsular recalcitrance, authorities in both Annapolis and Richmond moved to assert Maryland's rights in Pocomoke Sound. Shortly after the incident of September 11, the commissioners of the Maryland fisheries dispatched to the sound armed vessels of the state police force. Bayly Browne's response to Maryland police boats in Virginia waters was a rebuke of the oyster policy of the Kemper administration:

> [T]he Maryland steamer has frequented our waters, drawn a line of limit to the oystering operations of our people, far different from the Walker-Bowie [Lovett-Davidson] line, and placed an armed sloop for its protection. ... The class of citizens excluded from our waters by this late action of the Maryland authorities is such as are industrious, honest men, depending entirely upon the catching of oysters for a support, and if they are not speedily relieved of the restriction imposed by armed forces of Maryland much suffering must follow. I will respectfully add that our oyster law is sadly deficient in many particulars, especially so in the protection it affords our citizens, and the early attention of the legislature is earnestly invoked by the oyster class for some permanent relief from the encroachments of non-residents. Maryland citizens rest secure in the enjoyment of these peculiar privileges behind the guns of a large steamer and seven sailing vessels, while Virginia oystermen have the private canoe of Captain Custis to aid them in the exercise of their rights and to prevent violations of our laws.

Somewhat chastened, Kemper successfully urged Governor Groome to remove the offending vessels.[37]

---

36 *Correspondence of the Governor of Virginia with the Governor of Maryland and the Authorities of Accomac County, Va.*, pp. 15-16, 20-26, 35-36 (Browne quoted on pp. 21-23); *Baltimore Sun*, November 4, 1874, January 25, 1876.

37 *Correspondence of the Governor of Virginia with the Governor of Maryland and the Authorities*

Having failed to coerce Eastern Shoremen into renouncing their insistence on Virginia's exclusive right to Pocomoke Sound, Kemper on December 2 recommended that, pending the settlement of the boundary controversy, the legislature pass "an act extending to the citizens of Maryland the privilege of taking oysters in all waters claimed by both states, and expressly including Pocomoke river and sound and bay." Tidewater legislators and oystermen, led by Louis C. H. Finney of Accomack County, strongly opposed Kemper's recommendation. Pocomoke River, Finney and his allies claimed, was neutral territory but Pocomoke Sound belonged to Virginia. They demanded a declaratory act that would "rigidly exclude" Marylanders from the sound. They also called for a reinstitution of the oyster police force. Eastern Shoremen again thwarted Kemper's wishes. Although the ensuing act of February 8, 1875, did not revive the oyster police, it denied Maryland any privileges in Pocomoke Sound. The law went into force without the governor's approval.[38]

Uplanders in the legislature had no interest in funding the oyster police. Revenue from the tax on oysters might be low, but the expense of enforcement was no longer increasing the size of the state debt. The declaratory act was well and good for stating a legal principle, but it had no practical effect on depredation in the oyster grounds. By the spring of 1877 lawlessness on Pocomoke Sound had surpassed the capacity of local officials to deal with it. Senator Finney prevailed on the legislature to issue a joint resolution authorizing the governor to provide to the authorities of Accomack County fifty rifles and 2,000 rounds of ammunition "to enable the citizens of said county more effectually to enforce the laws of this commonwealth for the protection of oysters, and for the general security of the citizens of said county."[39]

---

of Accomac County, Va., pp. 22 (quotes Browne), 27-29.

38 James L. Kemper, *Annual Message and Accompanying Documents of the Governor of Virginia to the General Assembly, December 2, 1874* (Richmond: R. F. Walker, Superintendent of Public Printing, 1874), pp. 11, 12-13; *Baltimore Sun*, December 9, 12, 16 ("rigidly exclude"), 23, 1874; *Acts and Joint Resolutions Passed by the General Assembly of the State of Virginia, at the Session of 1874-5* (Richmond: R. F. Walker, Superintendent of Public Printing, 1875), pp. 64-65.

39 *Baltimore Sun*, December 16, 1874, February 20, 1877; *Journal of the Senate of the Com-*

Since 1870 Virginians had been prohibited from dredging for oysters in all state waters except Pocomoke and Tangier sounds. Constant dredging had a deleterious effect on the oyster beds of the sounds. Baltimore journalist Richard H. Edmonds complained in 1881 of "the almost total exhaustion of the once famous beds of Tangier and Pocomoke sounds. Year after year these beds were dredged by hundreds of vessels, and even the summer months afforded them but little rest. The result of this has been plainly seen during the past few years, and more especially during the season of 1879-'80, in the great scarcity of oysters in these sounds." Dredgermen – both Virginians and interlopers from out of state – now began to encroach on waters elsewhere in the bay country. "[T]hese incursions," reported fisheries expert Marshall McDonald, "have become more frequent, and finally have culminated in an organized invasion of the forbidden grounds by armed vessels, in open, flagrant defiance of the laws of the State. ... As the dredging grounds become exhausted these incursions will become more frequent, and the destruction of the tonging interest is imminent, unless the State adopts and enforces a stringent measure of police to repress this organized piracy." In addition to an oyster police force, McDonald also recommended as a conservation measure an act temporarily prohibiting dredging in all waters of the commonwealth.[40]

On March 6, 1881, the General Assembly banned the dredging of oysters everywhere in the commonwealth including Pocomoke and Tangier sounds. The act condemned violators to one to three years in prison and their vessels to sale at public auction. Proceeds from the sale

---

monwealth of Virginia, 1876-1877 (Richmond: R. F. Walker, Superintendent of Public Printing, 1876), pp. 196, 360; *Acts and Joint Resolutions Passed by the General Assembly of the State of Virginia at its Session of 1876-77* (Richmond: R. F. Walker, Superintendent of Public Printing, 1877), p. 243.

40 *Acts of the General Assembly of the State of Virginia, 1869-1870*, pp. 448-451; Ingersoll, "The Oyster Industry,", p. 159 (quotes Edmonds); Francis Winslow, "Deterioration of American Oyster-Beds," *Popular Science Monthly* XX (November, 1881), p. 38, (December, 1881), p. 153; Winslow, "Report on the Oyster Beds," p. 42; *Baltimore Sun*, January 14, 1882; Marshall McDonald, *Report upon the Fisheries and Oyster Industries of Tidewater Virginia, with Recommendations of Such Legislation as is Necessary to Regulate the Same and Derive a Revenue from Them* (Richmond: R. F. Walker, Superintendent of Public Printing, 1880), pp. 15-16; *Richmond Dispatch*, February 13, 1884.

were to be split between the boat's captor and the state. The act contained no provision for an oyster police force. McDonald blamed the legislature's reluctance to fund a police force on the constitutional article excusing tongmen from the payment of a license fee: "It has been a serious blow to the tonging interest that such a provision was ever embodied in the constitution. It was not to be expected that those portions of the State not directly interested would submit to be taxed to protect, by efficient police, an industry that gave back to the State nothing in the shape of taxes; consequently the tongmen have been left to a ruinous competition with the products of unlicensed, untaxed and unrestrained dredging."[41]

Before the passage of the act, an Accomack man asserted his region's point of view: "The people of Tidewater ought to be allowed to appropriate to their use the gifts of nature that are to be found in our waters. Instead of that they are annoyed by many laws, too many, and most of them daily violated; but now and then some poor unfortunate is hauled up, fined, and imprisoned, where ninety-nine out of one hundred go unpunished." After the act had been in force for a year, he described its ironic effect: "The dredged oysters have gone to enrich the Maryland dredgers. The law which prohibits dredging for oysters in Virginia waters has been in force, so far as our people are concerned, because they are within Jurisdiction of our courts. The Maryland dredgers, however, work in Tangier and Pocomoke sounds because there is no force to keep them out."[42]

The dredging law exposed class and professional contention between Eastern Shore oystermen. Tongmen, most of whom were relatively poor men living on the upper Accomack bayside near the shores of Pocomoke Sound, believed that unrestricted dredging would ruin their livelihoods by stripping bare the oyster rocks. Dredgeboat owners and skippers, who lived on bayside creeks to the south of the sound and were relatively more well-to-do than the tongmen, complained that the new law threatened their ability to support their families, meet the mortgage

---

[41] *Acts and Joint Resolutions Passed by the General Assembly of the State of Virginia during the Session of 1879-80* (Richmond: R. F. Walker, Superintendent of Public Printing, 1880), pp. 197-198; McDonald, *Report upon the Fisheries and Oyster Industries of Tidewater Virginia*, p. 15.

[42] *Richmond Dispatch*, February 2, 1880, February 2, 1881.

and maintenance payments on their boats, and pay their crews. Indeed, the law now made the practice of their profession a criminal act. In early 1882 the dredgermen forwarded to the legislature several petitions praying for repeal of the law. The tongmen of the upper bayside countered with a petition containing 800 signatures asking not for repeal but for guard boats to protect the oyster grounds.[43]

Driven by necessity, Eastern Shore dredgermen set sail in contempt of what they regarded as a discriminatory and unenforceable law. In February, 1882, Governor William E. Cameron responded to the dredgermen's effrontery and to the pleas of outraged tongmen by leading a punitive expedition composed of two hired steamboats outfitted with cannon and a detachment of armed militia. Off the mouth of the Rappahannock River, Cameron and party pursued and captured five schooners and two sloops, all of which were manned by Eastern Shoremen. Tried and convicted in Mathews County Court, forty-six skippers and crewmen were sentenced to a year in the penitentiary and their vessels were condemned and sold at auction. Shortly after the prisoners' incarceration, Cameron pardoned the crewmen and commuted the sentences of the skippers. All the auctioned vessels were purchased by their owners. In November, the Virginia Supreme Court of Appeals, citing trial error, ordered the reimbursement to the owners of the purchase price.[44]

Cameron's raid of 1882 and a subsequent, farcical one of 1883 were political theater. The governor's expeditions did nothing to dissuade determined dredgermen. In a message to the General Assembly in December, 1883, Cameron admitted that he had pardoned the convicted oystermen "because the law theretofore had been a dead letter." Drummondtown editor John W. Edmonds also considered the law a "dead letter." He identified the immediate cause of the chaos on the Chesapeake: "With our water thrown open, as it were, to the world, and everyone reaping

---

43 *PE*, January 26, 1882. See also George Toy, Eastville, to William Mahone, February 21, 1882, Mahone Papers, Duke.

44 For Governor Cameron's expeditions of 1882 and 1883 see James Tice Moore, "Gunfire on the Chesapeake: Governor Cameron and the Oyster Pirates, 1882-1885," *Virginia Magazine of History and Biography* 90 (July, 1882), pp. 367-377.

the benefits which belong to our citizens, is there not some excuse for them if they have dredged in forbidden waters even, which for want of protection has become the common property of all mankind?"[45]

While the governor chased Eastern Shore dredgers, pirates from Maryland and elsewhere trespassed in Pocomoke Sound. The marauding reached an apogee in the fall and winter of 1883-1884. The Saxis Island correspondent of the *Peninsula Enterprise* reported in November that "Byrd's Rock in Pocomoke Sound is being daily dredged by citizens of Maryland, New Jersey, and elsewhere. The oyster beds in this section have been sadly depredated upon by the dredgers, and our tongers do not get as handsome returns for their labor as they did earlier in the season." The *Baltimore Sun* reported that the dredgermen were driven to desperation by a widespread scarcity of oysters and that Virginia boats were more troublesome than those of Maryland.[46]

The tongers, backed by Accomack County authorities, resolved to eject the dredgermen. On December 4, the county court appointed George W. Hinman, a fifty-three-years-old oysterman from Marsh Market on Messongo Creek, inspector of oysters for the district embracing Pocomoke Sound. Hinman was to be paid not only from the collection of official fees but also from a subscription raised among the tongmen. The day following his appointment, Hinman manned three canoes and a sloop with a posse of twenty-five tongers armed with rifles previously supplied by the commonwealth. Hinman's flotilla sailed into the sound where it attacked a fleet of sixteen dredge boats. Most of the boats immediately fled but five remained to exchange fire with Hinman's party. Having perhaps sustained casualties, three of the dredge boats left the fight, but two schooners, one out of Baltimore and the other from Tangier Island, were captured and their crews imprisoned.[47]

The following month Hinman encountered a check when his posse

---

45 *Journal of the House of Delegates of the State of Virginia For the Session of 1883-4* (Richmond: R. V. Deer, Superintendent of Public Printing, 1883), doc. 4 (quotes Cameron); *PE*, March 16, 1882 (quotes Edmonds).

46 *PE*, November 15, 29 (quotation), 1883; *Baltimore Sun*, December 5, 1883, April 12, 1884.

47 Accomack County Court Order Book, 1881-1883, p. 682; *Baltimore Sun*, December 7, 8, 12, 1883; *Richmond Dispatch*, December 9, 1883; *Alexandria Gazette*, December 12, 1883.

was out-gunned by an organized fleet of dredge boats. He regained the upper hand a few days later by mounting a six-pound cannon on his canoe. "The boom of Inspector Hinman's cannon is now heard echoing along the flats and fens of Pocomoke," rejoiced a Mappsville man, "warning the wily denuder of the rocks that the iron avenger is on his track." In the meantime, the Virginia General Assembly granted Hinman a salary of $150 per month. The legislators justified the expenditure by stating that "the citizens of Accomack county have been, and are now at great expense protecting the oyster interests of their locality, and repelling invasions of depredations from citizens of other states in violation of the oyster laws of the state of Virginia, and destructive of their rights as citizens."[48]

By the early 1880s the continued existence of the Chesapeake Bay oyster industry seemed in doubt. Unrestricted dredging had impoverished the oyster beds and the sale of seed oysters to the North had crippled the prospects of their recovery. Richard H. Edmonds of Baltimore noted in 1882 that "The dredgers that come to this city are complaining very much of the difficulty that they experience in catching a load of oysters, and of the length of time necessary to do it. ... The beds have been scraped to such an extent that but very few oysters are left on them, and the dredgers say that they hardly know where to look for them." In 1884 Governor Cameron told the General Assembly that "The merchantable oysters for sale to be eaten would amount to nothing, but the dredges scrape the rocks, take off the seed, and it is only a question of a few years when Virginia shall have to buy back from other states the wealth that had been her own. Already most of the natural rocks on the Eastern Shore have been denuded. It is only a question of time, with seventy or eighty vessels constantly poaching on our preserves, when the Western Shore will be naked of natural products." Having closely studied the oysters grounds of Pocomoke and Tangier sounds, scientist Francis Winslow concluded that the condition of the industry was "bad" and its prospects "worse."[49]

---

48 *PE*, January 26, February 2, 9, March 8, 1884; *Baltimore Sun*, January 30, 1884; *Acts and Joint Resolutions Passed by the General Assembly of the State of Virginia During the Session of 1883-84* (Richmond: R. V. Deer, Superintendent of Public Printing, 1884), p. 64.

49 *Alexandria Gazette*, January 17, 1884; *PE*, November 23, 1882; *Baltimore Sun*, January 16 (quotes Edmonds), 1882, February 19, 1884; *Journal of the Senate of the Commonwealth of*

Their livelihoods endangered, Eastern Shore tongmen expressed through their representatives in the legislature a willingness to dispense with the clause in the state constitution exempting them from payment of a license fee. "This section of the State has contributed to the internal improvements, for which they have reaped no benefit," an Accomack man reminded the *Richmond Dispatch*. "As a matter of justice Tidewater is entitled to something in return; and in asking to have the oyster-beds protected she is not doing so to be an expense to the State. We are willing to pay tax sufficient to cover the protection." John W. Edmonds of the *Peninsula Enterprise* asserted that "No member of the legislature surely can longer doubt that protection is necessary when a class of her citizens ask, as the tongmen do, for a tax to be imposed upon them to defray the expenses incurred thereby. Will they give it? Have they the right to refuse to furnish the means of protecting, not only the property but the lives of the citizens[?] Without it, it has been demonstrated often since the passage of the dredging law, that both were in peril."[50]

The Virginia General Assembly responded to the devastation on the oyster grounds by passing on March 4 "An Act for the preservation of Oysters, and to obtain revenue for the privilege of taking them within the waters of the commonwealth." The act echoed recommendations by leading figures concerned with the oyster industry including Governor William E. Cameron, Orris A. Browne, Marshall McDonald, Francis Winslow, and Hampton dealer W. N. Armstrong. It sought to solve immediate problems while looking toward the future growth of the industry. To stimulate the planting of oysters, the legislation more closely defined the privileges and protections afforded planters. To raise revenue, it required tongmen to register with local inspectors and to pay either a tax on their estimated harvest or a fee of fifty cents every three months. It thus evaded the constitutional prohibition against a direct

---

Virginia, 1883-1884 (Richmond: R. V. Deer, Superintendent of Public Printing, 1884), p. 278 (quotes Cameron); Winslow, "Report on the Oyster Beds," p. 40; Winslow, "Deterioration of American Oyster-Beds," p. 32; Winslow, "Present Condition and Future Prospects of the Oyster Industry," p. 148 (quotation).

50 *PE*, November 29, December 13 (quotes Edmonds), 1883, January 12, 1884; *Richmond Dispatch*, December 9, 1883; *Baltimore Sun*, December 10, 1883.

license tax on tongmen. The recent repudiation of a portion of the state debt also must have eased the fiscal qualms of upland legislators. To secure the oyster grounds, the act created a Board on the Chesapeake and its Tributaries, which was authorized to spend $30,000 to create a permanent naval police force. It also provided that, after January 1, 1885 (by which time the oyster police should be on station), the board might permit the dredging of oysters in Chesapeake Bay except in designated areas including Pocomoke and Tangier sounds. Although "An Act for the preservation of Oysters" was an improvement on earlier legislation, it failed to define clearly the powers of the Board on the Chesapeake and its Tributaries, an omission that in the future would hinder the board's ability to respond to changing circumstances on the oyster grounds. At the time, however, the prospect of an oyster police force in the waters of the sounds gave encouragement to bayside tongmen.[51]

On the Seaside – The coming in 1876 of the Maryland, Delaware and Virginia Railroad to Franklin City accelerated the growth of an already dynamic oyster industry in Chincoteague Bay. The number of oysters planted in the Virginia portion of the bay jumped from 36,000 bushels to 300,000 in 1884. Much of the bay became an immense planting ground staked off in plats indicating individual ownership. Every spring and fall, Chincoteague planters imported seed oysters from the James River and spread them in the bay. In two or three years, tongmen in their employ harvested the oysters, which were shipped to Philadelphia and New York. During the winter of 1879-1880, shipments from Chincoteague Bay totaled 318,113 bushels, 166,113 going by rail and 152,000 by sail. Fat and salty, the best Chincoteague oysters brought premium prices in urban saloons and restaurants. "The cultivation of these oysters is very profitable," wrote a Chincoteague correspondent to

---

51 *Acts and Joint Resolutions Passed by the General Assembly of the State of Virginia During the Session of 1883-84*, pp. 324-339; Moore "Gunfire on the Chesapeake," pp. 375-376. For Cameron's recommendations see *Journal of the Senate of the Commonwealth of Virginia, 1883-1884*, pp. 278-279, and *Baltimore Sun*, February 6, 1884; for Browne's see *Baltimore Sun*, January 7, 1884; for McDonald's see *Report upon the Fisheries and Oyster Industries of Tidewater Virginia*, p. 16; for Winslow's see "Deterioration of American Oyster-Beds," pp. 154-155; and for Armstrong's see *Notes on the Oyster Industries of Virginia* (Hampton: Author, 1879), pp. 10-11.

the *Richmond Dispatch*, "generally yielding a profit of from 200 to 300 per cent. on the outlay, and the business last year reached somewhere in the neighborhood of $300,000 from this point."⁵²

The oyster industry also boomed on the seaside below Chincoteague Bay. Buy boats from New Jersey descended on the Broadwater to purchase seed oysters to replenish the depleted grounds adjacent New York City. In 1875 Alexander Hunter asserted that "There are four hundred oystermen in and around Cobb's [Island], in the winter time, who gain their living by gathering oysters; they do not haul seines, nor yet use oyster tongs, but simply go to the flats, on low tide, and gather them by the barrel full and boat load; the supply, they say, is inexhaustible; they dispose of them to the vessels at forty cents per bushel, and all of the oysters are shipped to New York." So extensive was the trade in seed oysters, a Chincoteague man worried that "if this state of things continues the entire destruction of our [public] oyster rocks is only a question of time."⁵³

Meanwhile, the planting of oysters by private individuals expanded extensively along the seaside. Some planters, particularly those living on the bays near Chincoteague, used seed from Chesapeake Bay. Others employed the tightly bunched local seed, which did well if separated and spread near the heads of creeks. A visitor to Orris A. Browne's home on Folly Creek noted that "An elegant terraced lawn led down to the water side and close by his wharf was a large bed of the most delicious oysters." Planters such as Browne sold their oysters to local dealers or to those in Norfolk or the North.⁵⁴

---

52 Survey of Chincoteague Bay, United States, House of Representatives, 48th Congress, 2nd Session, Ex. Doc. 107 (1885), p. 7; "Chincoteague Island," Elkton (Md.) *Cecil Whig*, September 9, 1876; Ingersoll "The Oyster Industry," p. 183; "Oysters of the James"; "The Teagues of Accomack"; "Chincoteague Island, Va.," *Baltimore Sun*, August 28, 1876; "The Lenten Oyster"; "The Eastern Shore," *Richmond Dispatch*, September 2, 1881.

53 Hunter, Cobb's Island, to editor, August 2, *Alexandria Gazette*, August 7, 1875 (quotation); Hunter, "Cobb's Island in Summer," *Forest and Stream* VII (August 31, 1876), p. 49; Hunter, "Birds at Cobb's Island, *Ibid.* XVIII (March 23, 1882), p. 146; *PE*, May 4, 1882, December 20, 1883 (quotation), March 1, April 26, 1884.

54 *Richmond Dispatch*, April 16, 1874; *Baltimore Sun*, April 25, 1877; *PE*, April 13, 1882, January 12, 1884; *Richmond Enquirer*, March 5, 1858; "The Future State" (quotation); *Norfolk*

The planting of oysters was costly. Grounds must be surveyed and registered with inspectors. Seed must be purchased, carried to the grounds, planted, and spread periodically to encourage growth. At maturity, the oysters must be harvested and transported to market. A poor man possessed of assiduity and acumen and blessed with luck might rise in the industry, but the odds favored the man with means to lease grounds, buy equipment, and employ labor. At the time of his death in 1883 William H. Harmon of Greenbackville owned 13,000 bushels of planted oysters, two bateau, two monitors [barges], four scows, two floats, and a half share in an oyster house and platform. He also owned seven pair of oyster tongs, shovels, measures, forks, and fifty or more barrels. In the 1870s and early 1880s a working capital of $500 to $1,000 seemed the necessary initial investment for the prospective planter. Access to money enabled risk-taking. The idea of planting in the tumultuous waters and sandy bottom of Tom's Cove at the southern end of Assateague Island was viewed as "a wildcat scheme, too ridiculous to be entertained." However, "The handsome profits realized from oysters planted at the place ... has changed the views ... of those who ridiculed this departure from the beaten path of their fathers, and the vacant grounds so long regarded as worthless, for oyster planting purposes, are likely to be monopolized [by planters] at no distant day."[55]

The large planters controlled hundreds of acres of ground and planted thousands of bushels of oysters. They often marketed the catch of small planters as well as their own. Some dealt in raw stock; others in processed. Harmon and his partner John F. Powell operated a shucking house at Greenbackville, John W. Ketcham a cannery at Brighton near Capeville, and Phillips and Bradford a pickling plant at Powellton. Ketcham's establishment was small. Alexander Hunter described it as "a little grocery and one-horse oyster and clam steamer built on piles in the bay." The planter-dealers sold directly to urban dealers, restaurants, and saloons. Small planters might bypass the local dealers by placing

---

Landmark, February 17, 1880.

55 *Baltimore Sun*, April 18, 1870; "Oysters of the James"; *PE*, March 1 (quotation), June 21, 1883; Mariner, *Once Upon an Island*, p. 43.

their oysters with commission merchants or by selling direct to city middlemen.[56]

Oyster planting having come to dominate Chincoteague Bay, the tongmen who comprised the great majority of bay oystermen found themselves increasingly under the planters' sway. Whereas most tongmen on the bayside were free agents working the public rocks of Tangier and Pocomoke sounds, most Chincoteague Bay tongmen were cash laborers working private grounds. On Chincoteague Bay, the romantic idea of the independent oysterman had become a chimera. Several of the large Chincoteague planters were Northerners. A newspaperman reporting from Chincoteague Island in 1876 maintained that "The business push and enterprise that now characterizes the place are chiefly supplied by the new comers." In 1884 tongers resolved that the twelve cents per bushel that the planters paid them for harvesting their crops was insufficient. The laborers downed tongs and rakes and struck for an increase of three cents per bushel. The planters acceded to their demands. Northern "push and enterprise" had brought in its wake adversarial labor relations along the cash nexus.[57]

Finfishing – Post-Civil War urban growth, expansion of steamboat and railroad service, and change in consumer dietary preference from salted to fresh fish brought Eastern Shore fishermen deeper into the national market. On seaside and bayside, Eastern Shoremen fished commercially. Louisiana traveler Fannie B. West noticed older black men handline fishing in Cherrystone Inlet. Robert Marshall of Saxis Island used gill nets to catch perch and rock fish. "Seine hauling with seventy-five fathom seines is a profitable business below Capeville," noted the editor of the Onancock *Eastern Virginian*. "They run the meshes straight out from the shore and let the tide sweep it in shore bringing the fish with it." At

---

56 *PE*, January 19, 1882, June 21, 1883, February 9, March 15, July 6, 1884; Chataigne, ed., *Virginia Business Directory and Gazetteer, 1880-1881*, p. 75; Hunter, "Bay Bird Shooting on the Chesapeake," *Forest and Stream* XX (June 7, 1883), p. 365; *Middletown (Del.) Transcript*, January 20, 1877.

57 Chincoteague Island, Va." (quotation); *PE*, February 9, 1884; Wilmington *Morning News*, February 11, 1884.

Pickett's Hole on the bayside above Cape Charles, a traveler witnessed large hauls of drum, hogfish, trout, and other species. Most Eastern Shore fishermen marketed their catch locally, but the larger operators packed their fish on ice and sent them by sail and steam to Baltimore, Washington, Norfolk, Philadelphia, and New York. Large shipments also went by rail to Philadelphia via Crisfield.[58]

Seine haulers, like most other watermen, demonstrated no great respect for the law. At Cape Charles in the summer of 1874 a Richmond man encountered "a 'rakish-looking schooner' ... a poacher, who, in spite of the laws to the contrary, has been hauling seine out of season, and infringing the rights of the people inhabiting the point. ...[H]er hold was apparently full of excellent fish, caught in a day and a half in these teeming waters." The Virginia legislature responded to such outrages in typical fashion. It set penalties for out-of-season seine hauling but left the law's enforcement to the initiative of paid informants. "[T]o secure conviction some one must first become an informer, and this is enough to prevent almost any honest man from interfering," sighed a correspondent of *Forest and Stream*. "Of course it is not to be supposed that the various Commonwealth's attorneys are to become spies and detectives; consequently the law is of no effect."[59]

More controversial than the seines were the pound-nets that infested the waters of the Eastern Shore bayside. A pound-net was constructed of wooden stakes supporting a tar-coated mesh. A fence leading from the shore directed fish into an opening at the top of a heart-shaped, false pound and thence through an opening at the point of the heart into a larger, square pound. Altogether, the pound-net extended for two or three hundred yards. The bewildered fish having imprisoned themselves in the pound, the fishermen untied the net, raised it from the bottom,

---

58 Mark T. Taylor, "Seiners and Tongers: North Carolina Fisheries in the Old and New South," *North Carolina Historical Review* LXIX (January, 1992), p. 12; Ward, "Red Letter Days, No. III: Summering at Old Point Comfort," New Orleans *Times-Picayune*, July 21, 1878; *PE*, March 29, 1883, March 15, April 12, October 4, 1884; *EV*, October 6, 1876; Washington *National Republican*, November 1, 1879; "My Own Trip"; *Baltimore Sun*, September 10, 1881, July 20, 1882; *Annual Report of the Commissioner of Fisheries, 1882* (Richmond: R. F. Walker, Superintendent of Printing, 1882), p. 13.

59 "My Own Trip"; *Forest and Stream* V (August, 1875), p. 4.

and, keeping the cornered fish before them, dipped them into their canoes. Pound-net fishermen often made large catches of 2,000 or more fish. They kept the marketable ones but cast the small or otherwise undesirable on the shore to rot.[60]

So efficient were the pound-nets and so wasteful their fishermen that the future of the Eastern Shore fisheries seemed in danger. Eastern Shoremen petitioned the legislature for relief from the menace, and their delegates, black Republican and white Democrats, united in championing their cause. Democrat Oswald B. Finney of Accomack told the House of Delegates that "one of the great nets set at the mouth of a creek will catch all the fish going in and out." Finney's Accomack colleague and fellow Democrat John Neely contended that "many of the kinds of fish ... were almost extinct, and if any other reason than the use of pound-nets had been assigned he had not heard it. ... [H]undreds of people are dependent upon [the fisheries] for their living and the support of their families. The pound-nets have almost destroyed their small fisheries." Republican Peter J. Carter of Northampton informed the delegates that "Prior to the war there were no pound-nets in Virginia waters. He was not opposed to all the Yankees have done since the war, but he was opposed to the mode of fishing brought here by them, and they did not come until Northern Legislatures had driven them off." Finney echoed Carter: "The pound-nets are Yankee contrivances which have destroyed the fish in the North, and are now brought down here to rob us." He asserted that the pound-nets were "great monopolies" while Carter argued that they were owned nominally by Virginians but the profits went to non-residents. Finney agreed that it was "a notorious fact" that the pound-nets belonged to non-residents who were "taking away the substance of his people."[61]

---

60 "The Chesapeake Shore"; *Annual Report of the Fish Commissioner of the State of Virginia for the Year 1877* (Richmond: R. F. Walker, Superintendent of Public Printing, 1877), p. 50; *Denton (Md.) Journal*, May 25, 1877; *Richmond Dispatch*, January 19, 26, 1878.

61 *Journal of the Senate of the Commonwealth of Virginia, 1876-1877*, pp. 131-132, 140. For synopses of the speeches of Carter, Finney, and Neely see *Annual Report of the Fish Commissioner of the State of Virginia for the Year 1877*, pp. 49-51, and *Richmond Dispatch*, January 19, 26, 1878.

The strong and united opposition to pound-nets illuminates the importance of finfishing to Eastern Shoremen, black and white, waterman and landsman. It also indicates that, although Eastern Shoremen generally welcomed Northern investment, they were not so bemused as to accept it in its most brazenly exploitative and destructive forms.

The Virginia legislature refrained from banning pound-nets, but in 1877 it prohibited the catching of fish by pound-net within two miles of the mouths of rivers or creeks. Pound-net fishermen adjusted to the new dispensation. In 1884 twenty-two pound-nets stood off the Eastern Shore bayside – four near Tangier Island, nine from Pungoteague Creek southward to Cherrystone Inlet, and nine from Cherrystone to Cape Charles. A correspondent informed the *Peninsula Enterprise* that "all the good runs are occupied. ... There is a very large capital invested in the business, and it gives employment to a large number of people." Now local men were among the investors, including Hallett and Warren near Cape Charles, Dr. John T. Wilkins at Hungars Wharf, Roberts, Wilkins and Company at Taylor's Wharf on Mattawaman Creek, and Carmine and West on Occohannock Creek. The lower bayside was a prime mackerel fishery. The *Eastern Virginian* reported in 1884 that "One hundred and thirty barrels of fine bay mackerel were shipped from Hungars and Occohannock creek[s] last Tuesday by the steamer *Eastern Shore* to Baltimore." The pound-nets also captured other marketable fish in abundance including drum, trout, and bluefish.[62]

Terrapin – In the spring Eastern Shore watermen drag-netted terrapin from deep tidal pools; after a hard frost they dug them from the mud in which the animals hibernated. Terrapin found a ready market locally and in Baltimore, Philadelphia, and New York. In early November, 1878, a sailboat left Onancock for Baltimore with thirteen barrels of terrapin, the first of the fall season. A New Yorker found the palates

---

62 *Acts and Joint Resolutions Passed by the General Assembly of the State of Virginia at its Session of 1876-77*, p. 330; *Annual Report of the Commissioner of Fisheries, 1882*, p. 12; *Report of the Commissioner of Fisheries of the State of Virginia for the Years 1884 and 1885* (Richmond: Rush U. Derr, Superintendent of Public Printing, 1885), p. 15; *Baltimore Sun*, August 25, 1884; *PE*, May 31, 1884; Wilmington *Morning News*, August 14, 1883; *PE*, May 31, 1884; *EV*, August 2, 1884.

of Baltimoreans and Philadelphians so educated they could "determine by its flavor whether it was raised in Maryland, Virginia, Georgia, or South Carolina." He added that "In New York we scarcely appreciate the distinction ... but we know that in our markets the Long Island and Chesapeake terrapins command much higher prices than their Southern congeners." Demand for Eastern Shore terrapin was so great that the species seemed threatened with local extinction. In 1880 the Virginia General Assembly decreed a closed season in Accomack and Northampton counties for terrapin and their eggs from May through October. A few years later, John W. Edmonds suggested that "an effort be made toward the propagation of the salt-water or diamond back terrapin. These are growing scarcer year by year. On the Jersey coast, where, forty years ago, they were very numerous, now one is seldom seen. At the present rate of extermination, the same will soon be said of our coast."[63]

Clamming – Watermen waded the tidal flats of bayside and seaside in search of buried clams. They indentified the tell-tale sign made in the sand by the clams and then gathered them with rakes. An Onancock man used a dog to help find clams. The harvests were abundant. During the summer of 1882 a dealer at Willis's Wharf on the Northampton seaside bought 120,000 clams. Clammers also sold their catch in the cities. In 1884 a group of young men from Muddy Creek on the upper Accomack bayside clammed at the Virginia capes before proceeding with their cargo to Baltimore.[64]

Increasingly, clammers on the seaside came into conflict with planters who expropriated the flats as oyster grounds. Throughout 1883 "hostilities" between clammers and planters disrupted business

---

[63] Howard Pyle, "A Peninsular Canaan," *Harper's New Monthly Magazine* 58 (May, 1879), p. 809; Wilson, "On the Eastern Shore," p. 239; *PE*, February 9, May 17 (quotes Edmonds), 1884; *EV*, November 9, 1878; "Terrapins," *Forest and Stream* III (December 10, 1874), p. 280 (first quotation); *Acts and Joint Resolutions Passed by the General Assembly of the State of Virginia during the Session of 1879-80*, p. 239.

[64] Curtis J. Badger, *A Culinary History of Delmarva: From the Bay to the Sea* (Charleston, S.C.: American Palate, 2021), p. 31; Snow Hill (Md.) *Democratic Messenger*, September 3, 1881; *PE*, December 7, 1882, March 29, 1883, April 26, July 26, 1884.

at Greenbackville. Rising post-war profits had made riparian owners and lessees less tolerant of intruders on their premises. A decade earlier a Richmond man had visited Fisherman's Island near Cape Charles in the company of its aging owner William H. Parker. Captain Parker, declared an Onancock editor, was "a rare specimen of the every-day, hospitable, strong-minded, don't-care-a-bullet, old fashioned, Virginia gentleman." Near the island the Richmond visitor noticed "A large body of fishermen ... gathering clams ... free of charge. Fifty dollars' worth of clams per day are borne off by these trespassers. That is old Virginia over. The Captain is genuine. He swore he wouldn't stand it, and yet he has stood it for years. When he comes down upon these fellows we shall believe that he is 'done standing it.'" By the 1880s riparian owners were much more likely to "come down" on alleged trespassers than those of Parker's generation. On the seaside, the transformation of the tidal commons to private property fostered class conflict.[65]

Crabbing – In the immediate post-Civil War years crabs were taken in Eastern Shore waters for local consumption only. Bayside and seaside marshes and guts offered an ideal habitat for crabs, but lacking were swift transportation that could reliably get them to distant markets before spoiling. Also, many potential urban consumers were put off by the crab's unsavory reputation as a bottom feeder. The coming of the railroad to Crisfield and Franklin City and expanded steamboat service along the peninsula helped solve the transportation problem. In 1873 or 1874 the crab industry began with shipments by rail from Crisfield to Philadelphia. An advertising campaign and the recommendations of satisfied users gradually overcame consumer reservations.[66]

Eastern Shore crabbing centered on the creeks and marshes of the

---

[65] *PE*, July 5 ("hostilities"), November 8, 1883; "My Own Trip" (second quotation); *EV*, October 6, 1876 (on Parker).

[66] L. Eugene Cronin, "Chesapeake Fisheries and Resource Stress in the 19th Century," *Journal of the Washington Academy of Sciences* 76 (September, 1986), p. 195; E. P. Churchill Jr., *Crab Industry of Chesapeake Bay*, Appendix IV to the Report of the U. S. Commissioner of Fisheries for 1918, Bureau of Fisheries Document No. 868 (Washington: Government Printing Office, 1919), pp. 5, 9; Wilmington *Morning News*, July 7, 1877.

upper bayside. During the warm months, local watermen caught soft crabs, which they sold at Crisfield. As crabs grow, they periodically retreat to shallow waters where they cast off their hard exterior skeletons. There they wait defenseless until a new skeleton forms. Men and boys ran their flat-bottomed skiffs into the shallows where they took the soft crabs with hand nets and small, toothless, iron scrapes with cotton-mesh receiving bags. Crabbers spent much of their time wading through marsh mud. A crabber told journalist Robert Wilson that "I wear wet breeches from Monday morning till Saturday night." Their daily take varied from a few crabs to a hundred or more. The size of the crabs was of no consideration. Early in the season, they caught young crabs the size of a thumbnail, which they packed ten dozen to a cigar box. "A dozen would hardly make a good mouthful," a reporter remarked, "but the epicures North must have the first, and we are very willing to supply their cravings."[67]

As demand grew, dealers sought a more efficient way of harvesting soft crabs than "mud-flapping." They tried impounding hard crabs in fenced areas near the shoreline to await their moulting. The experiment failed due to excessive labor expenditure and high crab mortality. The dealers eventually settled on confining hard crabs in wooden floats, a practice that in modified form continues to this day. "Nurseries for crabs about to shed their jackets and become soft have multiplied wonderfully," the *Baltimore Sun* reported in 1881. Dealers also further combated the problem of spoilage during transportation by shipping soft crabs in stackable trays packed on ice. The number of soft crabs shipped from Crisfield grew from 1,000 dozen weekly in 1880 to 5,000 to 8,000 dozen at mid-decade. "Crabbing is the most remunerative of all the bay fishing," declared the *Sun*.[68]

67 William W. Warner, *Beautiful Swimmers: Watermen, Crabs and the Chesapeake Bay* (Boston: Little, Brown and Company, 1976), p. 21; "The Crab and His Curious Haunts: Some Interesting Inside History of This Great Virginia Industry," Richmond *Times-Dispatch* in Irvington *Virginia Citizen*, October 4, 1907 (second quotation); Churchill, *Crab Industry of Chesapeake Bay*, p. 5; "Spearing Fish in Maryland Waters," Forest and Stream XVI (May 12, 1881), p. 289; Wilson, "On the Eastern Shore," p. 238; "Washington's Oyster Trade," Washington *Evening Star*, January 26, 1889.

68 Warner, *Beautiful Swimmers*, pp. 79-80; Churchill, *Crab Industry of Chesapeake Bay*, pp.

The soft crab industry on the Eastern Shore also extended along the route of the Eastern Shore Steamboat Company on the bayside and to the waters around the railhead at Franklin City on the seaside. "J" of Taylor's Wharf told the *Peninsula Enterprise* in 1884 that crabbing on the steamboat route was developed "entirely by the capital and labor of Baltimoreans." He suggested that "The soft shell crab which has become such a profitable business around Crisfield, might be made as profitable in either of the creeks where the steamers of the Eastern Shore Steamboat Co., run. We call attention to this growing business with the hope of seeing some of our enterprising business men take hold of it." Steamboat clerk Tully A. T. Joynes believed that oyster tongers "who have heretofore remained idle during the summer, living on the store laid up in winter, can find this [crabbing] a more profitable employment than the oyster business." The exhortations of "J" and Joynes were prescient but premature. The rise of a peninsula-wide crabbing industry would await developments in the canning of the meat of hard crabs.[69]

Tourism

As cities grew in population and wealth, increasing numbers of their well-to-do residents sought recreation in the countryside. Improved transportation allowed them to indulge their desires. The Eastern Shore of Virginia became an accessible destination. Vacationing families came to the peninsula to swim, sail, and fish its waters, walk its beaches, ride its smooth roads, and enjoy its sea breezes. Visitors interacted with hospitable rustics living in picturesque communities. They found local food simple but delicious; lodgings rough if not downright primitive. The atmosphere was hardly fashionable and night-life non-existent, but vistas of field, woods, marsh, and water soothed the frayed nerves of refugees

---

5-6; Philadelphia *Times*, July 6, 1880; *Baltimore Sun*, September 10, 1881; *PE*, July 14, 1884. For the term "mud-flapping" see Richard L. Parks, "Eastern Shore of Virginia" in *Duck Shooting Along the Atlantic Tidewater*, ed. Eugene V. Connett (New York: William Murrow, 1947), p. 143.

69 *PE*, May 10, 1883, May 31 (quotes "J"), July 19 (quotes Joynes), 1884; Snow Hill (Md.) *Democratic Messenger*, June 17, 1882.

from the clamor and hustle of city life. "One never gets tired of watching nature in her varying beauty; the mighty ocean in her gentlest moods," wrote Alexander Hunter from Cobb's Island. "The surf mourning softly against the beach, and even the roar of the breakers, come to the ear mellowed by the gentle winds, and as softly as the memory of a dream. Then the ships, those freighted argosies, outward bound, the[ir] snowy sails gleaming against the far blue sky like the wings of the sea gulls."[70]

Sportsmen came in larger numbers than vacationers. For many Philadelphians and New Yorkers, the hunting resorts of Long Island and New Jersey had become overcrowded and costly. The Eastern Shore, inexpensive, teeming with game, and now relatively close at hand, offered an inviting alternative. "There is, perhaps, no portion of the country presenting a greater attraction to the sportsman in quest of small game, such as quail and waterfowl, than this little strip of land," asserted a writer for *Forest and Stream*. Hunters shot quail on the mainland and wildfowl on bayside and seaside waters. They bagged stunning amounts of game. Hunter found that on Cobb's Island in 1876 the usual bag per gunner was 20 to 30 black ducks, 40 to 60 brant, and 75 to 140 red-breasted snipe. A Wilmington journalist noted that on the Broadwater "At times the shooting is very great, and the sportsman has all he can do to load and fire."[71]

Hunters boarded with peninsula families or stayed at hotels in Horntown, Nashville, Drummondtown, Onancock, Pungoteague, Belle Haven, Powellton, and Eastville and on Cobb's and Chincoteague islands. Urban hunt clubs leased sloops from which they gunned on the Broadwater. In 1883 Hunter reported on clubmen from Baltimore, Richmond, and Norfolk bound for the Virginia capes. The hunters came prepared for a good time. Two New Yorkers observed in 1876 at Franklin City awaiting the steamboat to Chincoteague "had three

---

70 Hunter, "Cobb's Island in Summer," p. 49.

71 "Brant Shooting on the Virginia Broad Waters," Wilmington *Daily Gazette*, November 12, 1881 (second quotation); T. Robinson Warren, "Bay Shooting," *Scribner's Monthly* XIII (December, 1876), p. 156; "The Eastern Shore of Virginia," *Forest and Stream* VII (November 16, 1876), p. 232 (first quotation); Hunter, "Cobb's Island in Summer," p. 49; "Snipe Shooting in Virginia," *Forest and Stream* I (August 28, 1873), p. 35.

trunks, 200 pounds of shot, ten gallons of whiskey, and other stores in proportion." Eastern Shoremen expected visiting hunters to behave as sportsmen. *Forest and Stream* warned its readers that they "welcome gentlemen who come for enjoyment and recreation, and furnish them gladly with every assistance in their power, but hold the pot hunter in detestation, and visit him, when caught, with the severest penalties of the law prohibiting hunting by non-residents."[72]

The railroad ignited a hitherto smoldering tourism industry in the Chincoteague Bay region. Before the rails came to Franklin City in 1876, Northern visitors were compelled to travel the latter legs of their journey by stagecoach and sailboat. Now, the trip from New York via Lewes, Delaware, could be accomplished wholly by steamboat and rail. Immediately, the island attracted vacationing families and day-tripping excursionists. "The recent completion of the line of railway to Franklin [City], and the employment of steam navigation in Chincoteague sound, are progressive steps in opening up this hitherto but little frequented section," a traveler told the *Baltimore Sun*. "Chincoteague is now within easy reach of Baltimore and Philadelphia in a day, and large excursion trains from Wilmington, Georgetown or Harrington, Del., to Ocean City [Maryland] or Chincoteague Island have been of frequent occurrence nearly every week this summer." The island also attracted junketing lawmakers, scientists anxious to study the local biosphere, invalids recruiting their strength, and journalists looking for a good story. The latter, especially author and illustrator Howard Pyle with his eye for the picturesque and his penchant for plausible hyperbole, called the attention of a national audience to the island's quaint customs and institutions such as pony penning.[73]

---

[72] "Honk! Honk! Honk!," *Forest and Stream* I (December 25, 1873; "The Eastern Shore of Virginia, *Ibid*. VII (November 16, 1876), p. 232 (second quotation); Chasseur [Hunter], Old Point Comfort, to editor, June 22, *Ibid*. XX (June 28, 1883), p. 425; "A Trip for Quail in Maryland," *Ibid*. VII (February 1, 1877), p. 402 (first quotation).

[73] "A Trip for Quail in Maryland," p. 402; *Forest and Stream* V (February 11, 1875), p. 42; *Wilmington Daily Commercial*, September 26, 1872; "Brant Shooting on the Virginia Broad Waters"; *PE*, July 26, August 23, 1883, April 26, 1884; "Chincoteague Island, Va." (quotation); Pyle, "Chincoteague: The Island of Ponies," *Scribner's Monthly* XIII (April, 1877), pp. 737-745. In 1875, before the coming of the railroad to Franklin City, a Richmonder found the two small

Chincoteague Bay's attraction to sportsmen gave the region a year-around hospitality industry. Hunters came at all seasons to pursue immense flights of waterfowl and shorebirds. Within a year of the coming of the railroad, *Forest and Stream* proclaimed that Chincoteague Island was "rapidly becoming a favorite resort for sportsmen not only from Washington, but New York, Philadelphia and Baltimore." Industrialist and speculator Hamilton Disston of Philadelphia frequently visited in his steam yacht *Mischief*. In 1881 Disston and his politician cronies killed 500 to 1,000 shorebirds daily. Two years later, *Mischief* returned to the island "with a pleasure party, who expect to do some fine gunning in this latitude. The party is well equipped, and 'a feast of reason and flow of soul' will be the order of the trip, judging from the well filled larders, and copious supply of the old 'stand by' which loomed up from her quarter deck as she approached the wharf." Some Eastern Shoremen contemplated presenting the trigger-happy Disston and party to the Accomack County Grand Jury for violating the Virginia statute prohibiting non-residents from shooting game. The irate Chincoteague correspondent of the *Peninsula Enterprise* retorted that "Seven-eights of the people on this island think that the law should be repealed, and will send a petition to that effect to the next Legislature." Apparently, Chincoteaguers cared less for maintaining the supply of birds than for the money that Disston and other hunters might spend on the island.[74]

Most over-night visitors to Chincoteague stayed at one of the island's three hotels. The Atlantic Hotel, built in 1876 in anticipation of the arrival of the railroad at Franklin City, was the largest on the Eastern Shore of Virginia. Four stories high, it accommodated two hundred guests and featured "large airy rooms," "home comforts," "a first-class bar," and a table laden with local seafood. It also provided its guests with ponies, hunting guides and decoys, and other sporting necessities. The

---

hotels on Chincoteague Island "crowded all the summer with visitors from Baltimore, Philadelphia and New York" (*Richmond Dispatch*, August 18, 1875).

74 *Forest and Stream* V (November 25, 1875), p. 252, X (May 30, 1878), p. 320; "Shooting on Chincoteague Island," *Ibid.* IX (September 13, 1877), p. 111 (quotation); Wilmington *Morning News*, May 12, 1881; Snow Hill (Md.) *Democratic Messenger*, May 14, 1881; *PE*, May 10 (second quotation), 17 (third quotation), 1883.

island was a gourmand's paradise of restaurants, oyster bars, cake shops, and watermelon stands. "Chincoteague, it was found, had plenty to eat, and of the best," a Baltimore man discovered. "The oysters, served on the half-shell, were fresh and dripping from Chincoteague bay. ... Fish fresh from the peter-boats, crabs deviled and possessing a delicious flavor such as I have never found on the Western Shore, and birds freshly killed in the morning formed part of the Chincoteague Sunday dinner, and after a cigar in the cool air on the porch Chincoteague began to rise in estimation."[75]

The railroad also stimulated tourism on the mainland shore of Chincoteague Bay. New hotels appeared at Nashville and at Girdletree, Maryland, and John Shivers, a New Jersey immigrant living on the bay, took in summer boarders. Thomas Pettit, innkeeper at Horntown, earned a reputation among sportsmen as "what a good landlord ought to be." A quail hunter noted that "He has plain comfortable quarters, ducking outfits, boats, teams, oyster beds, &c., and voluntarily and heartily does every thing to further his guests' pleasure and comfort. ... I have struck upon so many cheerless, unhomelike hotels, when on hunting trips that I always like to hear of good places and to let others know of them." At the Red Hills near Nashville, a pavilion and bath houses attracted both Northerners and locals. In 1882 members of the Methodist Protestant Church at Pocomoke City, Maryland, picnicked at the Red Hills. The Pocomoke City *Record and Gazette* reported that "Bathing, sailing, etc., were indulged in by the pleasure seekers and all seemed to enjoy themselves."[76]

Further down the peninsula, expanded steamboat service brought increased numbers of tourists and sportsmen. In the mid-1870s the Eastern Shore Steamboat Company carried travelers bound for the

---

75 *EV*, July 7, 1876; "Chincoteague Island, Va." (quotation); "A Trip for Quail in Maryland"; Wilmington *News Journal*, April 10, 1878; "Shooting on Chincoteague Island"; Snow Hill (Md.) *Democratic Messenger*, May 14, 1881; *PE*, May 4, 1882, June 7, 1884.

76 *EV*, July 7, 1876; *PE*, July 28, 1881, July 5, 1884; "A Trip for Quail in Maryland" (quotation); Ralph T. Whitelaw, *Virginia's Eastern Shore: A History of Northampton and Accomack Counties* (Richmond: Virginia Historical Society, 1951), II, 1371; Pocomoke City *Record and Gazette* in Snow Hill (Md.) *Democratic Messenger*, July 22, 1882

Battle Point Hotel in Occohannock Neck. The hotel's manager boasted that "The Fishing in August and September cannot be surpassed, and as the Point is entirely exempt from fever and ague, it is a very desirable location for Families to spend the most pleasant part of the year. Besides the splendid Beach Bathing, the Hotel is furnished with Steam and Hot Salt Water Baths so efficacious in Rheumatic complaints." At the new town of Powellton on the seaside visitors boarded in private residences or, beginning in 1882, in A. S. Kellam's Powellton Hotel. Kellam catered especially to sportsmen gunning or fishing on the Broadwater and the Barrier islands. Meanwhile, Abel W. Kellam hosted at the Belle Haven Hotel quail hunters to whom he guaranteed "choice fare, fine liquor and courteous attention."[77]

The Cobb's Island Hotel remained the Eastern Shore's premier resort. In the mid-1870s its accommodations consisted of hotel, clubhouse, and perhaps as many as a dozen guest cottages situated 150 yards from the surf. Near the buildings were old willows, a grape arbor, fig bushes, and cantaloupe and watermelon patches. The hotel and cottages housed 150 to 200 guests. In the summer, people came to the island to swim, sail, hunt, and fish. Shark fishing from small boats was a much enjoyed pastime. Hotel and cottage guests were joined by yachting parties and steamboat excursionists. Some excursionists came for the day, but others stayed for extended periods. In 1875 the steamer *Jane Moseley* made five "Grand Excursions" to the island from Washington via Norfolk. The *Moseley* arrived at the island on a Saturday and left the following Monday. "The hotel on the island was crowded," remarked an excursionist. "This, however, did not at all interfere with our party, as we had the pleasure of carrying one of the best hotels in the country with us in the shape of the steamer and its admirable *cuisine*." Throughout the year came the Cobbs' bread and butter – sportsmen intent on hunting wildfowl and shorebirds. A Richmonder encountered on the island "shooting parties from Baltimore, with hunting suits and long-legged

---

77 "Snipe Shooting in Virginia"; *Baltimore Sun*, August 5, 22, 1873, July 27, 1875 (first quotation); *PE*, August 18, December 15, 1881, March 23, April 27, June 8 (quotation), 1882, December 6, 20, 1883, February 2, May 17, 1884.

boots." A writer for *Forest and Stream* considered Cobb's Island the best locale for shorebird shooting on the peninsula.[78]

Hotel guests included leading businessmen, politicians, and jurists. Most visitors came from Baltimore, Washington, and Richmond, but localities from Maine to Florida were also represented. During the summer of 1880 Alexander Hunter was aghast to find the hotel occupied by Yankees. "They are like bitters one places in his cocktail, an admirable infusion, but when taken simon pure, rather unpalatable to the Southern taste," he groaned. "The Northern ladies are decidedly pretty as a general thing but they haven't the development of the female form divine that is so alluring and captivating to the masculine eye, besides most of them have big feet and hands, and, but come to think of it, it is ungallant to draw comparisons which Mrs. Malaprop says are oderus."[79]

In contrast to the more fashionable seaside resorts, life at the Cobb's Island Hotel was rudimentary. Guests enjoyed an abundance of surf, sport, and sea breezes but went without such amenities such as daily mail, telegraph service, and gas lighting. They also went without formalities of manners and dress. "No 'fashion' there," asserted an Alexandria journalist, "fishing, gunning and bathing, rolling ten pins and playing billiards – are the pastimes – eating all the time and drinking between times." A visitor from Baltimore observed that "Here one's whole soul does not appear to be absorbed in the matter of dress, but a simple *negligee* style is generally adopted, which, beside being really more graceful, is certainly more convenient in the bowling alley, croquet grounds and various other amusements of the place." Hunter maintained that "There

---

78 Amine Kellam, "The Cobb's Island Story," *Virginia Cavalcade* XXIII (Spring, 1974), p. 23; *Norfolk Landmark*, July 18, August 15, 1874, July 13, 1875 (first quotation); Joseph F. Morgan, "Trip to Cobb's Island, *Chronicles of St. Mary's: Monthly Bulletin of the St. Mary's Historical Society* 17 (April, 1969), p. 288; Richard H. Meade to Mrs. Meade, July 19, 23, 1874, private collection; *Baltimore Sun*, August 1, 1872, August 23, 1879; "Cobb's Island," Washington *Evening Star*, August 15, 1871; *Ibid.*, August 3, 1877; Alexander Hunter, *The Huntsman in the South, Volume I: Virginia and North Carolin*a (New York: Neale Publishing Company, 1908), p. 145; Washington *Critic-Record*, July 29, August 3, 6, 12, 1875; *Alexandria Gazette*, March 22, 1876; "My Own Trip" (second quotation); "Eastern Shore of Virginia," *Forest and Stream*, November 16, 1876, p. 232.

79 Kellam, "The Cobb's Island Story," p. 23; Chasseur [Hunter], Cobb's Island, to editor, July 18, *Alexandria Gazette*, July 21, 1880.

was no conventionality at Cobb's, no grades of social position; every one was on an equal footing."[80]

The Cobb's Island Hotel passed through a crisis in the mid-1870s. The resort's egalitarian simplicity had commercial limits. In the minds of paying guests, the Cobbs' geniality and the island's natural endowments were finely balanced against inconvenience and discomfort. "As it is now, under the present owners," Hunter told the *Alexandria Gazette* in 1875, "the system of entertainment is simply abominable, the dirt, flies and vermin abound. The hotel is exactly like an old Virginia country tavern, a long two-story frame dwelling with a rickety porch in front and small rooms, which are not looking to the sea. There is a lamentable lack of neatness and the absence of a woman's love of order is visible everywhere. At the meals, for instance, the flies swarm in thousands, and you have to fight them with one hand and eat with the other." Conversely, Hunter acknowledged that "Cobb's Island presents attractions that no place on this continent possess; the view of the sea is sublime – beyond the power of words to describe; the breakers outside dashing over the reefs with a booming sound, the wide expanse of water, the pure salt air, the surf bathing (which is unequalled), the fishing and hunting, and all those sea luxuries that an epicure delights in." Writing home in 1874, Richard H. Meade of Richmond summed up the dichotomy in a more succinct and homely fashion: "The fare and accommodations are not as good as they were or ought to be by a great deal. The coffee is execrable & the butter is usually rancid. But everybody puts up with it on account of the delicious air and bath."[81]

Around the time of Meade's letter, family patriarch Nathan Cobb Sr. inadvertently upset the equilibrium by dividing his interest in the resort between his sons Warren, Nathan Jr., and Albert. The three did not see eye-to-eye on the hotel's future. As a result, Warren and Nathan Jr. left the management of the hotel to Albert whose business partner

---

80 Hunter, "Cobb's Island in Summer," p. 49; *Alexandria Gazette*, August 8, 1871; *Baltimore Sun*, August 6, 1873; Hunter, *The Huntsman in the South*, p. 144.

81 *Baltimore Sun*, August 6, 1873; Chasseur [Hunter], Cobb's Island, August 2, to editor, *Alexandria Gazette*, August 7, 1875; Meade to Mrs. Meade, July 21, 1874, private collection; Washington *Evening Star*, August 3, 1877.

Thomas G. Segar ran the resort on a daily basis. According to Hunter, Segar conducted business

> on the Boss Tweed principle. He actually did not keep account books, and the Cobbs were in profound ignorance of the outlay as well as the income, and the profit and loss were utterly unknown to them. Under his sway Cobb's Island became almost a robber's den, and woe to the unlucky sportsman who fell into their clutches. All, from the chief clerk to the boot-black, took a hand in plundering him. It was legalized robbery. ... Then the guides charged the sportsman ... $5 per day, and even more, if they thought they could bleed him, and besides, they took half the game he killed. ... It was simply outrageous.

Cobb & Segar also raised the lodging rate to that of a first-class resort while neglecting the upkeep of buildings.[82]

The Cobb's Island Hotel fell into a spiral of diminished patronage and shrinking revenue. In late December, 1876, the firm of Cobb & Segar dissolved, and in 1877 the resort closed for the season. In Hunter's words, "the whole concern busted. Mr. Segar left with some ten thousand dollars, the Cobbs tell me, that he grabbed as his share, leaving them literally nothing, nay, leaving them deeply in debt. In perfect disgust the Cobbs threw the whole thing up. They sold the tugboat [that connected the island with the mainland] for a mere song, and went back to their occupation of oystering, hunting and fishing." The resort nonetheless reopened in 1878 under the management of guide John Thomas Spady in association with Elkanah Cobb, a grandson of Nathan Cobb Sr. Hunter considered Tom Spady "a sensible man [who] has remedied all the former abuses. There is absolutely no extortion, and everything is open and without guile. The rates of board are cheaper than any resort on the Atlantic coast." Under the Spady regime the guides reduced their

---

82 Hunter, "Cobb's Island in Summer," p. 49; Washington *Evening Star*, August 3, 1877; Morgan, "Trip to Cobb's Island," p. 288; *Baltimore Sun*, August 23, 1879; *Richmond Dispatch*, June 6, 1876; *Norfolk Landmark*, July 6, 1876; Hunter "All about Cobb's Island," *Forest and Stream* XV (August 26, 1880), p. 65 (quotation).

rates but declined to abandon their insistence on keeping for themselves half of the sportsman's daily bag.[83]

Conditions for visitors improved under Spady & Cobb, but as a new decade opened the resort was still paying a price for mismanagement. "Never was there such an illustration of killing the goose that laid the golden egg as this place presents," Hunter wrote from the island in January, 1881. "The Cobbs, by the extortion and high prices charged sportsmen, have effectually killed their island; for five years ago there were dozens of Northern sportsmen who rendezvoused here for duck shooting, now there are none, I being the sole, solitary visitor." The Cobbs were shrewd Yankee opportunists and resourceful wreckers, guides, and market hunters, but they lacked the financial means to run a first-class resort. Hunter believed that the Cobb's Island Hotel run by men possessed of capitol and vision would become "a grand watering place." Early in 1882, in his single term as a member from Alexandria County of the Virginia House of Delegates, he successfully promoted an act incorporating the Cobb's Island Seaside Company. Hunter and the other incorporators, most of whom were prominent Virginia politicians, proposed to purchase the island from the Cobbs and build a new hotel. They also intended to connect the resort by steamboat with Old Point Comfort and by telegraph with Cherrystone in anticipation of the eventual extension of the railroad down the peninsula. Their dreams came to naught. The Cobbs refused to sell, and Spady & Cobb continued in their management of the resort.[84]

---

[83] *Norfolk Virginian*, December 12, 1876; Norfolk *Weekly Virginian and Carolinian*, July 5, 1877; *Richmond Dispatch*, July 22, 1878; *Baltimore Sun*, August 23, 1879; Allen B. Hamilton, comp., *The Northampton County, Virginia, 1880 Census* (Millsboro, De.: Colonial Roots, 2016), p. 96; Chasseur [Hunter] to editor, July 28, *Forest and Stream* XV (August 5, 1880), p. 11; Hunter, "All about Cobb's Island," p. 65 (quotation); One Who Has Been There, Poughkeepsie, N.Y., to editor, August 7, *Forest and Stream* XV (August 12, 1880), p. 31; Adirondack to editor, *Ibid.*, XV (September 2, 1880), p. 88; Hunter, "A Trip Through North Carolina," *Ibid.* XIX (November 9, 1882), p. 237.

[84] *Alexandria Gazette*, August 7, 1875, July 21, 1880, January 18, 19, 23, 1882; Chasseur [Hunter], Cobb's Island, January 1, to editor *Forest and Stream* XV (January 27, 1881), p. 511 (quotation); *Acts and Joint Resolutions Passed by the General Assembly of the State of Virginia During the Session of 1881-82* (Richmond: R. F. Walker, Superintendent of Public Printing, 1882), pp. 42-43; Hunter, "Birds at Cobb's Island," *Forest and Stream* XVIII (March 23, 1882),

Tourism's economic impact on the Eastern Shore was slight overall but significant to the communities involved. Restaurants, liveries, and mercantile firms operating near resorts and hotels gained additional customers while local residents found employment attending to guests. Seven people (four fewer than in 1870) worked at the Cobb's Island Hotel in 1880. Their responsibilities split along racial lines. Managers – two male hotel keepers and a female housekeeper – were white; domestics – a male cook, a male waiter, and two female servants – were black.[85]

The influx of sportsmen created opportunities for watermen to supplement their income by working as guides. Successful guides possessed attention to detail, knowledge of the haunts and habits of game, and an ability to handle politely but firmly wealthy and privileged clients. Besides their expertise and patience, guides provided blinds, boats, and decoys. They loaded their clients' guns and gathered their game. Once when Nathan Cobb was retrieving downed birds for Postmaster-General John A. J. Creswell, the accidental discharge of Creswell's shotgun put nine No. 10 shot in Cobb's backside. The guides might also pack the game on ice and send it to the hunter's home. Guides were well compensated, earning in a week what a farm worker might earn in a month. Alexander Hunter at times considered the guides' rates extortionate but he nonetheless appreciated their stamina and discipline: "I know of no manual labor that is equal to their duties of crouching close behind a blind on a salt meadow with the blazing sun beating down, straining their eyes to catch sight of the [shore]birds, so as to whistle them to the decoys, and almost blinded by the dazzling glare, and then chasing wounded birds, often waist deep in water. All this in cold blood, they not having guns, and, of course, not being braced up with the excitement and stimulus that the shooter feels." The writings of Hunter and others made famous among sportsmen the names of several Eastern Shore guides – George D. Hitchens and Sandford Spady at Smith's Island, Kenneth McKown at Capeville, the Cobbs and Tom Spady at Cobb's Island, Decatur Birch, John Snead, and Sumner Jeffries

---

p. 146; *Norfolk Landmark*, August 15, 1874; *PE*, June 14, 1883.

85 Hamilton, comp., *The Northampton County, Virginia, 1880 Census*, p. 96.

at Chincoteague. Also celebrated were Jake, "the colored Adam" who worked the Broadwater from Hog to Wallop's islands, and William J. Clayville of Chincoteague, described by a client as "guide, philosopher and friend."[86]

Transformation

From 1873 through the remainder of the decade, the United States struggled in the grip of economic depression. The Eastern Shore of Virginia, however, did not share equally in the national misery. Urban growth created an increasing demand for Eastern Shore agricultural produce, seafood, lumber, and recreational opportunities. An enhanced transportation network satisfied that demand. "[T]his part of Virginia ... in ten years has developed surprisingly, and [its] people are comfortable and prosperous as well as important producers," remarked a Baltimore man in 1881. "For the greater part of this prosperity the section is indebted to the Eastern Shore Steamboat Company of Baltimore, whose steamers are at present taxed to their utmost to meet the demands of the trade."[87]

By the early 1880s Accomack and Northampton counties carried on an estimated commerce of $1,000,000 with Baltimore and Norfolk alone. The Eastern Shore's population grew as its expanding economy encouraged young people to remain at home and outsiders to settle on the peninsula. New communities appeared near railroad depots at Crisfield and Franklin City, near steamboat wharves on bayside

---

86 *Alexandria Gazette*, August 7, 1875; *PE*, February 28, 1885; *Forest and Stream* XV (August 5, 1880), p. 11; Hunter, "Shore Birds off Cape Charles: I. Summer Shooting," *Ibid*. XXI (August 23, 1883), p. 64; Hunter, "All about Cobb's Island," p. 65 (quotation); Hunter, "In the Highlands of Virginia," *Forest and Stream* XIII (November 27, 1879), p. 844; Hunter, "A Summer Idyl in Virginia," *Ibid*. XI (October 31, 1878), p. 257; "Shooting on Chincoteague Island," p. 111; *PE*, October 18, 1883; *Forest and Stream* XXIII (August 14, 1884), p. 48; "Snipe Shooting in Virginia," p. 35 (on Jake); "Brant Shooting on the Virginia Broad Water" (on Clayville).

87 Roy F. Nichols, *The Stakes of Power, 1845-1877* (New York: Hill and Wang, 1961), p. 208; *Norfolk Landmark*, November 20, 1873; Wilmington *News Journal*, March 10, 1873; *Richmond Dispatch*, April 13, 1874; *Baltimore Sun*, September 5, 1881.

and seaside, and near sawmills in the interior. Commercial buildings, wharves, houses, and churches sprang up in communities old and new. Land values increased and farms were sub-divided. Travelers from off the peninsula frequently remarked on improvements that farmers had made to their property. A Baltimorean ascribed these signs of prosperity to the culture of Irish and sweet potatoes: "The war left these people crippled in fortune and with a demoralized labor system. Yet in this one crop they have recovered all losses and have made themselves comparatively rich." From the confusion of Confederate defeat and the chaos of Union occupation emerged a vibrant economy.[88]

---

[88] *Baltimore Sun*, February 28, 1883; *PE*, August 10, October 12, December 14, 1882, August 16, 1883; Washington *National Republican*, November 1, 1879; *Richmond Dispatch*, August 13, 1875, January 22, 1879; Charles H. Barnard and John Jones, *Farm Real Estate Values in the United States by Counties, 1850-1982* (Washington: United States Department of Agriculture, 1987), pp. 102, 104; "Future State"; "On the Peninsula"; "A Land of Promise," *Baltimore Rambler* in *Southern Planter* 44 (March, 1883), pp. 152 (quotation).

Chapter IV

Landscape Change

In the years from 1870 to 1884 emancipation, economic growth, agricultural innovation, government expansion, and enhanced transportation services combined to reshape the Eastern Shore landscape. Population grew significantly. Farms became smaller and more numerous. New wharves and new communities appeared along the waterfront. Crossroad villages experienced building booms. Contractors raised new houses, stores, churches, and schools. Sawmills exhausted stand after stand of timber. New roads linked sawmill and wharf and village. Meanwhile, the federal government surveyed dredging projects, opened post offices, and established Life-Saving Service stations. Burgeoning commerce brought Eastern Shoremen in closer contact with the outside world. That world, rich and bountiful and exciting, delighted them with new products, pleasures, and conveniences. It also gently ensnared them in desire and dependency.

Between 1870 and 1880 the total population of Accomack and Northampton counties grew by 17.9 percent from 28,455 to 33,560. The rate of growth exceeded by 10 percent that of any decade since the first federal census in 1790. Accomack's population increased from 20,409 to 24,408 (19.6 percent); Northampton's from 8,046 to 9,152 (13.7 percent). Accomack remained a white-majority county (62 percent) while Northampton retained its black majority (58 percent). Among blacks, population growth in Accomack slightly surpassed that of whites, 19.8 percent to 19.5 percent while in Northampton it lagged behind that of whites 8.6 percent to 21.6 percent. The higher rate of growth of the black population in Accomack probably reflected the relative demand for labor vis-à-vis the two counties in the seafood and lumbering industries.[1]

Population increase was relatively uniform along the peninsula except in the district embracing the islands of Assateague and Chincoteague where the booming oyster industry attracted a flood of newcomers. Between 1870 and 1880 the population of the islands grew from 1,122 to 1,662, a rate of 48.1 percent. Howard Pyle reported that "many strangers ... are pouring in from the main-land to settle there." Another observer noted an "immigration from Delaware, New Jersey and Maryland. ... A few New Englanders and some negroes are also included in the population." In 1880 around 30 percent of the population of Assateague and Chincoteague were born outside of Virginia. On the mainland, newcomers were scattered the length of the peninsula, but their numbers were small, comprising about 6 percent of the population.[2]

The booming oyster industry stimulated population growth in seaside waterfront communities. It does not follow, however, that the corresponding boom in agricultural production was exclusively responsible for population growth on the mainland. A prime mover in Eastern Shore farm population growth between 1870 and 1880 was the shift to fruit and vegetables on land hitherto devoted to the production of grain. By turning to truck crops, farmers could make a living on fewer acres than required by general farming. They could now more safely sub-divide their land among offspring, rent to tenants (including freed slaves), or sell excess acres to fellow Eastern Shoremen or to newcomers.

The impact of the shift to truck farming is revealed in the federal

---

1 James E. Mears, Statistics from Federal Censuses in "Shoreline Column," Onancock *Eastern Shore News* (hereafter cited as *ESN*), October 11, 1940.

2 *Statistics of the Population of the United States at the Tenth Census (June 1, 1880)* (Washington: Government Printing Office, 1883), pp. 356, 359; Pyle, "Chincoteague: The Island of Ponies," *Scribner's Monthly* XIII (April, 1877), p. 738; "Chincoteague Island, Va.," *Baltimore Sun*, August 17, 1876 (quotes N. E. F.); analysis of Census of Population, Accomac and Northampton Counties, Virginia, 1880, microfilm, National Archives, Washington, D.C.

agricultural censuses of 1870 and 1880. In the intervening decade, the number of farms on the Eastern Shore grew from 2,096 to 2,926 (an increase of 39.6 percent) while the average acreage per farm declined from 128.5 to 86.6 (a decrease of 32.6 percent). Comparison of data from Accomack and Northampton indicates that the counties were proceeding in generally the same direction but at a different pace. The number of farms in Accomack grew during the period from 1,456 to 2,145 (an increase of 47.3 percent); in Northampton from 640 to 781 (22 percent). Average farm size declined in Accomack from 112 to 79.2 acres (a decrease of 29.3 percent); in Northampton from 167 to 106.9 acres (36 percent). Total farm acreage in Accomack rose by 4.4 percent as did improved acreage by 7.1 percent. In contrast, total farm acreage declined in Northampton by 21.8 percent and improved acreage by 32.3 percent. Also, the value of farms rose in Accomack by 35.4 percent while it fell in Northampton by 17.2 percent. The statistical discrepancies between the two counties probably reflect the more brisk rate of population growth in Accomack and the relatively larger number of undercapitalized freedmen assuming the management of farms in Northampton.[3]

FROM THE EARLIEST DAYS OF ENGLISH SETTLEMENT, bayside and seaside wharves had been the conduits of commerce on the Eastern Shore. The coming of the railroad to Crisfield and Franklin City and, more important, the expansion of steamboat service along the peninsula stimulated the construction of new wharves. By 1884, thirty or more wharves served both steamboats and sailboats while others served sailboats exclusively. Between 1876 and 1884 at least ten wharves were built on the shores of Chincoteague Bay to facilitate primarily the oyster and lumbering industries. Farther down the seaside, wharves at Powellton, Willis's

---

3 *The Statistics of the Wealth and Industry of the United States ... Compiled From the Original Returns of the Ninth Census (June 1, 1870)* (Washington: Government Printing Office, 1872), pp. 266, 270, 364; *Report on the Productions of Agriculture as Returned at the Tenth Census (June 1, 1880)* (Washington: Government Printing Office, 1883), pp. 137-138; E. H. Stevens, *Soil Survey of Accomac and Northampon Counties, Virginia* (Washington: Government Printing Office, 1920), p. 18.

Wharf, and other points handled the trade of ocean-going steamers. On the bayside, a dozen or more new wharves joined existing structures in meeting the needs of the Eastern Shore Steamboat Company. Increased commerce occasioned new construction; new construction occasioned increased commerce. William G. Hoffman and Henry C. Walker built a new steamboat wharf at Hoffman's Wharf (now Harborton) in 1871. The wharf extended 450 feet into Pungoteague Creek. It was 16 feet wide, expanding to 125 feet at the docking point. In 1884 Frank T. Boggs and Bros., in order to alleviate crowding at Boggs's Wharf on Pungoteague Creek, raised, enlarged, and extended their wharf while Peter H. Davis at Davis's Wharf on Occohannock Creek added ninety feet to his wharf. A correspondent of the *Peninsula Enterprise* commended "the enterprise of Capt. Davis. The more convenient and roomy a wharf is, the more it will be patronized. ... The increased value of the property around the neighborhood on account of such improvements is not to be forgotten. ... If I were looking for land to buy, one of the first things I should inquire about would be the distance from the point of shipment and the facilities at that point for shipping."[4]

Large quantities of fruits and vegetables passed from the wharves

---

4 Kirk Mariner, *Almost an Island: The History of Saxis, Virginia* (Onancock, Va.: Miona Publications, 2011), p. 37; *Acts and Joint Resolutions Passed by the General Assembly of the State of Virginia at the Session of 1874-5* (Richmond: R. F. Walker, Superintendent of Public Printing, 1875), p. 209; *Acts and Joint Resolutions Passed by the General Assembly of the State of Virginia at the Session of 1875-6* (Richmond: R. F. Walker, Superintendent of Public Printing, 1876), pp. 20, 23, 143; *Acts and Joint Resolutions Passed by the General Assembly of the State of Virginia at the Session of 1876-77* (Richmond: R. F. Walker, Superintendent of Public Printing, 1877), pp. 37, 53, 166, 243; *Acts and Joint Resolutions Passed by the General Assembly of the State of Virginia during the Session of 1877-78* (Richmond: R. F. Walker, Superintendent of Public Printing, 1878), pp. 150, 277; *Acts and Joint Resolutions Passed by the General Assembly of the State of Virginia during the Session of 1879-80* (Richmond: R. F. Walker, Superintendent of Public Printing, 1880), pp. 27, 86, 260; *Acts and Joint Resolutions Passed by the General Assembly of the State of Virginia during the Session of 1881-82* (Richmond: R. F. Walker, Superintendent of Public Printing, 1882), p. 164; *Acts and Joint Resolutions Passed by the General Assembly of the State of Virginia during the Session of 1883-84* (Richmond: R. v. Deer, Superintendent of Public Printing, 1884), pp. 485, 509, 681; *Journal of the House of Delegates of the State of Virginia, For the Session of 1878-9* (Richmond: R. F. Walker, Superintendent of Public Printing, 1879), p. 446; *Norfolk Virginian*, August 21, 1873; Snow Hill (Md.) *Democratic Messenger*, August 5, 1882; Accomac C. H. *Peninsula Enterprise* (hereafter cited as *PE*), June 22, 29, 1882, June 21, 1883, April 12, June 14 (quotation), July 5, 19, August 16, 1884; James Egbert Mears, *Hacks Neck and Its People Past and Present* (Chicago: Author, 1937), p. 35.

onto steamboats, sailboats, and railroad cars. Collector of Customs George Toy reported 78,000 barrels of sweet and Irish potatoes shipped from Onancock alone in 1878. Five years later, a visiting journalist informed the *Baltimore Rambler* that a conservative estimate for Onancock was 100,000 and for the entire peninsula 745,000 barrels. From Finney's Wharf on Onancock Creek on a single day in May, 1884, vessels carried away 8,000 quarts of strawberries, 60 barrels of peas, 85 barrels of radishes, and 17 boxes of crabs.[5]

Come the harvest, the fields were full of pickers and the roads crowded with carts loaded with produce. "I dig 100 barrels [of Irish potatoes] and start to the wharf," a correspondent told the *Peninsula Enterprise*, "[where] the air rings with the whistle of steamboats, the banging of wheels, the chuck and roar of enginery, the striking of message bells and the hiss of steam." A traveler related that as soon as the steamboat made fast to the Onancock dock "a bewildering confusion begins. Every one of our thirty-eight deckhands seizes a [hand-] truck and rushes from steamer to landing and back again, exchanging merchandise, molding and store goods for sweet potatoes, fish, eggs, and garden 'truck.'" A local man boasted in June, 1882, that "A thousand barrels or more of peas and about five hundred crates of berries were shipped from Onancock to Baltimore on last Monday by the steamer *Tangier*. Pratt Street, in Baltimore, never presented a more business-like appearance than did the Onancock steamship wharf on that occasion. Every available space around the wharf for a hundred yards or more was so crowded with carts that one walking could with difficulty thread his way through them." On a similar occasion a visiting parson making his way among the carts complained of being "exposed to the mule-heels and ox-horns of the vast sea of teams and vehicles."[6]

---

5 Onancock *Eastern Virginian* (hereafter cited as *EV*), June 29, 1878; "Trade of Port of Baltimore," *Baltimore Sun*, July 15, 1879; *Ibid.*, June 17, 1880; "Land of Promise,' *Baltimore Rambler* in *Southern Planter* 44 (March, 1883), pp. 151-152; *PE* May 24, 1884.

6 *Baltimore Sun*, June 10, 1882; "The Eastern Shore," Richmond *State*, July 24, 1883; *PE*, April 27 (first quotation), June 8 (third quotation), September 14, 1882; "A Virginian Atlantis," *American Traveler and Tourist* in *PE*, October 8, 1887 (second quotation); *EV*, July 7, 1876; "Seashore Gossip," *Richmond Dispatch*, August 16, 1872 (fourth quotation).

Despite their busyness at harvest time, wharves generally were too geographically remote to support substantial local communities. Farmers of necessity hauled their produce to the wharves but met their everyday needs at the heads of the necks. Thus, stores located at wharves served mainly steamboat travelers and nearby residents. The scene recorded at Pitts's Wharf on the Pocomoke River in 1883 – "a freight shed, a store with dwelling above, and a stable. In the distance ... one or two farm houses" – was frequently replicated at wharves on both sides of the peninsula. Some wharves, however, were better favored by geography or circumstance. Hoffman's Wharf on the deep waters of Pungoteague Creek was the site of the oldest continuous steamboat dock in Accomack County. In 1880 a fish factory located nearby. A few years later, a visitor described Hoffman's Wharf as "quite a village. It consists of several good dwellings, three first-class stores, two bar-rooms, [and] one eating saloon."[7]

Onancock was the most advantageously located of the wharf communities. Its steamboat wharf and four or five sailboat wharves stood at the head of navigation of Onancock Creek. In town was a crossroad where the north-south bayside road intersected with an east-west road running from the seaside. Over these roads came tons of produce for Onancock's wharves and hundreds of customers for its stores. In 1865 a Philadelphian had described Onancock as a "dingy village" of 150 souls with four stores, three churches, a female seminary, and a "diminutive hotel." In the mid-1880s another traveler found the community a "thriving business place" with twenty stores, seven churches, two drug stores, a "good hotel," a barrel factory, a cannery, a public school and a private academy. After the General Assembly incorporated Onancock in 1882, municipal authorities laid sidewalks and spread oyster shells on the streets. As the town's population grew to 500 or more, residential development expanded from its original locus east of North Street westward along Kerr, Main (now Market), and Johnson streets. The local correspondent of the *Baltimore Sun* proudly declared in 1883 that "it

---

7 "The Eastern Shore," Richmond *State*, July 24, 1883; *PE*, December 7, 1882, December 6, 1883; Snow Hill (Md.) *Democratic Messenger*, July 16, 1881.

seems settled that Onancock is to be commercial and educational centre of the Eastern Shore of Virginia."[8]

Powellton emerged as Onancock's equivalent on the seaside of the peninsula. In 1872 brothers John T., George W., and Henry F. Powell purchased twenty-nine acres of land on Finney's Creek opposite Wachapreague Inlet. The Powells erected a wharf, a warehouse, and a store on the waterfront while dividing the remainder of the property into building lots. They also improved the road running from the creek inland to the nearby crossroad village of Locustmount. Located on water sufficiently deep for ocean-going vessels and linked by roads via Locustmount to an extensive hinterland, Powellton by the early 1880s was the emporium of the lower Accomack County seaside. It contained several mercantile establishments, a millinery, a drug store, a barber shop, a wheelwright shop, a hotel, and a saloon. A commercial and residential building boom was underway as the town expanded northward from the original settlement. In 1882 Collector of Customs Toy remarked that Powellton "is a thriving village ... of about 200 inhabitants. ... [It] is the largest grain shipping point on the Eastern Shore, and the second [to Onancock] in trucks. More than nine tenths of the business of the neighborhood is done there."[9]

Increased commerce and population brought growth to many of the crossroad hamlets in the Eastern Shore's interior. In 1884 a correspondent

---

[8] *Philadelphia Inquirer*, August 19, 1865 (first quotation); *Norfolk Virginian*, August 17, 1883; *Baltimore Sun*, June 5, 1882 (second quotation); February 28, May 7 (third quotation), 1883; *PE*, August 11, 1881, April 5, May 17, October 25, November 15, 1883, March 29, July 5, 1884; Wilmington *Morning News*, March 13, 1883; T. C. Morton, "Life in a Level Land," *Staunton Vindicator*, June 23, 1882; "A Virginian Atlantis"; Anne B. Nock, *Child of the Bay: Past, Present, and Future* (Norfolk, Va.: Hampton Roads Publishing Company, 1992), pp. 178, 181; Kirk Mariner, *Revival's Children: A Religious History of Virginia's Eastern Shore* (Salisbury, Md.: Peninsula Press, 1979), pp. 521-523; *Acts and Joint Resolutions Passed by the General Assembly of the State of Virginia during the Session of 1881-82*, pp. 127-130.

[9] Ralph T. Whitelaw, *Virginia's Eastern Shore: A History of Northampton and Accomack Counties* (Richmond: Virginia Historical Society, 1951), II, 782-783; Kirk Mariner, *Wachapreague, Virginia: Then and Now* (New Church, Va.: Miona Publications, 1995), pp. 9, 13, 14; Accomack County Order Book, 1870-1873, p. 699; *PE*, October 27, 1881, July 5, 12, September 6, December 20, 1883, January 12, March 1, 1884; Wilmington *Morning News*, August 26, 1884; Toy to William Mahone, February 21, 1882, Mahone Papers, Manuscript Department, William L. Perkins Library, Duke University, Durham, N.C.

boasted to the *Peninsula Enterprise* of improvements along the seaside road in lower Accomack County. Grangeville (near present-day Keller), he noted, had recently added a store, and shops for a blacksmith, a wheelwright, and a carriage maker. A mile south, near the sawmill and store of Stockley and Coleburn, had appeared blacksmith and carriage maker's shops and Francis T. Stockley's "magnificent private residence." Farther up the peninsula in northern Accomack, Spencer R. Nelson in 1882 purchased Helltown and adjacent acreage on the middle road. Nelson both honored himself and enhanced the attractiveness of his property by changing the place's name to Nelsonia. He proposed to replace its "rickety hut with a single inhabitant" with dwellings, a store, and a blacksmith shop by way of converting it into a "first class business place." To the northward on the middle road, the community of Seaside (also known as Mappsville) experienced a building boom. "The spirit of improvement seems to abide with our little village," a resident told the *Peninsula Enterprise* in 1884. "[W]ith the opening of another road soon, more buildings will be put up during the year." Nearby Assawoman, an old village at the head of Assawoman Creek, seems to have been uninfected by the "spirit of improvement." Besides a mill, a traveler passing through in 1883 found there "a store and a bar-room, two or three ancient houses with brick ends and wooden sides and as many modern houses of wood. Everything about the place looks as dead as a neglected graveyard."[10]

No locality on the Eastern Shore experienced greater growth than uppermost Accomack County where enhanced transportation facilities stimulated agriculture, lumbering, and the fisheries. "Oysters are the living of the people," a visitor to Chincoteague Island declared in 1881, "and there are not probably 150 of the 1,700 people who do not directly derive their support from the oyster trade. I can only think of the employees at the Assateague light-house and the United States signal-station and the life-saving station, and the proprietors and employees of

---

[10] *PE*, September 21, 1882 (second quotation), February 15, 1883, February 2, May 24 (third quotation), August 9 (first quotation), 1884; Oliver J. Lucas to William Mahone, August 15, 1882, Mahone Papers, Duke; "The Eastern Shore," Richmond *State*, July 24, 1883 (fourth quotation).

the fish-fertilizer factories who have a living independent of the oyster trade." An officer in the United States Army Corps of Engineers counted 107 sloops and 31 schooners on Chincoteague Bay, most of them engaged in the transport of oysters and clams. The island produced only about one-tenth of the agricultural products consumed there. Mainland farmers received better prices for their crops on Chincoteague than in Philadelphia or New York. By the early 1880s the community along the island's bay waterfront had become "quite a town, with its dozen stores, a large and handsome hotel, six churches ... while the steamboats, schooners, fishing smacks, and smaller sail vessels that fill the channel and crowd against the wharves, convey an idea of commercial importance which the stranger is not prepared to find there."[11]

On the western shore of Chincoteague Bay stood the adjacent villages of Franklin City and Greenbackville. Founded in 1876 and incorporated by the Virginia General Assembly in 1878, Franklin City was a planned community laid out in a grid pattern on either side of the rails leading to a pier extending into the bay. Its founder, Maryland Judge John R. Franklin, envisioned a town of 2,000 people, but its marshy terrain and the difficulty of obtaining fresh water retarded development. In 1880 Franklin City, despite the large quantities of seafood and agricultural produce shipped from its pier, was still "a small place" with a hotel, a store, and a post office. Many of the oysters shipped from Franklin City were harvested by people from nearby Greenbackville and vicinity. Founded around 1865, the population of Greenbackville proper had reached 300 by 1880. The great majority of the area's inhabitants, many of whom hailed from the North, derived their livings from the water.[12]

---

11 "The Eastern Shore," *Richmond Dispatch*, September 2, 1881 (quotations); Chincoteague Bay, Va., United States, Senate, 46th Congress, 2nd Session, Ex. Doc 90 (1880), p. 12; *PE*, March 29, August 9, 1884; "The Teagues of Accomack," Wilmington *Delaware State Journal*, April 7, 1881; Wilmington *Morning News*, August 24, 1881.

12 Kirk Mariner, "Ghost Town on the Marsh," *Chesapeake Bay Magazine* 10 (December, 1980), pp. 41-42; Mariner, *Once Upon an Island: The History of Chincoteague* (New Church, Va.: Miona Publications, 1996), p. 70; *Acts and Joint Resolutions Passed by the General Assembly of the State of Virginia during the Session of 1877-78*, p. 73; Samuel Sanford, "The Underground Water Resources of Coastal Plain Province of Virginia," Virginia Geological Survey *Bulletin* V (1913), p. 120; Chincoteague Bay, Va., United States, Senate, 46th Congress, 2nd Session, Ex. Doc 90 (1880), p. 12 (quotation); "The Sussex Railroads," Wilmington *News Journal*, July 17, 1877; Er-

By the early 1880s the crossroad communities in the agricultural interior of uppermost Accomack County were also flourishing. Atlantic on the seaside road saw in 1884 the construction of ten or twelve new houses. At New Church on the middle road in 1882 merchants Marshall and Brittingham built a new store house said to be the largest of its kind in the county. The traveler who found Assawoman so derelict praised the middle road community of Temperanceville: "There are two stores, steam saw, flour and grist mills, a smith's shop, post office, etc., and about a dozen scattered dwellings. The stores seem to carry large stocks and the village dwellings have the outward appearance of life and prosperity."[13]

Change came also to the communities of watermen and small farmers ("laboring poor people," a politician called them) on the upper bayside. In 1887 a correspondent styling himself "Drummer" alerted the *Peninsula Enterprise* to "marks of progress" in Messongo Neck (also known as Freeschool or Pocomoke Neck) between Holden's and Messongo creeks:

> [T]here is no section of Accomac covering the same amount of territory that has made the same amount of improvement in ten years. ... Where there were but two stores a few years ago on the mainland and one on [Saxis] island, now there are nine on the mainland and three on the island – perhaps an oversupply – where there was no mantua maker or millinery establishment in that section, now there are two good ones. ... The dwelling houses a few years ago were unattractive, and many of them uncomfortable. To-day they are not only comfortable but tasty, and many of them would be attractive anywhere.

A resident of Marsh Market on Messongo Creek commented in

---

nest Ingersoll, "The Oyster Industry" in *The History and Present Condition of the Fishery Industry*, by G. Brown Goode (Washington: Government Printing Office, 1881), p. 183. Franklin City was the first community on the Eastern Shore of Virginia to be incorporated by act of assembly.

13 *PE*, September 29, 1881, August 2, 1884; Snow Hill (Md.) *Democratic Messenger*, August 19, 1882; "The Eastern Shore," Richmond *State*, July 24, 1883 (quotation).

1883 on the "many evidences of improvement" in the neck. He listed thirteen new dwellings, four new stores, two sawmills, blacksmith and shoemaker shops, and two churches with two more under construction. On Saxis a building boom raged as houses went up on every part of the island. From Tangier Island in the midst of Chesapeake Bay came word that "In the history of the island our people were never more thrifty than at present. There are two schools, a first-class church edifice, lands being improved, our dwellings are neat and comfortable, and, what is better than anything else, our people are happy and contented."[14]

Economic growth and increased population created demand on the Eastern Shore for the goods supplied by urban mercantile wholesalers. Their representatives, known as drummers, were ubiquitous. A visitor noted that "The drummers from the cities, with their buggies, rejoicing in the fast trotters of the country, scour the country and are hardly ever out of sight of the dust of each others' wheels." Between 1870 and 1880 the number of stores on the Eastern Shore doubled. In 1880 *Dun's Mercantile Agency Reference Book* listed in the two counties 162 dealers in general merchandise (including liquor, tobacco, and groceries). Accomack accounted for 122 of the stores and Northampton 40. Most general stores served only their immediate neighborhoods. Accomack averaged 200 persons per store and Northampton 229. The proliferation of new retail businesses resulted in a combined average for the counties of 207 persons per store, down from the 356 per store of 1870. In Messongo Neck in 1882 ten or twelve stores operated in eight localities within a three-mile radius of the village of Sanford. While in most places one to three stores might meet the needs of the community, the more heavily trafficked localities featured half a dozen or more. *Dun's* listed thirteen general stores on Chincoteague Island, eleven in Onancock, nine in Eastville, seven in Drummondtown, and six in Belle

---

14 Abel T. Johnson to William Mahone, January 27, 1882. Mahone Papers, Duke (first quotation); "Pocomoke Neck and Sykes, *PE*, July 23, 1887 (second quotation); *PE*, May 17 (fourth quotation), November 15, 29 (third quotation), 1883; "A Peninsular Tour: Tangier Sound and the Chesapeake Oyster Beds," Wilmington *News Journal,* June 19, 1878; *EV*, November 23, 1878, in *ESN*, February 21, 1930.

Haven and in the Locustmount-Powellton area. The increased number of stores not only developed local dependence on the merchandise of the urban North but also introduced its fashions and mores.[15]

Most of the stores were small and undercapitalized. Of the 212 general stores and other businesses rated by *Dun's* in 1880, 54 percent were capitalized at $2,000 or less and 76 percent at $5,000 or less. Only 19 percent achieved a "high" or "good" credit rating while 54 percent received a "fair" rating and 27 percent no rating at all. On *Dun's* scale of 1 (highest credit rating) to 4 (lowest), Eastern Shore businesses averaged 3.3. Their respective places of business reflected the disparity between the relatively wealthy merchants and their less well-to-do brethren. The store houses of the lesser merchants were often low, narrow, single-story edifices. Those of the greater merchants were more commodious – a building of 1,500 square feet was considered large and of 2,500 "mammoth." They also were more elegantly appointed. When opened in Drummondtown in 1884 Charles B. Lilliston's new store "took the cake" for beauty and convenience – "glass front, gaslight, all the modern improvements."[16]

With no banks on the peninsula, Eastern Shoremen largely depended on merchants for credit. "The great want of the lower Peninsula is capital," a Wilmington man averred in 1884. "This want is noticeable everywhere below the Pocomoke river. The people live hand to mouth, having hardly enough ready cash at any time with which to buy a horse or a cow. The costly, tyrannous credit system prevails, and the few professional and business men control the bulk of the circulating money." Most merchants possessed little capital and so were themselves dependent on the credit extended them by the urban wholesalers from whom they bought their stock. The merchants, in turn, extended credit to their

---

15 Morton, "Life in a Level Land" (quotation); *Dun's Mercantile Agency Reference Book* 47 (July, 1880); John D. Parsons to John W. H. Parker, July 12, 27, in Parker to William Mahone, August 3, 1882, Mahone Papers, Duke; Chataigne listed 182 general stores – 131 in Accomack and 51 in Northampton (J. H. Chataigne, ed., *Virginia Business Directory and Gazetteer, 1880-81* [Richmond: Baughman & Bros., 1880], pp. 75-76, 399-400.

16 *Dun's Mercantile Agency Reference Book* 47 (July, 1880); *PE*, January 19, 1882, November 22, 1883, February 16 (quotation), April 19, 1884.

cash-strapped customers. Tongue-in-cheek, a correspondent informed the *Peninsula Enterprise* that storekeeper Albert F. Mears of Muddy Creek "blends business with philanthropy. He has furnished promiscuously to our small farmers tons of fertilizer 'on time.'" The usual profit earned by local merchants such as Mears was 25 percent over Baltimore store prices. Nonetheless, there were too many storekeepers, many of whom lived on a close margin. Miscalculation, competition, or a bad crop year might lead to bankruptcy. Rapid turnover among Eastern Shore merchants was endemic.[17]

As they had since the early colonial period, the merchant-shippers with their stores, wharves, warehouses, and sailboats remained at the top of the Eastern Shore's mercantile pyramid. Firms such as Frank T. Boggs & Bros. at Boggs's Wharf on Pungoteague Creek, John T. Finney & Bro. at Finney's Wharf on Onancock Creek, and Powell Bros., Hopkins & Bro., and John M. Fosque & Bro. at Onancock bought, shipped, and sold produce. Themselves enjoying top ratings from *Dun's*, they extended credit to others. The activities of the Powell brothers give an idea of the varied enterprises of the merchant-shippers. The Powells managed stores, engaged in the vessel trade, invested in real estate, developed Powellton, and introduced sweet potato culture to St. Mary's County, Maryland. In 1875 George W. Powell affirmed the family's status by purchasing Ker Place, a Federal mansion in Onancock. Several merchant-shippers also served as agents of the Eastern Shore Steamboat Company. Hopkins & Bro. sold their sailboats when in 1876 they assumed the agency at Onancock. The *Eastern Virginian* reported in 1878 that Hopkins & Bro. "are engineering the freight traffic ... with marvelous success."[18]

Urban sales representatives pursuing orders, commission merchants

---

17 Wilmington *Morning News*, November 19, 1884 (first quotation); *PE*, August 25, 1881, February 23, 1882, March 14 (second quotation), November 15, 1884.

18 Benjamin T. Gunter, "Produce Exchange Keystone of Prosperity," PE, August 8, 1936; *Dun's Mercantile Agency Reference Book* 47 (July, 1880); Mariner, *Wachapreague*, p. 9; John J. Wise to William Mahone, March 14, 1882, Mahone Papers, Duke; *Baltimore Sun*, April 8, 1884; Leonard Town (Md.) *Saint Mary's Beacon*, June 5, 1884; *PE*, July 19, 1884; Nock, *Child of the Bay*, p. 134; Elizabeth H. Smith, "Century-Old Firm Retains Charm of Yester-Years," *Southern States Cooperative* in *ESN*, January 23, 1942; *EV*, June 29, 1878.

importuning consignments, and tourists and sportsmen seeking recreation required overnight accommodations. In 1880 eleven hotels served travelers to the Eastern Shore. The hotels were located on Cobb's and Chincoteague islands, in the courthouse towns of Eastville and Drummondtown, and in the principal crossroad communities. Their managers conveyed their guests from steamboat wharf to hotel where they supplied them with room, food, and drink. When James Ambler Jarvis took charge of the Taylor House in Eastville in 1875 he announced that the hotel "has been refitted with new Furniture and Bedding of the latest style. The table will always be laid with the best of eatables, for which taste the Eastern Shore of Virginia has been often justly complimented. ... His Bar will always be supplied with the best of Liquors, Wines, and Cigars, and prompt attendance." Jarvis and other managers also arranged livery service for commercial travelers and for vacationers interested in touring the countryside. Busy entertaining their guests, the hotel-keepers had neither the time nor inclination to ponder the long-term implications of providing lodgings, food, drink, and conveyance to the advance agents of Yankee imperialism.[19]

THE CONSTRUCTION OF NEW AND THE IMPROVEMENT of old dwellings, churches, wharves, and commercial buildings assumed by the early 1880s the aspect of a boom. In 1882 John W. Edmonds of the *Peninsula Enterprise* exclaimed that "Building in our county at present is booming to such an extent that it is impossible to secure mechanics enough to meet the demands of the people." Two years later, he reported that "G. Welly Coard, architect and builder, has now thirty mechanics in his employ, and is having built under his supervision, store houses, hotels, dwellings, etc., in Maryland and Virginia. ... [H]owever, he is still unable to meet the demand for his services." The *Enterprise's* Chincoteague correspondent commented that times on the island were so "lively" for carpenters that help was being "imported" from Maryland and

---

19 Chataigne, ed., *Virginia Business Directory and Gazetteer, 1880-81*, pp. 74, 399; *Norfolk Landmark*, December 22, 1875 (quotation); Morton, "Life in a Level Land"; *PE*, June 14, 21, November 22, 1883, March 15, April 12, 1884.

Delaware. At Powellton an abundance of work enticed a master builder from New Jersey to settle in the rising town. Bricklayers also had more work than they could handle. To meet the need for bricks, large kilns were erected near Onancock and in lower Accomack County near Sturgis (present-day Mappsburg). The boom increased pressure on contractors who, in turn, increased pressure on their employees. The mechanics of Onancock and vicinity circulated in 1882 a petition "looking to the restriction of a day's labor to 10 hours."[20]

The building boom required large quantities of lumber. At seemingly every crossroad a sawmill arose to meet local demand. In the two counties the number of sawmills increased from eleven to nineteen between 1870 and 1880 and grew by an additional half-dozen or more between 1880 and 1885. The sawmills supplied lumber for stove wood, for furniture, for boats and carts, for fence rails and dock pilings, for churches, wharves, stores, houses, and outbuildings. Sawmills sold all the lumber that they could produce but still struggled to meet demand. Builders were forced to import shingles and laths from North Carolina and a merchant on Hunting Creek bought plank from Georgia for use as oyster tong shafts. In 1881 the Onancock partnership of Waples, Hopkins and Company found a local market for 150,000 feet of timber imported from Lynn Haven Bay on the Western Shore.[21]

The shift from grain to potatoes also stimulated lumber production. Unlike grain, potatoes were shipped to market in barrels to guard against bruising in transit. Into the mid-1870s commission merchants supplied most of the barrels used by Eastern Shore farmers. In 1876 T. W. and G. B. Jones opened a barrel factory as part of their new sawmill at Sunnyside (now Cheriton). During the next few years additional

---

20 *PE*, April 13 (fourth quotation), September 21 (first quotation), 1882, June 7 (third quotation), 21, October 25, December 6, 1883, March 1, April 26, May 3 (second quotation), October 4, 25, November 15, 1884.

21 Products of Industry, Accomac and Northampton Counties, 1870 and 1880, microfilm of manuscripts, National Archives, Washington, D.C.; Washington *National Republican*, November 1, 1879; *EV* in *Norfolk Virginian*, November 17, 1880; *PE*, July 28, December 22, 1881, July 13, 1882, February 15, June 21, 1883, February 23, March 29, April 5, 26, July 6, August 23, September 27, October 4, 25, November 15, 1884. Some builders might have preferred cypress shingles from North Carolina to indigenous shingles.

barrel factories opened at or near Onancock, Grangeville, and Shadyside (adjacent to present-day Machipongo). With the exception of Frank T. Stockley and Company's factory near Grangeville, all were established by men from the Eastern Shore of Maryland. The Miles-Taylor-Lankford family connection operated a barrel factory as part of its Onancock Mill Company. "Activity and system" characterized their enterprise. The mill could manufacture 1,000 barrels daily; its barrel makers turned out a completed barrel every three and a half to four minutes. From its wharf, the company shipped its barrels to other waterfront locales.[22]

Meanwhile, Northern demand for Eastern Shore lumber expanded exponentially. The Chincoteague Bay region remained a prime supplier. In 1882 entrepreneurs from Bishopville, Maryland, established a "lumber shipping depot" on Chincoteague Island with Joseph T. Kenney as agent. On the peninsula's creeks, lumbermen rafted oak planks and pine stove wood to waiting schooners bound for the North. The lumbermen sold direct to boat captains and urban dealers or on contract to builders and manufacturers. In the fall of 1883, the firm of John O. Selby & Edward H. Conquest of Oak Hall in upper Accomack County filled "a large contract for oak timber for the Northern market."[23]

Sawmills were a dynamic force in the landscape. Near the mills, the smell of freshly-sawn lumber sweetened the air and the whine of the blade and the thump and whistle of the steam engine disturbed the quiet. In wet weather, the heavily-laden timber carts made a morass of the public roads. Sawmills fostered the establishment of new communities

---

22 Wilmington *Morning News*, November 19, 1881; Henry Riley Parker, "Transportation and Communication on the Eastern Shore," *ESN*, August 30, 1929; Louise Savage Mapp, "Eastern Shore of Virginia," *Washington Post*, June 16, 1935; W. A. Whelan, "Cheriton: Possesses Ideal Advantages as a Place of Residence," Eastville *Eastern Shore Herald* (hereafter cited as *ESH*), February 26, 1909; Katherine D. Wilson, "The Origin of Cheriton," *ESN*, September 22, 1922; *EV*, May 21, in *Norfolk Virginian*, May 26, 1881; *Baltimore Sun*, September 10, 1881; Snow Hill (Md.) *Democratic Messenger*, September 3, 1881, April 1, May 20, 1882; *PE*, August 11, 1881 (quotation), February 9, March 30, May 4, 18, July 13, 1882, June 7, 1883, September 14, 1884.

23 *Wilmington Daily Commercial*, September 26, 1872; *Baltimore Sun*, July 4, 1873; Philadelphia *Times*, September 7, 1875; Washington *National Republican*, August 18, 1879; *PE*, October 12 (first quotation), 19, 1882, March 29, December 13 (second quotation), 1883; June 14, 1884.

and the expansion of old. Cheriton at the head of King's Creek grew up around T. W. and G. B. Jones's mill, which in 1880 employed thirty-one hands. Leemont (formerly Woodstock) at the head of Hunting Creek experienced a building boom after the opening in early 1883 of two nearby sawmills. From the mills, roads (some of which became permanent) reached into the woods and down to the waterside. In 1884 S. M. Hancock and Company built in Wallop's Neck a road and wharf to facilitate the shipment of lumber to Chincoteague Island.[24]

In some places, the voraciousness of the sawmills depleted the supply of timber. The inroads on Eastern Shore woodlands led John W. Edmonds to believe that "No section of Virginia is to-day more poorly off for timber for all purposes than this Peninsula." Edmonds overstated the case. Some localities experienced a shortage of merchantable timber, but Eastern Shore farmers, ever more involved in sweet potato culture, continued to cherish their supplies of pine shatters and other woodlot "resources." Moreover, in the "mid-woods" along the spine of the peninsula and especially in the low grounds of upper Accomack County stood extensive woodlands awaiting ax and saw.[25]

DURING THE PERIOD 1870 TO 1884, NORTHAMPTON County lagged behind Accomack in population and community growth and in the construction of new buildings. Thomas M. Scott, editor of the Eastville *Eastern Shore Herald* complained in 1883 of "a sad lack of enterprise in our county. We need more mills and factories. A good strong push out of the old ruts would do the county incalculable good. There must be more grass and better stock. The farms are too large. They must be divided, and labor, capital and enterprise must be invited to come here." In its specifics Scott's analysis had merit but it overlooked crucial factors. Black-majority Northampton was in the process of integrating a proportionally large number of freedmen into a free labor economy.

---

24 Washington *National Republican*, November 1, 1879; Whelan, "Cheriton"; Wilson, "The Origin of Cheriton"; Products of Industry, Accomac and Northampton Counties, 1880; *PE*, February 16, March 30, 1882, February 15, 22, March 8, April 5, May 10, October 4, 11, 1883, March 29, April 5, 19, September 13, 1884.

25 *PE*, May 11 (quotation), 1882; Snow Hill (Md.) *Democratic Messenger*, November 12, 1881.

More important, the county's transportation system was underdeveloped. Northampton lacked waterfront railheads such as Crisfield and Franklin City to stimulate its seafood industry, and steamboat service on both sides of the county was not as extensive as that of Accomack. When, shortly, Northampton's labor and transportation difficulties were resolved, Scott would find that his county possessed an abundance of "enterprise."[26]

A CONSEQUENCE OF FEDERAL VICTORY IN THE Civil War was a greatly enlarged role for the state and federal governments in Southern localities. The dominant Republican Party intended to employ government power to meet the needs of business while enhancing the party's electoral prospects through an increased federal patronage. State and federal mandates initiated and facilitated change. On the Eastern Shore of Virginia during the period 1870 to 1884, government expenditures funded schools, roads, post offices, dredging projects, and life-saving stations. Government activity was another engine that reconfigured the Eastern Shore countryside.

THE EXPANDING ECONOMY OF THE 1870S AND early 1880s increased local demand for good roads. Farmers, watermen, and lumbermen wanted convenient access to shipping points while consumers wanted access to commercial centers. Rising vehicular traffic required frequent road maintenance. By order of the Accomack County Court, new roads were built in the oystering communities of Saxis, Chincoteague, and Greenbackville. In 1874 a new road connected Sanford with the nearby sawmill and steamboat wharf at the Hammocks on Messongo Creek. A year later a causeway, built at relatively great cost to the county, extended from the Hammocks across the marsh to Saxis Island. On the south side of Messongo Creek, the county court in 1884 ordered the construction of a road giving lower Cattail Neck an outlet on the Bayside Road. In anticipation of a brisk trade, Albert F. Mears established a store at the new crossroad that would soon bear his name. On the lower seaside,

---

26 *ESH* in Wilmington *Morning News*, July 31, 1883.

farmers in Bradford's Neck successfully petitioned the court for a road joining the neck with the steamboat wharf at Powellton.[27]

Local boosters believed good roads a basic tenet of the cult of progress. "The Boggs' wharf road, that is the road from the neck road to the creek, if it were made wider and [oyster-] shelled would make a beautiful street," "J. A." told the *Peninsula Enterprise*. "There are some fine locations on either side of this road. There are fish, soft and hard crabs enough in Pungoteague Creek to supply a dozen small settlements, at this important shipping point. With a good road here, and the ground laid off in neat building lots, we should soon see a baby city sneezing and giving evidence of life."[28]

IN THE LATE ANTEBELLUM PERIOD, VIRGINIA MAINTAINED a rudimentary system of public schools for white children. The schools were supported by the state Literary Fund for the education of paupers, by tuition collected from those disqualified from taking the pauper's oath, and by whatever monies the counties might allocate. In 1850 Accomack County had twenty-seven one-room schools and Northampton thirteen. Virginia's Reconstruction constitution of 1868 required free public education for children of both races to be sustained by the Literary Fund, the capitation tax, and optional local property taxes. Political uncertainty in Virginia delayed the inauguration of the free school system until 1871. In its first year of operation, Accomack funded thirty-two public schools and Northampton nine.[29]

The commonwealth's vain struggle to repay its public debt, the concomitant reluctance of taxpayers to support the schools, and the

---

27 *PE*, July 5, September 27, October 4, 11, 1883, January 26, March 1, April 26, May 10, 1884, June 29, 1907; Mariner, *Almost an Island*, pp. 37, 44; Mariner, *Wachapreague*, p. 9.

28 J. A. to editor, *PE*, August 16, 1884.

29 Leonard W. Johnson. *Ebb and Flow: A History of the Virginia Tip of the Delmarva Peninsula, 1561-1892* (Verona, Va.: McClure Printing Co., 1982), p. 185; Jack P. Maddex Jr., *The Virginia Conservatives, 1867-1879: A Study in Reconstruction Politics* (Chapel Hill: University of North Carolina Press, 1970), p. 59; James C. Weaver, "An Epitomized History of Education in Accomac County, Va.," *Fifteenth Annual Report of the Superintendent of Public Instruction for the Year Ending July 31, 1885* (Richmond: Superintendent of Public Printing, 1885), pp, 50, 51; J. B. Dalby, "The History of Education in Northampton," *Ibid.*, p. 246.

necessity of poor people to put their children to work at an early age hamstrung the efforts of educators to serve an enlarged student population. By 1878 the number of schools in Accomack had climbed only to forty-six (thirty-eight white and eight black) and in Northampton to twenty (thirteen white and seven black). The number of pupils in Accomack had reached 3,178 (2,524 white and 654 black) and Northampton 1,038 (523 white and 515 black). The ratio of pupils to the school-age population was 41.3 percent in Accomack and 36.1 percent in Northampton. While non-attendance was general across racial lines, black participation lagged well behind white. In Accomack 51.7 percent of eligible white children attended school versus 23.3 percent of black; in Northampton 45.9 percent of white versus 29.6 of black. That the white school trustees and superintendents discriminated against black schools seems likely, but the prime reason for the low attendance among blacks was the need of impoverished black parents for their children to earn their keep.[30]

In 1876 a journalist noted the tendency among the sons of the predominantly white watermen of Chincoteague to leave school: "Although the native population is generally illiterate, schools are established on the island, to which some parents have been induced to send their children, but the boys generally take to the water and its fascinations at so early an age that they have no time to learn to read and write." In the post-Civil War period, advocates of free public schools battled attitudes and imperatives that discounted reading, writing, and the higher forms of ciphering as unnecessary to most people who made their livings by sweat and toil.[31]

The idea of free schools gradually gained acceptance among Eastern Shoremen. The penetration of the peninsula by the forces of modernity convinced increasing numbers of people that schooling was essential to

---

30 *Eighth Annual Report of the Superintendent of Public Instruction for the Year Ending July 31, 1878* (Richmond: Superintendent of Public Printing, 1878), pp. 90, 91, 93, 94; *Ninth Annual Report of the Superintendent of Public Instruction for the Year Ending July 31, 1879* (Richmond: Superintendent of Public Printing, 1878), p. ix; *Journal of the Senate of the Commonwealth of Virginia, 1877-1878* (Richmond: Superintendent of Public Printing, 1878, Doc. No. 3.

31 "Chincoteague Island, Va.," *Baltimore Sun*, August 28, 1876.

the well-being of children and the economic advancement of the community. "Under our admirable public school system, the children of parents residing in heretofore comparatively isolated districts are rapidly coming out from beneath the cloud of ignorance," an Onancock man told the *Norfolk Landmark*, "and now the march of mind and growth of intellect is plainly visible upon every hand." The commonwealth's repudiation in 1882 of a portion of the state debt freed for school use monies that heretofore had stuffed the pockets of creditors. By 1885 the number of schools had increased to eighty-two in Accomack and twenty-six in Northampton. The ratio of pupils to the school-age population edged up to 57.5 percent in Accomack and 41.7 percent in Northampton. James C. Weaver, superintendent of the Accomack schools, enthused about educational gains among the children of the watermen of the upper county:

> Tangier ... before the adoption of the present system, with scarcely a score of inhabitants that could read and write, now has a graded school of two teachers, with an enrolment of 96 pupils. Chincoteague ... has a graded school with three teachers and 219 pupils enrolled; another white school on the north end of the island, with 51 pupils, and a colored school, with 87. On Syke's [Saxis] island ... there is a school with 35 pupils. Greenbackville ... that 18 years ago had a single log dwelling, now has a population of almost 600 inhabitants and a graded school, with two teachers and an enrolment of 112 pupils.

Two years later, "Drummer" declared that the children in Messongo Neck "are being educated, not merely a few but the masses."[32]

In 1880 at least five private schools and academies – the schools of Mrs. J. F. Nottingham and Mrs. Mary A. Thomas in Northampton and the Locustville Academy, the Onancock Academy, and the Margaret

---

32 *Norfolk Landmark*, November 20, 1873; Wilmington *Morning News*, May 12, 1881; Weaver, "An Epitomized History of Education in Accomac County, Va.," pp. 50 (quotation), 51; Dalby, "The History of Education in Northampton," p. 246; *Journal of the House of Delegates of the State of Virginia For the Session of 1883-4* (Richmond: Superintendent of Public Printing, 1883), Doc. No. 8; "Pocomoke Neck and Sykes" (quotes "Drummer").

Academy at Bobtown in Accomack – tutored the children of the affluent on the Eastern Shore. Superintendent Weaver considered the academies a complement to the public schools. He cited Onancock Academy as "where the branches higher than those taught in the public schools could be pursued. ... The primary and higher branches of English are taught, together with the languages, ancient and modern, mathematics, and music. The school deserves to be ranked as a valuable assistant to the educational progress of the day. Its teachers are two gentlemen and a lady of culture, refinement, and progress, and deserve the hearty support of the community."[33]

A child's "being educated" consisted of more than the sum total of hours spent in a classroom. Orestes Brownson, a New England educational maverick, emphasized the primacy of home, community, and landscape: "[O]ur children are educated in the streets, by the influence of their associates, in the fields and on the hill sides, by the influences of surrounding scenery and overshadowing skies, in the bosom of the family, by the love and gentleness, or wrath and fretfulness of parents, by the passions or affections they see manifested, the conversations to which they listen, and above all by the general pursuits, habits, and moral tone of the community." Eastern Shore children learned the fundamentals of life from parents and elders, from field and wood, marsh and water. The words, figures, and angles that they mastered in classrooms helped them better negotiate an increasingly impersonal, complex, and competitive world in which the emerging deities were money, technology, statistics, and "expert" opinion.[34]

IN 1870 THE FEDERAL ESTABLISHMENT ON THE Eastern Shore consisted of a handful of customs officers and lighthouse keepers and two dozen postmasters. Over the ensuing decade and a half, the federal presence expanded dramatically. The number of post offices more than doubled,

---

33 Chataigne, ed., *Virginia Business Directory and Gazetteer, 1880-81*, pp. 74, 399; Nock, *Child of the Bay*, pp. 178-179; Weaver, "An Epitomized History of Education in Accomac County, Va.," p. 49.

34 Christopher Lasch, *The Revolt of the Elites and the Betrayal of Democracy* (New York and London: W. W. Norton & Company, 1995), p. 157 (quotes Brownson).

the Life-Saving Service established stations on the barrier islands, and the Army Corps of Engineers commenced the dredging of peninsula waterways. Federal activity created jobs, facilitated business, and enhanced public safety. It also brought Eastern Shoremen more tightly into national commercial and political orbits while increasing their dependence upon federal largess.

BEFORE THE CIVIL WAR, MOST SOUTHERNERS REJECTED the idea of using federal money to fund internal improvements such as turnpikes and railroads and the dredging of channels and harbors. In the persuasive light of Union victory, they decided that, if the federal pie was to be sliced and divided, they wanted a share to help rebuild their war-worn country. On the Eastern Shore, the demands were for harbor and channel improvements. Projects contemplated on the seaside included the dredging of a canal (or inland waterway) between the barrier islands and the mainland from Delaware Bay to Chincoteague Bay and the less ambitious undertaking of dredging a channel between the railhead at Franklin City and Chincoteague Island. Reports to Congress of the Army Corps of Engineers effectively killed both proposals by emphasizing their expense, divided public support, and uncertain outcome. Corps officers pointed out that powerful currents and storms endlessly reshaped the channels and islands of the seaside. Inlets opened and closed periodically and changing currents made the permanence of dredging doubtful. Considering the proposed Franklin City-Chincoteague channel, Major William P. Craighill warned that cross currents might require the construction of expensive dikes and breakwaters. He also commented that, while "navigation" interests supported the project, "those who own and work the extensive and very productive and valuable oyster-beds are very much opposed to any change which would disturb them."[35]

On the bayside, Eastern Shore commerce benefited from Corps-endorsed improvements at Baltimore and Crisfield and along the

---

35 *Baltimore Sun*, January 21, 1879; *PE*, October 11, 1884; Chincoteague Bay, Va., United States, Senate, 46th Congress, 2nd Session, Ex. Doc 90 (1880), p. 13 (quotes Craighill); Survey of Chincoteague Bay, Va., United States, House of Representatives, 48th Congress, 2nd Session, Ex. Doc. 107 (1885), p. 5.

Pocomoke River. A *Baltimore Sun* reporter noted in 1881 that Crisfield, "so important today," was fifteen years earlier "an inaccessible mud flat." Government aid, he continued, had in the meantime provided "a fine harbor ... for the bay trade." In home waters, the Corps in 1879 recommended the dredging of a channel through the sandbar at the mouth of Onancock Creek and the dredging of a channel and turning basin in Onancock harbor. The work was completed in 1880 at the cost of $8,000. Before the dredging at the mouth of the creek, steamboats and large sailboats had to await high tide before crossing the bar.[36]

THE NUMBER OF POST OFFICES IN THE two counties grew from twenty-six in 1870 to sixty-six in 1884. The Post Office Department created the new offices to meet the business needs of a growing population and to satisfy the importunities of politicians. Many of the twenty-three offices opened during the years 1882 to 1884 owed their existence to pressure applied by United States Senator William Mahone. Having won control of the federal patronage in Virginia, Mahone used it to build a Republican machine. He saw right-minded postmasters as grass-roots ambassadors, organizers, and intelligence agents of the party. They informed Mahone of local politics, disbursed funds, disseminated party propaganda, and herded loyal voters to the polls. The postmasters had an incentive to work hard for the party. A takeover of the national administration by the Democrats would deprive them of their places.[37]

The storekeepers who ran these post offices earned little money - $75 to $125 per annum – from handling the mail. They found the office attractive because it brought potential customers into their stores.

---

36 *Baltimore Sun*, August 23, 1881 (quotation); "Trade of Port of Baltimore"; *EV* in *Norfolk Virginian*, April 16, 1880; Surveys of Certain Rivers in Virginia and North Carolina," United States, House of Representatives, 45th Congress, 3rd Session, Ex. Doc. 68 (1879), pp. 10-11; Onancock Harbor, Va., United States, House of Representatives, 51st Congress, 1st Session, Ex. Doc. 83 (1889), p. 3; *Norfolk Virginian*, April 23, 1880.

37 United States, Post Office Department, Record of Appointment of Postmasters, 1832-September 30, 1971, Microfilm Publication, M841, National Archives, 1973; Brooks Miles Barnes, "Triumph of the New South: Independent Movements in Post-Reconstruction Politics," Ph.D. dissertation, University of Virginia, 1991; Johnson, *Ebb and Flow*, pp. 211-213; *Wilmington Morning News*, April 25, 1883.

Patrons who came in to pick up their mail might also purchase merchandise. "Rusticus" told the *Peninsula Enterprise* that he suspected that his postmaster deliberately failed to deliver mail in a timely manner in the hope that by compelling patrons to call repeatedly they might eventually see something they wanted to buy. Storekeepers also realized that a postmastership aided in debt collection. Aware of when farmers and watermen received checks from commission merchants, postmasters knew the most propitious time to dun their debtors.[38]

The new post offices were a convenience to those who previously had to walk or ride four or five miles to pick up their mail. In 1881, for example, some of the people living in Messongo Neck had to travel several miles to Jenkins Bridge to post or retrieve a letter. By 1885 they had recourse to post offices at Sanford (1885), Marsh Market (1882), or on Saxis Island (1884). Mail generally arrived semi-weekly or tri-weekly. During the harvest, the communities at the steamboat wharves received a daily mail. Besides personal and business correspondence, Eastern Shoremen received newspapers, magazines, farm journals, religious bulletins, and mail-order catalogs. Thus, urban mores and attitudes diffused throughout the countryside.[39]

As the American economy grew in the years following the Civil War, the number of vessels plying coastal waters multiplied. Shipwreck, always a danger of maritime life, became more commonplace. In 1872 citizens of Accomack County informed the governor of Virginia of "the recent large number of wrecks." The United States Congress responded in 1873 and 1874 to the loss of life and property by appropriating funds to expand the country's rudimentary public life-saving capabilities. The

---

38 John E. Bradford to First Assistant Postmaster General, in James E. Brady to William Mahone, July 4, 1881, John J. Wise to Mahone, March 14, Bradford to Mahone, March 16, August 5; Wilbur F. Nottingham to Mahone May 18, 1882, Mahone Papers, Duke; "Rusticus" to editor, *PE*, February 23, 1884.

39 John H. Snead to William Mahone, September 12, 1883, John E. Bradford to Mahone, February 8, 1884, Mahone Papers, Duke; "Pocomoke Neck and Sykes"; *Baltimore Sun*, March 10, 1874; *PE*, June 21, 1883, February 9, 16, 1884; G. Terry Sharrer, *A Kind of Fate: Agricultural Change in Virginia, 1861-1920* (Ames: Iowa State University Press, 2000), p. 92.

Revenue Marine Bureau of the Treasury Department, succeeded in 1878 by the United States Life-Saving Service, commissioned life-saving stations in hitherto neglected regions including the Eastern Shore. Stations opened in 1875 on Assateague, Cedar, Hog, Cobb's, and Smith's islands; in 1883 on Wallop's Island; and in 1884 on Parramore Island. An excursionist described the arrangement of the Cobb's Island station:

> [A] frame house just on the edge of the beach, which you would mistake for a summer cottage but for its massive timbers and solid appearance, bolted as it is to the ground, braving the force of wind and storm. Entering through large double-doors facing the sea, you first catch sight of the lifeboat resting on a great broad-wheeled truck, for rolling the boat along the beach to a point opposite the distressed vessel, and from there out into deep water. You are amazed at the sight of great piles of rope, cannon, and mortar, for shooting a line across the stranded vessel, carrying instructions written in every language, a water-tight car for sliding over the rope between the vessel and station, great life-saving suits of the Boydton patent dangling from the ceiling like thieves from a gallows, cork jackets, sky-rockets, lanterns, and axes in profusion – every article as bright as a mirror. The crew consists of six men and a captain – on duty eight months of the year and off four. While on duty they eat and sleep at the station. The second floor consists of three rooms, one large dormitory, with six nice iron-framed bedsteads for the use of the crew. The captain occupies the other two, one for his bed-room, the other for his office, containing the library and medicine-chest, together with official books for keeping meteorological records for each day, with the health and attendance of the crew. We were struck with the immense number of blankets hanging from the rafters with the inevitable U.S. brand on it. We were told that they were kept for the use of the survivors from the wreck.[40]

---

40 Richard A. Pouliot and Julie J. Pouliot, *Shipwrecks on the Virginia Coast and the Men of the*

SUMNER I. KIMBALL OF MAINE OVERSAW THE establishment and growth of the Life-Saving Service. Upright, dynamic, and iron-willed, Kimball ensured that the service, unique among government agencies of the era, remained free of patronage politics. The *New York Times* described him as "not only an officer of exceptional ability, whose energies are entirely devoted to the preservation and improvement of the service which he has developed, but also one who has always stood between his subordinates and the spoilsmen, defending the organization against the attacks of politicians who would have ruined it if they could have worked their will." Kimball demanded that the men employed by the service be experienced watermen, that they be housed in stations substantial enough to withstand storms, and that they use equipment best suited to function. On the Eastern Shore, several of the stations employed an improved surf boat designed by Benjamin S. Rich, superintendent of the service on the peninsula. By 1885 four of the original stations had been remodeled and rebuilt, and a telephone had replaced the telegraph that relayed periodic weather reports from the Assateague station to Washington via the United States Signal Office on Chincoteague.[41]

The crew at each station was on duty from September 1 through April 30. The keeper received in wages $50 per month and the surfmen $40. In the off-season, surfmen worked as watermen or guides or lived on their wages. In the summer of 1883 surfmen living on Chincoteague

---

United States Life-Saving Service (Centreville, Md.: Tidewater Publishers, 1986), pp. 4, 6-7; Petition of Citizens of Accomac County requesting the appointment of Charles S. Jester as Wreck Master, June 13, 1872, Executive Papers of Gilbert Carlton Walker, 1869-1873, Library of Virginia, Richmond; *Baltimore Sun*, December 26, 1874; *PE*, October 25, November 15, 22, 1883; "Demon" to editor, *Richmond Dispatch*, August 22, 1879 (quotation). See also the letter of E. H. F. in the *Dispatch* of the same date.

41 Pouliot and Pouliot, *Shipwrecks on the Virginia Coast*, p. 5; *New York Times*, n.d., clipping in Memorandum for Senator Mahone, April 5, 1885, Mahone Papers, Duke; Ron M. Kagawa and J. Richard Kellam, *Cobb's Island, Virginia: The Last Sentinel* (Virginia Beach: The Donning Company, 2003), p. 29; *PE*, February 9, November 30, 1882, May 10, July 19, September 20, 1884; *Norfolk Virginian*, August 4, 1884; *Richmond Dispatch*, December 7, 1884; "The Teagues of Accomack"; Snow Hill *Democratic Messenger*, October 14, 1882. For Senator Mahone's unsuccessful attempt to gain control of the Life-Saving Service patronage on the Eastern Shore see Barnes, "Triumph of the New South," pp. 202-204.

contemplated organizing "a 'lazy man club' for the purpose of fining any man caught at manual labor previous to the opening of stations in the fall."[42]

The daily life of station crewmen was a routine of watch, drills, and nocturnal patrols. It exposed keepers and surfmen to cold and wet and to hard slogs along sandy beaches and strenuous pulling at oars in rough waters. Attending shipwrecked vessels subjected them to frostbite, broken bones, and death by drowning or exposure. On January 9, 1883, Keeper George D. Hitchens and his crew of the Smith's Island Station attempted in freezing weather and high seas to rescue eight men (four crewmen and four employees of the Cobb Wrecking Company) lashed to the rigging of the stranded schooner *Albert Daily* of Augusta, Maine. Waiting for sufficient light, Hitchens and his men remained on the beach through the night without food or fire. They periodically immersed their feet in sea water to keep them from freezing. At daybreak they launched their surf boat into seas so heavy that only on their fourth approach were they able to reach the *Albert Daily* and effect a rescue.[43]

The rescue of professional wreckers aboard the *Albert Daily* by the men of the Life-Saving Service was not without irony. Life-Saving Service crewmen warned off potentially endangered vessels, and, when feasible and as a public service, employed their surf boats to free stranded vessels. Wreckers naturally resented the loss of business. On the night of August 27, 1879, shortly before the Cobb's Island Station was to be reopened for the season, arsonists burned it to the ground. A federal agent investigated and, although unable to identify the perpetrators, concluded that "the incendiaries were, without much doubt, persons who are opposed to having a life-station there to save vessels from being wrecked." The Life-Saving Service immediately rebuilt the station, and the arson was not repeated. The business of wrecking would continue

---

[42] Pouliot and Pouliot, *Shipwrecks on the Virginia Coast*, pp. 15, 16; *Baltimore Sun*, September 3, 1879; "The Teagues of Accomack"; *PE*, May 17, 1883 (quotation).

[43] Marinus James, "A Day at a Coast Guard Station," *PE*, August 4, 1928; *PE*, February 23, April 12, 1884; *EV* in Nashville *Tennessean*, January 29, 1883.

on the barrier island, but it would have to accommodate itself to the priorities of modern government.[44]

ON THE EASTERN SHORE FROM 1870 TO 1884, physical and mental landscapes underwent rapid change. Long on the periphery of national life, the Eastern Shore was now being subsumed and transformed by the American economy and government. New appetites, expectations, and dependencies were being formed. Old customs, attitudes, and liberties were being abandoned. An old world was fading away as a new world emerged.

---

[44] *Baltimore Sun*, September 3, 5, 10 (quotation), 1879; *Philadelphia Inquirer*, September 5, 1879; *Richmond Dispatch*, September 5, 1879; Washington *National Republican*, September 10, 1879; *Norfolk Virginian*, September 15, 1880.

Chapter V

Social Change

Marked alterations in social structure and attitudes occurred on the Eastern Shore of Virginia in the post-Civil War years. Black emancipation and citizenship required racial adjustments in politics and in labor relations. The paternalism of the old regime began to fade as processes of segregation and self-segregation shaped new boundaries in race relations. Northern values and mores insinuated themselves into the local psyche through the mediums of newspapers and periodicals, traveling lecturers and showmen, national fraternal organizations, and steamboat excursions to nearby cities. The founding of black churches and the opening of new white churches transformed the religious landscape. The desire for social progress fueled the temperance movement. The formality of the Code Duello gave way to the chaos of shoot-on-sight. Crime and hooliganism belied the promise of human progress.

THE COURSE OF RECONSTRUCTION ON THE EASTERN Shore, relatively brief but punctuated by theft, arson, affray, murder, and intimidation from the terror of which neither race was spared, convinced the peninsula's citizens that political, institutional, and economic accommodation was necessary if the races were to live together in peace and plenty. During the period 1870 to 1884 Eastern Shoremen negotiated these accommodations, not without contention but seldom with violence. The negotiations never reached a definitive settlement (they continue today), but they determined approximate, if shifting, boundaries of rights and responsibilities. Blacks and whites cooperated because they were dependent on each other. Whites needed labor and blacks needed work and neither could depend on finding what they needed elsewhere.

A political arrangement was the most easily accomplished and clearly understood. In his study of politics and voting in the Virginia Tidewater, 1865-1900, historian Joseph Patrick Harahan concluded that emerging from Reconstruction was "a changed set of assumptions which endorsed universal manhood suffrage, competitive political parties, Negroes in public office, and political democracy." Accomack and Northampton counties were no exception. In both counties, black voters almost universally enjoyed a free vote and a full count. In 1885 a Wilmington man, having visited several election precincts in Accomack, noted "The general attendance, the good order, [and] the free expression of sentiment through the ballot box." Only at Guilford precinct on the upper Accomack bayside were blacks afraid to vote. There, they were intimidated by white oystermen possessed of "an intense feeling of hostility to the negro."[1]

In white-majority Accomack, blacks failed to elect a man of their race to public office, but they participated avidly in local, state, and national elections. While acknowledging that "De whites is powerfu' strong Democrats round about heah," black farmer George T. Annis of near Metompkin Station [now Parksley] denied vociferously that he was a Democrat. Drawing himself up, he declared "No, Sir! De cull'd men votes de Republica' ticket." In heavily black Northampton, blacks might have elected one of their own to almost every office in the county. Peter J. Carter and other black leaders realized, however, that such a course would incite racial strife, something that neither they nor their Democratic counterparts desired. The result, then, was a tacit fusion agreement. Black Republicans received some of the district offices

---

1 Joseph Patrick Harahan, "Politics, Political Parties, and Voter Participation in Tidewater Virginia During Reconstruction, 1865-1890," Ph.D. dissertation, Michigan State University, 1973, pp. 297-298; Brooks Miles Barnes, "Triumph of the New South: Independent Movements in Post-Reconstruction Politics," Ph.D. dissertation, University of Virginia, 1991, p. 96; "Rambler Through Accomac," Wilmington *Daily Republican*, June 2, 1885; William Mayo to William Mahone, September 8, 1882 (quotation), John E. Bradford to Mahone, March 30, John J. Wise, List of the Most Prominent Accomac Readjusters, May, 1883, Mahone Papers, William L. Perkins Library, Duke University, Durham, N.C.

–constable, justice of the peace, overseer of the poor – while their white Republican allies shared with Democrats the higher positions – sheriff, treasurer, commonwealth's attorney, clerk of the court, commissioner of the revenue, and the three district supervisor positions. For his part, Carter claimed the county's seat in the state legislature. Carter and other black leaders countenanced an unequal arrangement, but their followers retained their right to cast a ballot and have it counted, and the pistol, the rope, and the faggot played no role in county politics.[2]

A voting majority gave Northampton blacks leverage among magistrates and office-holders that was probably denied their compatriots living in white-majority counties such as Accomack. "Here," white Republican Israel Townsend of Capeville proclaimed with doubtless some hyperbole, "they are protected in all necessary and proper rights ... and in all matters in dispute a negro can get as free, full and clear justice as a white man can."[3]

ON THE ANTEBELLUM EASTERN SHORE WHERE SLAVEHOLDINGS were almost uniformly small, white masters and black slaves were likely to break bread together in the home, work together in the field, worship together in church, and drink together at the crossroad store. Under such an intimate regime, racial segregation was impossible. What slaves (and free blacks) endured was not segregation but exclusion – exclusion from education, political participation, and institutional leadership.[4]

---

2 Wilmington *Morning News*, November 19, 1884 (quotes Annis); Barnes, "Triumph of the New South," pp. 103-104. Historian Steven Hahn wryly commented that fusion had less to do with fusing together than with dividing up (Hahn, *A Nation under Our Feet: Black Political Struggles in the Rural South from Slavery to the Great Migration* (Cambridge and London: Harvard University Press, 2003), pp. 385-387. Historian Armstead L. Robinson noted that "conservative politics of survival served legitimate political interests within the Afro-American community, interests as legitimate as the more radical politics of immediate equality and every bit as worthy of careful analysis" (Robinson, "Beyond the Realm of Social Consensus: New Meanings of Reconstruction for American History," *Journal of American History* 68 (September, 1981), p. 295).

3 Townsend, Capeville, to editor, August 9, Wilmington *News Journal*, August 10, 1877.

4 Kirk Mariner, *Slave and Free on Virginia's Eastern Shore from the Revolution to the Civil War* (Onancock, Va.: Miona Publications, 2014); Philip Leigh, *Southern Reconstruction* (Yardley, Pa.: Westholme Publishing, 2017), pp. 154-155; Howard N. Rabinowitz, *The First New South, 1865-1920* (Arlington Heights, Ill.: Harlan Davidson Inc., 1992), p. 135.

Emancipation occasioned segregation of the races. Whites and blacks now desired to relinquish responsibilities for and limit associations with each other. Intent on restricting contact with what they regarded as an inferior race, whites segregated themselves from blacks. They insisted that schools, lodges, fairs, and even some churches be segregated. Meanwhile, to escape white oversight, blacks self-segregated. If they continued on the farm, they left the quarters near the owner's dwelling to reside in tenant houses scattered about the property. If they chose to work as casual laborers, they joined older communities where free blacks had gathered during antebellum days or newer settlements formed since emancipation. A traveler discovered a black section on the outskirts of Onancock: "A number of streets or lanes run from the main one, and end in a forest of scrub pine in which are numerous negro huts fairly alive with noisy pickaninies." In and near these communities, blacks established their own churches and fraternal organizations, and they cherished the segregated schools that the state provided them. Black leaders now would direct the activities of their own communities and institutions. At this moment in history, segregation constituted for blacks a kind of freedom.[5]

Within this segregated society emerged a cadre of black leaders. Some came from off the Eastern Shore, but most were native to the peninsula. They had imbibed the pride and discipline required for leadership from service in the Union Army, from post-war studies at the Hampton Institute and other seats of learning, or from succeeding at business in a white man's world. In the ironic liberty afforded by segregated schools, churches, lodges, and political offices, their now unfettered talents flourished. Their successes gave the black community reasons to be proud of their institutions and themselves. The leaders gave the community the strength it needed to endure the long march toward equality.[6]

---

5 "A Virginian Atlantis, *American Traveler and Tourist* in Accomac Court House *Peninsula Enterprise* (hereafter cited as *PE*), October 8, 1887 (quotation); Frances Bibbins Latimer, *Landmarks: Black Historic Sites on the Eastern Shore of Virginia*, eds. Brooks Miles Barnes and Barbara G. Cox (Eastville, Va.: Hickory House, 2006).

6 For black community leaders see Latimer, *Landmarks*; Latimer, *Life for Me Ain't Been No*

Emancipation revolutionized labor relations on the Eastern Shore. The freedmen were now clear of the masters' schedule and discipline. They controlled their own working lives. Moreover, laborers, of whom blacks comprised eighty percent or more of the male casual work force, were sellers in a sellers' market. In the 1870s and early 1880s a local economy flourishing in all sectors gave Eastern Shore laborers, black and white, options off the farm unavailable in most regions of the South. They might work in the seafood or lumbering industries as well as in agriculture. The more independent among them might move from job to job and industry to industry in pursuit of higher wages and more congenial work. Summertime jobs in the tourist trade might take them off the peninsula. In the early 1880s blacks from Atlantic left annually for seasonal work in the resort town of Long Branch, New Jersey. Some of the casual laborers worked steadily but others, certain that means of making a living always would be available, enjoyed their leisure until driven by necessity.[7]

Eastern Shore farmers, most of whom were white, found themselves in an uncomfortable position. The accelerating shift from general to truck crops in the postbellum years placed a premium on the availability of labor. Farmers needed help throughout the year but especially at planting and harvest. Vegetables must be planted promptly in order to ripen in time for the early markets. Fruits and vegetables must be gathered, packed, and shipped quickly to insure fresh delivery to those markets. Unhappily for the farmers, planting and harvest times coincided with periods of activity in the seafood industry where workers earned more than in agriculture. "[G]rowers are unable to compete in wages with the more profitable vocations adopted by the male portion of their laborers," "J. T. B." told the *Wilmington Every Evening*. "Indeed the waters of the ocean and bay and their tributaries abound in salt

---

Crystal Stair: Stories from Virginia's Eastern Shore African-American History, eds. M. N. Mitchell and Brooks Miles Barnes (Eastville, Va.: George A. Latimer, 2013); and Kirk Mariner, *Revival's Children: A Religious History of Virginia's Eastern Shore* (Salisbury, Md.: Peninsula Press, 1979).

7 *PE*, November 29, 1884. Statistical analysis derived from Manuscript Censuses of Population, Accomac and Northampton Counties, 1880.

water luxuries to such extent that the more robust laborer reaps such rate of compensation as to preclude his employment on the land. This traffic from the waters has grown so rapidly with the increased facilities of transportation that a small army of laborers find there employment during the larger portion of the year." Farmers sought to assure themselves of reliable labor by offering monthly or annual contracts but laborers often preferred to preserve their autonomy by working by the day.[8]

Farmers attempted to compensate for the scarcity of labor by limiting the acreage of land under cultivation and by enlisting the aid of all capable family members at the harvest and other moments of crisis. Otherwise there seemed little that the farmers could do. Raising the wages paid labor to a point commensurate with the burgeoning seafood industry was, at this point, impossible. Farmers had not yet discovered a system of marketing their crops that would earn them enough to offer competitive wages.[9]

As the cost of labor continued to rise in the early 1880s, farmers desperately sought an alternative supply. Early in 1882 John W. Edmonds of the Accomac Court House *Peninsula Enterprise* suggested that they turn to European immigrants:

> If a few of our farmers club together and charter a boat for New York, or Boston, or Philadelphia, they can obtain all the labor they wish – in the household or on the farm. Hundreds of German families would be proud of the chance to hire out to our farmers. They can work just as cheap as any other race. Irishmen, too, make good farm hands; they understand the care of horses, and when necessary can use the hoe. In fact they are "hedgers and ditchers" by nature.

---

8 *PE*, March 23, May 18, 1882, February 28, 1885; *Wilmington Every Evening* in *PE*, May 17, 1884; Ernest Ingersoll, "The Oyster Industry" in *The History and Present Condition of the Fishery Industry*, by G. Brown Goode (Washington: Government Printing Office, 1881), pp. 160, 182; *Richmond Dispatch*, January 21, 1873; *Baltimore Sun*, June 10, 1882; Eastville *Eastern Shore Herald* (hereafter cited as *ESH*) in Salisbury (N.C.) *Carolina Watchman*, May 3, 1883; *ESH* in Wilmington *Morning News*, January 15, 1884. For the labor demands of potato culture see E. J. T. Collins, "Migrant Labour in British Agriculture in the Nineteenth Century," *Economic History Review* 29 (February, 1976), p. 39.

9 *Richmond Dispatch*, January 21, 1873, April 16, 1874.

Try the Celt, try the German, try the Swede. So soon will a new prosperity dawn upon this land, and you will ever after have the help you now so much desire.

Over the next several months, Alfred J. Mears of Grangeville, acting as an agent for farmers in lower Accomack County, made several trips to New York City from whence he returned with around 150 German male laborers. By May, however, Edmonds realized that "We have made ... mistakes in this. Foreign labor, differing in language, manners and customs, coming as it does without any ties of family, and without that home-feeling and steadying influence which family intercourse naturally brings with it, soon wearies, and, singly or in groups, gradually disappears." He went on to reveal the cultural naivete of Eastern Shore farmers: "These laborers, although merely laborers, have not been raised on 'hog and hominy,' and *will not* live on it. ... The huts with which our negroes are familiar, and to them are *homes*, are what these not only do not expect, but will not accept."[10]

Having failed with immigrant labor, Eastern Shore farmers soon found a partial solution at home. "Colored women are taking more to field work than formerly," an Onancock correspondent told the *Baltimore Sun* in the spring of 1884,

> In most any part of the county you can find entire neighborhoods cultivated by the labor of colored women and boys. The most successful farmers are giving up men and looking to this class, which can be held with some certainty. These farmers are building comfortable huts in out-of-the-way places on their farms and rent them to colored women having children large enough to work. This movement is very

---

10 Wilmington *Morning News*, November 29, 1881; *Baltimore Sun*, December 1, 1881; *PE*, February 9 (quotation), March 2, 16, 23, April 20, May 4 (quotation), 18 (quotation), 1882; Snow Hill (Md.) *Democratic Messenger*, June 24, 1882. In 1883 Orris A. Browne tried to stir up interest in importing Hungarian laborers, but the idea seems not to have gained traction (PE, March 29, April 26, 1883; Wilmington *Morning News*, April 7, 30, 1883). For the many reasons that the South failed to attract European immigrants in the post-Civil War years see E. Merton Coulter, *The South During Reconstruction, 1865-1877* (Baton Rouge: Louisiana State University Press, 1947), pp. 104-105.

general here now, and is thought to be productive of much good. It is the only labor that can be held with any certainty.

This "movement" indicates the almost complete mobilization of black labor. It meant a larger income for black families but at the cost of dashing the freedmen's dream that their women might be kept out of the fields. It also hints at the frequent absence of adult males from family circles and at the emergence of a black matriarchy.[11]

Another area of economic adjustment involved the growing number of blacks operating farms. Between 1870 and 1880 the number of black farmers in the two counties increased from about 300 to 735. In 1880, the total number of farm operators, white and black, was 2,730, of whom 1,097 (40.2 percent) were farm owners, 1,010 (37 percent) were renters, and 623 (22.8 percent) were sharecroppers. Blacks comprised 27 percent of the farm operators. Ten percent of blacks were farm owners while 42 percent were renters and 32 percent sharecroppers. That blacks comprised 10 percent of land owning farmers in 1880 indicates significant progress. Land tax records for Northampton County confirm the upward trend. Black landownership increased in the county from 3 percent (16 landowners) in 1870 to 12 percent (81 landowners) in 1880.[12]

The renter enjoyed more autonomy than the sharecropper. The renter financed some or all of his own work and at the harvest paid the landlord in cash or in a share of the crop. He disposed of his share as he wished. The sharecropper was, in effect, a wage laborer. The landlord financed and supervised the cropper's work and paid him his share after disposing of the crop. Whether the prospective tenant achieved the

---

11 *Baltimore Sun*, May 5, 1884; *Wilmington Every Evening* in *PE*, May 17, 1884.

12 The statistical elements of this and the following paragraphs devoted to farm tenure are based on an analysis of the Manuscript Censuses of Agriculture, Accomac and Northampton Counties, 1880. The figures given differ slightly from those in *Report on the Productions of Agriculture as Returned at the Tenth Census (June 1, 1880)* (Washington: Government Printing Office, 1883), pp. 94-97. The increase in the number of black landholders in Northampton is derived from work by Stacia Childers based on Allen B. Hamilton, comp., *Northampton County, Virginia, Land Tax Records, 1851-1870* (Berwyn Heights, Md.: Heritage Books, 2021), pp. 397-422, and Hamilton, comp., *Northampton County, Virginia, Land Tax Records, 1875, 1880, 1885, and 1895* (Berwyn Heights, Md.: Heritage Books, 2021), pp. 76-118.

independence of a renter often depended on the assets – equipment, working stock, and credit with which to obtain seed and fertilizer – he brought to negotiations with the landlord. So necessary did agricultural paraphernalia seem to Henry Hope, a black would-be farmer living near Woodberry on the middle road in central Accomack County, that he allegedly participated in a house-breaking in order to invest "the spoils in a farming outfit (horse, cart, &c.)."[13]

In 1878 a journalist visiting the Eastern Shore supplied a classic description of sharecropping:

> What were formerly large estates, worked by slaves, are now divided into sections and the owners occupy the mansion houses; the negroes cultivate the sub-divisions. They are furnished by the owners with guano, seeds, teams and implements, and cultivate the land under the superintendence of the owner and receive one-third of the crop; the owner receiving the remaining two-thirds. It is found that a much larger yield is had under this system, and we are assured that this co-operative plan is in every way satisfactory.

A few years later, another journalist interviewed a renter:

> A faint idea of what a small farmer may do in this country is gleaned from the statement of George T. Annis, an intelligent colored man who rents a place of 25 acres clear and as many more acres of 'resources,' timber land, near Matomkin station [now Parksley]. He pays $60 rent a year, which is the interest and tax on about $800. He works his own place, keeps one mule and a horse and a couple of cows. He raises enough corn for bread, but sweet potatoes are his saleable crop. He looked fairly flourishing and said that he was doing 'right smart.'[14]

---

13 *PE*, January 5, 1884. For comparisons of renters and sharecroppers see Harold D. Woodman, "Sequel to Slavery: The New History Views the Postbellum South," *Journal of Southern History* 43 (November, 1977), pp. 553, and Woodman, "Post-Civil War Southern Agriculture and the Law," *Agricultural History* 53 (January, 1979), p. 325.

14 "The Future State," Wilmington *News Journal*, February 28, 1878; Wilmington *Morning*

On the Eastern Shore in 1880 sharecropping was a more productive mode of farming than renting. Landlords were better able than renters to spend money on wages, fence, and fertilizer. As a result, the average value of produce harvested on sharecropped farms was $352 compared to $268 on rented farms (owner-operated farms averaged $374). The average value of sharecropped farms was $1,927 compared to $1,403 of rented farms (owner-operated farms averaged $2,223). Sharecropping seemingly was of financial advantage to the landlord. Yet, the number of renters, white and black, surpassed that of sharecroppers 1,010 to 623. If possessed of sufficient assets, tenants chose to preserve their independence from landlord supervision. They preferred to manage their own work and broker their own sales. In a tight labor market, the landlord must bow to their wishes.[15]

Black people chose to farm because they had experience in agricultural work and because they viewed it as a better way than casual labor to oversee the family and preserve its integrity. Then, too, intangibles such as the rich smell of broken earth and the satisfactions of the harvest might have had played a part. Black farm operations were small when compared to those of white. In 1880 the average white farmer resided on a larger holding (103 acres to 47 for the average black farmer), worked more improved acres (54 to 23), paid more in wages ($122.59 to $84.82) expended more on fence ($15.91 to $5.67) and fertilizer ($26.60 to $9.23), and sold more produce ($391 to $183). Still, blacks had their feet in the door of an industry on the rise. Whites would employ them as tenants and sell them land. Black farmers had reason to believe that with hard work, thrift, and luck they might continue to improve their station.[16]

Despite the scarcity of labor, white Eastern Shore farmers came

---

News, November 19, 1884.

15 How much the landlord gained from letting his land to sharecroppers is unclear. Against income would be some or all of the cost of seed, fertilizer, fence, implements, work stock, etc.

16 For farming and the black family see Orville Vernon Burton, *In My Father's House Are Many Mansions: Family and Community in Edgefield, South Carolina* (Chapel Hill and London: University of North Carolina Press, 1985), p. 259.

to regard the end of slavery as a boon. The transition from slave to free labor enabled the rise of a more numerous, productive, and prosperous yeomanry. Money hitherto expended in the purchase, hire, and maintenance of slaves exceeded that now spent in wages to laborers and in the outfitting of tenants. From the Eastern Shore in 1884, came the story of Tom, a field hand who had taken to heart a rumor that blacks would shortly be re-enslaved. Tom told his employer, the son of his former master, that "I has been free so long that I can't stan' slavery again and me and my ole woman is a-gwine to Canady." "Very good," replied his employer, "you look into this thing well, Tom, and if slavery is to be reestablished, let me know, and I'll go with you, for I'll be shot if I'm going to support the big gang of idle negroes my father had hanging on him during his lifetime." The emancipation of the slaves was in certain respects the emancipation of their masters.[17]

Emancipation replaced master and slave with employer and employee. The ethics of Northern-style labor relations began to supersede the duties and moral responsibilities (albeit often honored in their breach) embedded in the slave regime. "When Northern capital penetrated the plantation country after the war, an unalloyed capitalist ethic also appeared," wrote historian James L. Roark. "The desperate search for renewed prosperity put a heavy strain on unprofitable traditional relationships. Paternalism did not wear well in the Gilded Age." Northampton County Clerk of Court William T. Fitchett in 1879 contrasted the pre-emancipation days with the present: "We all had to be kind to our niggers then, they was worth so much. They ain't as well treated now as they was then, I reckon."[18]

---

17 Coulter, *The South During Reconstruction*, p. 211; *Norfolk Landmark* in Wilmington *Morning News*, December 9, 1884; Richard M. Weaver, *The Southern Tradition at Bay: A History of Postbellum Thought* (n.p.: Regnery Gateway, 1989 [reprint of 1968 ed.]), p. 249. "An agricultural reorganization that could have raised a prosperous yeomanry in the place of dependent laborers and marginal farmers with minimal purchasing power would have required, above all, the elimination of slavery" (Eugene D. Genovese, *The Political Economy of Slavery: Studies in the Economy and Society of the Slave South* [New York: Vintage Books, 1965], pp. 138-139, 246).

18 James L. Roark, *Masters Without Slaves: Southern Planters in the Civil War and Reconstruction* (New York and London: W. W. Norton & Company, 1977), pp. 198-199; Allen Tate, "Faulkner's *Sanctuary* and the Southern Myth" in *Memoirs and Opinions, 1926-1974* (Chicago: The Swallow Press, 1975), p. 151; Howard Pyle, "A Peninsular Canaan," *Harper's New Monthly*

Although weakened, paternalism lingered in the interstices of Southern life for generations. Especially in the farmyard and in the kitchen with their daily routines, employers knew employees as persons. They valued the employees' reliability and thus, combining philanthropy and self-interest, rewarded them with bonuses, gifts, and favors. Farmers also extricated hands from legal difficulties. In 1881, for example, white farmer John Wesley Hurst qualified as surety for Esau Riley, a black laborer who had been arrested for being "drunk and rioting" at a black camp meeting at Savageville near Onancock. Hurst was the brother-in-law of Riley's employer. In a passage written in 1941 South Carolinian Archibald Rutledge revealed the reciprocal nature of such paternalism: "Every employer of Negroes in the South is *expected* by his employees to stand between them and the statutes. A lot of my time and effort and some of my money go toward keeping my people out of jails and off chain gangs. They really behave no worse than we do, they are singularly defenseless."[19]

THROUGHOUT THE 1870S AND EARLY 1880S EASTERN Shoremen continued to pursue their traditional pastimes. They gathered together in homes and stores where they gossiped, drank, danced, and played cards. They hunted and fished. They attended horse races, boat races, and beach parties. To these they added activities facilitated by growth in income and population, improved transportation, and more widespread literacy. Local participation in these activities resulted from the peninsula's vastly increased contact with the outside world and signified an implicit acceptance of the national cult of progress.

Baseball was the most innocuous of Northern imports. Indeed, it seemed of native growth. The peninsula's level terrain, spacious fields,

---

Magazine 58 (May, 1879), p. 807 (quotes Fitchett).

19 Robert Penn Warren, "The Briar Patch" in *I'll Take My Stand: The South and the Agrarian Tradition by Twelve Southerners* (New York: Harper and Row, 1962 [reprint of 1930 ed.]), p. 262; *PE*, August 18, 1881; Rutledge, *Home by the River* (Indianapolis: Bobbs-Merrill, 1983 [reprint of 1941 ed.]), p. 122 (quotation; emphasis added). The connection between John Wesley Hurst and Esau Riley was established from research in the Manuscript Census of Population, Accomack County, 1880, and the genealogical database The Miles Files.

encompassing woods, and immense skies provided an ideal setting. The game's leisurely pace suited the Eastern Shore temperament. Players and spectators alike were mesmerized by baseball's beauty, grace, and rhythm. Interest on the peninsula grew rapidly and within a couple of decades would become a mania.

Kinsmen and neighbors formed local "nines," and the clubs took names – Chincoteague Continental, Modestown Modocs, Metompkin Blues, Onancock Stars. Usually a team exchanged visits with rival nines from nearby villages but occasionally it would travel a considerable distance for a game. In 1877, for example, the Onancock Stars ventured to Franktown in upper Northampton County only to lose 22 to 21. As community rivalries intensified, clubs brought in "ringers" from other Eastern Shore villages and even from other states. At Woodberry in 1882 the Stars, aided by ringers from Guilford, Modestown, and Delaware, took on the Combination Club, consisting of players from Woodberry, Drummondtown, Pungoteague, and Maine. The Stars overcame the Combination 30 to 26. In the early 1880s competition reached an apogee when picked nines from Accomack and Northampton clashed during the agricultural fair. Accomack came out ahead in 1884 by the score of 12 to 6. The score of most games generally was higher, the winning team often scoring twenty runs or more. The bare-handed baseball of the era was not conducive to what is regarded today as good fielding. Catchers who backstopped fast pitchers often emerged from games with blistered hands. In the 1882 fair grounds match, Dr. John W. Bowdoin of Woodberry, captain of the Accomack nine, "got his right hand split from the centre of the palm to the end of the middle finger." Surely, Dr. Bowdoin's discomfort was assuaged by his having played for the winning team.[20]

Closer connections with the outside world combined with a growing, more literate population and an expanding village life to encourage

---

20 Wilmington *Morning Herald*, July 17, 1876; July 28, 1877, July 22, 1878, Charles Albert Van Ness Journals, 1874-1885, transcription in Eastern Shore of Virginia Heritage Center, Eastern Shore Public Library, Parksley, Va.; Onancock *Eastern Virginian* (hereafter cited as *EV*), September 1, 1877, July 13, 1878, August 2, 1884; *PE*, June 15, July 13, 27, August 31, 1882, March 29, May 17, June 28, July 12, August 9, 1883, March 15, April 19, May 17, 31, August 1, 1884; *Baltimore Sun*, September 1, 1884 (quotation).

the formation of chapters of national fraternal organizations. Families were eager to relieve the isolation of rural living, and villages were near enough at hand to make attendance at fortnightly lodge meetings convenient. During the post-Civil War years, Eastern Shore whites joined the Patrons of Husbandry (Grange), the Masons, the Heptasophs, the Rechabites, and the Knights of Honor; blacks joined the Masons, the Odd Fellows, and the Good Samaritans. Women of both races participated in lodge auxiliaries while black women in Northampton formed a chapter of the United Order of Tents. The orders met in churches, schools, and vacant buildings, but when possible they erected their own lodge halls. In 1883 the Odd Fellows dedicated their new hall at Drummondtown "in the presence of a vast assemblage estimated at 2,000." A year later the white Masons of Eastville built a new hall to replace the one vandalized by Union troops during the war while on Saxis Island a recently organized chapter of the Independent Order of Rechabites erected "a handsome and imposing structure."[21]

The lodge activities gave participants the satisfaction of ritual, regalia, and responsibility. They alleviated boredom and engendered a sense of belonging. They aided churches, schools, and the indigent. They encouraged upright living. The Rechabites and the Good Samaritans placed abstention from alcohol at the center of their creed. Perhaps most important, the lodges provided sick and death benefits for dues-paying members.[22]

Young people formed private clubs. In the summertime, the unmarried men and women who composed the Drummondtown Jolly Club sponsored moonlight cruises out of Folly Creek and beach parties on Cedar and Metompkin islands. Throughout the year, the club members organized dances. The Led Astray Club of Chincoteague in 1883 recruited a brass band to entertain the crowd attending the annual sheep penning on Assateague.[23]

---

21 *EV*, July 13, 1878; *PE*, March 9, 1882, April 5, July 5 (first quotation), 12, December 20, 1883, February 9, March 1, 15, August 2, September 13, October 18 (second quotation), November 15, 1884; Latimer, *Landmarks*, pp. 73-74, 77-78; "A Quaint Town: Eastville, Va., Contains Many Historical Buildings," *Detroit Free Press* in *ESH*, February 14, 1914.

22 Thomas J. Schlereth, *Victorian America: Transformations in Everyday Life, 1876-1915* (New York: HarperCollins, 1991), pp. 212-213; Latimer, *Landmarks*, p. 74.

23 L. Floyd Nock III, *Drummondtown, "A One Horse Town," Accomac Court House, Virginia*

Civil War veterans also organized. Black Union veterans founded Grand Army of the Republic posts at several locations on the peninsula. Typical was the post established in 1885 at Savageville near Onancock. A G.A.R. mustering officer from Norfolk worked with Rev. Peter Shepherd and the congregation of Gaskin's Chapel African Methodist Episcopal Church to organize local veterans. The founding membership consisted of fifty veterans led by a commander, two vice-commanders, and a chaplain. The mustering officer was impressed by what he experienced on the Eastern Shore. According to a member of the Savageville post, the officer "spoke in the highest praise of Rev. Mr. Shepherd's congregation for being so hospitable in entertaining strangers. He also spoke of the prosperous condition of the people, and assured them that he had traveled a good deal, but at no place had he found the colored people so prosperous. He says also, that the white people are always approachable and ready to give information at all times."[24]

The organization of Confederate veterans lagged behind that of their black Union counterparts. In 1883 Confederate veterans established at Drummondtown the Accomack Camp with forty members. The veterans declared that "It is for us ... to rescue from fatal decay the memory of the deeds of the noble men, who by their courage shed lustre upon the arms of the Confederacy and sealed their devotion with their blood." They resolved to compile an honor roll of those who fell in active service and a roster of those who survived the war. Both projects moved slowly and the roster remained far from complete when camp secretary George T. Scarburgh issued a last call for registration in 1884. The Confederate effort was premature. Not enough time had passed, not enough veterans had passed away, for dejection to become nostalgia. In the immediate post-war years, the difference between the enthusiasm of black veterans and the apathy of white was the difference between victory and defeat.[25]

Expanded steamboat service made the peninsula easily accessible to

---

(Verona, Va." McClure Press, 1976), pp. 292-293; *PE*, June 7, 1883.

24 Latimer, *Landmarks*, p. 74; *PE*, June 13, 1885 (quotation).

25 *PE*, June 14 (quotation), 28, July 5, 26, August 23, 1883, April 26, June 7, August 16, November 22, 1884.

professional entertainers. In 1881 Dr. George W. Bagby, the Richmond humorist, gave lectures at Onancock and Drummondtown. His subjects were "Bacon and Greens" and the "Comic Side of Negro Life." An advertisement for the lectures promised "a rare intellectual treat for those who favor him with their presence." The Weston Combination in 1882 played three consecutive nights to a crowded house in Drummondtown. The Combination featured Professor Frank Weston, a prestidigitator who performed sleight-of-hand and mind reading, and "the Lilliputian family, seven midgets whose tricks delighted old and young." At Pungoteague in 1881, an illusionist entertained his audience by manipulating a large mirror to produce the image of a ghost. The exhibition ended prematurely when a stranger in the audience, producing a pistol, fired at the ghost and broke the mirror. Aware that the mirror was "the only means which the poor man had to eke out a very precarious living," the people of Pungoteague and vicinity raised a subscription to cover the cost of its replacement.[26]

Meanwhile, local amateurs performed for the public. A "grand soiree and musical entertainment" occurred at the Onancock Academy in 1881 and a dramatic association organized on Chincoteague in 1882. In the latter year, Austin H. Merrill, a graduate of Princeton, gave a reading and recitation on behalf of the building fund of Onancock's Market Street Methodist Episcopal Church, South. "Go and be convinced as to the beauty of our mother tongue when presented by a gentleman who understands and appreciates it," declared the notice in the *Peninsula Enterprise*. At the school house in Temperanceville in 1884 Rev. Montcalm Oldham lectured on "Evolution." A listener, persuaded by Rev. Oldham's argument, told the *Enterprise* that he "greatly deplored" the recent demise of Charles Darwin "that he might realize how fallacious the theory was upon which he spent so many years of study and research in natural history."[27]

---

26 PE, September 1, 8 (first quotation), December 15, 22 (third quotation), 1881, October 5, 12 (second quotation), 1882, August 30, 1883.

27 *PE*, December 15, 1881 (first quotation); March 2 (second quotation), April 13, 1882, March 15, 1884 (third quotation).

Improved railroad and steamboat service at once stimulated the curiosity of Eastern Shoremen in the outside world and helped satisfy that curiosity by facilitating delivery on the peninsula of urban newspapers and magazines. Through the railhead at Franklin City came a steady stream of newspapers. "Area and population considered, Chincoteague stands first, perhaps, of any place on the Eastern Shore in the encouragement of newspaper literature," boasted an islander. "Every household, almost, has the weekly visits of some paper, and very many of our people subscribe to the dailies." On the bayside the vessels of the Eastern Shore Steamboat Company served as conduits for the printed expression of Northern ideals and mores. "Drummer" declared that in Messongo Neck "The great circulating educators are doing their work. ... Many of the leading secular and religious journals can be found there."[28]

The Eastern Shore's first newspaper was the *National Recorder* established at Drummondtown in 1860. The *National Recorder* continued in operation until 1862 when occupying Union troops confiscated the press for use in producing a camp newspaper. In the post-war years, a vigorous economy and a growing and more literate population encouraged the publication of local newspapers. The Onancock *Eastern Virginian* appeared in 1873 and the Eastville *Eastern Shore Herald* and the Accomac Court House *Peninsula Enterprise* in 1881.[29]

While the post-war influx of urban newspapers and magazines tightened bonds between the Eastern Shore and the nation, local newspapers strengthened those between the peninsula's communities. Readers weekly learned what was happening in business, society, and politics not only in their own neighborhood but also in other villages from New Church to Townsend. Local newspapers documented change and were themselves agents of change. Their editors – Charles W. B. Marshall of the *Eastern Virginian*, Thomas M. Scott of the *Eastern Shore Herald*, and

---

28 *PE*, March 29 (quotation), December 6, 1883, March 29, 1884; "Pocomoke Neck and Sykes," *Ibid.*, July 23, 1887 (quotes Drummer).

29 Lester J. Cappon, *Virginia Newspapers, 1821-1935: A Bibliography with Historical Introduction and Notes*, Guide of Virginia Historical Materials, Pt. 1 (New York: D. Appleton-Century Company, 1936), pp. 41 63, 83, 145; Wilmington *News Journal*, August 28, 1873; Snow Hill (Md.) *Democratic Messenger*, May 14, 1881.

John W. Edmonds of the *Peninsula Enterprise* – subscribed wholeheartedly to the cult of progress. They advocated Northern immigration and investment, improved transportation and communications, and the development of towns and industry. Local newspapers also facilitated the transformation of the Eastern Shore from an oral to a written culture. News, gossip, and legal notices now were broadcast in the public prints.

Nothing better represented the quest for improvement than the annual agricultural fair established near present-day Keller by the Pungoteague Grange in 1878. The fair began as a one-day exhibition of Granger farm produce. By 1881 the Grange had formed the Eastern Shore Agricultural Association which leased a twenty-acre plot, erected a two-storey exhibition hall, laid out a race track, and arranged for a boarding tent. The association also made the fair a four-day event. Exhibitions included farm produce, livestock, machinery, and ladies' handiwork. Entertainment regularly featured orators, baseball games, and horse racing. "Among the numerous attractions" in 1881 were a bicycle race, musicians from Baltimore, and "a living skeleton, twenty-six years old, who weighs only seventeen pounds." Besides white Eastern Shoremen, the fair attracted excursionists who came by steamboat from Baltimore. In 1883 nearly 3,000 people attended the fair on its busiest day."[30]

The Eastern Shore Agricultural Fair, maintained John W. Edmonds, was important to everyone on the peninsula "whatever his avocation" because "agriculture is the foundation stone upon which every industry is built, and from which it derives its sustenance and support." Edmonds urged all farmers to compete for premiums. Fairs, he insisted, "were intended to stimulate us to ... advance our interests by the lessons

---

30 J. E. Mapp, "Interesting Letter about Keller Fair," Onancock *Accomack News*, August 19, 1921; James Egbert Mears, "The Eastern Shore of Virginia in the Nineteenth and Twentieth Centuries" in *The Eastern Shore of Maryland and Virginia*, ed. Charles B. Clark (New York: Lewis Historical Publishing, 1950), pp. 618-619; Ralph T. Whitelaw, *Virginia's Eastern Shore: A History of Northampton and Accomack Counties* (Richmond: Virginia Historical Society, 1951), II, 795; *EV* in *Norfolk Landmark*, July 26, 1876; *Norfolk Virginian*, April 14, 1880; *PE*, August 25, 1881 (quotation), August 24, 1882; *Baltimore Sun*, August 23, 1880; Wilmington *Morning News*, September 1, 1883. The "living skeleton" probably was Josh Gunter of Occohannock Neck (*EV* in Westminister (Md.) *Democratic Advocate*, September 16, 1882).

taught by those whose experience is riper and success greater than ours, and while we may not secure premiums, those who do will have their reward – if they ... are thereby taught to improve and till their lands more skillfully, to sow their seeds at times most suitable to their germination, how to cultivate their crops, when to reap them." The lessons the fair taught went down easily. The agricultural exhibits, various and competitive, entertained as well as edified. Bands, baseball games, horse races, promenades along the midway, and visiting with kinsmen and neighbors made the fair the most exciting social event of the year. Many Eastern Shoremen treasured memories of the fair for the rest of their lives.[31]

The people of the Eastern Shore further edified and amused themselves by joining steamboat excursions to nearby cities and watering places. On the seaside, summer excursions frequently left Wishart's Point for the new resort at Ocean City, Maryland, via Chincoteague and Franklin City. A trip to Ocean City in 1883 left Wishart's Point at 8.00 a.m. and returned at 7.00 p.m. A round-trip ticket cost 75 cents. Ice cream and other refreshments were for sale on board the steamer. In the fall of 1884 the Old Dominion Steamship Company carried excursionists from Powellton to Norfolk and from Chincoteague to New York. On the bayside, vessels of the Eastern Shore Steamboat Company frequently embarked excursionists for Baltimore. The city's Order of the Oriole Festival attracted hundreds from the Eastern Shore in 1883. In the summer of 1884 black excursionists traveled by steamer from Cherrystone to Norfolk. The success of the excursions benefited from publicity in the peninsula's newspapers.[32]

Also publicized in the newspapers were notices of numerous local parties and festivals. Readers learned of corn gatherings at Atlantic; a quilting party at Muddy Creek where "both sexes were well represented,

---

31 *PE*, August 10, 1882 (quotation), March 1, August 16, 1883. For the social aspects of agricultural fairs see Charles S. Sydnor, *The Development of Southern Civilization, 1819-1848* (Baton Rouge: Louisiana State University Press, 1948), p. 267.

32 *EV*, July 7, 1876, September 22, 1877, July 27, 1878; *PE*, September 8, 1881, August 3, 1882, June 14, August 9, September 13, 1883, July 19, 26, October 4, 18, 1884; *ESH* in *Norfolk Virginian*, August 23, 1884.

and as the saying goes, a vast 'number of old coals rekindled'"; and water parties at Guilford, on Saxis, and at Guard Shore at the confluence of Guilford, Young's, and Muddy creeks. The organizers of the party on Saxis promised a boat race and, by way of variety, a race to catch a greased pig. The events often served as fundraisers. The issue of the *Peninsula Enterprise* for July 27, 1882, advertised festivals for the benefit of Sunday schools at Atlantic and at Oak Grove (near present-day Melfa) and for the erection of a Methodist Church at Powellton. Under a spacious arbor near the wharf at Cherrystone, the women of the Lower Northampton Baptist Church in the late 1870s hosted an annual fair and feast that attracted excursionists from Norfolk and Portsmouth. Perhaps the most spectacular and certainly the most archaically romantic of the occasions were the tournaments held at Onancock in 1876 and 1882, at Cherrystone in 1877, and at Pastoria (near present-day Parksley) in 1883. The champion knight of the Pastoria tournament won a fine bridle and saddle while the winners of all three events gained the privilege of crowning the Queen of Love and Beauty. The tournaments were dreamy anachronisms in this new world of the wide awake. They celebrated horsemanship, exalted an idealized womanhood, and recalled the heroism of the late war.[33]

Eastern Shoremen continued to enjoy public holidays. On Christmas Eve, 1883, the inhabitants of Marsh Market greeted the coming of the Christ Child with food, drink, and the nocturnal firing of pistols and shotguns. Earlier that year, the people of Northampton County gathered in Eastville for August court day. A citizen of the town reported that the holiday "was observed here ... with more than antebellum sanctity. By 10 o'clock the streets of the village were one mass of moving humanity, and, considering the quantity of the usual concomitant

---

33 *PE*, July 27, August 3, September 21, 1882, July 19, August 23, 1883, January 26, November 29, 1884; Snow Hill (Md.) *Democratic Messenger*, September 30, 1882; *EV*, September 1, 1876; Norfolk *Landmark*, August 2, November 20, 1877; *Norfolk Virginian*, August 1, 1879; Coulter, *The South During Reconstruction, 1865-1877*, p. 297. According to Elizabeth Fox-Genovese and Eugene Genovese, the post-war tournaments represented a means of "coping with the trauma of defeat, frustration, impoverishment, and military occupation" (*The Mind of the Master Class: History and Faith in the Southern Slaveholders' Worldview* [Cambridge: Cambridge University Press, 2005], p. 357).

evil dispensed, the crowd was orderly to a fault." In Accomack County, March had displaced August as the great court day. The popularity of the August camp meetings and agricultural fair probably accounts for the change. In 1884 March court day attracted 1,000 people from all over the county. "March court day is the great fete day of the year," a correspondent told the *Baltimore Sun*.

> It is the only time when this little village of 250 inhabitants becomes thoroughly aroused. The session of the court is a matter of secondary importance. The exhibition of stallions and live stock is the great feature of the occasion. There were fully seventy-five stallions here on Monday. There were trials of speed, comparison of points, buying, selling, trading of horses. ... Drummondtown ... has not even the ferment of excitement which Onancock has when the boat comes in. Only once a year is it lively here, and that is when March court begins.[34]

In the immediate post-war years, white Eastern Shoremen were little inclined to celebrate the Fourth of July. "The glorious Fourth has come and gone," Delaware native and Union veteran Israel Townsend wrote from Capeville in 1867. "And I think, from all I can learn, I and my family were about all here who kept the glorious anniversary. It appears strange to these Virginians that any one could keep it. I have inquired pretty freely among them, and one and all admit that they never did keep or celebrate the day, and I am convinced that a good many did not and do not know what the 4th of July means." It seems likely that decades of Yankee contempt and abolitionist calumny culminating in Union military invasion, occupation, and reconstruction had tempered the enthusiasm of Townsend's neighbors for the "glorious Fourth." Yet, time passed, war wounds healed, the sting of defeat eased, and a growing economy encouraged reconciliation. Eastern Shoremen accepted the predominance of the Northern idea of progress and so began to feel again a sense of citizenship. By the early 1880s, some had

---

34 *PE*, August 16, 1883 (quotes "K."), January 5, 1884; *Richmond Dispatch*, May 31, 1879; *Baltimore Sun*, April 3, 1884.

begun to celebrate the Fourth of July. Chincoteague and Franklin City, home to large populations of immigrants from the North, hosted elaborate affairs attracting free-spending excursionists who arrived via the railroad. Celebrations elsewhere on the peninsula were more sedate, but by 1884 the merchants of Onancock had woke to the commercial value of patriotism. "For the first time in the history of this town," a resident exclaimed, "the merchants closed their stores on the 4th. They wish to show that they are becoming more patriotic."[35]

EMANCIPATION, AN EXPANDING ECONOMY, AND A GROWING population transformed the Eastern Shore's religious landscape. Blacks responded to the push of segregation and, more important, to the pull of self-segregation by forming congregations independent of white supervision. Illustrative of push and pull was an incident occurring on Sunday, January 14, 1866, at Garrison's Chapel in Mappsburg on the seaside road in lower Accomack County. Garrison's white congregation was not meeting that day, and Rev. T. L. Tompkinson, the church's pastor, was willing that Elder James H. A. Johnson, a missionary of the African Methodist Episcopal Church, and his followers might use the building for worship. Tompkinson, however, locked the doors to the lower floor of the chapel and informed the blacks that they must enter by the side door and ascend to the gallery. Turning to his flock, Elder Johnson declared that "It is degrading to our manhood to go up into that gallery. If you say so, I will go right over there into the woods and preach." Despite cold weather, the party accompanied Johnson into the woods where they sang, prayed, and listened to the Elder's sermon.[36]

---

35 Townsend, Capeville, to editor, July 6, Wilmington *Delaware State Journal*, July 16, 1867; Wilmington *Daily Gazette*, June 22, 1882; *PE*, July 13, 1882, July 5, 12, 1883, May 31, July 5 (quotation), 12, 1884.

36 Mariner, *Revival's Children*, pp. 135-136, 138-139; Mariner, *Slave and Free*, p. 227; James H. A. Johnson, *The Pine Tree Mission* (Memphis, Tenn: General Books, 2012 [reprint of 1893 ed.]), p. 7. "Racial separation advanced steadily within the Southern churches after emancipation, and when blacks left, most whites, despite marked emotional wrenching, breathed a sigh at having been relieved of a burden. Blacks left in droves, in part doubtless to express their religious feelings in their own way and so develop their own institutions and leadership, but also because most whites who wanted integrated churches simply assumed that blacks would have to accept secondary status as wards of their paternalistic brothers (Eugene D. Genovese, *A*

Between 1865 and 1883 blacks established thirty-four churches in the two counties. Faithful to the Eastern Shore's historical pattern, Methodist churches predominated, twenty-two Methodist to twelve Baptist. The churches served as engines of liberation. Within their walls, black worshipers were no longer abased or excluded. The churches encouraged a sense of belonging and developed leadership cadres. They affirmed Christian values, supported the needy, and sponsored lodges and schools, social gatherings and political rallies. Kirk Mariner, historian of religion on the Eastern Shore of Virginia, stressed the significance of the black exodus:

> [W]ith the creation of the black churches the single greatest schism in the religious history of the Shore occurred. The division of the churches sealed the virtually total separation of the two races for a century to come. Cut adrift from one another, the black churches and the white churches developed along different lines, evolved different styles, and ministered to completely different worlds. On the Shore, as elsewhere in the nation, the black church became the real center for the hopes and dreams and aspirations of the black people, one of the few places the black citizen had to go to voice his feelings about anything. It was in the church that his social, economic, and political as well as his spiritual life was discussed and molded.[37]

White churches emerged from the Civil War bereft of vigor and vision. "In matters pertaining to their *spiritual interests* the blacks are manifesting an energy which would be well if we would emulate," an Eastern Shoreman told the *Richmond Dispatch* in 1867. "The churches of the whites, desolated and worn out by the war and stagnations

---

Consuming Fire: The Fall of the Confederacy in the Mind of the White Christian South [Athens and London: University of Georgia Press, 1998], p. 92).

37 Mariner, *Revival's Children*, pp. 135-144 (quotation on p. 138); Burton, *In My Father's House Are Many Mansions*, pp. 228, 230, 242. See also the penetrating commentary of novelist James Gould Cozzens, *By Love Possessed* (New York: Harcourt, Brace and Company, 1957), pp. 517-518.

thereof, are still in many places remaining as they were, though in some instances unfit to be occupied, while everywhere our colored people are earnestly at work building their houses of worship. In the two counties I know of five colored churches being built. One of these stands in sight of and between two other churches that have never been used since the war." The malaise ended in the mid-1870s as a stable political situation, an improving economy, and a growing population restored confidence. By 1884 twenty-three new white congregations had been formed while twelve existing churches erected new buildings. Other existing churches repaired their sanctuaries and built parsonages. Activity on the Accomack bayside in the fall of 1884 reflected renewed fervor. An Episcopal church was under construction at Onancock and Methodist churches at Sanford and Pungoteague. Meanwhile, Methodist churches were remodeled at Onancock and Chesconnessex. The white religious establishment on the Eastern Shore remained predominantly Methodist. Of the sixty-one white churches in operation in 1884, six were Episcopalian, six Presbyterian, fourteen Baptist, and thirty-five Methodist.[38]

The church brought its congregators, black and white, closer to God. It gave meaning, structure, and fellowship to the lives of the faithful. The church fulfilled needs spiritual and secular. Sunday school, Sunday service, Wednesday prayer meeting, and church get-togethers were at once sacred and sociable, each in its way a communion of the saints. Everyone there was equal before the Lord. Men assumed formal leadership roles, but women often were the more powerful disciples of Christ. They raised their children in the faith and raised funds for the faith. Through quiet ministries, they strengthened the bonds of fellowship. They visited the spiritually needy, nursed the sick, and, at church feasts, fed the multitudes. Women also assumed the role of moral arbiters.

---

38 *Richmond Dispatch*, July 18, 1867; Mariner, *Revival's Children*, pp. 158-163, 244-637 passim; *PE*, August 10, October 26, November 23, 1882, July 5, December 6, 1883, February 2, March 1, September 20, 27, October 18, November 15, 1884; Wilmington *Morning News*, December 3, 1884. Evidence from newspapers and from *Revival's Children* indicates that Mariner was partially mistaken when he wrote that "for the most part the two decades following the Civil War were, for the white Christians of the Eastern Shore of Virginia, a period of struggle, retrenchment, and standstill" (*Revival's Children*, p. 144).

They were the hidden wheel that drove the great temperance crusade that began to roil the peninsula in the early 1880s.[39]

Religious leaders understood that an active church was a living church. They filled the church calendar with events that relieved tedium, sustained the Holy Spirit, and attracted potential converts. Besides fairs and festivals, the churches sponsored more intimate gatherings such as suppers, picnics, and concerts. They also held revivals and protracted meetings, which encouraged the cathartic experience of repentance and conversion. In August, 1884, four ministers conducted a protracted meeting at the new Sanford Methodist Church where "The attendance was large, the deportment commendable, and the sermons preached were excellent. Ten persons professed religion during the time, and many were seeking it."[40]

For Methodists, the camp meeting remained central to their religious experience. Camp meetings attended by whites occurred on Tangier and Chincoteague islands, at Johnsontown, Drummondtown, and Woodberry, at Wise's Point near Onancock, and at Turlington's camp grounds near Dunkirk (south of present-day Melfa) in lower Accomack County. Held annually in August from 1871, the eight-days-long meeting in Turlington's woods attracted crowds averaging 2,000 daily with 3,000 to 4,000 present for service on the concluding Sunday. Ministering to the throngs were teams of preachers from both sides of Chesapeake Bay. So great was the need for wood for fences, stoves, camp fires, benches, and shed-tents that the proprietors of a nearby sawmill were "taxed to their utmost capacity in supplying the daily calls for thousands of feet of lumber for camp meeting purposes." A visitor described improvements made for the meeting of 1883: "The grounds are neat and clean, the tents are larger and not so much crowded together as in previous years, a tabernacle well ventilated, with good seats and having the capacity to accommodate 1,500 people or more, takes the

---

39 For the role of women in the church see Burton, *In My Father's House Are Many Mansions*, pp. 23, 131.

40 *Wilmington Daily Commercial*, September 26, 1872; *PE*, December 15, 22, 29, 1881, March 16, 1882, May 17, September 27, 1883, August 30 (quotation), September 13, November 22, 1884.

place of the pine bower, and the grounds are lighted by eight large lamps instead of the pine knots of other years. Rules for the government of the camp are posted on the grounds, and a vigilant police force has been appointed to look after evil doers."[41]

Black Eastern Shoremen established their own camp meetings. They met annually at Wattsville and Savageville in Accomack County and possibly elsewhere on the peninsula. The meeting at Savageville served as a homecoming for black expatriates. "The Eastern Shore [Steamboat Company] steamers have brought to the county a large number of colored people. The Savageville camp meeting offered the usual attraction for them to visit their old homes at this season of the year," a correspondent informed the *Peninsula Enterprise* in 1883. The Savageville meeting also drew black excursionists from Crisfield and Baltimore. In 1884 the *Enterprise's* Temperanceville correspondent attended the Sunday meeting at the nearby Wattsville camp ground. He reported a large attendance and "Some ten or twelve ministers ... among them we recognized Bro. Birch of Fairmount, Md., Bro. Ames of Cambridge, Md., [and] Bro. Jas. Cluff of Temperanceville. Bro. Ames preached the afternoon sermon, his text being, 'In hell he lifted up his eyes [Luke 16:23].'"[42]

Religious activity on the peninsula increased during the post-war period. An extensive black ecclesiastical establishment appeared seemingly overnight. White churches made a vigorous recovery from the dislocation and despair of occupation and Reconstruction. The camp meeting, the ultimate expression of Methodist revivalism, flourished. Yet, despite the construction of new churches, despite the popularity of camp meetings, many Eastern Shoremen remained unchurched. Writing from Washington in 1884, a Drummondtown woman lamented the spiritual lethargy of the home folks: "The churches here are always full. ... It is with great difficulty you can get a seat. Such a contrast

---

41 *Norfolk Virginian*, August 7, 1874, July 29, 1884; Wilmington *Morning Herald*, August 2, 1876; *PE*, July 28, August 4, 1881, July 13, 27, August 3, 1882, July 12, 19, 26, August 9 (quotation), 16, 23, 1883, July 19, August 9, 16, September 6, 1884; Mariner, *Revival's Children*, pp. 147-152. The Turlington Camp Meeting was not held in 1882 (*PE*, March 23, 1882).

42 *PE*, May 4, 1882, June 7, August 9, 23 (first quotation), 1883, August 16, 1884 (second quotation); *EV*, August 18, 1883.

to the congregation at home." Attendance was good on Chincoteague, but a visitor to the island in 1876 considered it more a function of form than of devotion. "I have never been in a community where there was a more general observance of the Sabbath. Not that the people generally are especially religious or devout, but they at least entertain a creditable regard for the observances of the Christian Sabbath, and a decent respect for its institutions." Another outside observer regretted "to learn that the *membership* of the churches is small in proportion to the population." Some islanders evinced little regard for prayer meeting. "There were rather strange proceedings at the Hall last Wednesday night – a prayer meeting above and a dance below," a critic remarked in 1884. "If our dancers had a little more respect for Christianity, they would select other nights for their reel than those on which prayer meetings are held."[43]

Although some Eastern Shoremen might avoid church services or go through the motions of worship, although others might neglect to show proper respect for the sensibilities of the devout, few were irreligious. The modern mind, self-exiled from heaven and earth, rational rather than pietistic, is baffled by the idea of religion. When not altogether dismissive, it relegates religion to "a small, specialized and insulated area of national life." To Eastern Shoremen, churched and unchurched, in the 1870s and early 1880s, God's presence was a commonplace, as manifest as the chapel at the crossroad.[44]

CRIME AND VIOLENCE ARE EVER-PRESENT IN society. The Eastern Shore in the post-Civil War years was no exception. Despite the peninsula's

---

[43] Sadie, Washington, to Hennie Parramore, April 12, 1884, Accomac Bicentennial, 1786-1986, Collection, Eastern Shore Heritage Center; "Chincoteague Island," Elkton *Cecil Whig*, September 9, 1876 (second quotation; italics added); J. P. Matthews, "Chincoteague Island," Baltimore *American* in Westminster [Md.] *Democratic-Advocate*, August 23, 1873 (third quotation); *PE*, February 2, 1884 (fourth quotation). A Wilmington man remarked that on Chincoteague "you will hear long scriptural disquisitions from men whom you would never have suspected of familiarity with the Bible" ("The Teagues of Accomack," Wilmington *Delaware State Journal*, April 7, 1881).

[44] J. C. D. Clark, *Revolution and Rebellion: State and Society in England in the Seventeenth and Eighteenth Centuries* (Cambridge: Cambridge University Press, 1986), p. 106 (quotation).

reputation for hospitality and conviviality, it had its criminal underworld. Thieves entered isolated farm houses on Sundays after the occupants had gone to church. Once inside, they forced the locks on furniture and took money, clothing, and "such property as struck their fancy." Burglars broke into stores and saloons after closing. Bolder criminals pilfered from stores during business hours. "For downright cheek an Onancock thief can 'take the cake,'" exclaimed Charles W. B. Marshall of the *Eastern Virginian*. "Our bed-room happens to be on the first floor. Some scoundrel reached in at the window and stripped the mattress of every vestige of covering, quilt and sheets – and it was a favorite quilt, too." Robbers made off with livestock. They plundered orchards and gardens, smokehouses and corn-cribs. Desperadoes undermined the foundation of the smokehouse at the Accomack County almshouse and carried off its contents. Although the petty larceny was never epidemic, it occurred frequently enough to be a public irritant. In 1884 an exasperated Leemont man declared that the village needed "a Vigilance Committee to take care of the hen roosts, dairies and woodpiles."[45]

Outbreaks of hooliganism constantly annoyed and outraged respectable Eastern Shoremen. Hooligans usually were young, white laborers or watermen who were landless and owned little personal property. They resented their neighbors whose affluence, thrift, or piety made them respected in the community. They despised blacks as racially inferior and feared them as potential competitors. Hooligans fought a guerilla war against society. They moved about in groups, egging on each other in their anti-social capers. They carried chips on their shoulders and pistols in their pockets. They filled public thoroughfares with profanity and played dangerous practical jokes. They were in their element at events such as the raucous post-wedding serenades of bride and groom where the milling crowd, the firing of pistols, and the dark of night provided cover for malevolent pranks.[46]

---

[45] *PE*, May 25, July 20, December 7 (first quotation), 1882, August 16, 1883, March 29, April 5 (third quotation), October 11, 18, 1884; Wilmington *Morning News*, May 8, 1883; *Richmond Dispatch*, May 31, 1879, *EV* in Snow Hill (Md.) *Democratic Messenger*, August 5, 1882 (quotes Marshall); *EV* in Norfolk *Weekly Virginian and Carolinian*, October 2, 1884.

[46] *Easton (Md.) Gazette*, June 16, 1877; *PE*, December 29, 1881, May 4, November 9, 1882,

Hooligans took pleasure in disrupting religious services and other public occasions. In 1879 a gang of toughs repeatedly impeded efforts to organize a Presbyterian church at Powellton. Presbyterian leaders responded by organizing a police force. "By this means," recalled the church's first pastor, "a tolerable degree of order was maintained. The law had to be given before they would receive the gospel and it proved a school master to lead them unto Christ." Despite the presence of a police force at the Turlington camp grounds in 1884, a worshiper from Onancock reported that "Thieves and devils were on hand, and some rascal stole the horse and harness of Mr. Alonzo Doughty of this town, while a malicious person cut to pieces the harness of Mr. Southey Wilkins of Northampton." On July 4, 1882, around 3,500 people, including 2,200 excursionists from Delaware and Maryland, gathered at Franklin City to celebrate Independence Day. The visitors found the whisky plentiful and the thugs active. An excursionist described the resultant pandemonium:

> Whisky, the "real old genuine tangle foot" or "Jersey lightning," flowed freely. [T. F.] Colborn of the Franklin House, with three assistants, couldn't begin to supply the demand. You may imagine what effect all this had on the Virginia and other roughs. ... About 2 o'clock the fun began, and men fought and brawled constantly till long after night. Israel Pollett, a young Franklin [City] oysterman and bully, was cock of the walk, and had things pretty well much his own way, knocking a man down here, choking or kicking another man there and trying his best to keep "things moving." ... The police force consisted of six men, who, when a row occurred, stood and looked at it, instead of trying to quell it and considering the meager strength of the force, acted wisely. A Georgetown [Del.] man was hurt severely in the afternoon. The excursion train arrived at Franklin at 2 o'clock and left there at 10 in the evening, arriving in Georgetown at about 3 o'clock this morning. "The Lord deliver us from

December 20, 1883, October 18, 1884.

Franklin City in the future," is the prayer of many who were there yesterday.[47]

The most notorious of the hooligans was a gang from the Guilford area who styled themselves the Charlestown Tigers. Guilford was known as the abode of hard-working and hard-living watermen and as the only election precinct in the two counties where blacks were afraid to vote. In 1877 the Tigers attempted to crash the performance of a traveling circus at Mappsville. The circus crew attempted to eject the interlopers and in the ensuing brawl a man was shot and the left ear of a Charlestown Tiger bitten by a circus performer called the "Man with the Iron Jaw." A year later, the Tigers assumed the role of enforcers of racial mores. After a black woman living near Guilford beat a white woman, several of the gang went to the black woman's home and, while a Tiger pointed a double-barrel shotgun at her husband, another thrashed her with "a screaming black gum."[48]

Arson occurred with disturbing frequency. Houses, stores, barns, stables, outbuildings, and fodder stacks went up in flames. Livestock, stored crops, and farm machinery were destroyed. Most acts of arson followed a dispute between the owner of the burned property and a customer, employee, or neighbor. In Northampton County in 1884 "an incendiary fire destroyed the barn and corn-crib of Mr. Bayley Bell ... together with forty barrels of corn and all his faming implements. Two negroes with whom Mr. Bell had had a misunderstanding, were arrested yesterday and committed to jail at Eastville on strong circumstantial evidence." More sinister were attempts by the arsonist to murder his victim. Peter Savage, a black tenant farmer living near Belle Haven, escaped through a window after fires had been set at both doors of his house.[49]

---

47 John G. Anderson, "History of Organization of Powellton Presbyterian Church," *PE*, December 6, 1956; *PE*, March 16, 1882, August 9, 1883; *EV* in *Norfolk Virginian*, August 4, 1884 (second quotation); Wilmington *Daily Gazette*, July 5, 6 (third quotation), 1882.

48 *EV*, September 22, 1877, June 29, 1878. The merchants of Onancock referred to their stock of pistols as "Guilford trifle" (*PE*, December 6, 1883).

49 *PE*, October 19, 1882, November 29, 1883, May 10, 17, 1884; *Richmond Dispatch*, December 13, 1884 (quotation).

Fear of arson haunted the public mind. The idea made people feel particularly vulnerable to the malice of their enemies. Other than keeping a dog, there was little in the way of protection. There were no electric lights, alarms, or cameras. There were no fire companies. An arsonist could murder a family in its home or jeopardize its livelihood by firing outbuildings and stored agricultural produce. The sound of stabled horses burning alive might ring in one's ears for a lifetime. Thus, the activities of a pyromaniac at Onancock and Drummondtown in 1884 filled people living in the area with dread and anger. The incendiary struck during a period of prolonged drought during which wells ran dry and woods fires raged along the peninsula. In a half-dozen incidents extending from mid-October to late December, he destroyed a house, a carriage house, stables, and other outbuildings. He failed in efforts to burn a dwelling, a hotel, and two stores. Charles Marshall of the *Eastern Virginian* reported that people in the vicinity of Drummondtown were "greatly agitated" and that "Several families packed up their valuables, and held themselves in readiness to move out on short notice, and vigilance committees were formed to guard against the fire fiend." Near the end of the incendiary spree, the Onancock correspondent of the *Peninsula Enterprise* commented that "Popular indignation runs very high ... and popular opinion has not yet decided what punishment should be meted out to one guilty of such a cowardly and terrible act." Soon thereafter, the fires ceased.[50]

Firearms were commonplace in Eastern Shore life. A Chincoteague man complained in 1883 that "the boys and youths of our community universally carry pistols in their hip pockets, and ... it is not an uncommon thing to find them in the possession of children at school." The careless handling of firearms occasionally led to injury or death. At Guilford in 1882 a seven-year-old boy, mistaking a real pistol for a toy, blew out the brains of his five-year-old brother. Inebriates and fools discharged weapons indiscriminately. A Northampton man in 1881 shot

---

50 *PE*, October 18, 25, November 22 (quotation), 1884; *Baltimore Sun*, October 20, 22, 1884; *EV* in *Norfolk Virginian*, October 28 (quotation), and November 12, 1884; *Richmond Dispatch*, January 2, 1885. The arsonist was perhaps responsible for the destruction of the public school at Leemont (Wilmington *Morning News*, December 3, 1884).

up a store until a clerk mollified him with a glass of rum. Firearms, however, were seldom employed in personal disputes and almost never to facilitate robbery. The would-be assailant or thief was well aware that his victim might be carrying a pistol in his pocket. An incident that occurred in lower Accomack County in 1878 underscored the hazards of initiating a gunfight. On a February night, constable and state tax collector George E. Bull drove his buggy from Belle Haven toward his home in Pungoteague. Shortly after crossing the bridge in the lonesome hollow formed by Taylor's Branch, Bull's horse shied and refused to go on. Two men emerged from the gloom, one of whom began firing his pistol at the collector. Bull, who never traveled at night without his pistols, returned fire, sighting on the highwayman's muzzle flashes. At a lull in the firing, Bull urged his horse forward, passed through another volley fired by comrades of the assailant, and made his way home in his bullet-ridden buggy. The next day Bull and a friend visited the scene of the assault where they found the ground and bushes stained with blood.[51]

Most Eastern Shore males, irrespective of race, possessed a Southern sense of honor. They responded forcefully when they believed themselves insulted. Scenes of violent personal conflict were frequently enacted. Most disputes that turned physical were settled, not by guns, but by fists, knives, razors, or other weapons at hand. At Concord Wharf on Occohannock Creek in 1881 a black man fractured the skull of another by smiting him with a hickory club. The sound of the blow was heard 100 yards away. A quarrel between individuals sometimes escalated into a general brawl. In 1884 a correspondent of the *Eastern Virginian* reported that "On Saturday night the laborers engaged in the fish factory at Hoffman's wharf commenced quarrelling for some trifling cause. A free fight was soon in full blast during which Mr. Andrew Sparrow had his arm broken with a bar of iron. One negro received an ugly gash on the body, while another got off with a scalp wound."[52]

---

51 *PE*, January 26, February 16, March 16, September 28, 1882, February 22, December 6 (quotation), 1883, May 3, July 19, October 18, 1884; Wilmington *Morning News*, April 7, 1883, Snow Hill (Md.) *Democratic Messenger*, June 11, 1881; *EV* in *ibid.*, October 28, 1882; *Baltimore Bulletin* in *Alexandria Gazette*, February 15, 1878.

52 *Richmond Dispatch*, February 5, 1880; Norfolk *Weekly Virginian and Carolinian*, July 5,

The points of personal honor most tender to Eastern Shoremen involved insults directed at their womenfolk and the infidelity of their wives or paramours. Near Muddy Creek in 1881 Thomas Northam, aged fifteen, died from a stab wound while defending his sister from the aspersions of a rejected suitor. In 1882 Captain Richard Miles, having learned that James Godwin had cursed him and slandered his daughter, confronted Godwin at Holland's Mill near Eastville. Captain Miles struck Godwin on the head with a shovel, cutting off an ear. He then threw Godwin into the millpond and held his head underwater until pulled off by a bystander. Also in 1882 the *Peninsula Enterprise* reported that "John James Taylor was shot and fatally wounded by some unknown person ... on the premises of Dennis Hart, in Cattail neck. No one witnessed the act. ... The presumption, however, is, that he was shot by Hart, with whose wife for months he has been accused of having a criminal intimacy."[53]

Black males were perhaps even more offended by sexual infidelity than white. Continually made to feel inferior by interactions with white employers, with white landlords, and even with white strangers, control of their domestic arrangements was crucial to their sense of manhood. Both their self-respect and the respect of their neighbors depended on it. At Crossroads (now Onley) in 1879 Lewis White entered the house of John Laws and brained him with an axe in culmination of a dispute over a woman. Near Newstown (now Metompkin) in 1882 Benjamin Young shot to death Gilley Bundick for seducing Young's wife Margaret. Curiously, two years earlier the then Margaret Downing had fought with Louisa Wise for the affections of Young. Downing was armed with a club and Wise a pitchfork. Both women emerged from the encounter seriously injured. Downing shortly married Benjamin

---

1877; *Norfolk Virginian*, April 14, 1880; Snow Hill (Md.) *Democratic Messenger*, April 2, 1881; Wilmington *Morning News*, July 12, 1881; *PE*, October 20, 1881, March 2, 9, 1882, July 19, 26, August 9, October 11, 1883, November 22, 29, 1884; Richmond *Whig*, April 7, 1883; *EV* in *Norfolk Virginian*, June 15, 1880 and August 4, 1884. For a discussion of Southern honor see Edward L. Ayers, *Vengeance and Justice: Crime and Punishment in the 19th Century South* (New York and Oxford: Oxford University Press, 1984), pp. 9-33.

53 *EV* in Snow Hill (Md.) *Democratic Messenger*, April 2, 1881; *Ibid.*, April 16, 1881, May 6, 1882; *PE*, September 1, 1881, September 7, 1882.

Young while Wise recovered from her wounds in the home of Gilley Bundick.[54]

Based on newspaper reports, incidents of violence appear to have been on the rise in the latter years of the period 1870-1884. Also, a rapidly growing population implies a commensurate growth in violent behavior. A definitive answer awaits systematic research in the court records. What seems clear is that during these progressive years all aspects of Eastern Shore life were increasingly driven by urgency, impatience, and truculence, be it the dredging of an oyster ground, the building of a railroad, or the settling of a point of honor. On March 28, 1878, an exchange of words on the main street in Eastville between scions of leading peninsula families led instantly to an exchange of gunshots. Major S. Pitts, aged twenty-one, fell dead, a bullet in his chest. Alfred P. Thom, aged twenty-four, suffered a painful wound to his jaw. Had the young gentlemen quarreled before the Civil War, the rules of the Code Duello would likely have been invoked. Days might have been consumed in ritual, and the duel perhaps averted by mediation. Now, the principals shot on sight. "Befo' the wah, sah, we folks of the Eastern Sho' were bad men in the juel," Judge William G. Riley of Accomack told the Washington *Critic* in 1881. "Times are changed now."[55]

EASTERN SHOREMEN, BY AND LARGE, ENJOYED THEIR liquor. Overindulgence usually resulted in little more than a hangover. Marshall of the *Eastern Virginian* repeated an age-old tale: "A rural individual came to Onancock on his birth day. He got drunk, busted, fell into a gutter, got a black eye, and woke up next morning in a mud puddle,

---

54 Ayers, *Vengeance and Justice*, pp. 234-235; Philadelphia *Times*, January 26, 1879; *EV* in New York *Daily Herald*, July 15, 1879; *PE*, March 23, 1882; New York *Sun*, February 11, 1880. For the Young-Bundick-Downing-Wise connection see Manuscript Census of Population, Accomack County, 1880, enumeration district 5, pp. 24, 56, and Barry W. Miles and Moody K. Miles III, comps., *Marriage Records of Accomack County, Virginia, 1854-1895* (Bowie, Md.: Heritage Books, 1997), p. 366.

55 Kirk Mariner, *True Tales of the Eastern Shore* (New Church, Va.: Miona Publications, 2003), pp. 116-119; Weaver, *The Southern Tradition at Bay*, p. 163; Ayers, *Vengeance and Justice*, p. 268; Washington *Critic*, October 26, 1881. For other resorts to firearms on points of honor see *Norfolk Virginian*, July 16, 1875 and *Baltimore Sun* in *Norfolk Landmark*, September 19, 1884.

looking as if a regiment of mules had walked over him." Marshall also told of "A well known inebriate returning from Baltimore recently, sought a retired nook in the fire department of the steamer, and under the combined influence of the heat and whiskey became unconscious. On opening his eyes to his surroundings, the smoking coal, hissing steam and blazing fire, he imagined himself in the infernal regions. 'Just as I expected,' he exclaimed, 'in hell at last.'"[56]

In 1885 twenty-six saloons dispensed ardent spirits in Accomack and twenty-five in Northampton. Perhaps typical was the barroom of the "old hotel" on Chincoteague Island. "I found it quite small, and also somewhat crowded," a traveler recalled. "The furniture of this room comprised a backless bench, several rickety chairs, a round table, and the floor was covered with saw dust and tobacco juice. ... [T]hey did not put on any airs at this place. Here I saw during the evening plenty of the genuine natives of the island. ... Whisky and applejack circulated freely and some of the more musical of the company began to sing nautical songs, while others reeled off yarns from their personal experience that were entertaining, if not edifying." Each saloon had its regular clientele. Alexander Hunter observed that in front of the barroom at Cherrystone "on any fine day you may see a crowd of idlers sitting on dry goods boxes grumbling at hard times, and of course discussing politics. They only move as the sun moves ... and the crowd follows in shadow all around the house, and later in the evening we find them sitting in the same spot you saw them in the morning. They don't get out of their chairs expect to splice the main brace and take four fingers of whiskey."[57]

Most habitués of saloons passed their time at the bar in convivial discourse or in quiet stupor. Occasionally, however, unpleasantness interrupted the flow of good cheer. "Easter Saturday was a field-day for the tangle leg veterans of this vicinity," reported a Mappsville man in 1884. "The brigade was out in full force, and performed the elbow

---

56 John J. Wise to William Mahone, September 12, 1883, Mahone Papers, Duke; *EV*, October 6, 1876; *EV* in *Norfolk Virginian*, August 26, 1884.

57 Mariner, *Revival's Children*, p. 174; "The Teagues of Accomack" (first quotation); Alexander Hunter, "Letter from Old Point," *Alexandria Gazette*, August 7, 1879; Pyle, "A Peninsular Canaan," p. 805.

drill with remarkable rapidity and effect. Some of the members retain very marked impressions of the day's festivities. Even their *vivandiere* escaped only by her agility in dodging swiftly thrown glass tumblers." On Chincoteague at about the same time, Bill Harrison, already on a protracted drunk, entered a barroom, drew his revolver, and shot in the arm Ikey Blake, "an inoffensive old colored man." The island constable swiftly placed Harrison under arrest but, according to a correspondent of the *Peninsula Enterprise*, "from the manner in which he carried the constable around from one bar room to another a casual observer would have supposed that the constable, and not Harrison was the culprit." Later, complaint was made that Harrison while "on his debauch ... entered the house of Richard Lind and assaulted his wife." Near Locustville in 1879, a dispute over a game of cards led to the death of shoemaker William H. Rose, his skull fractured by a stool wielded by saloon owner John T. Rayfield. "The saloon is situated in a lonely place, and bears a hard reputation," noted a local man.[58]

Drunkenness also occasioned regrettable events outside of the barroom. The drunk might mistake a neighbor's house for his own and endeavor to make a forcible entry. He might accidentally injure or kill a friend. He might do himself harm or even do himself in. Benjamin F. Evans of Wagram in upper Accomack accidentally shot and killed himself while on one of his sprees. Tom Brodwater, a black laborer of Mappsville, froze to death while laying out drunk on a December night. Within days of each other in 1881 Keely Budd and Captain William Chance fell into ditches and drowned while walking home from barrooms. When, a few weeks later, drunks drowned a mule by driving it into a ditch, Marshall declared that the citizens of Accomack "must kick Dick Tanglefoot out of their company, or they will have to do away with the ditches which drain the county."[59]

---

58 *PE*, April 19, 1884 (first and second quotations); *Baltimore Herald* in *Richmond Dispatch*, March 13, 1879 (third quotation).

59 *PE*, December 22, 29, 1881, December 14, 21, 1882, October 25, 1883; *Newton (Md.) Record* in *Middletown (Del.) Transcript*, October 27, 1877; *Richmond Dispatch*, August 31, 1883; *Easton (Md.) Star-Democrat*, February 22, 1881; *EV* in *Richmond Dispatch*, February 23, 1881; *EV* in Wilmington *Morning News*, March 15, 1881 (quotation). In 1884 George Budd, son of

Notwithstanding the foregoing episodes, Eastern Shoremen appeared to most strangers as relatively sober. A Washingtonian traveling in Northampton in 1879 reported that "In every settlement there is a saloon, but I saw very little drinking and not a case of drunkenness." A Gumboro, Delaware, man, having encountered only one drunken man on a visit to the peninsula in 1884, observed that "there is not one-tenth as many drunkards in Virginia as in lower Sussex county [Del.]. ... Bellhaven [sic], the size of Gumboro, has three saloons, but very little drunkenness, while this place has no saloons, but more drunkards, despite the fact that the people from here have to go two miles into Wicomico county [Md.] to get their liquor."[60]

Yet, on the Eastern Shore of Virginia, temperance advocates were organizing to abridge "the prerogatives of King Alcohol." Methodism was at the heart of Eastern Shore temperance agitation. Methodist asceticism meant to strip the individual of sin, thus preparing society for the coming of Christ the King. Temperance attracted the interest of local Methodists before the Civil War, but only in the postbellum years, as yearning for God's kingdom on earth coincided with the peninsula's embrace of the cult of progress, did the temperance movement gain momentum. It seemed apparent to many that sobriety was both good for the soul and necessary for social betterment. In 1882 Rev. L. E. Barrett of Cokesbury Methodist Church in Onancock denounced the liquor trade as "a voracious wolf ... eating out the life of the country." Barrett indicted "this traffic as the deadly foe of religion, morality, education, national and individual prosperity; the deadly foe of all social, domestic and individual peace and happiness."[61]

Keely, while under the influence of alcohol, fell into Chesconnessex Creek and drowned (*EV* in Wilmington *News Journal*, November 25, 1884).

60 Washington *National Republican*, November 1, 1879; Wilmington *Morning News*, September 22, 1884.

61 *PE*, February 2 (first quotation, 9 (quotes Barrett), 1882; William H. Williams, *The Garden of American Methodism: The Delmarva Peninsula, 1769-1820* (Dover, Del.: Scholarly Resources for the Peninsula Conference of the United Methodist Church, 1984), pp. 147-148; Mariner, *Revival's Children*, pp. 75-76, 87; Louis D. Rubin Jr., *The Wary Fugitives: Four Poets and the South* (Baton Rouge and London: Louisiana State University Press, 1978), pp. 6-7. "Antebellum southern religion had been characterized by an emphasis on personal morality as the key to

The temperance crusade on the Eastern Shore flourished from the mid-1870s onward. Councils of the Friends of Temperance organized in communities large and small, and at their meetings orators from on and off the peninsula stoked the fires of enthusiasm. "[E]loquent, logical and replete with statistical information," William T. Bundick of Onancock served not only locally but also as the Friends' state lecturer. Bundick, Barrett, and other temperance advocates championed the cause of local option, whereby each county or magisterial district within the county would be granted authority by the commonwealth to regulate the sale of alcoholic beverages. Citizens from the two counties frequently petitioned the Virginia General Assembly asking for a local option law. During the legislative session of 1881-1882 they submitted eight petitions, those from Accomack containing 104 *feet* of names.[62]

Although the petitions failed to persuade the legislature to enact local option on the peninsula, temperance advocates won some victories at home. They discouraged the opening of new saloons in Pungoteague and Temperanceville, and a supporter boasted of Grangeville that "there is not a single 'gin mill' in our midst and it is the rarest thing imaginable to see one of our young men under the influence of any intoxicating liquor." More important, in August, 1884, the Accomac Baptist Association, which included churches in both counties, resolved to "prevent the reception of and compel the expulsion of any member engaged in the liquor traffic." Later that year, George W. Mason, a retired Savageville farmer and an elector on the National Prohibition Party

---

salvation. In contrast to many of their northern counterparts, southern evangelicals had shied away from advocating fundamental structural or institutional transformations in society" (Drew Gilpin Faust, *The Creation of Confederate Nationalism: Ideology and Identity in the Civil War South* [Baton Rouge: Louisiana State University Press, 1988], pp. 29-30).

62 Mariner, *Revival's Children*, p. 174; July 26, 1876, Van Ness Journals, typescript in Eastern Shore Heritage Center; *EV*, July 27, 1878; *PE*, December 15, 1881, January 5, 26, February 16, August 3, October 5, November 23 (quotation), 1882, February 15, 22, March 1, 1883, January 26, 1884; *Journal of the House of Delegates of the State of Virginia, For the Session of 1877-8* (Richmond: R. F. Walker, Superintendent of Public Printing, 1877), pp. 320, 349, 398, 416, 432; *Journal of the House of Delegates of the State of Virginia, For the Session of 1881-2* (Richmond: R. F. Walker, Superintendent of Public Printing, 1882), pp. 200, 223, 254, 278, 302, 320, 351, 399; C. C. Pearson and J. Edwin Hendricks, *Liquor and Anti-Liquor in Virginia, 1619-1919* (Durham, N.C.: Duke University Press, 1967), p. 173.

ticket, expressed the opinion that "intemperance was gradually being weeded out on the Eastern Shore."63

Declining or not, King Alcohol had its loyal subjects. In Onancock, the seat and throne of the Eastern Shore temperance movement, a public meeting in 1882 regarding the incorporation of the town proceeded harmoniously until "A conflict of views in regard to the sale of liquor gave rise to an acrimonious debate, in which each party was alternately the victors, and finally the matter was dropped." A few weeks later, John W. Edmonds of the *Peninsula Enterprise* remarked that "Local option agitates us much. On Monday last, Rev. Mr. Barrett preached the doctrine, and now choose whom ye will serve, Option or Rye? Optionally, we expect Rye." On Chincoteague, another temperance stronghold, Charles W. Duncan assumed management of the Atlantic Hotel in September, 1881, with the intention of operating it as a temperance establishment. After six months the idealistic Duncan had grasped the reality of running a hostelry dependent on the patronage of vacationers, sportsmen, and traveling salesmen. "The 'Temperance Hotel,' on Chincoteague Island, is a thing of the past," announced the Snow Hill *Democratic Messenger*, "its name has been changed to the 'Chincoteague House,' and a 'first class bar' is now one of its many attractions. Mr. Charles W. Duncan still holds the tiller, and is ready at all times to make his guests comfortable." In 1883 the Chincoteague correspondent of the *Peninsula Enterprise* reported that

> considerable talk of temperance reform and local option laws in our community of late ... has greatly disturbed the 'Wheelbarrow Club,' whose pride and mission it is to look after the weary who have gazed on the "wine when it was red," and tasted of "the whisky that stingeth like an adder." This charitable organization have determined to fight it out

---

63 *PE*, July 19, 1883, May 3, August 9 (first quotaton), 1884; Wilmington *Delaware Gazette and State Journal*, August 21, 1884 (second quotation); Wilmington *Morning News*, November 19, 1884 (quotes Mason); National Prohibition Ticket, November 4, 1884, Mahone Papers, Duke. Formerly White's Crossroads, Temperanceville took its name in 1824 when an order of the Sons of Temperance organized there (Bernice E. Hall, "History of Temperanceville," *PE*, May 13, 1922).

on the wheelbarrow front if it takes all summer, and between the local option and "wheelbarrowism" the latter is considerably ahead.[64]

Segments of the population among whom temperance advocates might have found support remained aloof. Black people generally demonstrated little enthusiasm for local option. Why should they deny themselves in freedom what many masters denied them in slavery? Some whites who might have been receptive to the message resented the messengers. Most of the leaders of the local temperance movement were affiliated with Methodist congregations that had remained with the Northern church when the denomination split into Northern and Southern divisions over slavery in 1845. To Southern loyalists there lingered about the temperance leaders the odor of collaboration with Union occupiers. Then there were those put off by the single-mindedness of awoken temperance zealots. In 1882 the *Democratic Messenger* related how

> Over in old Virginia the other day an old-time sort of a fellow was sitting out on the porch in front of his house during a heavy rain and thunder storm. It appears that the old fellow was a heavy drinker, being pretty full at the time. On this occasion he was in his usual condition, when in the twinkling of an eye, he was struck dumb by lightning. His family and friends thought he was killed, but in the course of half an hour he recovered. Opening his eyes and looking all around, he said to a friend who was standing by: "I am mighty glad I am not killed, because if I had been all the temperance people would have said it was whisky that did it."[65]

---

64 *PE*, January 12 (first quotation), February 2 (second quotation), 1882, April 26, 1883 (fourth quotation); Wilmington *Morning News*, September 24, 1881; Snow Hill (Md.) *Democratic Messenger*, April 1, 1882.

65 Kirk Mariner, *Methodism in Onancock; A Brief History* (Onancock, Va.: Miona Publications, 2015), p. 92; Mariner, *Revival's Children*, pp. 126, 146, 325; Snow Hill (Md.) *Democratic Messenger*, October 7, 1882.

Union victory in the Civil War compelled the acceptance on the Eastern Shore of Virginia of Northern cultural values. In 1881 "M." provided a partisan description of the ideological infiltration of Chincoteague:

> The people [of the island] are remarkably thrifty, temperate, honest, and law-abiding citizens. This desirable state of things is comparatively recent. Twenty-five years ago civilization was at a low ebb. ... At that time the island was much given to dissipation and lawlessness, and drunken rows were of common occurrence, while ignorance and irreligion predominated to a distressing degree. That was very much the state of things until after the war. ... [T]he work of changing the picture was at first largely, if not almost entirely, that of one man (Mr. J. T. Kenney), who came here from Baltimore to live about fourteen years ago. He at once commenced a war upon rum, was shortly after made a magistrate, and, aided by the arm of the law, gradually got the better men of the place to work with him to crush out the vices of the people and build up the churches and schools. He is now one of the supervisors of the county of Accomac, and though a Republican, elected by Democratic votes, the most influential man on the island, the pillar of the Methodist Church, trusted and esteemed by every one, and the head of every laudable enterprise.

In concentrating on the efforts of Joseph T. Kenney, "M." ignored the cumulative effects of enhanced transportation facilities, of expanded commercial relations, and of the increased availability of Northern newspapers and periodicals. Nonetheless, he captured the combination of social benevolence and self-righteousness driving the Yankee impulse toward social uplift. He also demonstrated the willingness of devotees of progress to use coercion as well as persuasion to encourage the recalcitrant along the way to human perfection.[66]

---

66 "The Eastern Shore," *Richmond Dispatch*, September 2, 1881. See also *Alexandria Gazette*, November 27, 1874; *Richmond Dispatch*, August 18, 1875; "Chincoteague Island, Va.," *Balti-

In April, 1881, William E. Greenly of Kent County, Delaware, "a devout leader of the Free Gospel sect," abandoned his wife, children, and grandchildren to elope with fellow church member Laura Cooper, who was also married with a child. The couple fled to Chincoteague where Greenly had previously purchased a house and lot. When citizens of the island learned of the presence of the illicit pair, they met to form a vigilance committee. Before the committee acted, however, Greenly and Cooper departed for parts unknown. "In the history of this island a number of such characters as the above fugitives from justice have taken up their abode here," a Chincoteague man told the Wilmington *Morning News*, "and we have been informed that these criminals of Delaware and Maryland have always looked upon Chincoteague as being a haven of security to which they could flee when pursued by the officers of the law. We should say for the information of this class that *in these days of Christianity, temperance, railroads, steamboats, corporations and vigilance committees,* Chincoteague is a dangerous harbor."[67]

---

more Sun, August 17, 1876; and "Chincoteague Island," Elkton (Md.) *Cecil Whig*, September 9, 1876.

67 Wilmington *Delaware State Journal*, April 14, 1881; Wilmington *Morning News*, April 21, 1881 (emphasis added); Snow Hill (Md.) *Democratic Messenger*, April 30, 1881. In 1887 "Drummer" commented of Messongo Neck that "the church, the school and the press" had worked a "wonderful" change in the people: "With them instead of drunkenness, there is sobriety – instead of laziness, there is energy – instead of thoughtless waste, there is thoughtful economy – instead of dishonor, there is honor. Sober, energetical, economical, honorable, could they be otherwise than thrifty?" ("Pocomoke Neck and Sykes").

Chapter VI

Bands of Steel

For decades, the vision of a railroad connecting Philadelphia and New York with Norfolk and the coastal South remained unfulfilled. The missing link in the chain was a railroad running from Maryland down the Eastern Shore of Virginia. The construction of the road and the formation of a seaboard rail system were hindered by regional and corporate rivalries and by the propensity of state legislatures to charter a plethora of underfunded rail corporations. "If charters were constructive as well as contemplative," wrote a journalist, "lower Delaware and the Eastern Shore [of Maryland] would long since have taken to itself wheels and steamed into the Atlantic at 60 miles an hour." In 1869 the editor of the Wilmington *Delaware Tribune* identified the problem and its solution:

> We have faith in a Peninsular *Through Line*, and believe it to be one of the certainties of the future, but we see very clearly that we can never have such a line while the roads which must constitute it are cut up into sections, owned by weak corporations, jealous of each other, and without any unity of action. We do not love 'monopolies' any better than other people, but we do wish to see the whole of the Peninsular Railroad system owned, or at least controlled, by some strong and wealthy corporation with the power and will to push it on to Cherrystone, and to maintain a ferry from there to Norfolk, whether it pays at first or not. ...

This, however, we must for a while regard as something belonging to the future.

A decade and a half later, the editor's prophecy came true.[1]

DURING THE RAILROAD FRENZY THAT GRIPPED THE Eastern Shore of Maryland in the mid-1830s, speculator Littleton D. Teackle of Princess Anne attempted to interest kinsmen and politicians on the Eastern Shore of Virginia in building a line through Accomack and Northampton counties. Teackle envisioned the Virginia road as a link between Norfolk and existing lines in Maryland, but the Virginians thought in bolder terms. An act of the Virginia General Assembly passed in 1836 incorporated the Eastern Shore Rail-Road Company for the purpose of constructing a railroad from Cherrystone to the Maryland boundary "and thence, with the consent of the states through which the route shall pass, to some other point on or near to the Delaware Bay or river, and thence to some other point not above the city of Philadelphia." The directors included prominent men from both the Eastern and Western shores of Virginia and from the Eastern Shore of Maryland. Unfortunately for the directors (one of whom was Teackle), the Eastern Shore Rail-Road Company came to naught in the financial Panic of 1837.[2]

The vision of a through line revived in the mid-1850s when joint action of the legislatures of Virginia, Maryland, Delaware, and New Jersey laid the groundwork for the projected New York and Norfolk Air-Line Railroad Company. The Virginia General Assembly led the way. On January 24, 1853, it passed an act incorporating the North and South Railroad Company of Drummondtown and Eastville. The act authorized the company to build a railroad beginning at a point in Northampton from which steamboats could run to Norfolk. At the

---

1 "The Sussex Railroads," Wilmington *News Journal*, July 17, 1877; Wilmington *Delaware Tribune*, November 18, 1869.

2 Littleton Dennis Teackle to Thomas R. Joynes, February 1, 1836, in Accomac Court House *Peninsula Enterprise* (hereafter cited as *PE*), February 23, 1882; *Richmond Enquirer*, February 11, 1836; *Acts of the General Assembly of Virginia, Passed at the Session of 1835-36, Commencing 7th December, 1835, and Ending 24th March, 1836, in the Sixtieth Year of the Commonwealth* (Richmond: Thomas Ritchie, 1836), pp. 130-140.

Maryland boundary the road would connect "with any railroad which may be constructed from any point or points north of that line." The General Assembly followed up with a resolution of February 28 authorizing the governor "to request the States of Maryland, Delaware and New Jersey, to take into consideration the expediency of granting respectively, such right of way to a railroad or railroads as may be necessary to connect the cities of Philadelphia, Baltimore or New York, or all three of these cities with the North and South Railroad." Each of the states complied with the request.[3]

The New York and Norfolk Air-Line Railroad Company, incorporated in New Jersey, coordinated the various state initiatives. The company's executive committee of eleven included seven members from New York and New Jersey and four from Virginia, Maryland, and Delaware. The projected route of the railroad extended from Key Port, New Jersey, opposite New York City, south to Cape May on Delaware Bay. Connecting by water with Lewes, Delaware, the line continued along the coast through Sussex County, Delaware, Worcester County, Maryland, and Accomack and Northampton counties to a point opposite Norfolk. The company estimated the cost of construction at $5,000,000.[4]

Civil engineer William Mahone (later Confederate Major-General, railroad magnate, and United States Senator) told a convention of potential investors meeting at the Astor House in New York in late May and early June of 1854 that "In the city of Norfolk will concentrate a vast network of railways penetrating the Southern and Western States, and this road is to connect that point with the commercial metropolis of the Union, by a route possessing unrivaled advantages." Mahone stated that

---

[3] *Acts of the General Assembly of Virginia, Passed in 1852-3, in the Seventy-sixth Year of the Commonwealth* (Richmond: William F. Ritchie, 1853), p. 153 (first quotation); *Journal of the Tenth Senate of the State of New Jersey, Being the Seventy-Eighth Session of the Legislature* (Freehold: James S. Yard, 1854), pp. 802-804 (second quotation); *Baltimore Sun*, August 13, 1853; *Richmond Dispatch*, March 6, 1854.

[4] "New York and Norfolk Air-Line Railroad" in *Plan and Charter of the North and South Air-Line Company, Incorporated by the State of New Jersey* (New York: Baker, Godwin & Co., 1855), pp. 11-12.

> The "Eastern Shore" is just beginning to have its capabilities known and appreciated. It enjoys a fertile soil and healthy climate. It is peculiarly adapted to the cultivation of the various products which find so ready a market, in their season, at the great cities of the North, and which, by this road, and the "Delaware Railroad," will be rendered accessible in a few hours. In fact, this important district, embracing portions of three States, which has hitherto been "a sealed book," and almost a *terra incognita*, will be placed on the completion of our road, upon "the highway of nations," through which the busy rush of travel of the whole coast of the United States will pulsate.[5]

In July, Mahone and his assistants surveyed the Virginia section of the projected railroad. The completion of the survey required seventeen days of hard labor in the oppressive heat and humidity of the Eastern Shore summer. Mahone ran the line straight down the spine of the peninsula. It passed close to Drummondtown, through Belle Haven and nearby Hadlock, and through Eastville where it split into two branches. One branch continued south to Cape Charles while the other proceeded southwest to the steamboat wharf at Cherrystone.[6]

Surveys for the entire line having been completed, the New York and Norfolk Air-Line Railroad Company in October opened its books for subscription. The sale of stock, however, failed to support the laying of rails. For the remainder of the 1850s, prospects of a through line advanced only by way of rumor.[7]

At the session of the Virginia General Assembly of 1859-1860,

---

5 *Ibid.*, p. 12. Thanks to Kellee Blake for drawing to my attention that "a sealed book" alludes to Revelation 5:1.

6 Nelson Morehouse Blake, *William Mahone of Virginia: Soldier and Political Insurgent* (Richmond: Garrett & Massie, 1935), pp. 33-34; Norfolk *Southern Argus*, August 15, 1854; Map and Profile of Instrumental Reconnaissance for the Virginia Section of the New York and Norfolk Air-Line Railway – by William Mahone, Civil Engineer, Library of Virginia, Richmond.

7 *Baltimore Sun*, October 11, 1854; Dover *Delaware State Reporter*, February 16, 1855; "Accomac and Northampton," *Richmond Enquirer*, August 27, 1858; *Richmond Dispatch*, April 12, 1859.

Dr. Arthur Watson of Accomack County introduced a bill to amend the charter of the North and South Railroad Company. He proposed that the commonwealth subscribe three-fourths of the $375,000 estimated cost of construction of the railroad through Accomack and Northampton counties. Dr. Watson addressed the House of Delegates on February 29, 1860. He ignored the idea of a through line directly linking Norfolk with New York via Lewes and Cape May. Instead, he stated that upon completion the North and South Railroad would connect with Philadelphia by way of existing railroads in Maryland and Delaware. Watson maintained that the North and South would benefit Virginia by diverting "a large part of the trade of the Eastern Shore, from Baltimore and New York ... to Norfolk." He pointed out that the Eastern Shore had never received from the state a single dollar for internal improvements. "Reject this application," he warned, "and the citizens of the Eastern Shore will feel as our forefathers felt towards England under the stamp act; that they are a mere province of Virginia; paying tribute to the State and not allowed to be equal participants in its favors."

Watson also asserted that a railroad on the peninsula would be a military necessity should "Northern fanatics" launch an invasion. "As Virginians, Mr. Speaker, we are ready to resent any insult to Virginia," he affirmed. "We are also ready to protect the Federal Constitution, to shield it from unhallowed hands, and under it to maintain all the rights, privileges and immunities which it guarantees Virginia. We are ready to draw the sword under that constitution, if necessary to protect these rights; and if the aggressions of the North and the usurpation of our rights ... force Virginia out of the Union, you will find the Eastern Shore hand in hand with you." Dr. Watson's bill failed to pass into law. Eastern Shoremen were not united behind the idea of internal improvements (see above, pages 107-108) and, even had they been, the geographically isolated counties lacked the political clout to win a place at the public trough.[8]

---

8 Arthur Watson, "Speech of Dr. A. Watson, of Accomac, Delivered in the House of Delegates, Wednesday, February the 29th, 1860, on the Bill to amend the Charter of the North and South

Subsequent events made ironic Dr. Watson's stirring oratory about Virginians drawing the sword against Northern aggression. After Union troops invaded the Eastern Shore in late 1861, Watson aided the federal regime in various capacities. A few days after the invasion, he lobbied to attach permanently Accomack and Northampton to Maryland. His brother, Gillet F. Watson, also collaborated with the occupiers. Gillet Watson served as a state senator in the rump legislature created by federal authorities to represent the "loyal" citizens of the occupied counties of the commonwealth. In 1862 he secured passage of an act creating "a general stock company to construct a railroad from Cherrystone Ferry ... to the Maryland line, in the direction of Salisbury, Maryland." This company also failed to stimulate anything more than another round of idle speculation.[9]

IN THE IMMEDIATE POST-BELLUM YEARS, THE idea of a through rail line connecting the Southern seaboard with the Northern via Norfolk remained a dream of boosters, speculators, and railroad executives. Their plans continued to involve a coastal route from Norfolk through Lewes to New York or a central route through Delmar to Philadelphia. These were the schemes of competing corporations and cities. Eastern Shoremen cared little what route won out. They thought in terms of new markets for their produce and of rising values for their real property. "This [Northampton] and Accomac counties are destined one day, to be the market gardens of the Northern cities, and a railroad, and only a railroad, will accomplish it," Israel Townsend of Capeville told a Wilmington editor. "With it, no place on this continent has facilities and

---

Railroad," *Richmond Enquirer*, March 13, 1860. See also Petition of Citizens, December 13, 1859, Accomack County Legislative Petitions, 1776-1862, Library of Virginia, Richmond.

9 Camp Wilkes (Accomac C.H.) *Regimental Flag*, March 6, 1862, in Darrell N. Middleton, comp., *The Second Regiment Delaware Volunteers* (Georgetown, Del.: By the Author, 2005); Leonard W. Johnson, *Ebb and Flow: A History of the Virginia Tip of the Delmarva Peninsula, 1561-1892* (Verona, Va.: McClure Printing Co., 1982), p. 166 (quotes act); *Philadelphia Inquirer*, May 19, 1862, August 8, 1865; James Egbert Mears, "The Eastern Shore of Virginia in the Nineteenth and Twentieth Centuries" in *The Eastern Shore of Maryland and Virginia*, ed. Charles B. Clark (New York: Lewis Historical Publishing Co., 1950), II, 589. For examples of Arthur Watson's activities during the federal occupation see Mears, "The Virginia Eastern Shore in the War of Secession and in the Reconstruction Period," typescript, 1957, in Eastern Shore Heritage Center, Eastern Shore Public Library, Parksley, Va., pp. 128-129, R280, R363.

advantages of soil, climate and seasons to suit the gardens, equal to these two counties. We are at least three weeks ahead of you in [the maturation of] almost all vegetables, and, with a railroad, we are only eight hours from Philadelphia. So you can see the great wants of these counties."[10]

At the prompting of Eastern Shoremen, the Virginia legislature in 1867 passed an act incorporating the Eastern Shore Railroad Company of Eastville and Drummondtown. The act authorized railroad corporations outside of Virginia to subscribe to the new company's capital stock. It also required that the rails laid on the line be of a gauge compatible with those of any line connecting with it at the Maryland boundary. Alas, these inducements failed to attract sufficient outside capital. The Eastern Shore Railroad Company fell quickly into the "contemplative" rather than the "constructive" category.[11]

The Eastern Shore Railroad Company proved nothing more than an expression of provincial wishful thinking. Without sufficient capital, local desire was not enough. If a railroad down the peninsula was ever to be built, it had to be a component of a larger program of organization and construction. United States Congressman Richard S. Ayer, Union veteran from Maine temporarily a resident of Virginia's Northern Neck, advanced such a program when he introduced in 1870 a bill to grant 800,000 acres of public land to finance the construction of the seemingly moribund ("even the map makers had forgotten it," exclaimed a newspaperman) New York and Norfolk Air-Line Railroad. Congress failed to pass Ayer's bill, but the idea of a direct route from Norfolk to New York had re-kindled in the imaginations of potential railroad developers and beneficiaries.[12]

---

10 Comfort L. G. Nottingham, Baltimore to "Auntie," July 22, 1873, Garrett Family Papers, 1786-1928, Special Collections Research Center, Earl Gregg Swem Library, College of William and Mary, Williamsburg, Va.; T. [Israel Townsend], Capeville, to editor, June 24, October 27, Wilmington *Delaware State Journal*, June 28 [quotation], November 8, 1867; *Richmond Dispatch*, March 19, 1875.

11 *Acts of the General Assembly of the State of Virginia, Passed in 1866-7, in the Ninety-First Year of the Commonwealth* (Richmond: James E. Goode, Printer, 1867), pp. 876-877; *Baltimore Sun*, April 17, 1867.

12 *Richmond Dispatch*, May 17, 1870; Wilmington *Delaware Tribune*, June 2, 1870 (quotation); T. [Israel Townsend], Capeville, to editor, June 20, in *Ibid.* June 23, 1870.

In 1872 the Virginia General Assembly attempted to prepare the southern end of the proposed route by incorporating the New York and Norfolk Railroad Company. The act of incorporation permitted the construction of a railroad from the Maryland boundary through Accomack to a point on the bayside of Northampton from whence the company's steamboats would connect with "some point in Norfolk or Princess Anne county, and thence by railroad to the port of Norfolk." The act enabled the company to own vessels, piers, wharves, and warehouses. It authorized Accomack to sell $300,000 in bonds and Northampton $200,000 if approved by a majority of the qualified voters in separate referenda. It provided that the company might lease its franchise to other railroad or steamboat companies. Finally, the act stipulated that the construction of the railroad commence within two years and be completed within five. To facilitate the Norfolk end of the project, the directors of the stock subscription included leading citizens of Norfolk as well as of Accomack and Northampton.[13]

Capital claims no country. The primary investors in the Virginia portion of the New York and Norfolk Railroad Company were "money kings" of Pennsylvania who put aside the rivalry between Philadelphia and New York City in the interest of profit. When the company was organized at Drummondtown in September, 1873, stockholders elected Hendrick B. Wright of Pennsylvania president. They also elected Wright and three other Pennsylvanians to the board of directors along with one man from Delaware and four from the Eastern Shore of Virginia. At the board's first meeting, it resolved to commence a survey of the proposed route. The board also resolved to ask the Virginia legislature to grant the corporation more fiscal flexibility. The directors probably were concerned that the voters of Accomack and Northampton might reject incurring a considerable bonded debt on behalf of the railroad.[14]

The General Assembly complied with the board's request in

---

[13] *Acts and Joint Resolutions Passed by the General Assembly of the State of Virginia at its Session of 1871-'72* (Richmond: R. F. Walker, Superintendent of Public Printing, 1872), pp. 265-267.

[14] Wilmington *News Journal*, March 10 (quotation), May 12, July 17, September 17, 1873; *Salisbury (Md.) Advertiser*, May 17, 1873; *Baltimore Sun*, September 20, 1873.

amendments to the act of incorporation. An amendment enabled the company to issue preferred stock and to borrow money. Others repealed the earlier clause authorizing Accomack and Northampton counties to subscribe to the project. Instead, they allowed the counties to raise taxes in order to reimburse the company the cost of the purchase of rights-of-way. Accomack was to donate no more than $20,000 and Northampton no more than $10,000. The donations required the approval in referenda of three-fifths of the qualified voters and a majority of the registered voters.[15]

Meanwhile, civil engineer Daniel Hudson and his crew surveyed the projected route through Virginia and Maryland. From Cherrystone the survey ran up the spine of the peninsula through Eastville and Drummondtown before veering northeasterly to pass through Horntown. Crossing into Maryland, it continued through Stockton, Snow Hill, and Berlin to Selbyville, Delaware, where the road would connect with the soon-to-be-completed Breakwater and Frankford Railroad. Except for the existing Worcester Railroad linking Snow Hill and Berlin, the route would be of new construction.[16]

In the fall of 1874 voters in the two counties approved donations to the railroad company for the purchase of rights-of-way. In Northampton the proposal passed 1,014 votes to 35. A few weeks after the vote, the judge of the Accomack County Court commissioned a board "to ascertain a just compensation to the owners of the land upon the line of the improvement." Eastern Shoremen had done what Northern investors had required, and in so doing had demonstrated their conversion to the cult of progress. Yet, their effort was unrewarded; their god unpropitiated. The failure of the financer Jay Gould in November, 1873, initiated a long and severe depression. Banks collapsed, the money supply contracted, and capital investment declined steeply. The New York and Norfolk Railroad Company died in the Panic of 1873.[17]

---

15 *Acts and Joint Resolutions Passed by the General Assembly of the State of Virginia at its Session of 1874* (Richmond: R. F. Walker, Superintendent of Public Printing, 1874), pp. 87-89.

16 *Norfolk Landmark*, January 31, 1874; Wilmington *Delaware State Journal*, February 28, 1874; John C. Hayman, *Rails Along the Chesapeake: A History of Railroading on the Delmarva Peninsula, 1827-1978* (n.p.:Marvadel Publishers, 1979), p. 34.

17 Northampton County Court Order Book, 1871-1876, pp. 475-476; *Norfolk Landmark*,

THE DREAM OF A GRAND TRUNK LINE revived in late 1875 when General William Painter of Philadelphia assumed control of the Worcester and Somerset Railroad. Completed in 1872 the Worcester and Somerset ran southward for nine miles from near Westover on Maryland's Eastern Shore Railroad to the north bank of the Pocomoke River opposite Newtown (present-day Pocomoke City). Painter was a Union veteran who at war's end was in charge of transportation for the Army of the Potomac. After the war, he worked as a banker specializing in railroad securities. He procured funds for the construction of several railroads and served as the president of the Philadelphia, Newtown [Pa.] and New York Railroad. He also engaged in the manufacture of pig iron and rails. His obituary described him as being "warm and genial in his disposition, of untiring energy and always of a buoyant, cheerful disposition." General Painter determined to close the seaboard gap by bridging the Pocomoke and extending the line of the Worcester and Somerset to Cherrystone. He also intended to tap the Chincoteague Bay oyster grounds by building a spur line terminating at Bloodgood's Wharf near Nashville (present-day Sinnickson).[18]

Throughout the remainder of the economically depressed 1870s, General Painter struggled to attract investors. An unsubstantiated rumor made the rounds that California magnate Collis P. Huntington might interest himself in the project. Painter managed only to issue a prospectus and to gain the support of the Virginia legislature. An act of the General Assembly of 1876 gave the Worcester and Somerset permission to run a line through upper Accomack County to Chincoteague Bay. An act of 1878 incorporated the Peninsula Railroad Company whose powers and

---

August 30, September 24, 1874; Accomack County Court Order Book, 1873-1877, p. 274; David Herbert Donald, *Liberty and Union* (Boston and Toronto: Little, Brown and Company, 1978), p. 241; Harry Taylor Gause, *Semi-Centennial Memoir of The Harlan & Hollingsworth Company, Wilmington, Delaware, U.S.A., 1836-1886* (Wilmington: Harlan & Hollingsworth Company, 1886), pp. 262-263.

18 Hayman, *Rails Along the Chesapeake*, p. 68; Wilmington *Delaware Tribune*, May 21, July 23, August 6, 1868; *Philadelphia Inquirer*, February 4, 1878, May 5, 1884; "A Pokomoke Sketch," Wilmington *News Journal*, April 29, 1879; *Wilmington Commercial* in *Baltimore Sun*, November 17, 1875; Snow Hill (Md.) *Democratic Messenger* in Middletown (De.) *Transcript*, July 22, 1876.

privileges explicitly encompassed all those granted to previous Eastern Shore of Virginia railroad companies – the North and South (1853), the Eastern Shore (1867), and the New York and Norfolk (1872).[19]

The Peninsula Railroad Company's prospectus, issued in May, 1878, included a map of a proposed route. From Newtown the line would proceed southeastward to Modestown, then along the seaside through Newstown (present-day Metompkin), Drummondtown, Locustville, and Locustmount before veering southwestward through Belle Haven, Hadlock, Bridgetown, and Eastville to Cherrystone. The prospectus estimated the cost of construction at $1,000,000.[20]

The projected course of the road along the Accomack County seaside and the Northampton bayside reflected Painter's belief in the economic potential of the peninsula's expanding oyster industry. On Chincoteague Bay, he envisioned "Oyster City" rising from the marsh. Some "shrewd and careful judges" believed that during the season the oyster trade would require twenty or thirty railroad cars running daily from Oyster City. William H. Kimberly, the Baltimore and Old Point Comfort entrepreneur who owned wharf, store, and real estate at Cherrystone, also anticipated a railroad-driven boom in bayside oystering. He accordingly mapped out a town adjacent the wharf, which he named Cherryton.[21]

The prospectus in circulation, the Peninsula Railroad Company opened its books for subscription in early July, 1878. Over the next four years, William Painter and his brother Uriah worked to make the project attractive to investors. They secured enabling legislation from Maryland and Virginia and a rail traffic agreement from the Pennsylvania Railroad Company. They surveyed the line, began obtaining rights-of-way, and graded a portion of the roadbed.[22]

---

19 Wilmington *News Journal*, May 31, 1878; *Baltimore Sun*, August 12, 1880; *Acts and Joint Resolutions Passed by the General Assembly of the State of Virginia at the Session of 1875-6* (Richmond: R. F. Walker, Superintendent of Public Printing, 1876), pp. 113-114; *Acts and Joint Resolutions Passed by the General Assembly of the State of Virginia at the Session of 1877-78* (Richmond: R. F. Walker, Superintendent of Public Printing, 1878), pp. 208-209.

20 Wilmington *News Journal*, May 31, 1878.

21 *Ibid.*; *Richmond Dispatch*, July 27, 1878.

22 *Philadelphia Times*, July 10, 1878; Washington *Critic*, July 25, 1881.

An act of the Maryland legislature of April 10, 1880, reorganized the Worcester and Somerset Railroad as the Peninsula Railroad Company. On February 14, 1882, the Virginia General Assembly authorized the Peninsula Railroad Company of Virginia "to consolidate as one corporation" with its Maryland counterpart. The act further stipulated that upon consolidation the company might change its name to the New York, Philadelphia and Norfolk Railroad Company "provided that said railroad company shall have its principal office within the borders of this state." The Virginia and Maryland companies formally united under the new name on September 19, 1882.[23]

Meanwhile, the Painters' project benefited from the dynamic in railroad management toward corporate consolidation, car interchange agreements, and other innovations. These trends increased railroad efficiency while creating corporate empires, such as the leviathan Pennsylvania Railroad Company. Hailed as "the first great self-sustaining system in the United States," the Pennsylvania absorbed some smaller lines by purchase or lease. It allied with others through interchange agreements cemented by investment in securities. In early 1881 the Pennsylvania purchased the Philadelphia, Wilmington and Baltimore Railroad Company and its subsidiaries, thus gaining control of all the principal railroads on the Delaware and Maryland peninsula except the Worcester and Somerset, the Eastern Shore Railroad Company, and the railroads operating between Franklin City and Lewes owned by the Old Dominion Steamship Company. Pennsylvania executives also considered expanding their empire southward by building a line from Delmar to Cherrystone. Company First Vice-President Alexander J. Cassatt championed the idea but it failed to gain the approval of President George B. Roberts.[24]

---

23 Hayman, *Rails Along the Chesapeake*, p. 71; Wilmington *News Journal*, January 21, 1882; *Acts and Joint Resolutions Passed by the General Assembly of the State of Virginia at the Session of 1881-82* (Richmond: R. F. Walker, Superintendent of Public Printing, 1882), pp. 110-111; *Baltimore Sun*, May 12, 1882; *PE*, April 10, May 18, November 16, 1882.

24 David L. Carlton, *Mill and Town in South Carolina, 1880-1920* (Baton Rouge: Louisiana State University Press, 1982), p. 22; Alfred Chandler Jr., *The Visible Hand: The Managerial Revolution in American Business* (Cambridge and London: Belknap Press of Harvard University Press, 1977), pp. 135-136 (quotation), 151-156; (Wilmington *Daily Republican*, July 11, 1881;

William Painter was no stranger to the Pennsylvania Railroad leadership, having worked with them in the operation of the Philadelphia, Newtown [Pa.] and New York Railroad. In May, 1882, General Painter entered into a contract with the Pennsylvania which obtained for the Peninsula Railroad (soon to become the New York, Philadelphia and Norfolk) "rights and privileges" that would allow its cars to run from the Eastern Shore to New York in nine hours. The contract also obligated the Pennsylvania to secure traffic for the Peninsula Railroad. Subsequent agreements in 1883 and 1884 bound the Pennsylvania to grant to the New York, Philadelphia and Norfolk preferred rates on through business and to rebate to the line for the payment of interest on its bonds twenty percent of the revenue earned from traffic interchanged between the two railroads. Most important, the Pennsylvania guaranteed principal and interest on its bonds.[25]

When queried prior to the original agreement, Pennsylvania Railroad officials denied any desire to buy or control the Peninsula Railroad Company. "[I]t is an entirely independent enterprise," insisted the Pennsylvania's superintendent, "though the rates and working arrangements will be thoroughly in accord with the Pennsylvania system." The Pennsylvania also influenced other aspects of the smaller company's operations. A *Baltimore Sun* correspondent reported that "the best equipment of rolling stock, engines, &c., will be secured in conformity with the equipment on the Pennsylvania system, and the train crews and other officials will be selected from the same school of railroad men."[26]

While the Painters engaged in legislative and corporate maneuvering, their principal associates, construction superintendent J. L. Bates

---

Patricia T. Davis, *End of the Line: Alexander J. Cassatt and the Pennsylvania Railroad* (New York: Neale Watson Academic Publications, Inc., 1978), p. 104.

25 *Philadelphia Times*, February 4, 1878; William Painter, President, Peninsula Railroad, to editor, *Norfolk Virginian*, April 13, in Wilmington *Delaware State Journal*, April 21, 1881; U. H. Painter, Vice President, Peninsula Railroad, to editor, April 3, PE, April 13, 1882; Hayman, *Rails Along the Chesapeake*, p. 71; Pocomoke City [Md.] Times in *PE*, March 22, 1884; *Philadelphia Inquirer*, December 1, 1884; Jim Lewis, *Cape Charles: A Railroad Town* (Eastville, Va.: Hickory House, 2004), p. 50.

26 *Baltimore Sun*, September 5, 1881.

and civil engineer Dr. E. W. Goerke prepared for the laying of rails. Dr. Goerke surveyed the route on four separate occasions and negotiated rights-of-way. Bates oversaw the repair of tracks above Newtown and the grading of secured rights-of-way near Franktown.[27]

THE PENNSYLVANIA RAILROAD COMPANY'S INTEREST IN A seaboard line and its alliance with the New York, Philadelphia and Norfolk Railroad Company made the latter an attractive investment. Chief among potential investors was William L. Scott of Erie, Pennsylvania. Scott had amassed a fortune in coal mines and railroad stock. He already was acquainted with William Painter, president of the New York, Philadelphia and Norfolk, and with A. J. Cassatt, first vice-president of the Pennsylvania. Like Cassatt, Scott indulged a passion for thoroughbred horse racing. Both men owned extensive stables, and they competed against each other during the racing season. Cassatt was a brilliant and innovative civil engineer whom his turf rival now queried on the feasibility of transporting railroad cars across the rough waters at the Virginia capes. Car floats hitherto had been used for short hauls in harbors. Negotiating northeast storms and northerly winds on open water was, in the words of historian John L. Lochhead, "something else again." Cassatt satisfied himself that powerful tugboats towing large barges would make regular crossings of the lower Chesapeake both possible and practical. For a second time he urged the Pennsylvania to undertake the building of the railroad. When President Roberts again refused, Cassatt resigned his vice-presidency in September, 1882. The New York, Philadelphia and Norfolk's potentialities and challenges might account for Cassatt's resignation. Or, perhaps, his departure was an act of corporate subterfuge intended to placate Maryland and Virginia politicians suspicious of the Pennsylvania Railroad's relentless expansion. Indeed, in 1899 Cassatt would resign the presidency of the New York, Philadelphia and Norfolk to return to the Pennsylvania as its president. In any case, Cassatt joined

---

27 Princess Anne (Md.) *Somerset Herald* in Snow Hill (Md.) *Democratic Messenger*, September 3, 1881; *Baltimore Sun*, September 5, 1881; Pocomoke City [Md.] *Record and Gazette* in Snow Hill (Md.) *Democratic Messenger*, January 28, 1882; *PE*, April 13, 1882; Snow Hill (Md.) *Democratic Messenger*, March 26, April 2, May 28, 1881; Wilmington *Morning News*, June 13, 1881.

Scott in investing in Painter's railroad and in urging their friends to purchase the railroad's bonds.[28]

For decades, the quest for a railroad down the peninsula amounted to nothing more than columns of newsprint and issues of defunct railroad stock. To some Eastern Shoremen, planning for a railroad seemed wishful thinking and promotion of the road's potential benefits smacked of flattery to deceive. In April, 1882, Uriah H. Painter, vice-president of the Peninsula Railroad, dissipated some of the cynicism in a letter to the *Peninsula Enterprise*. Painter informed the public that his line had allied with the Pennsylvania Railroad (the long-awaited "strong and wealthy corporation" [see above, page 255]) and that capital had become sufficiently interested "to make the inquiry as to the probable cost of the construction and the future business of the road." Editor John W. Edmonds greeted Painter's announcement with enthusiasm: "At the back of this enterprise there is no want of pluck, money and brains, and its completion is simply a matter of time. ... The doubters may now throw their doubts to the wind, in the full conviction that the Peninsula [Railroad] is a fixed fact."[29]

Edmonds believed that the road would be in operation "within a very few months." He was overly optimistic. For the next year and a half, laborers grubbed and graded the roadbed while lumbermen felled and sawed timber for railroad ties. Dr. Goerke continued to obtain rights-of-way in the two counties. Most of the approximately 250 effected landowners put Goerke to little trouble. Anxious to see the railroad built, the great majority settled for small compensation. Meanwhile, the Painters, Scott, and Cassatt worked to solve corporate and engineering problems standing in the way of the projected line.[30]

---

28 *Baltimore Sun*, April 22, 1882, March 27, 1884; Mark Walgren Summers, *Party Games: Getting, Keeping, and Using Power in Gilded Age Politics* (Chapel Hill and London: University of North Carolina Press, 2004), pp. 157-158; *PE*. January 19, 1882; "N. Y., P. & N. Has Done Much to Improve Territory," Norfolk *Virginian-Pilot* in Onancock *Accomack News*, March 24, 1922; *Philadelphia Times*, December 16, 1884; Davis, *End of the Line*, pp. 103-104, 105; Lewis, *Cape Charles*, pp. 6, 15; John Teichmoeller, "Pennsylvania Railroad Chesapeake Bay Barge Service," *Keystone Magazine* 26 (1992), p. 20; Lochhead, "The Boat Trains,' National Railway Historical Society, *Bulletin* 43 (1978), p. 18; *Philadelphia Inquirer*, September 14, 1882; *Pittsburgh Post-Gazette*, March 5, 1884.

29 Painter to editor, April 3, *PE*, April 13, 1882; *PE*, April 27, May 18 (quotes Edmonds), 1882; *Baltimore Sun*, October 4, 1882.

30 *PE*, May 18 (quotes Edmonds), November 16, December 7, 14, 1882, January 18, July

The Painter brothers retained the presidency of the New York, Philadelphia and Norfolk until 1884 when William L. Scott succeeded Uriah Painter. William Painter served as vice-president under Scott until he died suddenly of a stroke on May 3, 1884. The Painters and Scott were far from figurehead presidents, but A. J. Cassatt largely was responsible for attending to essential details of the railroad's construction. Cassatt retained Dr. Goerke as chief engineer and William Bauman as superintendent of bridges. He hired James McConkey as superintendent of the line and R. B. Cooke as general traffic and freight agent with offices in Norfolk. He contracted with the Lancaster, Pennsylvania, firm of John Keller and L. L. Bush for the construction of the railroad. Having witnessed first-hand the success of the Pennsylvania Railroad Company, Cassatt resolved that the New York, Philadelphia and Norfolk would conform to Pennsylvania standards in every aspect of its operations.[31]

Cassatt and Scott considered it necessary to gain control of the Eastern Shore Railroad, which ran from Delmar to Crisfield. The New York, Philadelphia and Norfolk connected with the Eastern Shore at Newtown Junction between Westover and Princess Anne. Its cars then traveled north on the Eastern Shore to its junction with the Pennsylvania Railroad at Delmar. The Eastern Shore Railroad was not part of the Pennsylvania system, its rails were below Pennsylvania standards, and its financial situation was precarious. The Pennsylvania having recently considered buying the Eastern Shore, Cassatt was familiar with the road. As was Scott, who had been involved in the negotiations on behalf of the Pennsylvania.[32]

In 1883 Scott and Cassatt began discussions with the Eastern Shore

---

5, September 13, November 22, December 6, 1883; *Norfolk Virginian*, September 13, 1882; Onancock *Eastern Virginian* (hereafter cited as *EV*) in *Ibid*, January 4, 1883; *Baltimore Sun*, October 4, 1882; Lewis, *Cape Charles*, p. 16.

31 Hayman, *Rails Along the Chesapeake*, p. 213; *Norfolk Virginian*, November 6, 1884; *Philadelphia Times*, May 4, June 28, 1884; Lewis, *Cape Charles*, pp. 15-16; *Baltimore Sun*, April 15, 1884; "N. Y., P. & N. Has Done Much to Improve Territory"; *New-York Tribune*, April 28, 1884.

32 *Baltimore Sun*, December 11, 1878, November 22, 1881; *Philadelphia Inquirer*, February 21, 1879; Snow Hill (Md.) *Democratic Messenger*, February 11, October 7, 1882; Princess Anne (Md.) *Marylander* in *Ibid.*, March 4, 1882.

Railroad's majority owners, the Harlan and Hollingsworth Company of Wilmington, the manufacturer of railroad cars and iron steamships. Harlan and Hollingsworth also owned the Eastern Shore Steamboat Company, the boats of which linked with the Eastern Shore Railroad at Crisfield. Although Scott and Cassatt refused to guarantee the steamboat company's continued connection with the railroad, Harlan and Hollingsworth agreed to sell the Eastern Shore Railroad for $450,000. Harlan and Hollingsworth executives probably disposed of the railroad because the Eastern Shore often struggled to turn a profit and because they feared that Scott and Cassatt, if thwarted, would bypass the Eastern Shore line by laying their own tracks south from Delmar. Perhaps more important, the shipbuilders did not wish to alienate a customer shopping for steamboats and tugs. Scott and Cassatt took control of the Eastern Shore Railroad Company on January 1, 1884, and formally merged it into the New York, Philadelphia and Norfolk on June 1.[33]

The spine of the Eastern Shore of Virginia was ideal for railroad building. The terrain was high, dry, and level. Known locally as the mid-woods, the spine was sparsely populated and covered with timber suitable for use as railroad ties. William Mahone, who in 1854 surveyed a route through the mid-woods for the New York and Norfolk Air-Line Railroad Company, found "no place upon a grade greater than eight feet ... upon a slight embankment, no cuts, no bridge, one culvert." Mahone stated that a line straight down the peninsula would be cheap and easy to build and maintain. He predicted that locomotives traveling the route would obtain a speed "greater than any other road in this country."[34]

The route chosen by A. J. Cassatt in 1882 traversed the mid-woods, but, unlike Mahone's survey, it avoided all existing communities including Drummondtown and Eastville. The railroad depots would stand from a quarter mile to four miles from the nearest village. Like that

---

33 *Baltimore Sun*, November 18, 1882, December 18, 1883, January 5, 1884; *Ibid.* in *PE*, March 15, 1884; *Norfolk Virginian*, January 12, 1884; Hayman, *Rails Along the Chesapeake*, p. 72.

34 Mahone, President, Atlantic, Mississippi & Ohio Railroad, Lynchburg, April, 19, to Dear Sir, *Wilmington Daily Commercial*, April 29, 1873; "New York and Norfolk Air-Line Railroad," p. 12 (second quotation). See also "Speech of Dr. A. Watson."

of Mahone and others, Cassatt's primary interest was in gaining access through Norfolk to the crops and natural resources of the southeastern seaboard. Local traffic was a secondary consideration. Cassatt's route was cold-bloodedly practical. Beggars could not be choosers. Eastern Shoremen must come to the railroad. The railroad would not come to them. To those who lived there, the Eastern Shore was a beloved home; to capitalists, it was a convenient thoroughfare.[35]

Determining a location for the railroad's terminus fell to William L. Scott. Nearest to Norfolk of the Eastern Shore's harbors, Cherrystone wharf had long seemed the logical choice. The Painters also considered Pickett's Hole near Cape Charles, but no final decision had been made when Scott invested in the company. Scott's primary interest in the terminus was to develop adjacent real estate. His retainers, having inspected likely locations, recommended William H. Kimberly's property at Cherrystone or that of the heirs of Governor Littleton W. Tazewell between nearby King's and Old Plantation creeks. Cherrystone had a natural harbor and Kimberly's Cherryton development. The Tazewell estate was nearer Norfolk and consisted of a large tract of undeveloped land. A salt pond on the property might be made into a suitable harbor. On May 12, 1883, Scott purchased from the Tazewell heirs for $55,000 the Old Plantation, King's Creek, and Old Quarter tracts totaling 2,107 acres. With the stroke of a pen, the Erie industrialist became the third largest landowner and largest payer of the land tax in Northampton County.[36]

In August, 1884, Scott sold forty acres including the salt pond and surrounding land to the New York, Philadelphia and Norfolk Railroad.

---

35 *PE*, May 3, September 13, 1884; Wilmington *Morning News*, September 22, 1884; *Baltimore Sun* in *Norfolk Landmark*, November 14, 1884; Mahone, President, Atlantic, Mississippi & Ohio Railroad, Lynchburg, April, 19, to Dear Sir, *Wilmington Daily Commercial*, April 29, 1873; *Norfolk Virginian*, May 14, 1882; Davis, *End of the Line*, p. 104. Cassatt's route was probably based on Dr. E. W. Goerke's final survey with Cassatt's emendations (*PE*, April 13, October 26, 1882).

36 *Baltimore Sun*, April 22, May 13, 1882, October 22, 1883, March 27, 1884; Eastville *Eastern Shore Herald* (hereafter cited as *ESH*) in Wilmington *Morning News*, July 25, 1881; *EV* in *Norfolk Virginian*, January 4, 1883; *ESH* in Wilmington *Daily Gazette*, May 3, 1883; May 12, 1883, Northampton County Deed Book 36, p. 150; Allen B. Hamilton, comp., *Northampton County, Virginia, Land Tax Records, 1875, 1880, 1885, and 1895* (Berwyn Heights, Md.: Heritage Books, 2021), pp. 266-267.

The indefatigable Dr. E. W. Goerke oversaw the dredging of the pond. Two of the largest machines of the American Dredging Company converted it into a rectangular harbor of a depth of eleven feet below the low water mark and covering about eleven acres. A dredged channel, ten to twelve feet deep, 200 feet wide, and 1,500 feet long, connected the harbor with the deep waters of Cherrystone Channel. Having failed to convince the federal government to fund the cost of the channel, A. J. Cassatt paid for it himself. A breakwater at the mouth of the harbor discouraged the accumulation of silt. The 500,000 cubic feet of spoil from the dredging was dumped in nearby shoal waters, creating Cherrystone (or Sandy) Island.[37]

Around the harbor, the railroad built bulkheads, offices, and two landing slips. On the north side, it erected freight and passenger depots and a mammoth wharf of 150,000 square feet. Vessels docked on the harbor side of the wharf while trains arrived and departed on the landward side. Civil engineer Adam Stierle in 1889 found the harbor "in many respects excellent for the purpose for which it was built, namely, the trans-shipment of heavy freight ... but it can not be enlarged except at great expense. ... In this connection, it may be stated that King's Creek, one mile to the north, and [Old] Plantation Creek, two miles to the south ... appear to have offered greater natural advantages for a harbor." But likely not for Scott's real estate development.[38]

Ferriage over the thirty miles of open water that lay between the new harbor and Norfolk was a novel undertaking for a railroad company. To meet the challenge, Cassatt contracted with the Harlan and Hollingsworth Company to build to his specifications a steamboat and

---

37 *PE*, August 30, 1884; Hamilton, comp., *Northampton County, Virginia, Land Tax Records, 1875, 1880, 1885, and 1895*, pp. 98-99; Philadelphia *Telegraph*, November 3, in Wilmington *Morning News*, November 4, 1884; *Ibid.*, November 13, 15, 1884; *Richmond Dispatch*, September 20, 1884; *Baltimore Sun* in *Norfolk Landmark*, November 14, 1884; Cape Charles Harbor, Va., House of Representatives, 51st Congress, 1st Session, Ex. Doc. 29 (1889), pp. 3, 6, 9-10; Davis, *End of the Line*, p. 105.

38 Cape Charles Harbor, Va., House of Representatives, 51st Congress, 1st Session, Ex. Doc. 29 (1889), pp. 3, 8 (quotes Stierle); "Through the New South Opened Up by the N. Y., P. & N. Railroad," Wilmington *Every Evening*, November 15, in Wilmington *Delaware Gazette and State Journal*, November 20, 1884; Lewis, *Cape Charles*, p. 16.

a tug. Constructed of iron, both vessels were powerful enough to navigate the heavy seas of lower Chesapeake Bay. The side-wheel steamer *Cape Charles* was 253 feet long and displaced 941 tons. Driven by a 1,115 horsepower engine, she was capable of reaching 20 miles per hour. The *Cape Charles* was much larger than comparable boats of the Eastern Shore Steamboat Company. She transported not only passengers and freight but also was equipped with railroad tracks for the accommodation of four sleeper cars. The *Cape Charles* was the first boat on the bay with electric lights. The screw tug *Norfolk* was 116 feet long and displaced 211 tons. Intended to tow barges carrying loaded freight cars, the *Norfolk's* engine generated 915 horsepower. Harlan and Hollingsworth delivered the vessels several months after the New York, Philadelphia and Norfolk commenced operations in November, 1884. In the interim, the railroad chartered the wooden, side-wheel steamboat *Jane Moseley*.[39]

Across the bay in Norfolk, Scott, Cassatt, and the Painter brothers endeavored to secure harbor and terminal facilities and to establish rail interchange agreements. They found Norfolk business and civic leaders eager to cooperate. Truck farmers and produce brokers appreciated the advantages of overnight shipment via rail to the Northern markets. "Heretofore this business has labored under the great disadvantage of delay and unsuitable accommodation incident to water transit," noted a Philadelphia reporter. "The early truck, though the first to be seen in Northern markets, could not be put there in first-class condition, and therefore could not command maximum prices. The packages were necessarily shut up in the holds of vessels, practically in air-tight compartments, and during the twenty to thirty hours required in transit they lost their first freshness. The early potatoes turned dark, the peas dried up, the radishes faded and the berries softened."[40]

---

39 Hayman, *Rails Along the Chesapeake*, p. 71; *Baltimore Sun*, August 21, 1884; "Through the New South Opened Up by the N. Y., P. & N. Railroad"; Davis, *End of the Line*, pp. 104-105; *PE*, October 18, 1884; Wilmington *Morning News*, November 13, 1884; A. Hughlett Mason, *History of Steam Navigation to the Eastern Shore of Virginia* (Richmond: The Dietz Press, Inc., 1973), pp. 22, 38, 47; "Cape Charles: A Town Built by the Railroad," Onancock *Eastern Shore News*, December 10, 1986.

40 *ESH* in Wilmington *Daily Gazette*, May 3, 1883; *Baltimore Sun*, April 26, 1884; *Philadelphia Inquirer*, May 5, December 1 (quotation), 1884; *Norfolk Virginian*, January 12, November

Norfolk railroad men anticipated that cooperation with the New York, Philadelphia and Norfolk would increase traffic along their lines to and from the South and West. The Norfolk and Western Railroad (formerly William Mahone's Atlantic, Mississippi and Ohio) had recently come under the control of Philadelphia and New York investors. The *Baltimore Sun* reported that "This syndicate, while not actually allied, is understood to be in sympathy with the projectors of the Philadelphia, New York and Norfolk Railroad [sic]." Capitalists contemplating the building of a new railroad linking Norfolk and Charleston saw the projected line as an extension of the New York, Philadelphia and Norfolk.[41]

Cassatt leased wharf and warehouse property at Town Point on which the New York, Philadelphia and Norfolk erected a passenger depot and additional storage facilities for freight. Cassatt also negotiated traffic interchange agreements with the major railroads serving the cities at the mouth of the James River. An agreement with the Norfolk and Western connected the New York, Philadelphia and Norfolk to Petersburg, Lynchburg, and Bristol and that with the Norfolk Southern Railroad to Elizabeth City and Edenton. From Old Point Comfort, the Chesapeake and Ohio Railroad linked with Richmond. From Portsmouth, the Seaboard and Roanoke Railroad connected at Weldon with the Atlantic Coast Line and thus south to Jacksonville and west to New Orleans. Cassatt also came to terms with local lines – the Norfolk and Ocean and the Elizabeth and Norfolk railroads. A Philadelphia reporter grasped the enormous significance of the New York, Philadelphia and Norfolk: "All the railroad systems of the South and Southwest, centering at Norfolk, are thus placed in direct communication with lines of the North reached by the Pennsylvania system, without breaking bulk or disturbing passengers."[42]

IN DECEMBER, 1883, A. J. CASSATT AND William L. Scott hired Keller

---

6, 1884; Wilmington *Morning News*, November 4, 1884.

41 Blake, *William Mahone of Virginia*, pp. 132-134; *Baltimore Sun*, March 12, 1884; *Pittsburgh Daily Post*, March 29, 1884; *EV* in *Goldsboro (N.C.) Messenger*, May 19, 1884.

42 Pocomoke City [Md.] *Times* in *PE*, March 8, 1884; *Baltimore Sun*, March 27, September 4, 1884; *PE*, July 5, October 25, 1884; *Philadelphia Inquirer*, March 8, November 14, December 1 (quotation), 1884; Elkton (Md.) *Cecil Whig*, November 22, 1884; *Pittsburgh Post-Gazette*, March 5, 1884.

and Bush as primary contractor for construction of the New York, Philadelphia and Norfolk Railroad. They directed the firm not only to build the seventy miles of track between Pocomoke City [formerly Newtown] and the road's terminus at Scott's Cape Charles City but also to replace the forty-seven miles of track between Pocomoke City and Delmar. Although busy with corporate aspects of the railroad's management, Scott and Cassatt occasionally inspected the laying of the rails. Cassatt's right-hand-man Dr. E. W. Goerke monitored construction on a daily basis. Uriah H. Painter aided by successfully lobbying United States Senator William Mahone to ensure that the governor of Virginia sign a bill extending the deadline for completion of the railroad.[43]

Keller and Bush employed contractors, some of them local, to supply railroad ties and to move houses and outbuildings from the right-of-way. For common labor, the firm contracted with brokers who supplied black and Italian workmen from the northeastern cities. By mid-1884, 1,100 men were at work on the line. Gangs of workers moved southward grading sections of the roadbed. Where the ground was particularly rough, they spread oyster shell ballast to even the grade. They were followed by men setting ties and cleaning and ditching the margins of the roadbed. Bringing up the rear and accompanied by a construction train, came the gang laying the rails. At Cape Charles City, laborers constructed terminal facilities. Along the line from Pocomoke City to Cape Charles City, another gang erected poles and strung telegraph wire. Except for a period during the Civil War, the Eastern Shore of Virginia heretofore had not experienced telegraphic communication with the outside world.[44]

---

43 Lewis, *Cape Charles*, pp. 15, 17; *Baltimore Sun*, January 19, March 27, 1884; Wilmington *Morning News*, November 13, 1884; *PE*, April 19, 26, September 13, 1884; *Philadelphia Inquirer*, August 29, 1884; Painter, West Chester, Pa., telegram to Mahone, January 3, 1884, Mahone Papers, William R. Perkins Library, Duke University, Durham, N.C.; *Acts and Joint Resolutions Passed by the General Assembly of the State of Virginia at the Session of 1883-84* (Richmond: R. F. Walker, Superintendent of Public Printing, 1884), pp. 115-116.

44 *PE*, May 17, June 14, 1883, May 17, June 14, July 5, 12, 1884; Orris A. Browne, Cape Charles, to Mayor A. P. Rowe, Fredericksburg, November 30, Fredericksburg *Free Lance*, December 10, 1889; *Philadelphia Times*, June 28, 1884; Pocomoke City (Md.) *Times* in *PE*, March 22, 1884; *Baltimore Sun*, August 19, 27, September 4, 1884; "Through the New South Opened Up by the N. Y., P. & N. Railroad"; Davis, *End of the Line*, p. 105; *ESH* in *Norfolk Virginian*,

The laborers were young men. They worked from dawn to dark and, when the moon was full, into the night. Their day's work done, they returned not to home and family but to temporary barracks or vacant houses. Many of the Italians spoke only their native language and all of the workers were strangers in a strange land. In their limited leisure time, some of them sought release from toil and loneliness in the bottle. A Leemont man reported that "The railroad employees at work opposite the town, came to see us last Saturday, and having indulged too much, a free fight was the result. The last time they were seen, they had drank all their whiskey and were fighting over the jug." The Italians, with their own language and customs, seemed to the locals a sinister lot. When someone fired into a house in the village of Seaside (also known as Mappsville), a correspondent told the *Peninsula Enterprise* that residents "supposed that the Italian laborers near by, may have been the perpetrators of the dangerous act." He quipped that "The Italians and measles are at present the terror of our little ones."[45]

Some workers acquired grievances against their employers. Italians on a tie-cutting gang near Temperanceville pursued the gang boss and another employee of the contractor until the pair sought safety in a private residence. Claiming that they had been defrauded of their wages, the Italians besieged the house and threatened "summary vengeance" on the fugitives. Danger of bloodshed passed when the contractor's men escaped through a back door. A magistrate and a constable soon arrived and dispersed the mob. The gang boss claimed that the money in question had been deducted from the Italians' pay to defray their travel expenses.[46]

Keller and Bush commenced operations shortly after the New Year. By early March, the firm had rebuilt the existing New York, Philadelphia and Norfolk Railroad between Delmar and Pocomoke City. Keller and Bush replaced old ties with new and iron rails with steel. The new rails conformed to Pennsylvania Railroad Company standards, as did new switches

---

February 9, 1884; Wilmington *Morning News*, May 15, 1883.

45 *PE*, May 3, 24 (second and third quotations), July 5 (first quotation), September 13, 1884; Pocomoke City (Md.) *Times* in *PE*, June 14, 1884; *Norfolk Virginian*, July 29, 1884.

46 *PE*, July 26, 1884 (quotation); *Norfolk Virginian*, July 29, 1884.

and sidings. "The steel rails weigh sixty pounds to the yard, which will admit of the running of very heavy loads," noted the editor of the Pocomoke City *Times*. "The building of the road in this substantial manner is a guarantee that it is something more than a mere speculation, and that it is to be made one of the most important trunk lines to the South."[47]

Contractors Joseph H. Coffrode and Francis H. Salyer of Pottstown, Pennsylvania, began building the railroad drawbridge over the Pocomoke River in mid-February. Their work involved the employment of a "monster pile-driver" with a three-thousand-pound hammer, the filling in of stone abutments, and the laying of a wooden span. At sixty feet in width, the draw was sufficient to accommodate the largest steamboat engaged in the river trade. Coffrode and Salyer finished the bridge on May 9. An onlooker told the *Peninsula Enterprise* that the first crossing by a train "was celebrated by the blowing of all the whistles of the mills and factories, and by firing a cannon salute. The banks of the river were crowded with people, including many ladies."[48]

The river barrier overcome, the rail-laying gang and accompanying construction train moved down the peninsula through Worcester County, Maryland. By June 7 rails had crossed the pond at Beaver Dam and gained the Virginia boundary. Meanwhile, the grading gang had forged ahead to the vicinity of Drummondtown. For the most part, the grading proceeded swiftly over the level terrain of the Virginia mid-woods. An exception was the sodden bottom lands of Sandy Run and Gum Swamp respectively north and south of present-day Hallwood. At the Gum Swamp, an "immense quantity of water" tried the stamina and patience of the Italians attempting to grade the roadbed. Thirty or more downed tools and quit, "swearing that they would not work in such a place."[49]

---

47 Pocomoke City (Md.) *Times* in *PE*, February 9, 23 (quotation), March 1, 1884; *PE*, February 16, 1884; *Baltimore Sun*, March 11, in *PE*, March 15, 1884; Davis, *End of the Line*, p. 105. Keller and Bush used the best of the discarded iron rails to make repairs on the railroad from Newtown Junction to Crisfield. They also improved grades and shortened curves and bridges on the line (Pocomoke City (Md.) *Times* in *PE*, March 1, 1884).

48 Pocomoke City (Md.) *Times* in *PE*, February 9, 23, March 1, 1884; Snow Hill (Md.) *Democratic Messenger* in *PE*, February 2, 1884; *PE*, May 10, 31 (quotation), 1884. The name of Coffrode and Sayler's firm was the Philadelphia Bridge Works.

49 Pocomoke City (Md.) *Times* in *PE*, March 1, 1884; *PE*, April 12, May 17 (quotations), June

With the grading gang preparing the way, the rail-layers pushed through the mid-woods at the rate of one-half to one mile per day. They laid tracks to the vicinity of Drummondtown on August 18, of present-day Keller on September 4, of present-day Exmore on September 29, and of Eastville on October 11. So smooth and straight was the roadbed that delays occurred only when the pace of construction outran the supply of ties and rails.[50]

Adjacent the tracks, carpenters erected stations named New Church, Hallston (present day Hallwood), Metompkin (present-day Parksley), Accomac (present-day Tasley), Pungoteague (present-day Keller), Belle Haven (present-day Exmore), Bird's Nest, Eastville, and Cape Charles City. The stations stood at intervals of around eight-miles. Built of native lumber, they encompassed platform, station house, freight house, and water tank. A traveler described the duplex station houses as "commodious buildings, as like each other as two peas, with ladies' and gentlemen's waiting rooms, [and] ticket and telegraph offices." The second storey served as living quarters for the station master.[51]

By mid-August, company management deemed New York, Philadelphia and Norfolk tracks and stations from Pocomoke City to Accomac Station ready for traffic. Beginning August 18 its trains kept a regular schedule of stops every day but Sunday. In early September, the railroad extended its service to Pungoteague Station. Stations below Pungoteague did not come on line until after the completion of the railroad to Cape Charles City in late October.[52]

Eastern Shoremen took immediate advantage of the new means of

---

7, November 29, 1884; Lewis, *Cape Charles*, p. 16.

50 *Norfolk Virginian*, July 29, 1884; *PE*, June 7, August 16, October 11, 1884; *Philadelphia Times*, June 28, 1884; *Baltimore Sun*, September 4, 1884; Henry V. Poor, *Manual of the Railroads of the United States for 1886* (New York: H. V. Poor, 1886), p. 512; Lewis, *Cape Charles*, p. 16.

51 Philadelphia *Evening Telegraph* in *Norfolk Virginian*, November 6, 1884; Lewis, *Cape Charles*, p. 16; "On the Peninsula," Wilmington *Morning News*, November 15, 1884; *Baltimore Sun* in *Norfolk Landmark*, November 14, 1884; *Baltimore Sun*, August 27, 1884; "Through the New South Opened Up by the N. Y., P. & N. Railroad" (quotation); *PE*, July 12, 26, 1884.

52 *Norfolk Virginian*, August 15, 1884; *PE*, August 16, September 6, 1884; *Baltimore Sun*, September 4, 1884; *Philadelphia Inquirer*, September 3, 1884.

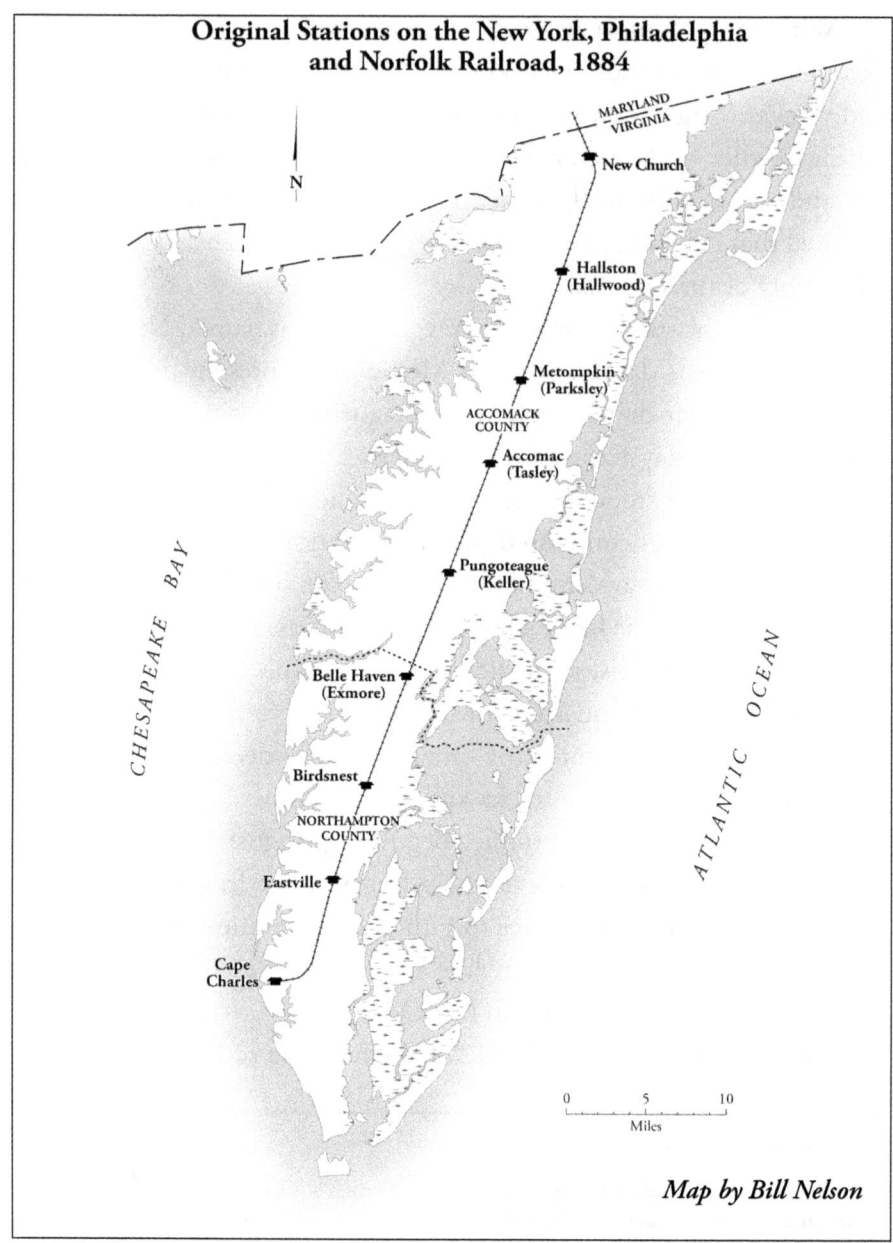

Map by Bill Nelson

trade and travel. The train departing Accomac Station on the line's formal opening carried three carloads of passengers on an excursion to the resort town of Ocean City, Maryland. Two weeks later, locals traveled at "greatly reduced rates" to Salisbury, Maryland, to experience "John Robinson's great circus show." Sweet potato season having commenced, farmers living near the tracks shipped their harvest via the rails to New York and Boston. The trains transported as many as 900 barrels of sweet potatoes daily. New locomotives manufactured by the Baldwin Locomotive Works pulled the freight and passenger cars. The locomotives, of course, conformed to Pennsylvania Railroad standards.[53]

While the coming of the railroad presented Eastern Shoremen with novel commercial and recreational opportunities, it also posed an unaccustomed danger to people, animals, and crops. Horses frightened by trains ran away with cart and driver. Livestock loitering on the tracks came to grisly ends. "Every few days we are supplied with fresh pork, as the swine have not learned to keep clear of the iron horse," sighed an Oak Hall man. Contrary to a recent act of the Virginia legislature, the New York, Philadelphia and Norfolk neglected to install cattle guards where the tracks passed through fence line. "Many of our farmers are in much trouble caused by the 'turning out' of their crops by the Railroad Company," the Oak Hall man reported. "No cattle guards have been put down, and hogs and cattle are at full liberty to run in upon the growing crops. Some are very indignant, and threaten to block the track unless something is done."[54]

One of the aggrieved did more than block the track. Under the cover of night, he derailed a construction train near Temperanceville by removing a pair of rails. Several of the train's crew were injured, the engineer severely. A farmer living near the scene was indicted for sabotaging the track. Intent on avoiding the trouble plaguing their Accomack brethren, some Northampton farmers obtained a court injunction restraining the railroad from removing fences until cattle guards were in place.[55]

---

53 *Baltimore Sun*, August 19, 1884; *PE*, August 30 (quotations), September 13, 1884; *Salisbury (Md.) Advertiser and Eastern Shoreman*, September 6, 1884; *Philadelphia Times*, August 24, 1884. In upper Accomack County, passenger service began early in August (*PE*, August 9, 1884).

54 *PE*, May 24, July 19 (second quotation), August 9, 16, September 13 (first quotation), November 15, 22, 1884.

55 *PE*, August 23, 30, September 27, October 18, 1884; *Baltimore Sun*, August 18, 19, 1884; *EV* in *Norfolk Virginian*, August 26, 1884; Wilmington *Morning News*, October 2, 1884

No one worked longer than Dr. E. W. Goerke and the Painter brothers to fulfill the old vision of a trunk railroad along the Atlantic seaboard. The dream, so long deferred, became reality on Saturday, October 25, 1884. "We have this afternoon reached the terminus with our railroad," Dr. Goerke at Cape Charles City telegraphed Uriah H. Painter at Washington. That evening John Keller invited a small party to ride with him on a construction train from the terminal to nearby Bay View. "This was the first train to leave Cape Charles," one of Keller's guests recalled, "stopping every few hundred yards to pick up laborers who had been filling in the tracks and carrying these men to their bunk houses about four miles from the harbor."[56]

On October 30 New York, Philadelphia and Norfolk Railroad President William L. Scott, Superintendent James McConkey, General Agent R. B. Cooke, and a group of stockholders traveled the new road on a tour of inspection. On November 3 the railroad opened to traffic its entire length from Delmar to Cape Charles City. A few days later, an excursion party of Delaware farmers and businessmen exploring investment opportunities came down on the cars. An accompanying journalist reported that at the terminal "The railroad is completed clear up to the high water mark, and is provided with all the necessary switches and side tracks. Ground is staked out for passenger, freight, engine and car houses, and a telegraph and express office is in use already."[57]

The ferrying of freight cars to Norfolk commenced on November 14. The steamer *Jane Moseley* began carrying passengers across the bay on November 17. Passengers now could leave Norfolk on the *Jane Moseley* at 6.30 p.m., transfer at Cape Charles City to the railroad at 9.00 p.m., and arrive in New York at 7.00 a.m. On November 21, Scott and Alexander J. Cassatt hosted at Norfolk a party of Pennsylvania Railroad Company executives and other industrialists who had traveled down the new line from Philadelphia. The Pennsylvania officials

---

56 "Pioneer Vision Brought P.R.R.," *PE*, August 8, 1936 (first quotation); W. D. Williams, "A Short History of Cape Charles," Cape Charles *Northampton Times*, June 13, 1946 (second quotation).

57 *Norfolk Landmark*, November 1, 1884; *Richmond Dispatch*, November 4, 1884; Wilmington *Morning News*, November 13, 1884 (quotation); *PE*, November 29, 1884.

included President George B. Roberts, four vice-presidents, and the general manager. Scott and Cassatt conducted the group on a tour of the terminal facilities at Norfolk, Portsmouth, and Old Point Comfort. The visit concluded with a banquet at the Hygeia Hotel on Old Point Comfort. President Roberts and his party gazed upon the tracks, the stations, the harbors, and the terminals and found them good. According to a Baltimore reporter, the industrialists spoke "in the highest terms of the new road and its possibilities."[58]

Despite its brief period of operation, at year's end the New York, Philadelphia and Norfolk reported to its stockholders a net profit, after construction expenses, of $50,236.34. Meanwhile, A. J. Cassatt departed for Europe on a business trip of several months, Northern capitalists and real estate agents descended on the rails, and John W. Edmonds of the *Peninsula Enterprise* remarked on an influx of tramps.[59]

THE COMPLETION OF THE NEW YORK, PHILADELPHIA and Norfolk Railroad was a quietly pivotal moment in the fortunes of cities and corporations and in the lives of millions of people. In the 1920s historian Vernon L. Parrington observed that "All over the land a spider web of iron rails was being spun that was to draw the remotest outposts into the common whole and bind the nation together with steel bands." The New York, Philadelphia and Norfolk connected the southeastern seaboard with the northeastern cities. By annihilating time and space, it stimulated the growth of a truck farming region stretching from north Florida to the lower Eastern Shore of Maryland. Its alliance with the Pennsylvania Railroad Company allowed that great corporation quick access to southeastern fields but also to the region's mines and forests.[60]

---

58 H. M. Schotter, *The Growth and Development of the Pennsylvania Railroad Company: A Review of the Charter and Annual Reports of the Pennsylvania Railroad Company 1846 to 1926, Inclusive* (Philadelphia: Pennsylvania Railroad Company, 1927), p. 209; Lochhead, "The Boat Trains,' p. 18; *PE*, November 22, 1884; *Philadelphia Inquirer*, November 14, 19, 21, 1884; *Baltimore Sun*, November 22, 1884 (quotation).

59 Davis, *End of the Line*, p. 105; *Philadelphia Times*, December 13, 1884; *Richmond Dispatch*, December 10, 1884; *PE*, November 22, 1884.

60 Vernon L. Parrington, *Main Currents in American Thought, Volume Three: The Beginnings*

In the Chesapeake country, the New York, Philadelphia and Norfolk upset the equilibrium between rival cities and corporations and between competing modes of transportation. An object of the railroad, noted a Philadelphia reporter,

> is to do for the great cities of Philadelphia, New York and Boston, by means of fast freight arrangements, what is now done for Baltimore by steamboats and other river and bay craft. It is to bring to Northern markets and housekeepers the fresh fruit and vegetable product of this prolific part of the country, where strawberries, spinach, lettuce and all the early spring fruits and vegetables are to be had months in advance of the Northern season. ... It will also open up in winter the great Norfolk, Cherrystone and Pocomoke oyster fields. The existing arrangement practically cuts off the Northern cities from participation in the best products of this region. Different lines of rival steamboats ... carry fruit and truck to Baltimore, where it has to be reshipped by rail, involving great loss of time and increased expense.[61]

On the Eastern Shore of Virginia, the New York, Philadelphia and Norfolk exponentially accelerated ongoing change in the local economy, culture, and landscape. With apparent unanimity, leading Eastern Shoremen embraced the idea of the railroad as an engine of progress. "Give us rapid transit and a judicious canvass of the advantages of the Eastern Shore, and we, so far from continuing a *terra incognita*, will become the prophetic realization of the Garden of the Hesperides," exclaimed a Northampton County man. Dr. John E. Mapp of Dunkirk in lower Accomack County predicted that "when steamboats ply on sea and bay, and steam mills and steam [railroad] cars occupy the central portion of this peninsula, better times must be in the near future for our people."[62]

---

of *Critical Realism in America, 1860-1920* (New York: Harcourt. Brace & World, 1930), p. 7. "[R]ailroads bind cities together with links of iron, therefore through trade and intercourse our country will eventually be firmly united" (Wilmington *Daily Republican*, December 3, 1866).

61 *Philadelphia Times*, January 9, 1884.

62 *Alexandria Gazette*, January 22, 1878 (first quotation); *PE*, May 18, 1882 (second quota-

Champions of the railroad argued that its presence would compel Eastern Shoremen to discard old ways for new. A Drummondtown man maintained that "The railroad completed will bring to light our undeveloped resources, improve our lands in productiveness and value. Thrift will follow it and our people be taught new lessons in economy. In a word it will force us from the groove in which we have spun for two centuries and a half and put us upon a level with this progressive age." "Farmer" insisted that "This is emphatically a progressive, practical and calculating age, in which dollars, cents and self predominate and actuate motives to perhaps all too great an extent. … The usages and habits of the people of the 'good old Colonial days,' of which the Virginian speaks so touchingly, have passed away. We have entered upon a new era of progress." John W. Edmonds found it gratifying to "behold the quiet, yet resistless struggle of the material energies of Virginia and the whole South, as step by step they advance to a final victory over the traditions, the prejudices and the sloth which have heretofore obstructed their progress."63

Local boosters sought Northern investment and immigration. A Temperanceville resident invited "Eastern capitalists … to visit our section. Here they can buy land cheaper than anywhere on earth, adapted to all kinds of fruit and produce, climate equal to Florida, oysters and fish in abundance. Canning establishments, fruit evaporators, glass factories and many other enterprises could be started in this section … and they could not fail to make money." Orris A. Browne told the *American Agriculturalist* that "there is nothing lacking here but people – new people, new blood, new ideas. We are as intelligent and industrious as most people, but we need new life to pull us out of the grooves and ruts, and turn us into different and more progressive channels. The writer, as a Southerner and a native, can see our shortcomings. How much more forcibly they would strike a man from the progressive North."64

---

tion). See also *PE*, March 9, 1882.

63 *PE*, February 23, first quotation), October 26 (third quotation), 1882, August 2 (second quotation), 1884.

64 *PE*, April 12, 1884; Browne, "The Eastern Shore," *American Agriculturalist* in PE, April 11,

No one on the Eastern Shore was more devoted to the cult of progress than John W. Edmonds. "When the railroad, the great artery of the Peninsula for its trade, shall be completed, we may look with absolute certainty to a surer, better and more profitable culture for our lands," he wrote. "Already we feel the grasp of the potent power of the hands of Philadelphia, New York and Boston." Edmonds and fellow Eastern Shoremen were soon to realize that progress is fraught with unintended consequences. They were made to understand that northeastern capital used its "potent power" for its own interest. They learned that in the Darwinian economy unleashed by Union victory in the Civil War survival required ceaseless vigilance and activity. Eastern Shoremen found their peninsula irrevocably linked by steam and steel to the nation. No matter the vicissitudes, they must cling to the progressive ethos of triumphant Northern capitalism. The "good old Colonial days" were gone forever.[65]

1885.

65 *PE*, August 24, 1882.

Index

A

Abbot, William W. iii
Accomac 285. See also Tasley
Accomac Baptist Association 256
Accomac C. H. 9, 19, 23, 32, 91, 136, 224, 235
Accomack (boat) 130
Accomack Camp 233
Accomack County v, vii, 1, 2, 3, 5, 6, 7, 8, 10, 13, 16, 17, 21, 23, 24, 27, 28, 30, 31, 32, 34, 36, 39, 41, 42, 43, 44, 45, 46, 48, 50, 51, 53, 54, 55, 56, 57, 63, 64, 65, 66, 69, 70, 73, 84, 86, 90, 95, 110, 111, 124, 127, 129, 131, 137, 140, 141, 142, 144, 145, 154, 155, 156, 157, 159, 161, 163, 164, 165, 171, 173, 179, 187, 189, 190, 191, 194, 195, 196, 198, 199, 203, 204, 205, 206, 207, 208, 209, 210, 213, 220, 221, 225, 227, 231, 239, 240, 242, 243, 244, 246, 250, 252, 253, 254, 256, 259, 262, 263, 265, 266, 268, 269, 270, 271, 287, 290
Accomack County Court 157, 206, 269
Accomack County Grand Jury 179
Accomack Peach Brandy 36
Accomac Station 285, 286
Accomac Steamboat Company 127
Accomac Wood and Kindling Company 49
Adams Express Company 113
African Methodist Episcopal Church 240
Alabama 44, 143
Albemarle County, Virginia 157
Albert Daily (boat) 216
Alexandria County, Virginia 185
Alexandria Gazette 183
Alexandria, Virginia 132, 182
Alice (boat) 130
American Agriculturalist 291
American Dredging Company 279
American Revolution 3, 15
Ames, [first name unknown] (Bro.) 244
Annapolis, Maryland 158
Annemessex 67
Annemessic Line 115, 121, 122, 123. See also Great Southern Inland Navigation Company
Annis, George T. 41, 220, 227
Armstrong, W. N. 165
Army of the Potomac 270
Assateague Island 72, 74, 138, 168, 190, 214, 232

293

Assateague Island Life-Saving Service Station 215
Assateague lighthouse 74, 196
Assateague ponies 73
Assawoman 196, 198
Assawoman Creek 12, 196
Astor House 263
Atlantic 2, 130, 223, 237, 238
Atlantic Coastal Plain 7
Atlantic Coast/coast 48, 61, 73
Atlantic Coast Line 281
Atlantic Hotel 179, 257
Atlantic, Mississippi and Ohio Railroad 281
Atlantic Ocean 2, 13, 25, 26, 37, 61, 110, 184, 287, 288
Augusta County 95
Ayer, Richard S. (Congressman) 267
Ayers, Edward L. ii, iii

B

Badger, Curtis i
Badger, Lynn i
Bagby, George W. (Dr.) 234
Baldwin, Furlong i
Baldwin Locomotive Works 287
Baltimore and Ohio Railroad 62, 117, 136, 142
Baltimore, Maryland v, vi, 5, 9, 23, 26, 37, 51, 59, 60, 62, 67, 72, 77, 83, 84, 85, 95, 100, 113, 115, 116, 117, 119, 121, 122, 123, 124, 126, 128, 131, 133, 136, 138, 141, 142, 143, 144, 147, 149, 160, 163, 164, 170, 172, 173, 176, 177, 178, 179, 180, 181, 182, 187, 188, 193, 201, 211, 236, 237, 244, 253, 259, 263, 265, 289, 290
Baltimore Rambler 193
Baltimore Steam Packet Company 123
Baltimore Sun 18, 108, 124, 136, 163, 175, 178, 194, 212, 225, 239, 273, 281
Baptist Church 85, 97, 241, 242
Barnes, Anne ii, iii
Barnes, Edward i, iii
Barrett, L. E. (Reverend) 255, 256, 257
Bates, J. L. 273, 274
Battle Point 54
Battle Point Hotel 181
Bauman, William 276
Baylor, John B. 76
Bayly, Thomas H. (Representative) 46
Bayside Road 10, 23, 206
Bay View 97, 288
Bearinger, David i
Beaver Dam, Maryland 284
Bell, Bayley 248
Belle Haven 35, 98, 142, 177, 199, 248, 250, 255, 264, 271, 285. See also Exmore
Belle Haven Hotel 181
Berlin, Maryland 129, 269
Birch, Decatur 186
Birch, [first name unknown] (Bro.) 244
Bird oyster rock 56, 163
Bird's Nest 285
Bishop, Nathaniel H. 25, 96
Bishopville, Maryland 204
Blake, Ikey 254
Blake, Kellee i

Bloodgood's Wharf 129, 130, 270
Blue Points (oysters) 148
Bobtown 210
Boggs's Wharf 192, 201, 207
Bone Island 80
Boston, Massachusetts 37, 131, 133, 141, 143, 224, 287, 290, 292
Bowdoin, John W. (Dr.) 231
Bradford's Neck 207
Bradley, Mary E. 3, 21, 22, 90, 91
Bradshaw, Severn 150
Breakwater and Frankford Railroad 269
Bridgetown 271
Brighton 168
Brig oyster rock 56
Bristol, Virginia 281
Broadwater 13, 56, 80, 82, 167, 177, 181, 187
Brodwater, Tom 254
Brown, Alexander Crosby 115
Browne, Orris A. 39, 67, 90, 139, 149, 154, 155, 157, 165, 167, 291
Browne, T. H. Bayly (Commonwealth Attorney) 91, 157, 158
Brownson, Orestes 210
Brownsville 54
Budd, Keely 254
Bull, George E. 250
Bundick, Gilley 251, 252
Bundick, William T. 256
Bunting, John W. 71
Butler, Benjamin F. (Major General) 49
Byrd's Rock 163. See also Bird oyster rock

C

California oyster rock 56
Cambridge, Maryland 244
Cameron, William E. (Governor) 162, 164, 165
Canada 147
Cape Charles 9, 17, 18, 80, 120, 131, 138, 170, 172, 174, 264, 278
Cape Charles (boat) 280
Cape Charles City 120, 282, 285, 288
Cape Charles Historical Society ii
Cape Cod, Massachusetts 75
Cape May, New Jersey 263, 265
Capeville 31, 33, 143, 168, 169, 186, 221, 239, 266
Capital (boat) 74
Caribbean 110
Carmine and West 172
Carter, Peter J. 28, 155, 171, 220, 221
Cassatt, Alexander J. 272, 274, 275, 276, 277, 278, 279, 280, 281, 282, 288, 289
Cattail Neck 206, 251
Cedar Island 74, 138, 139, 140, 214, 232
Chance, William (Captain) 254
Charleston, South Carolina 137, 281
Charlestown Tigers 248
Chatham (house) 21
Cheriton 203, 205
Cherrystone 80, 82, 100, 113, 114, 117, 120, 127, 128, 129, 131, 145, 172, 185, 237, 238, 253, 261, 262, 264, 269, 270, 271, 272, 278
Cherrystone Channel 279

295

Cherrystone Creek 55, 61, 113
Cherrystone Ferry 266
Cherrystone Inlet 169, 172
Cherrystone Island 279
Cherrystone oysters 61, 148, 290
Cherrystone Wharf 92, 96
Cherryton 271, 278
Chesapeake and Ohio Railroad 281
Chesapeake Bay v, 2, 15, 17, 18, 19, 25, 56, 59, 61, 62, 64, 65, 66, 67, 70, 78, 80, 100, 117, 119, 120, 121, 123, 124, 132, 138, 140, 143, 146, 147, 148, 149, 150, 151, 152, 157, 162, 164, 166, 167, 173, 199, 243, 274, 280, 290
Chesapeake oysters 148
Chesapeake terrapins 173
Chesconnessex 242
Chesconnessex Creek 124
Chesser, Grayson i
Chester River 119
Chicago, Illinois 136, 142
Childers, Stacia i
Chincoteague 70, 71, 166, 167, 211
Chincoteague Bay 23, 49, 70, 71, 114, 129, 130, 131, 148, 166, 167, 169, 178, 179, 180, 191, 197, 204, 211, 270, 271
Chincoteague Continental (baseball team) 231
Chincoteague Island 18, 21, 23, 71, 72, 74, 75, 96, 100, 129, 130, 131, 138, 139, 144, 154, 166, 167, 169, 177, 178, 179, 180, 187, 190, 196, 197, 199, 202, 204, 205, 206, 208, 209, 211, 215, 234, 235, 237, 240, 243, 245, 249, 253, 254, 257, 259, 260
Chincoteague oyster dealer 71
Chincoteague oystermen 70, 96
Chincoteague oysters 70, 71, 129, 148, 166, 270
Chincoteague planters 166, 169
Chincoteague ponies 73
Cincinnati, Ohio 142
City of Norfolk (boat) 121
City Point, Virginia 114
Civil War iii, v, 1, 4, 29, 31, 37, 38, 67, 78, 80, 81, 88, 94, 97, 103, 105, 106, 107, 108, 110, 112, 113, 116, 124, 128, 132, 143, 144, 149, 153, 169, 174, 206, 208, 211, 213, 219, 232, 233, 241, 245, 252, 255, 259, 282, 292
Clayville, William J. 187
Cluff, Jas. (Bro.) 244
Coard, G. Welly 202
Cobb, Albert 183
Cobb, Elkanah 184
Cobb family 75, 80, 82, 181, 183, 184, 185, 186
Cobb, Nathan Jr. 183
Cobb, Nathan Sr. 82, 183, 184, 186
Cobb & Segar 184
Cobb's Island 15, 16, 18, 70, 74, 75, 80, 81, 82, 92, 167, 177, 182, 183, 184, 186, 202, 214
Cobb's Island Hotel 181, 182, 183, 184, 185, 186
Cobb's Island Life-Saving Service Station 18, 214, 216
Cobb's Island Seaside Company 185
Cobb's Landing 92

Cobb, Warren 183
Cobb Wrecking Company 216
Code Duello 219, 252
Code of Virginia 73
Coffrode, Joseph H. 284
Cokesbury Methodist Church 99, 255
Colborn, T. F. 247
Combination Club (baseball team) 231
Compact of 1785 150
Concord Wharf 250
Confederate States of America ix, 1, 49, 97, 107, 108, 112, 188, 233, 263
Connecticut 62, 139
Cooke, R. B. 276, 288
Cooper, Laura 260
Corbett, Theodore ii
Costin, Robert S. 40, 43
Councils of the Friends of Temperance 256
Cox, Peter 43
Craighill, William P. (Major) 211
Craven, Avery 42
Creswell, John A. J. (Postmaster-General) 186
Crickett (boat) 75
Crisfield, John W. 122
Crisfield, Maryland 58, 60, 67, 84, 114, 115, 117, 119, 120, 121, 122, 123, 126, 128, 133, 141, 147, 150, 151, 170, 174, 175, 176, 187, 191, 206, 211, 212, 244, 276, 277
Critic (Washington, D.C.) 252
Crockett, Henry L. 140
Crockett, Thomas "Sugar Tom" 78

Crossroads 251. See also Onley
Custis, Dennis i
Custis, [first name unknown] (Captain) 158
Custis's Neck 131
Custis, William P. (Inspector) 156

D

Dakotas 136
Darwin, Charles 234
Davidson, Donald ix
Davidson, Hunter (Commander) 69
Davis, Peter H. (Captain) 192
Davis's Wharf 192
Dawson's (Dorson's) Shoal 74
Delaware 6, 7, 20, 31, 32, 45, 50, 109, 111, 119, 137, 141, 190, 203, 231, 239, 247, 260, 261, 262, 263, 265, 268, 272, 288
Delaware Bay 114, 129, 157, 211, 262, 263
Delaware Railroad 119, 120, 121, 264
Delaware River 157
Delaware State Journal 87
Delaware Tribune 120, 261
Delmar, Delaware 119, 266, 272, 276, 277, 282, 283, 288
Delmarva Peninsula 114, 115, 119, 121, 129
Delmay (boat) 84
Democratic Messenger (Snow Hill) 257, 258
Dennis, George R. (Dr.) 122
Detroit, Michigan 147
Disston, Hamilton 179
Dize, John W. 67
Dock Point 124

297

Doughty, Alonzo 247
Doughty, Jerry i
Drummondtown 23, 49, 65, 91, 98, 131, 137, 156, 162, 177, 199, 200, 202, 231, 232, 233, 234, 235, 239, 243, 244, 249, 262, 264, 267, 268, 269, 271, 277, 284, 285, 291
Drummondtown Jolly Club 232
Duke University ii
Duncan, Charles W. 257
Dunkirk 243, 290
Dun's Mercantile Agency Reference Book 199, 200, 201

E

Eastern Shore Agricultural Association 236
Eastern Shore Agricultural Fair 236
Eastern Shore (boat) 123, 124, 126, 172
Eastern Shore Herald 205, 235
Eastern Shore Heritage Center ii
Eastern Shore of Virginia Produce Exchange vi, viii
Eastern Shore Public Library ii
Eastern Shore Railroad 115, 117, 119, 120, 121, 122, 262, 267, 270, 271, 272, 276, 277
Eastern Shore Steamboat Company v, 113, 115, 122, 123, 124, 126, 127, 128, 133, 141, 142, 176, 180, 187, 192, 201, 235, 237, 244, 277, 280
Eastern Virginian 15, 17, 169, 172, 201, 235, 246, 249, 250, 252
Eastville 23, 43, 88, 91, 143, 177, 199, 202, 205, 232, 235, 248, 251, 252, 262, 264, 267, 271, 277, 285
Edenton, North Carolina 281
Edmonds, John W. 9, 162, 165, 173, 202, 205, 224, 225, 236, 257, 275, 289, 291, 292
Edmonds, Richard H. 77, 152, 160, 164
E. Flye and Company 50
Elizabeth and Norfolk Railroad 281
Elizabeth City, North Carolina 281
Elkton, Maryland 117
emancipation 1, 17, 28, 38, 45, 69, 91, 100, 103, 110, 111, 189, 219, 222, 223, 229, 240
Eolus (boat) 128
Episcopal Church 97, 98, 242
Erie, Pennsylvania 274, 278
Evans, Benjamin F. 254
Exmore 285

F

Fair Haven, Connecticut 62, 64, 65
Fairmount, Maryland 244
Fauquier County 155
Finney, Charles P. 37, 83
Finney, Louis C. H. (Senator) 159
Finney, Oswald B. 171
Finney's Creek 195
Finney's Wharf 83, 193, 201
Fisherman's Island 174
Fitchett, William T. (Clerk of Court) 229
Fitzhugh, George 4, 78, 85, 86, 110
Florida 182, 289, 291
Folly Creek 90, 167, 232
Fooks, Thomas H., V ii
Foote, Edwin J. 139

Forest and Stream 170, 177, 178, 179, 182
Forman, H. Chandlee 21, 22
Fort Monroe 23, 122
Fowler, Foote and Company 139, 140
Fox Island 15, 18, 56
Frankford and Breakwater Railroad 129
Franklin City 93, 114, 129, 130, 133, 141, 144, 166, 174, 176, 177, 178, 179, 187, 191, 197, 206, 211, 235, 237, 240, 247, 248, 272
Franklin City-Chincoteague channel 211
Franklin House 247
Franklin, John R. (Judge) 197
Frank T. Boggs & Bros. 192, 201
Franktown 231, 274
Frank T. Stockley and Company 204
Frazer, Alexander 148
Freedmen's Bureau 43, 45, 91, 96
Free Gospel (sect) 260
Freeman, Douglas Southall 97
Free School Marsh 13
Freeschool Neck 198. See also Messongo Neck
Fulton Fish Market 149

G

Garrison's Chapel 240
Gaskin's Chapel African Methodist Episcopal Church 233
Gause, John Taylor 127
Genovese, Eugene iii
Georgetown, Delaware 129, 178, 247

Georgia 143, 151, 173, 203
Gillet, John W. 8, 17, 20
Girdletree, Maryland 180
Gloucester County 70, 128
Godwin, James 251
Goerke, E. W. (Dr.) 274, 275, 276, 279, 282, 288
Good Samaritans (lodge) 232
Gould, Jay 269
Grand Army of the Republic 233
Grangeville 196, 204, 225, 256
Great Depression viii
Great September Gust of 1822 18
Great Southern Inland Navigation Company 115
Greenbackville 72, 131, 168, 174, 197, 206, 209
Greenly, William E. 260
Grey, Emily i
Groome, James Black (Governor) 157, 158
Guard Shore 238
Guilford 220, 231, 238, 248, 249
Guilford Creek 238
Gulf Stream 16
Gumboro, Delaware 255
Gum, John A. 139
Gum Swamp 284

H

Hack's Neck 18
Hadlock 264, 271
Hagley Museum ii
Hallett and Warren 172
Hallston 285. See also Hallwood
Hall's Wharf 133
Hallwood 284, 285
Hamalainen, Pekka 106

299

Hamilton, Allen i
Hammocks 50, 133, 206
Hampton 88, 165
Hampton Institute 222
Harahan, Joseph Patrick 220
Harborton 124, 138, 192
Harlan and Hollingsworth Company 115, 121, 122, 123, 124, 126, 127, 128, 129, 143, 277, 279, 280
Harlan family 122
Harlan, Samuel Jr. 115, 121, 122, 127
Harmon, William H. 168
Harrington, Delaware 129, 141, 178
Harrison, Bill 254
Hart, Dennis 251
Haupt, Herman (General) 113
Havran, Martin J. iii
Helen (boat) 123, 124, 126
Helltown 196
Heptasophs (lodge) 232
Herman, Bernard i
Hinman, George W. 163, 164
Hitchens, George D. 186, 216
Hoffman's Wharf 138, 139, 192, 194, 250. See also Harborton
Hoffman, William G. 192
Hog Island 55, 74, 91, 187, 214
Hog Island lighthouse 74
Holden's Creek 198
Holland, Edward i
Holland's Mill 251
Holmes Presbyterian Church 97
Hope, Henry 227
Hopkins & Bro. 37, 51, 201
Hopkins, John P. L. 139
Hopkins, Thomas S. 51

Hopkins, William 139
Horntown 93, 177, 180, 269
Hudson, Daniel 269
Hungars Creek 172
Hungars Wharf 128, 172
Hunter, Alexander 17, 74, 75, 167, 168, 177, 182, 183, 184, 185, 186, 253
Hunting Creek 6, 12, 203, 205
Huntington, Collis P. 270
Huntsville, Alabama 97
Hurst, John Wesley 230
Hygeia Hotel 289

I

Independent Order of Rechabites (lodge) 232
Individual Enterprise Steamboat Company 124
Ingersoll, Ernest 77
Institute for Advanced Studies in the Humanities at the University of Virginia ii
Iowa 42

J

Jacksonville, Florida 281
James River 114, 166, 281
Jane Moseley (boat) 181, 280, 288
Jarvis, James Ambler 202
Jeffries, Sumner 186
Jenkins Bridge 131, 213
J. L. Chadwick 145
Job's Island 15
John M. Fosque & Bro. 201
John O. Selby & Edward H. Conquest 204
Johnson, James H. A. (Elder) 10, 35,

52, 240
Johnsontown 26, 243
John T. Finney & Bro. 201
Jones, G. B. 203, 205
Jones, John Beauchamp 110
Jones, T. W. 203, 205
Joynes, Maria S. 98
Joynes, Tully A. T. 124, 126, 176
J. T. H. Colburn (boat) 84
Junction and Breakwater Railroad 129

K

Kearney, James (Lieutenant Colonel) 117
Keeney, W. Robert ii
Kellam, Abel W. 181
Kellam, A. S. 181
Keller 196, 236, 285
Keller and Bush 276, 281, 282, 283
Keller, John 288
Kelso, John (Captain) 83
Kemper, James Lawson (Governor) 153, 157, 158, 159
Kendall Grove 43
Kenney, Joseph T. 139, 204, 259
Kent County, Delaware 260
Kentucky 149, 151
Ker Place (house) 201
Ketcham, John W. 168
Key Port, New Jersey 263
Key Port Steamboat Company 131
Kimball, Sumner I. 215
Kimberly, William H. 113, 115, 271, 278
King's Creek 205, 278, 279
Knights of Honor (lodge) 232
Krawczel, Elizabeth iii

L

Lady of the Lake (boat) 121
Lancaster, Pennsylvania 276
Landis, Charles i
Laslett, Peter 88
Latimer, Frances i
Laws, John 251
LeCato, Nathaniel J. W. 145
Led Astray Club of Chincoteague 232
Leemont 136, 205, 246, 283. See also Woodstock
Lewes, Delaware 114, 126, 129, 131, 141, 144, 178, 263, 265, 266, 272
Library of Virginia ii
Lilliston, Charles B. 200
Lincoln, Abraham 106, 108
Lind, Richard 254
Literary Fund 207
Little Annemessic River 115, 117, 119
Lizzie Bell (boat) 84
Lochhead, John L. 274
Locustmount 195, 200, 271
Locustville 254, 271
Locustville Academy 209
Long Branch, New Jersey 223
Long Island, New York 21, 139, 173, 177
Long Island Sound 148
Long Island terrapins 173
Louisiana 169
Lovett-Davidson Line 69, 154, 158
Lovett, William H. C. (Chief Inspector) 68, 69
Lower Northampton Baptist Church 238

Luraghi, Raimondo iii
Lynchburg, Virginia 281
Lynn Haven Bay 203
Lytle, Andrew 44, 47, 99

M

Machipongo 131, 204
Machipongo River 131
Maddex, Jack P. Jr. 107
Maggie (boat) 123, 124, 126
Magothy Bay bean 34, 40
Mahone, William (United States Senator, Confederate Major-General) 143, 212, 263, 264, 277, 278, 281, 282
Maine 49, 50, 96, 104, 182, 215, 216, 231, 267
Mapp, George B. 145
Mapp, John E. (Dr.) 290
Mappsburg 203, 240
Mappsville 140, 145, 164, 196, 248, 253, 254, 283
Margaret Academy 209
Mariner, Kirk C. i, 87, 241
Market Street Methodist Episcopal Church (Onancock) 234
Marshall and Brittingham 198
Marshall, Charles W. B. 15, 235, 246, 249, 252, 253, 254
Marshall, Edward W. (Dr.) 86
Marshall, Robert 169
Marsh Market 133, 163, 198, 213, 238
Martin, Worthy ii
Marvel, William iii
Maryland 2, 3, 6, 9, 49, 55, 56, 57, 63, 64, 67, 69, 72, 78, 79, 82, 86, 110, 113, 115, 117, 119, 124, 129, 141, 142, 146, 149, 150, 151, 152, 154, 155, 156, 157, 158, 159, 161, 163, 173, 190, 202, 247, 260, 261, 262, 263, 265, 266, 267, 268, 269, 270, 271, 272, 274, 289
Maryland, Delaware and Virginia Railroad 166
Maryland oyster police 69
Maryland-Virginia boundary 69
Maryland-Virginia legislative commission 69
Mason, George W. 256
Masons (lodge) 232
Massachusetts 49, 139
Massachusetts (boat) 124
Mathews County Court 162
Mathews County, Virginia 128, 162
Matomkin Station 227. See also Parksley
Mattassippi 21
Mattawaman Creek 115, 126, 141, 172
McConkey, James 276, 288
McConnell, Thomas M. 95
McCready, Nathaniel L'Hommedieu 114, 117, 128
McDonald, Forrest 105
McDonald, Marshall 78, 160, 161, 165
McGowan, John (Commodore) 67
McKown, Kenneth 186
McLeary, Harry 130
McMath, George i
McWhiney, Grady 105
Meade, Richard H. 183
Mears, Albert F. 201, 206
Mears, Alfred J. 225

Mears, James E. i
Melfa 238, 243
Merrill, Austin H. 234
Messongo Creek 48, 50, 84, 133, 163, 198, 206
Messongo Neck 198, 199, 209, 213, 235
Methodist Church 85, 97, 99, 101, 238, 241, 242, 243, 244, 255, 258, 259
Metompkin 251, 271. See also Newstown and Parksley
Metompkin Bay 90
Metompkin Blues (baseball team) 231
Metompkin Island 232
Metompkin Station 220. See also Parksley
Mexico 65
Middle Road 10
Middlesex County 128
Middletown, Delaware 50
Middletown Transcript 88
Miles, M. K. i
Miles, Oscar Coles 26, 27
Miles, Richard Jr. (Captain) 251
Miles, Richard Sr. 26
Miles-Taylor-Lankford 204
Miles Wharf 50
Minnesota 136
Minor, Berkeley 108
Mischief (boat) 179
Mockhorn Island 80
Modestown 231, 271
Modestown Modocs (baseball team) 231
Montpelier (house) 98
Monumental City 119. See Baltimore, Maryland
Morgan, Charles 115, 121
Morning News (Wilmington) 260
Morse, Albro J. 139
Morton, T. C. x, 142
Mount Pleasant, Pennsylvania 144
Muddy Creek 173, 201, 237, 238, 251
Murphy, Lieutenant Eld. 45

N

Nancock 137. See also Onancock
Nash, Daniel D. 48, 49
Nashville 177, 180, 270. See also Sinnickson
National Archives-College Park ii
National Prohibition Party 256
National Recorder (Accomac C. H.) 235
Navy Yard (Norfolk) 122
Neely, John 171
Nelson, Bill i
Nelsonia 196
Nelson, Spencer R. 196
Nelson, William 15
Newberne (boat) 131
New Church 198, 235, 285
New Era (Washington) 28
New Jersey 21, 131, 137, 163, 167, 177, 180, 190, 203, 262, 263
New Orleans, Louisiana 85, 281
Newstown 251, 271. See also Metompkin
Newtown 270, 271, 274, 282. See also Pocomoke City, Maryland
Newtown Junction 276
New York 32, 48, 63, 72, 74, 75, 84, 113, 114, 115, 128, 131, 139,

303

142, 167, 172, 173, 177
New York and Norfolk Air-Line Railroad 262, 263, 264, 267, 277
New York and Norfolk Railroad Company 268, 269
New York harbor 71
New York Herald 66
New York, New York vi, 5, 37, 49, 51, 60, 70, 71, 116, 117, 121, 126, 128, 129, 133, 141, 142, 143, 144, 145, 147, 148, 149, 166, 167, 170, 172, 178, 179, 197, 224, 225, 237, 261, 263, 265, 266, 267, 268, 273, 281, 287, 288, 290, 292
New York, Philadelphia and Norfolk Railroad v, 271, 272, 273, 274, 276, 277, 278, 280, 281, 282, 283, 285, 287, 288, 289, 290
New York Times 215
New-York Tribune 57
New York World 45
Norfolk and Ocean Railroad 281
Norfolk and Western Railroad 281
Norfolk Argus 65
Norfolk (boat) 280
Norfolk City Council and Board of Trade 122
Norfolk County 70
Norfolk Landmark 209
Norfolk oysters 290
Norfolk Southern Railroad 281
Norfolk, Virginia 3, 4, 68, 80, 83, 93, 95, 100, 114, 115, 117, 119, 121, 122, 123, 128, 129, 133, 137, 138, 140, 141, 142, 143, 147, 167, 170, 177, 181, 187, 233, 237, 238, 261, 262, 263, 265, 266, 267, 268, 276, 278, 279, 280, 281, 288, 289
Northampton County i, v, vii, 1, 2, 5, 6, 7, 8, 16, 21, 23, 26, 27, 28, 30, 31, 32, 34, 36, 40, 42, 43, 50, 51, 53, 54, 55, 57, 63, 64, 66, 69, 70, 75, 78, 80, 84, 86, 88, 91, 97, 99, 110, 111, 112, 114, 115, 120, 126, 127, 128, 129, 131, 137, 140, 141, 143, 144, 145, 155, 171, 173, 187, 189, 191, 199, 205, 206, 207, 208, 209, 220, 221, 226, 231, 232, 238, 247, 248, 249, 253, 255, 262, 263, 265, 266, 268, 269, 271, 278, 287, 290
Northampton County Clerk of Court 229
Northam, Thomas 251
North and South Railroad Company 262, 263, 265, 271
North Carolina 203
Nottingham, Mrs. J. F. 209
N. P. Banks (boat) 128

O

Oak Grove 238
Oak Hall 204, 287
Occohannock Creek 50, 61, 172, 192, 250
Occohannock Neck 54, 181
Ocean City, Maryland 178, 237, 286
Odd Fellows (lodge) 232
Old Bay Line 123, 128, 143. See also Baltimore Steam Packet Company
Old Dominion Steamship Company

113, 114, 115, 117, 126, 128, 129, 130, 131, 141, 143, 144, 237, 272
Oldham, Montcalm (Reverend) 234
Old Plantation 278
Old Plantation Creek 278, 279
Old Point Comfort 113, 128, 185, 281, 289
Old Quarter 278
Olive (boat) 128
Onancock x, 15, 17, 23, 27, 36, 37, 38, 50, 51, 84, 99, 142, 155, 156, 157, 169, 172, 173, 174, 177, 193, 194, 195, 199, 201, 203, 204, 209, 212, 222, 225, 230, 233, 234, 235, 238, 239, 240, 242, 243, 246, 247, 249, 252, 255, 256, 257
Onancock Academy 209, 210, 234
Onancock Creek 6, 37, 132, 140, 141, 193, 194, 201, 212
Onancock Mill Company 204
Onancock Stars 231
Onley 251
Order of the Oriole Festival (Baltimore) 237
Oyster 92. See also Cobb's Landing
Oyster City 271

P

Painter brothers 272, 273, 275, 276, 278, 280, 288
Painter, Uriah H. 271, 275, 276, 282, 288
Painter, William (General) 270, 271, 273, 274, 275, 276
Panic of 1837 119, 262
Panic of 1873 269

Parker, William H. (Captain) 174
Parksley ii, 220, 227, 238, 285
Parksley Railroad Museum ii
Parramore Island 74, 214
Parrington, Vernon L. 289
Pastoria 238
Patrons of Husbandry (Grange) 232
Peninsula Enterprise 9, 136, 163, 165, 172, 176, 179, 192, 193, 196, 198, 201, 202, 207, 213, 224, 234, 235, 236, 238, 244, 249, 251, 254, 257, 275, 283, 284, 289
Peninsula Railroad 270, 271, 272, 273, 275
Peninsula Railroad Company (of Virginia) 272
Pennsylvania vi, 148, 151, 268
Pennsylvania Railroad v, 271, 272, 273, 274, 275, 276, 281, 283, 287, 288, 289
Petersburg, Virginia 281
Pettit, Thomas 180
Philadelphia, Newtown [Pa.] and New York Railroad 270, 273
Philadelphia, Pennsylvania vi, 5, 8, 32, 37, 51, 60, 65, 70, 71, 83, 95, 109, 116, 117, 119, 121, 122, 123, 126, 129, 133, 141, 142, 143, 144, 147, 148, 166, 170, 172, 173, 174, 177, 178, 179, 194, 197, 224, 261, 262, 263, 265, 266, 267, 268, 270, 280, 281, 288, 290, 292
Philadelphia, Wilmington and Baltimore Railroad 115, 117, 119, 120, 121, 129, 272
Phillips and Bradford 168

Piankitank Line 128
Pickett's Hole 170, 278
Piedmont 157
Pierpont, Francis H. (Governor) 68
Pietism 104
Pittsburgh, Pennsylvania 142
Pitts, Major S. 252
Pitts's Wharf 124, 194
Pocomoke City, Maryland 127, 129, 138, 180, 270, 282, 283, 284, 285
Pocomoke Neck 198. See also Messongo Neck
Pocomoke oysters 57, 290
Pocomoke River 48, 115, 122, 124, 126, 129, 144, 150, 151, 157, 159, 194, 200, 212, 270, 284
Pocomoke Sound 15, 23, 30, 56, 57, 58, 61, 62, 63, 64, 65, 68, 69, 120, 131, 146, 147, 148, 149, 150, 151, 152, 154, 156, 157, 158, 159, 160, 161, 163, 164, 166, 169
Pollett, Israel 247
Port Penn, Pennsylvania 144
Portsmouth, Virginia 83, 114, 238, 281, 289
Pottstown, Pennsylvania 284
Powell Bros. 201
Powell family 195, 201
Powell, George W. 139, 195, 201
Powell, Henry 139
Powell, Henry F. 195
Powell, John F. 168
Powell, John T. 139, 195
Powellton 18, 131, 139, 140, 144, 168, 177, 181, 191, 195, 200, 201, 203, 207, 237, 238, 247.
See also Wachapreague
Powellton Hotel 181
Power, Joseph P. 113, 115
Presbyterian Church 97, 242, 247
Princess Anne, Maryland 117, 262, 268, 276
Princeton University 234
Protestant Church 85, 97
Prout's Island 80
Providence, Rhode Island 143
Pungoteague 95, 99, 126, 133, 142, 177, 231, 234, 242, 250, 256, 285
Pungoteague Creek 6, 10, 83, 124, 140, 172, 192, 194, 201, 207
Pungoteague Grange 236
Pungoteague Station 285. See also Keller
Putalik, Erin i
Pyle, Howard 5, 19, 86, 100, 178, 190

R

Rappahannock River 26, 78, 152, 162
Rattlesnake Ridge 23
Rayfield, John T. 254
Reconstruction 1, 29, 79, 96, 98, 103, 107, 110, 111, 207, 219, 220, 244
Record and Gazette (Pocomoke City) 180
Red Hills 180
Red Star viii
Rich, Benjamin S. 139, 215
Richelieu, Armand Jean du Plessis (Cardinal) 156
Richmond Dispatch 68, 98, 112, 137,

142, 165, 167, 241
Richmond, Virginia 9, 24, 63, 81, 90, 92, 114, 142, 143, 158, 170, 174, 177, 181, 182, 183, 234, 281
Richmond Whig 107
Riddleberger, Harrison H. 153
Riggin, Thomas 156, 157, 158
Riley, Esau 230
Riley, William G. (Commonwealth Attorney and Judge) 88, 252
Roark, James L. 229
Roberts, George B. 272, 289
Roberts, Wilkins and Company 172
Rose, William H. 254
Ross, Frederick Augustus (Dr.) 97
Ross, Samuel T. 27
Ruffin, Edmund 7, 34, 37, 74
Runnymeade (house) 21
Rutledge, Archibald 230

S

Sadie Bell (racehorse) 95
Salisbury, Maryland 266, 286
Salisbury University ii
Salyer, Francis H. 284
Sandy Island 279
Sandy Run 284
Sanford 199, 206, 213, 242
Sanford Charity 48, 50
Sanford Methodist Church 243
Savage, Peter 35, 54, 248
Savageville 230, 233, 244, 256
Saxis Island 13, 15, 57, 69, 133, 163, 169, 198, 199, 206, 209, 213, 232, 238
Scarburgh, George T. 233
Scott, Thomas M. 205, 206, 235

Scott, William L. 274, 275, 276, 277, 278, 279, 280, 281, 282, 288, 289
Seaboard and Roanoke Railroad 281
Sea Fish and Oil Company 139
Seaside 196, 283. See also Mappsville
Seaside Road 10
Segar, Thomas G. 184
Selbyville, Delaware 269
Shadyside 204
Shenandoah County, Virginia 155
Shenandoah Democrat 153
Shenandoah Valley 9
Shephard, E. Lee ii
Shepherd, Peter (Reverend) 233
Shivers, John 180
Shore History ii
Simpkins, Jesse J. 6, 81
Sinnickson 129, 270
Skin Point 133
S. M. Hancock and Company 205
Smith Island, Maryland 69, 150
Smith's Island 55, 74, 80, 186, 214
Smith's Island Life-Saving Service Station 216
Smith's Island lighthouse 74
Snead, John 186
Snow Hill, Maryland 124, 126, 129, 144, 257, 269
Somerset County, Maryland 50, 154
Somers's Cove 115, 117
South Carolina 173, 230
Spady & Cobb 185
Spady, John Thomas 184, 186
Spady, Sandford 186
Sparrow, Andrew 250
Spears, John R. 21, 25, 75
Staunton Vindicator x, 142

307

Staunton, Virginia 95
St. Charles Trotting Park 95
Sterling, Captain William 15
Sterling, Isacc 15
Stevens, E. H. 7, 16
Stierle, Adam 279
St. Mary's County, Maryland 201
Stockley and Coleburn 196
Stockley, Francis T. 196
Stockton, Maryland 269
Sturgis 203. See also Mappsburg
Sue (boat) 114, 123, 124, 128
Sunnyside 203. See also Cheriton
Sussex County, Delaware 255, 263
Swan's Gut Creek 49

T

Tangier (boat) 123, 124, 193
Tangier Island 15, 20, 56, 58, 63, 67, 78, 79, 80, 100, 138, 139, 140, 163, 172, 199, 209, 243
Tangier oysters 57
Tangier Sound 15, 56, 57, 61, 62, 63, 65, 68, 69, 84, 131, 146, 147, 149, 151, 152, 154, 160, 161, 164, 166, 169
Tanner, Lou i
Tar Bay 78
Tasley 285
Tawes, Leonard S. 84
Taylor, Bayard 90
Taylor House 202
Taylor, John James 251
Taylor's Branch 250
Taylor's Wharf 126, 128, 172, 176
Tazewell heirs 278
Tazewell, Littleton W. (Governor) 278

Teackle, Littleton D. 262
Temperanceville 198, 234, 244, 256, 283, 287, 291
terra incognita 264, 290
The Countryside Transformed: The Railroad and the Eastern Shore of Virginia, 1870-1935 (website) ii
The Folly (house) 19
Thom, Alfred P. 252
Thomas, Mrs. Mary A. 209
Thomas's Wharf 131
Thomas, William G., III ii
Thompson, Willard 122
Tidewater/tidewater 5, 7, 43, 55, 66, 70, 73, 149, 153, 159, 161, 165, 220
Times (Philadelphia, Pennsylvania) 148
Times (Pocomoke City, Maryland) 284
Times (Smyrna, Delaware) 119, 144
Tobacco Island 15
Tompkinson, T. L. (Reverend) 240
Tom's Cove 168
Town Point (Norfolk) 281
Townsend 50, 235
Townsend family 109, 110, 111
Townsend, George Alfred 111
Townsend, Israel 33, 50, 54, 87, 88, 95, 109, 110, 120, 143, 221, 239, 266
Townsend, John J. 31, 32, 33, 35, 45, 88, 92, 109
Toy, George (Collector of Customs) 193, 195
Transcendentalism 104
Tredegar (boat) 155

Truitt, Barry ii
Tuckahoe (boat) 131
Turlington's Camp Meeting 243, 247

U

Unitarianism 104
United Order of Tents (lodge) 232
United States Army Corps of Engineers 197, 211
United States Bureau of Soils 7, 16
United States Congress 46, 103, 117, 211, 213, 267
United States Life-Saving Service 74, 139, 189, 211, 214, 215, 216
United States Life-Saving Service stations 18, 74, 139, 189, 196
United States Signal Office 196, 215
University of North Carolina ii
University of Virginia ii, iii
University of Virginia's Virginia Center for Digital History ii
Upshur, Abel Parker 27
Upshur, Thomas T. 54

V

Vincent, Carol ii
Virginia General Assembly 63, 64, 73, 152, 153, 155, 160, 162, 164, 165, 173, 194, 197, 256, 262, 263, 264, 268, 270, 272
Virginia House of Delegates 63, 111, 171, 185, 265
Virginia Museum of History and Culture ii
Virginia Oyster Police 67, 68, 149, 156
Virginia oysters 148
Virginia Supreme Court of Appeals 162

W

Wachapreague 130. See also Powellton
Wachapreague Inlet 195
Waddy, John R. 143, 145
Waddy & Saunders 145
Wade, John Donald 107
Wagram 254
Walker-Bowie Line 158. See also Lovett-Davidson Line
Walker, Gilbert C. (Governor) 150, 155, 157
Walker, Henry C. 192
Wallop's Island 187, 214
Wallop's Neck 205
Wall Street 154
Walsh, Harry 79
Waples, Hopkins and Company 203
Warren, Robert Penn 106
Washington, D.C. 28, 67, 82, 83, 100, 110, 143, 170, 179, 181, 182, 215, 244, 252, 255, 288
Watson, Arthur (Dr.) 265, 266
Watson, Gillet F. 266
Watts Island 15, 18, 56
Wattsville 244
Weaver, James C. (school superintendent) 209, 210
Weaver, Richard 1
Weldon, Virginia 281
Wesleyan Female College (Wilmington, DE) 99
West, Fannie B. 169
Weston Combination 234
Weston, Frank (Professor) 234
Westover, Maryland 270, 276
West Virginia 154
Whealton, John A. M. 71

309

"Wheelbarrow Club" 257
White, Lewis 251
Whitman, Walt 106
Widgeon (boat) 18, 130
Wilkins, John T. (Dr.) 172
Wilkins, Southey 247
Williamsport, Pennsylvania 132
Willis, Nathaniel Parker 104, 105
Willis's Wharf 173, 191
Wilmington, Delaware 4, 24, 32, 85, 86, 114, 119, 120, 121, 122, 126, 129, 133, 141, 143, 144, 147, 177, 178, 200, 220, 260, 261, 266, 277
Wilmington Every Evening 223
Wilson, Robert 53, 58, 67, 93, 175
Wiltse, Charles M. 116
Winder, John W. 64
Winder's Neck 49
Winslow, Francis 164, 165
Winter Quarters 74
Wise, Henry A. (Governor) 45, 63, 66, 68, 96, 150, 153, 157
Wise, John S. 24
Wise, Louisa 251, 252
Wise's Point 243
Wishart's Point 130, 237
Witham, James 50
Woodberry 39, 227, 231, 243
Woodstock 205. See also Leemont
Woodward, C. Vann iii
Worcester and Somerset Railroad 270, 272
Worcester County, Maryland 86, 263, 284
Worcester Railroad 129, 130, 269
World War I viii
Wright, Hendrick B. 268

Wynona (house) 21

Y

Yarrington, Jonna ii
Yerby, George Teackle (Dr.) 111, 112
York County, Virginia 70
Young, Benjamin 251
Young, Margaret Downing 251
Young's Creek 238

www.ingramcontent.com/pod-product-compliance
Lightning Source LLC
Chambersburg PA
CBHW050102170426
43198CB00014B/2430